BRITISH & IRISH TRAMWAY SYSTEMS

since 1945

Previous page:
Southampton's last new trams were three delivered in 1931-32. One of the three, No 32, is seen at Swaythling on 8 January 1949. The domed roof was typical of Southampton's double-deck trams and was a profile specifically dictated by the Bargate. No 32 was another of Southampton's trams sold to Leeds, where it became No 298.

This page:
The last service train leaves St Helens station with the 9.55am from Rutland Street to South End. This train was followed by a special tram, carrying VIPs, for which special souvenir tickets were issued. The special left Rutland Street at 11.30am and returned there at 12.30pm. In the background the Central Wales line (ex-London & North Western Railway) from Shrewsbury to Swansea Victoria runs parallel to the Swansea & Mumbles. *H. Daniel*

Below:
With its crew posing for the cameraman, SHMD No 64 illustrates well the dilapidated state that many tramcars operated in the months prior to a system's closure. *The Late J. H. Roberts/Courtesy Martin Jenkins*

BRITISH & IRISH TRAMWAY SYSTEMS

since 1945

Michael H. Waller and Peter Waller

IAN ALLAN Publishing

Contents

Abbreviations

BEC	British Electric Car Co Ltd
CT	Corporation Transport (or variants)
EE	English Electric Co Ltd
EMB	Electro-Mechanical Brake Co Ltd
ERTCW	Electric Railway & Tramway Carriage Works Ltd
GNR(I)	Great Northern Railway (Ireland)
LCC	London County Council
LUT	London United Tramways
MCTD	Manchester Corporation Transport Department
M&G	Mountain & Gibson
M&T	Maley & Taunton
MER	Manx Electric Railway
MET	Metropolitan Electric Tramways
STD	Sheffield Transport Department
UCC	Union Construction & Finance Co Ltd
UEC	United Electric Car Co Ltd

First published 1992

ISBN 0 7110 1989 4

Published by Ian Allan Ltd, Shepperton, Surrey; and printed by Ian Allan Printing Ltd at their works at Coombelands in Runnymede, England.

Dedication:

This book is dedicated to the memory of my Father, Michael H. Waller, whose knowledge of and enthusiasm for the tram did so much to stimulate my own interest in the subject.

In 1985, just before I joined Ian Allan Ltd, the company had published very successfully R.J.S. Wiseman's *Classic Tramcars* and was obviously keen to look for further possible subjects of tramway interest. I happened to mention that during the 1940s and 1950s my father had travelled widely photographing the then surviving British tramways and had, indeed, been an Ian Allan author in the early years of the 1950s.

From these discussions the idea of a book examining the history of the postwar British tram developed and a contract for my father to produce the book was drawn up. Unfortunately, increasing ill-health made it impossible for my father to persevere with the project, although he had started to progress it, and at the time of his death the manuscript was barely started.

With my access to the archives that Ian Allan Ltd possesses I had already assisted my father with some of the factual research and it seemed logical to try and complete the work as a tribute to him. The book, as I have written it, is not the book that he would have compiled; I lack some of the personal knowledge that he would have brought to the subject — the anecdotes and the minutiae that were so much a part of British tramway life — but his greatest contribution was his photographs, and I hope that I have managed to make a reasonable selection from the many hundred that he took. I have supplemented those with other photographers' work in those cases where my father did not visit the tramway or, occasionally, where his visits coincided with a failure of his photographic equipment.

I hope that the finished work helps to bring across the flavour of the two decades of dramatic change.

Peter Waller
April 1991

KEY TO MAPS

LINES OPEN
LINES CLOSED
ADJACENT OPERATORS LINES CLOSED
LINES OPENED AFTER 1945
CLOSED LINES RETAINED FOR DEPOT WORKINGS

Acknowledgements

This is very much a secondary history and numerous printed sources have been referred to in the book's preparation. A detailed bibliography at the end will help those wishing for further information on individual systems.

I am particularly grateful to J. H. Price for permission to quote material from the detailed fleet lists that he has prepared for the LRTA's series of regional histories of Britain's tramway systems. I am also grateful to the PSV Circle for permission to cite details obtained from the Circle's highly detailed and indispensable fleet histories. A further debt is owed to Mr. Price for agreeing to read through the galleys and for making many useful comments thereon.

I would also like to thank the following for their assistance: R. C. Ludgate for photographs and advice on the various Irish sections; J. W. P. Rowledge and R. J. S. Wiseman for information on Dublin; to A. D. Packer for photographic help on those systems that my Father did not visit; and to G. E. Baddeley, R. Brook, A. W. Brotchie, F. N. T. Lloyd-Jones and C. C. Thorburn for permission to use photographs. Information for the maps has been kindly provided by J. C. Gillham, whose highly detailed maps should be referred to for further information.

All uncredited photographs were taken by Michael H. Waller.

Finally, it goes without saying, that if, despite all the efforts made, any errors have slipped through, these are entirely my responsibility.

Author's note

Although the book is entitled *British and Irish Tramway Systems since 1945*, and all the photographs (bar a handful) date from the post-1945 period, the text covers the full history of each operator back to the 19th century. It was felt that the comprehensive text would allow the reader to put the post-1945 events into their proper historical context.

If, in 1945, a transport enthusiast, or even a professional within the industry, had been told that within 17 years the number of tramcars in Britain would have declined from almost 7,000 to less than 300 he would have wondered at the sanity of the messenger. True, the number of trams in the country had declined from a peak of some 14,000 and erstwhile tram operators had converted completely to bus or trolleybus systems, but there were still more than 40 towns and cities in the British Isles that had some form of tramway system. Whilst some of these systems were already under threat, others, most notably Leeds, Sheffield, Glasgow, Blackpool and Aberdeen, could be considered as bastions for this form of transport. That the position so radi-cally altered in less than a generation is one of the most remarkable aspects of British transport history.

In 1945 there were probably four distinct types of tramway operator. There were those, like Blackpool, Leeds and Glasgow, where the tramways had received substantial investment in the prewar decade and which still considered the tram to form the basis of future public transport needs. There were those small town systems, like Dundee and Stockport, which had seen little in the way of investment but which remained stalwart in their belief in the tram. There were those cities, like Hull and Manchester, where the war had intervened to prevent the already accepted closure procedure being completed. And, finally,

Right:
Although the majority of Britain's tramways were constructed to the standard gauge of 4ft 8½in, a significant number were constructed to other gauges. Of the other gauges, those of 3ft 6in and 4ft 0in were the most common. The authorities often set detailed limits on the trams that the narrow-gauge systems could operate. These limits tended to prevent the most modern fully-enclosed cars operating over the system and therefore made the comparison with the fully-enclosed bus or trolleybus much less favourable for the tram. One of the systems so limited was Bradford, where the adoption of the 4ft 0in gauge meant that the Corporation was forced to operate trams such as No 195 (seen at Bradford Moor on 6 November 1948), whilst Blackburn, another 4ft 0in system, was empowered to operate fully-enclosed cars, such as No 50 seen at Intack depot on 18 April 1949.

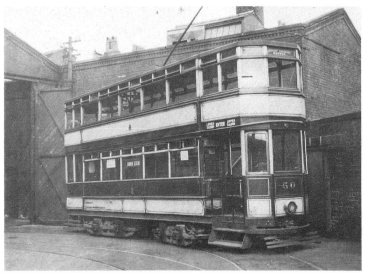

there were those systems, like the Snaefell and the Great Orme, which owed their existence to the tourist industry.

With peace in 1945 there came the opportunity for those systems for whom closure was already an agreed policy to wield the final axe. It came as little surprise when the cities of Manchester and Birmingham confirmed that the prewar closure policies were to be maintained. That the closures took time may, in hindsight, be a surprise, but at the time the austerity programme and the general 'make do and mend' policy meant that funds were not available for huge replacement fleets, even if the actual vehicles were available. The real question that needs to be addressed is why the apparently secure systems fell by the wayside.

There were a number of reasons why this occurred. In the first place, the war had imposed a great strain upon all transport undertakings. The decline in standards of maintenance was particularly noticeable on tram track and overhead and it was inevitable that there was a backlog of work required. At the same time, the cost of track and overhead had more than doubled from the prewar levels, making the restoration of prewar standards costly. Likewise, the cost of vehicles had increased so that whilst a double-deck bus could, by 1950, cost something like £4,500, the new single-deck trams, Nos 601/602, introduced by Leeds cost on average £12,500 each, whilst Dundee was quoted a staggering £21,000 in 1951 for a single articulated tramcar. There was little competition when it came to comparing these costs at a time of austerity.

Some of the tramway operators were able to avoid this inflation by the judicious acquisition of second-hand tramcars at a fraction of the price of new trams (although the costs of maintenance of second-hand trams were unfavourable compared to similar costs for brand-new buses) and by reusing recovered track from abandoned sections. Thus the Belle Isle/Middleton extension in Leeds was partly built using track from the closed Beckett Street section. But this policy was self-defeating; it delayed the investment needed to ensure the long-term survival of the trams and undermined the domestic manufacturing industry. By 1945 many of the best known tramcar manufacturers, such as English Electric and Brush (although Brush Coachworks did not finally close until 1951 and were capable of building trams, no orders came), had ceased to construct new vehicles, and whilst new builders emerged, such as Roberts and Roe, the market had declined to such an extent that the number

Above:
All British tramways were governed by the provisions of the 1870 Tramways Act. Amongst the clauses of the Act was one which made the tramway operator responsible for the maintenance of the public highway for a distance of 18in outside the running track. This inevitably added a considerable cost burden for all tramway operators — especially as the tram track was itself liable for rates — for something that was of no practical use to the tramway. Typical of most of Britain's street tramways is this section near Walmersley, with the 18in section clearly visible to the right of Bury No 11.

of new trams produced was minimal. Significantly, the largest batch of postwar trams, the Glasgow 'Cunarders', were constructed (like many of their predecessors) in the Corporation's own workshops — the powers that many operators had to construct their own tramcars adding to the plight of the manufacturing industry. The problem of the industry was compounded by the remarkable efforts that certain operators made to keep the old cars running; in Dundee, for example, by the closure in 1956 no tram was less than 26 years old and many were past their 50th anniversary — no wonder it came as a shock to the city authorities when, in the early 1950s, prices were sought for possible replacement vehicles!

The financial position of the tramways was further undermined by the provisions of the 1870 Tramways Act. In particular there were two aspects that played a significant role. The first of these was that the tramway operator was responsible not only for the maintenance of the track upon which the trams operated, but also the public highway for a distance of 18 inches outside the running tracks. This had the effect of loading additional costs upon the tramway opera-

Left:

A number of relatively small systems, such as Stockport, did not have any definite withdrawal plans prior to World War 2 and indeed undertook investment in the years immediately after the cessation of hostilities. But even these operators were not able to reverse the decline, especially when a large neighbour — Manchester in the case of Stockport — was determined on conversion. Stockport No 28 is seen in Mersey Square, hub of the Stockport system, on 14 May 1949.

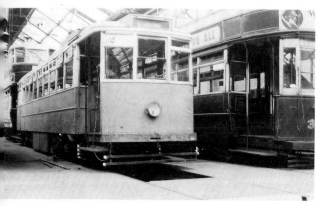

Above:
The increased congestion in city centres, along with the needs of postwar reconstruction, allowed for the development of plans to improve the provision of public transport. Although never reaching fruition, a number of cities had positive plans for the development of trams after 1945. One of the most notable were the proposals for tramway subways in Leeds. In furtherance of these plans, Sunderland No 85 was acquired by Leeds in 1944. Numbered 288 in the Leeds fleet, it was progressively rebuilt between 1949 and 1954. By the time it entered service, the car's *raison d'être* had passed, and as No 600 it eked out a shadowy existence on the Hunslet shuttle - a far cry from the earlier hopes.

amended, but with no success. Indeed, this particular provision of the Act remains in force and will affect the development of the new generation of Light Rail schemes. The second financial penalty imposed upon the trams was their liability for payment of rates for the track. Thus, whilst the public purse benefited, the overall financial position of the operator was weakened. Moreover, it was common for the profits made by the transport department, if municipally owned, to be transferred to the central funds to alleviate the overall rates bill rather than being used to fund future development of the system. In Blackpool, the perceived threat of Nationalisation was used as a reason to transfer the transport department's reserves, with the result that the acquisition of the 'Coronation' cars could only be funded by borrowing and thus leading to additional debt charges on the transport department.

The threat of Nationalisation was real. The Nationalisation of the electricity industry in the 1940s was an additional factor in the decline of electric street transport, both trams and trolleybuses, in Britain. Most local authorities had built power stations to generate power for transport, such as Valley Road in Bradford and Kirkstall in Leeds, and so long as these remained in municipal ownership the council was happy to see municipal enterprise supported. This was one factor behind the growth of trolleybus operation in the 1930s, since it allowed for the replacement of the trams whilst still supporting the municipal power station. Nationalisation and the imposition of national tariffs meant that the same principle no longer applied. In Leeds the introduction of national tariffs led to a sizeable increase in the costs of power, whilst the Nationalisation of Pinkston power station in Glasgow, in 1958, accelerated the decline of both tram and trolleybus operations in that city.

No doubt these factors could have been surmounted, but the tram was increasingly seen as old-fashioned and out of place in a modern society. When Lord Latham proclaimed at the closing

tor and also, because the rest of the road may not have been maintained to a similar standard, of funnelling other road transport onto the centre of the road and thereby making it appear again that the trams were contributing to congestion. There were efforts, most notably sponsored by Leeds in the early 1950s, to get this legislation

Left:
Whilst certain operators were eagerly disposing of their trams, others, such as Sunderland, were taking advantage to acquire second-hand bargains. One of Sunderland's more notable acquisitions was one of the prototype 'Felthams', ex-MET No 331. In its new guise as No 100, the tram is seen at Seaburn in May 1950. Whilst the policy of acquiring second-hand trams may have made economic sense in an era of austerity, it did little to sustain the domestic tramcar industry.

ceremony in London 'Goodbye, old tram' he was merely reflecting the widely held view amongst many influential transport executives. Without a doubt, there were people who were positive in their view of the future of trams in Britain — figures like W. Vane Morland in Leeds, E. R. L. Fitzpayne in Glasgow and W. G. Marks in Liverpool come readily to mind — but they were increasingly outnumbered by those who had grown up with systems that relied on buses to provide the basic public transport or whose views on tramcars were negative. The views of such people were officially supported by the Report of a Royal Commission in 1930. This important doc-

ument not only rejected the pleas that tramway operators be relieved of their duty to maintain the highway, but also argued that no further tramways should be constructed and that trams should gradually disappear in favour of other forms of transport. There were opponents to closure, such as Councillor Mather in Leeds, and local pressure groups, for example in Sheffield and Liverpool, did emerge to contest the issue, but these campaigns were too little and too late to save the tramcar. In many cases the public seemed to welcome the comfortable new buses or trolleybuses, which ran in the place of the old and noisy trams: a fond farewell but a hearty welcome to the rubber tyre.

With the rubber tyre came the flexibility that seemed to promise the end of city centre congestion. Trams tied to their rigid track were widely perceived as being a major contributory factor in the increasing congestion of city centres. As early

Right:
With most of the central area tracks built on-street and lacking the resources — or political will — for major central redevelopment, the tram was always going to be perceived as a major contributory factor to road congestion. Typical of the urban street-scape through which the majority of British trams operated is this view of Sheffield, with cars Nos 118 and 272 passing each other in September 1949. Where proposals were made to accommodate the tramcar in the postwar city, such as in Liverpool and Leeds, the lack of resources meant that such schemes were still-born.

Left:

One of the most significant factors in the increasing cost of tramcars after 1945 was the disappearance of many of the leading tramcar manufacturers in the prewar period. One such casualty was Brush, whose batch of streamlined trams delivered in 1937 to Blackpool, typified by No 292 seen at Cleveleys on 9 September 1948, were destined to be the last tramcars manufactured by the company.

Centre left:

As early as 1914, certain operators became aware of the problem of traffic congestion and the possibility that trams might contribute to the problem. In the pre-World War 1 days the congestion was caused by horse-drawn vehicles; increasingly as the century progressed the motor vehicle was to be the cause. In Liverpool, the general manager appreciated that public transport would involve a choice between buses and light rapid transit, with trams removed from city centre streets such as Old Haymarket. The radical solutions proposed, however, enabled the anti-tram lobby to gain the advantage.

as 1914 there had been attempts to analyse the problem and determine solutions. With many of Britain's city centres arising in a haphazard fashion with little thought to overall town planning, it was inevitable that many of the streets served by trams would be unsuitable and the proponents of tramway development and the adoption of reserved sections were always faced by the unwillingness of city authorities to contemplate the wholesale redevelopment of central areas. Moreover, after the destruction of World War 2 when the prospects of reconstruction opened up great possibilities, such as those proposed by W. G. Marks in Liverpool and by W. Vane Morland in Leeds, the ultimate decision never went in the tramcars' favour.

British and Irish Tramway Systems since 1945 is the story of failed endeavour, of the constant victory of rubber over steel and of the dramatic change in public transport over a 20-year period.

Left:

To avoid traffic congestion and to improve passenger access, segregated reserved track sections were a solution. But these were costly to provide and difficult to create on the existing radial roads. One of the few postwar extensions, that to Belle Isle in Leeds, was built upon those principles: this was one of the few contemporary housing estates, built in the suburbs, to be served by the trams. Elsewhere, the cost of providing a tram service to these outlying estates was considered prohibitive and so buses or trolleybuses were adopted instead.

The Granite City of Aberdeen was destined to be the northernmost of all Britain's postwar tramway operators and the penultimate tramway to operate in Scotland. Regarded for many years, even after 1945, as one of the most secure of Britain's tramway systems, the ill wind that swept many of the other systems meant that the promise that Aberdeen displayed during the 1940s came to nothing.

The Aberdeen District Tramways Act was passed in 1872. This allowed for the construction of a number of horse-tram routes within the city. The first two routes — from Queens Cross to Union Street and from St Nicholas Street to Kittybrewster — both opened, under private operation, in 1874. By 1898 further horse-tramways had been opened from St Nicholas Street to Woodside, from Castle Street to Mannofield and Queens Cross (via both Rosemount and Union Street) and from Bridge of Don to Bridge of Dee. A total of some 30 horse-trams were now in operation. On 26 August 1898 the Aberdeen Tramways Co sold out to the Corporation, and the latter took immediate steps to modernise the system through the Aberdeen Corporation Tramways Act of 1898.

On 23 December 1899 the first electric car operated on the route from St Nicholas Street to Woodside and further routes quickly followed. Amongst these was the line from Castle Street to Sea Beach, which opened on 4 July 1901. This route was of particular interest in that it saw the experimental use of stud contacts, rather than conventional overhead, for current collection. This experiment was, however, soon deemed to be a disappointment and overhead was erected within a fortnight of the opening. By 1902, with

the electric tramcar fleet now numbering 32, all the erstwhile horse tramway routes had been converted to electric traction. The cost of conversion had been £156,000. During 1903 two further extensions — to Ferryhill and Torry — were opened, taking the fleet strength to 56. There was now a period of consolidation, the most important development prior to the outbreak of World War 1 being the experimental use of Pay As You Enter on a number of routes during the period 28 April 1913 to 15 March 1915. This was not popular and was not repeated.

As elsewhere, the years 1914-18 witnessed a decline in the standards of maintenance. But the building of a brand-new depot at King Street (on the site of disused barracks) in 1919 (extended in 1932) was indicative of the return to postwar normality. However, the tram was no longer destined to remain dominant since, in 1920, it was decided that all new routes were to be operated by buses. The first bus service, an experimental circular tour, was launched on 19 July 1920 and the first proper bus service, from Castle Street to Footdee, opened on 10 January 1921. The aim was to generate the traffic and then, if it materialised, the investment in the tramway could be justified. The potential of the scheme was borne out by the opening of a two-mile extension of the Rubislaw route on 16 July 1924 to Hazlehead, an extension which replaced a bus service introduced in 1921 to serve the housing estate. The commitment of Aberdeen to the tramway was demonstrated by the acquisition in 1926 of 16 new trams.

1931 was to witness the first contraction in the tramway system with the conversion of two routes to bus operation: that to Torry on 28 February; and that to Duthie Park on 30 May. This did not, however, mean that Aberdeen's policy was now tramway abandonment, but rather to develop the tramways on the most heavily trafficked services. In 1935 bow collectors started to replace the conventional trolley boom, whilst the following year the first second-hand trams, from Nottingham, were acquired. In 1937 two major track alterations were started. The first, to construct a loop to serve the football ground at Pittodrie, was completed quickly. The second, to provide a more direct route from the city centre to Sea Beach, saw construction suspended on the outbreak of World War 2, and, whilst it was confidently expected that construction would resume on the cessation of hostilities, this route was never completed. However, 1938 did witness the extension of the Woodside route to Scatterburn, along the route of the erstwhile Aberdeen Subur-

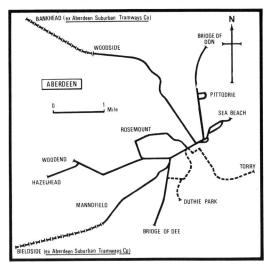

Left:
After their withdrawal in Manchester, 14 of the 'Pilcher' cars migrated northwards to Aberdeen where they were to give the Granite City almost a further 10 years of service. No 45, originally Manchester No 274, is seen at the Bridge of Don terminus on 24 January 1949.

Below left:
Aberdeen No 89, one of 12 open balcony double-deck trams delivered in 1920, is seen on Castle Street in January 1949.

the route to Mannofield, which was scheduled for early closure. This closure was not to be undertaken immediately due to the delay in obtaining replacement buses, with the consequence that in 1948 part of the route was relaid.

For supporters of tramways, during the late 1940s, Aberdeen remained one of the high spots. In 1948 the Corporation was one of several nationwide to take advantage of the contraction of the Manchester tramway system when it acquired 14 of the 'Pilcher' cars, whilst in 1949 20 new streamlined cars, manufactured by Pickerings on EMB bogies, entered service. At the time these were amongst the first tramcars to be manufactured by Pickerings and despite the forecast that Pickerings would have a future in tramcar manufacturing, no further orders resulted.

On 3 March 1951 the long expected closure of the route to Mannofield took place. At the same time, however, the Corporation reaffirmed that its policy was to retain tramcars on the main routes. This policy was destined to be relatively short-lived as the pro-abandonment lobby gradually gained influence. In February 1955 it was announced that the new policy was to see all trams withdrawn by the end of the decade. Indeed, the first abandonment, that of the Rosemount circle, had already taken place on 2 October 1954. The introduction of the new streamlined cars in 1949 had already seen the elimination of many of the older tramcars, the new policy of abandonment was to lead to the rapid withdrawal of many more. The ex-Nottingham cars had been withdrawn by 1951, whilst the 'Pilcher' cars were to follow by 1956. The mid-1950s were also to witness the demise of many of the trams built during the 1920s.

The next closure, on 26 November 1955, saw the route from St Nicholas Street to Woodside converted to bus operation. At the same time St Nicholas Street ceased to be a terminus. This closure was followed in September 1956 by the withdrawal of services to Sea Beach. This closure was, however, destined to be temporary due to

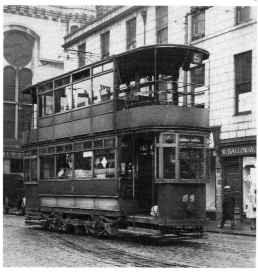

ban Tramways Co — a route that had been abandoned originally, along with the rest of the Suburban network, in 1926. The Suburban Co had originally operated two routes, effectively extensions of the Mannofield and Woodside lines.

It was also decided in 1938 to buy a further 20 new trams. Only four were delivered at this stage, however, but with their streamlined design they were to revolutionise tramways in Aberdeen. Manufactured by English Electric and delivered in 1940, Nos 138-141 were the only additions to the tram fleet during the war. In 1945 the Corporation decided that the tram system would be retained and modernised, with the exception of

the Suez crisis, and the trams were restored on 17 December 1956 for a further four months. Despite Suez, the next closure, that to Hazlehead, took place on 7 October 1956, to be followed on 17 November 1956 by the route to Woodend. The line to Sea Beach finally succumbed on 13 March 1957, leaving the primary north-south route — from Bridge of Don to Bridge of Dee — to become the last tram route. By this stage the Aberdeen fleet had declined to primarily the streamlined cars of 1949 along with a number of oddments from other types, and the final closure was not to be long delayed. With closure now the avowed policy, maintenance standards declined; and with the worsening condition of the track it was decided to bring forward the closure to 3 May 1958. The official last car was, appropriately, one of the streamlined cars which had seemed to promise so much when introduced — No 36.

Although by the late 1950s the tramcar preservation movement had gained ground, none of Aberdeen's fleet of electric tramcars survives. The Scottish Tramway Museum Society acquired 1913 J. T. Clark-built balcony car No 73, but this was subsequently scrapped. All the streamlined cars went for scrap as did all the second-hand trams. One Aberdeen tram does, however, survive. This is horse car No 1. This particular tram was one of the horse cars acquired by the Corporation from the Aberdeen District Tramways Co. Rebuilt in c1900 for use on the newly electrified line to Woodside, it was reconverted back to a horse car in 1924 and subsequently preserved. Even this

Above:
On 28 May 1955 No 115 is seen at the Hazlehead terminus of route 4. The car, one of a batch of nine supplied by Brush in 1925, is adorned by adverts, which by this time were beginning to appear on Aberdeen's trams. The service to Hazlehead would continue for another 18 months, being withdrawn in October 1956.

could not, however, find a home in its home town and was displayed for many years in Edinburgh before returning north to the Grampian Transport Museum at Alford.

Below:
The first of two streamlined double-deck bogie trams delivered in 1940, No 138, is pictured at the Bridge of Don terminus on 24 January 1949 awaiting its next turn of duty on the route to Bridge of Dee.

Aberdeen Closures	
3 March 1951	2 — Mannofield
2 October 1954	3, 5, 6 — Rosemount Circle
26 November 1955	7 — Woodside
7 October 1956	4 — Hazlehead
17 November 1956	4 — Woodend
13 March 1957	9 — Sea Beach (service had been suspended from September 1956 but was reintroduced due to Suez crisis on 17 December 1956)
3 May 1958	1 — Bridge of Don to Bridge of Dee
Last tram: No 36	

Aberdeen

Fleet Numbers	Date	Trucks/Bogies	Body	Withdrawn
1-18[1]	1936 (acquired)	Peckham P22	EE	1949-51
19-38[2]	1949	EMB bogies	Pickering	1958
39-52[3]	1948 (acquired)	Peckham P35	Manchester CT	1955-56
33-56 (i)[4]	1903	Brill 21E	Dick Kerr	All by 1950
57-61	1922	Peckham P35 (originally Brill 21E)	Aberdeen CT	1953-54
62-3	1923	Peckham P35 (originally Brill 21E)	Aberdeen CT	1958
66-7	1919	Peckham P35 (originally Brill 21E)	Aberdeen CT	1951 (66), 1953 (67)
72-7[5]	1913	Peckham P35/Brill 21E (not all converted from 21E)	J. T. Clark	1952-55
78-83	1914	Peckham P35 (originally Brill 21E)	Brush	1949-53
84-6[6]	1915	Brill 21E	Aberdeen CT	?
87-98[7]	1920	Peckham P35/Brill 21E (not all converted)	Aberdeen CT	1950-53
99	1923	Peckham P35 (originally Brill 21E)	Aberdeen CT	1956
100-106[8]	1924-25	Peckham P35 (originally Brill 21E)	Aberdeen CT	1956-58
107-15	1925	Peckham P35	Brush	1953-58
116-22[9]	1925-29	Peckham P35 (originally Brill 21E)	Aberdeen CT	1955
123	1930	EMB	Aberdeen CT	1958
124	1931	Peckham P35 (originally Brill 21E)	Aberdeen CT	1958
126-37	1929	Peckham P35	Brush	1955-58
138-39[10]	1940	EMB bogies	EE	1956-58
140-41	1940	EMB 4-wheel	EE	1956-58

1 Ex-Nottingham 181-94, 196-9 built 1926-27. Delivered in three sections and therefore not identifiable. 19th car bought as spares. No 18 used as works car post-1950.
2 Streamlined.
3 Ex-Manchester 'Pilcher' cars built 1930-32. Respective MCT numbers 121, 493, 420, 671, 161, 610, 274, 669, 141, 270, 106, 225, 510, 502.
4 Originally open top, converted to top cover. No 54 to railgrinder 4A in 1948 — withdrawn 1958.
5 No 73 sold to STMS for preservation but scrapped.
6 Converted to snowploughs — withdrawn 1952.
7 No 87 withdrawn in 1952 converted to snowplough and withdrawn in 1958.
8 No 102 exchanged number with 120.
9 No 120 exchanged number with 102.
10 Prototype streamline cars.

Left:
Aberdeen No 2, one of the ex-Nottingham cars, is seen at the Castle Street terminus of route 5 to King's Gate (via Rosemount) on 24 January 1949. No 2 was destined to be the last of the type withdrawn.

The city of Belfast has a number of claims to fame in transport history. It was the only Irish tramway to adopt the British standard gauge of nominally 4ft 8½in (it was actually 4ft 9in), it was the only Irish operator of trolleybuses, and it was the last tramway to operate in Northern Ireland. Belfast was, however, a relatively late entrant into the history of electric street transport.

The origins of tramways in Belfast go back to the early 1870s. On 22 December 1871, powers were obtained for the construction of a horse-tramway system. This was constructed during the following year, and on 28 August 1872 the first horse-trams, operated by the Belfast Street Tramways Co, ran on a route from Botanic Gardens to Castle Place. Further routes quickly followed. Although these initial routes were constructed to the Irish standard gauge of 5ft 3in, further powers obtained in the late 1870s allowed for the conversion to '4ft 8½in'. Further extensions to the horse-tramway network continued to be built through the 1880s and early 1890s.

In 1896 the company obtained powers for the conversion of the horse-tramway network to electric traction, although only with the Corporation's permission, and these powers were never exercised. In 1899 an act was passed which empowered the Corporation to construct tramways, and these were initially operated by the horse-trams of the Belfast Street Tramways Co. Finally, in 1904 the corporation obtained the Belfast Corporation (Tramways) Act which, amidst much acrimony, allowed for the Corpora-

tion to take over the Belfast Street Tramways Co, convert the lines to electric traction and build a number of extensions. On 1 January 1905 Belfast Corporation became the proud owner of some 170 horse-trams and two horse-buses. The process of conversion could go ahead.

Work proceeded rapidly, both in terms of vehicle delivery and route conversion, and on 30 November 1905 new electric tramcar services were introduced on Stranmillis Road, Malone Road, Springfield Road and Ormeau Road. The rest of the system was opened a week later on 5 December 1905. To operate the new services, 170 trams from Brush, with Brill 21E trucks, had been ordered. In addition, a number of ex-horse-trams were also converted. The first of the extensions authorised under the 1904 Act, that to Queens Road, opened on 11 August 1908. This route was ultimately destined to be the last route to operate.

Apart from the Belfast Street Tramways Co there were a number of other tramways in the city, but all, apart from one, had been operated by the Belfast Street Tramways Co. The exception was the Cavehill & Whitewell Co and this company also retained its independence after the 1904 Act. The Cavehill & Whitewell operated from Chichester Park to Glengormley. The line opened on 1 July 1882 and was initially operated by steam-trams. Subsequently operation was by a combination of horse- and steam-trams and from 1895 until 1906 by horse-trams alone. The line was converted to electric traction in 1906. During its independent existence the Cavehill & Whitewell was a thorn in the side of the Corporation and, consequently, the Corporation sought to take it over. This was achieved by the passing of the Belfast Corporation Tramways Act in 1910, and Corporation took over operation of the line (and the company's 10 trams) from 2 June 1911. The final settlement did not take place until the following year. It was from the Cavehill & Whitewell that the Corporation Tramways inherited their most peculiar asset — the estate at Bellevue which was developed (under the aegis of the Tramways Department!) into zoological gardens as a means of generating extra business onto the route. The Transport Department retained ownership of the zoological gardens well after the demise of the tramways, a fact which often led to Belfast's senior management being the butt of humour from their colleagues in other operators.

Following the acquisition of the Cavehill line, further extensions were built to the systems during 1913. These extensions included Donegall

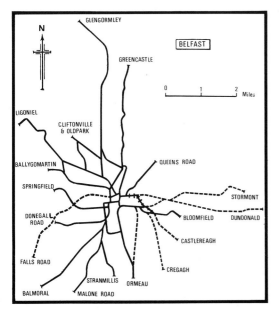

Road, Botanic Avenue (which led to the abandonment of the Ormeau Avenue line, the first closure of a section of electric tramway in the city), Castlereagh Road, Old Park Road and along Ravenhill Road to Ormeau Road. Two extensions to existing routes were also completed — Stranmillis Road and Ligoniel.

The process of tramway improvement continued after World War 1. In September 1923 the Belmont route was extended to Stormont, in July 1924 the Knock route was extended to Dundonald and on 18 December 1924 the section of track along Chichester Street in the city centre was completed. Belfast's last tramway extension, to Ballygomartin, was opened on 23 July 1925.

In 1926 the Corporation decided that it would adopt motorbuses to act as feeders to the tramways. There was still no overt intention of abandoning the tramways. The first buses appeared on 4 October 1926 on a route from the city centre to Cavehill. One factor in the fairly conservative view of tramway development was the inclusion of the so-called 'Aberdeen' clause in the 1904 Act. This clause had the effect of preventing the subsidising of the tramways from the rates (although the latter could be subsidised by profits from the tramways) and, thus, if the tramways had a period of continuing trading losses, they could have been forced to close. This meant that the risks involved in extending the tramway network were considerable. Moreover, the relatively parlous condition of the tramways was revealed in the bus wars that ran in the city between June and December 1928. They were a result of the 1926 Motor Vehicles (Traffic & Regulations) Act, with private bus operators undercutting the fares on the Corporation routes. If the wars had continued unabated the the tramways of Belfast would have suffered severely.

As it was, the drafting of new licensing laws (itself a cause of considerable controversy) and the appointment of a new General Manager, William Chamberlain, in November 1928, led to a more stable situation in which further investment in the tramways could be considered. The most conspicuous sign of this investment was the acquisition of 50 brand-new trams, Nos 342-91, from Brush and Service Motor Works Ltd, which inevitably became known as 'Chamberlains'. Despite this investment the Corporation simultaneously obtained powers, under the Belfast Corporation Act 1930, to operate trolleybuses.

Chamberlain's tenure at Belfast was relatively short; he resigned in 1931 to join the Traffic Commissioners in London and he was replaced by Col Robert McCreary. It was McCreary who laid down the specification for the next batch of trams, 50 streamlined cars delivered from Service Motor Works and from English Electric. Nicknamed 'McCrearies', they were delivered in 1934 in the new blue-and-cream livery pioneered by Chamberlain. These 50 trams, numbered 392-441, were to be the last trams delivered to Belfast.

1 October 1936 was to witness the first tramway abandonment since the closure of the Ormeau Avenue line before World War 1, when the outer section of the Cregagh Road route (from Gibson Park to the original terminus) was converted due to the poor state of the track. This was followed during 1937 by the diverting of services away from the Mountpottinger Road line. Yet 1937 was the peak year for Belfast's trams, with some 350 vehicles covering 9.7 million miles in service. However, in October 1936 the Transport Committee approved the conversion of one route to provide a trial for trolleybus operation. The Falls Road route was converted to trolleybus

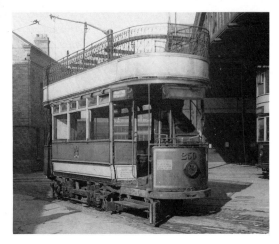

leybus operation during 1941. On 26 March 1942 the Stormont route was converted to trolleybus operation, followed on 16 November by the Dundonald via Queen's Bridge route. The alternative route to Dundonald, via Albert Bridge, was also converted to trolleybus operation on 8 March 1943.

1945 dawned with Belfast retaining a still considerable tramway network. Although the majority of the tramcar fleet was relatively modern, a number of the converted horse-trams remained in service. The next casualty was the Ormeau Road route via Botanic Avenue. The need to replace a sewer on Botanic Avenue led to the tram service being suspended on 5 January 1945 — and it was never reinstated.

The next casualty, on 5 May 1946, was the Bloomfield route, which was converted to trolleybus operation. This was followed on 20 April 1947 by the Donegall Road route, although this route was taken over by motorbuses. A second casualty of 1947 was the Cliftonville route, which was abandoned on 31 August. There was no direct replacement for this service as the existing bus services to the area were augmented. The next closure was that of Ormeau Road via Cromac Street, which was converted to trolleybus operation on 19 April 1948. Despite the closures, which had effectively reduced the tram network to about half its maximum, the trams still carried about half of the 257 million passengers in the year — and 1948 was the peak year for passengers carried overall.

The only closure of 1949, on 23 January, saw the end of the long route north to Glengormley that had been inherited from the Cavehill & Whitewell Tramway Co. This period also witnessed the final demise of the ex-horse-trams, four of which (Nos 213/244/249/250) had been retained for works duties. No 249 was retained as

operation on 28 March 1938, and less than a year later, in January 1939, the decision was made to convert the rest of the tram system over a five-year period.

Although the war did mean that the original five-year programme was impractical, Belfast, unlike most other cities in Britain, witnessed a considerable diminution of its tramway system during the war. On 5 September 1940 the Ravenhill Road route was converted to motorbus operation. Two routes, to Cregagh (on 13 February) and Castlereagh (on 5 June), succumbed to trola museum piece and was to appear again, in 1953, during an LRTL tour when it was made available for photography.

On 21 August 1950 the service into the NCC station (via Corporation Street) was converted to bus operation. From this date the Stranmillis route (which had been linked with the NCC station) now ran to Queens Road via the High Street instead of along Chichester Street. This closure was followed on 1 October 1950 by the conversion of the Greencastle route. With this closure there also disappeared the siding into the BCDR station; with this siding and the one serving the NCC station, Belfast was probably unique in providing such an undercover interchange facility between tram and rail.

1951 was to witness the closure of three more routes, but the first event of significance was the renumbering of all services to avoid any confusion. The remaining tram routes were allocated service numbers in the range 50-69. The first closure of 1951, on 29 April, was the route to Oldpark. This was followed on 29 July by the service to Stranmillis. The Queens Road route was now linked with Springfield Road. Finally, on 4 November, the Malone Road route saw trams for the last time.

Significantly, all the closures of 1951 saw the trams abandoned in favour of motorbuses — indeed, the last tram to trolleybus conversion was the Greencastle route in 1950 — and the final abandonment of the Belfast trams was significantly delayed due to problems in obtaining replacement buses. There were, therefore, no further abandonments until 9 November 1952 when four routes — Ballygomartin, Balmoral, Harbester Park and Springfield — were converted simultaneously. During early 1953, some 100 ex-London Transport buses were acquired, and these started to appear on the Crumlin Road route from 9 February, although the trams were to remain for a further eight months. On 3 July

Belfast Closures

5 September 1940	Ravenhill Road
13 February 1941	Cregagh
5 June 1941	Castlereagh
26 March 1942	Stormont
16 November 1942	Dundonald (via Queens Bridge)
8 March 1943	Dundonald (via Albert Bridge)
5 January 1945	Ormeau Road (via Botanic Avenue) (service initially suspended due to sewer work in Botanic Avenue then abandoned completely)
5 May 1946	Bloomfield
20 April 1947	Donegall Road
31 August 1947	Cliftonville Road
19 April 1948	Ormeau Road (via Cromac Road) (in 1948, despite the closures, Belfast trams still carried more passengers than the buses and trolleybuses combined)
23 January 1949	Glengormley
21 August 1950	LMS railway (via Corporation Street)
1 October 1950	Greencastle
29 April 1951	Oldpark Road
29 July 1951	Stranmillis
4 November 1951	Malone Road

9 November 1952	Balmoral
9 November 1952	Ballygomartin
9 November 1952	Springfield
9 November 1952	Harberton Park
3 July 1953	Withdrawal of limited peak hours services from Queens Road to Windsor Park (Lisburn Road) Queens Road to Mackie's Foundry (Springfield Road) Queens Road to Fortwilliam
10/11 October 1953	All day services on the remaining routes to Ligoniel (via Crumlin Road and via Shankill Road) and Queens Road
28 February 1954	Official last tram

Pre-1940 closures:

1 October 1936	Outer part of Cregagh route (Gibson Park to terminus)
1937	Mountpottinger to Castlereagh trams diverted via Albert Bridge.
28 March 1938	Falls Road (first trolleybus conversion)

Last tram: No 389

1953 the final trams along the Lisburn Road (Balmoral) and Springfield routes were replaced — after the withdrawal of the full services a number of peak-hour services had continued to be operated due to the lack of buses. To ease further the vehicle shortage, 11 second-hand trolleybuses were bought from Wolverhampton. The stage was set for the final rites.

On 10 October 1953 all-day services were withdrawn from the Queens Road route, although peak-hour services continued for a further four months, representing the only tram services in Belfast for that period. Then on 11 October, services were withdrawn from the Ligoniel, Crumlin Road and Shankill Road services. Even the remaining peak-hour trams were gradually phased out as the ex-London Transport buses

were rebodied for service, so that by the middle of February 1954 all tram operation had ceased, the last regular services occurring on 10 February. On 28 February 1954 the official ceremony took place, a procession of 12 'Chamberlain' cars running from Queens Road to Ardoyne depot, with No 389 being the official last car. Although a number of the 'McCreary' cars survived until February 1954, none were represented in the closure procession. As elsewhere, the official last tram did not mark the final movement — for a number of months following, until 17 June, the remaining trams processed from Ardoyne depot to Mountpottinger depot for scrapping. The last car into the depot, 'Chamberlain' No 357, was preserved and now resides with ex-horse-tram No 249 in the Belfast Transport Museum.

Belfast

Fleet Numbers	Date	Trucks/Bogies	Body	Withdrawn
2-5/10/2-4/6-8/23/6/7/9/30/2/ 33/6/7/40/2/3/46/8-51/4/5/7/ 58/61-5/73/80/88/9/94/5/8 100-5/7/8/10/1/3/4/6/8/ 9-22/4/6/8/30/2/4-7/40/1/ 4/6/147/9/51/3/5-8/162/3/6-70 [1]	1905	Brill 21E	Brush	1945-51
172-4/6-80/2/5/7-9/91/2 [2]	1908-10	Brill 21E (Brush-built)	Belfast CT	1948-51
194/5/7-200 [3]	Acquired 1911	Originally Lycett & Conaty radial (Long) or Brill (short), all retrucked to Brush Brill-type	Brush	1948-51
207/8/12/3/8/20-3/7/32/7/8/ 44-50 [4]	1905	Brush Brill-type	?	1946-54
251-91 [5]	1913-19	Brush Brill-type retrucked to Brush 7ft 6in 1929-32	Belfast CT, rebuilt by BCT or Service Motor Works	1951-54
292-341 [6]	1920-21	Brush Brill-type 7ft 6in retrucked to Maley and Taunton swinglink 8ft 0in	Brush	1951-53
342-91 [7]	1930	M&T Swinglink 8ft 0in	Brush 342-81; Service MW 382-91	1951-54
392-441 [8]	1935-36	M&T Swinglink 8ft 0in	EE 392, 423-41; Service MW 393-422	1950-54
21/2/31/5/78/123/59/64/86 [9]	Rebuilt 1929-32	Brush 7ft 6in	Brush, rebuilt by BCT or Service MW	1951-54

1 Remaining cars from original batch 1-170.
2 Remaining cars from batch 171-92.
3 Batch 193-200 — Belfast acquired eight of 10 trams from Cavehill & Whitewell Tramway in 1911 — five were C&W 1-5 (small) and three were from C&W 6-10 (large). The remaining two large cars had been sold to Mansfield in 1909. The large cars were unsuitable but one plus the five small cars were rebuilt as Belfast 'Standard' cars. Dated originally from 1906.
4 Batch 201-50 — originally horse-trams but rebuilt on the electrification of the system. Originally open top, some later received top covers. No 249 retained as snowplough until 1954 and preserved.
5 Rebuilt by Chamberlain as part of the 'DK1' class.
6 'Moffett' class.
7 'Chamberlain' class. No 357 preserved.
8 'McCreary' class.
9 'DK1' rebuilds dating from 1929-32 of 'Standard Reds' dating originally from 1905. Initially constructed with Brill 21E trucks.

Of the four tramways in Northern Ireland to survive into the postwar era, none were typical: the Fintona line was an archaic survival; the Belfast system adopted the British, rather than Irish, standard gauge; and the remaining two were amongst the oldest surviving electric railways in the British Isles. The first of these two survivors to close, indeed the first closure in all of Ireland after 1945, was the Bessbrook & Newry.

The development of the line was linked closely with the development of the Bessbrook spinning mills. These had been acquired in 1846 by the Richardsons, the concept of the line developing as a means of carrying coal and other raw materials from the quay at Newry to the mills and to transport the finished linen in the reverse direction. Initially, as shown in the Provisional Order of 1881, the line was intended to be steam-powered, but following the advice of Dr Edward Hopkinson the decision was made to adopt the new means of propulsion — electricity. Work started on building the line on 8 September 1883, and the necessary powers to use electricity were obtained on 26 May 1884. The power was to be generated through an hydro-electric power station at Millvale, on the Camlaugh Stream, and the third rail was to be adopted as a means of transmitting the power to the cars. By July 1885, laying of the conductor rail was completed, and, following an inspection on 10 September, public services started on 1 October 1885.

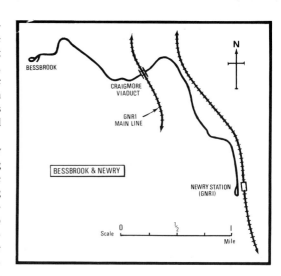

The total length of the line was some three miles, and it was built to the 3ft 0in gauge. It was fitted throughout with a centre third-rail, except

Below:
Bessbrook & Newry car No 1 hauls a typical train, comprising van No 7 and trailer No 6 in the early 1930s. Although the Bessbrook & Newry was predominantly a third-rail operation, there were a number of sections, at road crossings, where overhead was required necessitating the fitting of a bow collector to No 1. *Real Photographs/IAL*

Above:
A view of Bessbrook station and sheds in the early 1930s. *Real Photographs/IAL*

at about a dozen road junctions where a gap was left. The power cars were fitted with collector shoes at both ends to enable them to bridge these gaps; there was only one point, at Millvale itself, where the gap, at 150ft, was too long for this approach, and, therefore, a short stretch of overhead was fitted at this point. Two motor cars, Nos 1 and 2, were manufactured by the Ashbury Carriage Co of Manchester, which eventually became Metropolitan Amalgamated. A third, unpowered, trailer car was supplied by Starbuck of Birkenhead. In addition, there were a number of wagons, reflecting the dual purpose of the line. The wagons were unusual in that they were built without flanges, to enable them to operate also on the public highway, and an ingenious arrangement with the running track, effectively putting a second running rail at a lower level outside the main running rail, was adopted to allow the wagons to run over the tramway.

Once completed, the tramway fulfilled its objectives successfully and profitably for the next 30 years. By the 1920s, however, the original rolling stock and equipment was becoming increasingly outmoded, and consideration was given to the line's modernisation. Following discussions with the government, agreement was reached whereby the authorities would fund the

replacement of the generating equipment and the company would replace the rolling stock. However, a dispute arose, and this led to the government refusing to sanction the expenditure. The board of the tramway responded by threatening to close down the tramway if the funds were not forthcoming. The government relented and the modernisation proceeded. In 1920, two new cars were ordered from Hurst Nelson. On delivery these became Nos 1 and 4; it is believed that No 4 incorporated certain parts from the original No 1 which was withdrawn at this time. Also, in 1920, a further trailer car, No 5, was also ordered, and this was joined by another trailer car, No 6, in about 1923. In 1927, car No 4 was re-equipped, and in 1928 two single-deck trailer cars were acquired from the then bankrupt Dublin & Lucan Electric Railway. These two trailers were originally built for the 3ft 0in gauge when the Dublin & Lucan was steam-operated, but on the electrification of the line were converted to 3ft 6in; on their transfer to the Bessbrook & Newry the trams were reconverted to 3ft 0in. For a short period both cars ran in their Dublin & Lucan livery of pale cream and green.

The two ex-Dublin & Lucan cars were numbered 24 and 27. On the withdrawal of the original Bessbrook & Newry car No 2, the body of No 24 was placed on the original underframes and extended to form a new car, again numbered 2. In this condition the tramway continued to operate. As elsewhere, World War 2 was to lead to a serious decline in maintenance and in the

21

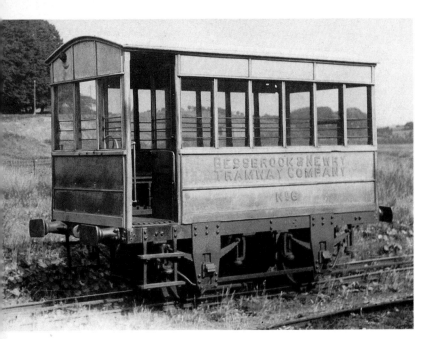

Left:
The rolling stock of the Bessbrook & Newry was a curious assortment. This is four-wheel trailer car No 6, which dated originally from the early 1920s and is pictured some 10 years later. *Real Photographs/IAL*

overall standard of the line, such that by 1947, competition, in the form of a frequent bus service linking the two termini operated by the Northern Ireland Road Transport Board, foreshadowed the demise of the tramway. On 5 October 1947 a new timetable was issued which showed only eight return workings per day, so it came as little surprise when the line closed completely on 10 Jan-uary 1948. There was no official ceremony to mark the closure and no last car was recorded.

After closure, the proprietors of the other historic hydro-electric line, the Giants Causeway, expressed interest in acquiring the Bessbrook & Newry fleet, but little progress was made. Of the cars, all bar the hybrid No 2 were scrapped. No 2 was acquired by the Manchester firm of Mather & Platt and was displayed for a time at its works. After the establishment of the Museum of Transport in Belfast, the car was returned to Northern Ireland where it remains on display in the company of Giants Causeway car No 5.

Bessbrook & Newry Closure

10 January 1948   Bessbrook to Newry

Bessbrook & Newry

Fleet Numbers	Date	Trucks/Bogies	Body	Withdrawn
1[1]	1920	Max traction bogies	Hurst Nelson	1948
2[2]	c1935	Max traction bogies	?	1948
3[3]	1885	—	Starbuck	1948
4[4]	1920	Max traction bogies	Hurst Nelson	1948
5[5]	1928 (acquired)	—	?	1948
6[6]	c1923	—	? (locally)	1948
7[7]	1920	—	Hurst Nelson	1948

1 Replaced original No 1 which dated from 1885.
2 Was rebuilt from the extended body of ex-Dublin & Lucan trailer No 24 which had been acquired in 1928, replacing the body from the original No 2. The new No 2 retained the original 1885 bogies and motors. Now preserved.
3 Non-powered trailer.
4 Originally received the 1885 bogies from 1 (i) but reconstructed 1927.
5 Originally Dublin & Lucan No 27. Built (as 2 above) for D&L when the line was 3ft 0in gauge and steam operated. Converted to 3ft 6in on the D&L electrification in 1900 and converted back to 3ft 0in when sold to the B&N. Non-powered trailer.
6 Four-wheeled, non-powered trailer.
7 Originally numbered 5; renumbered c1930. Small, open non-powered trailer car.

Situated at the heart of the West Midlands, Birmingham was, eventually, to become the single largest operator of 3ft 6in gauge trams in Britain. Its tramway history was, however, complex, involving a variety of operators, gauges and forms of traction, but showing that even the constraints imposed by the Board of Trade on narrow gauge tramways need not preclude meaningful investment.

On 20 May 1872 the Birmingham & District Tramways Co Ltd introduced a standard gauge horse-tramway from the Birmingham boundary at Hockley Brook to Dudley Port and Hill Top. The Corporation then sponsored the construction of a number of tramways in the city, authorised by the 1872 Tramway Orders Confirmation (No 3) Act, which were leased to the Birmingham & District company. The first section, which eventually linked Colmore Row in the city centre to Hockley Brook, opened on 11 September 1873. However, the Birmingham & District company soon hit financial difficulties, and on 24 May 1876 the leases passed to another company, the Birmingham Tramway & Omnibus Co Ltd, which also acquired the lease of the Corporation-built route along the Bristol Road, on 17 June 1876. This line, too, was also constructed to standard gauge.

The first appearance of 3ft 6in gauge trams, the gauge that was the Midlands' standard gauge, came on 26 December 1882 when the Birming-

ham & Aston Tramways Co Ltd opened its steam tram route linking Aston Manor with Old Square, Birmingham. Over the next three years a large 3ft 6in gauge system developed in the region, operated by the South Staffordshire & Birmingham District Steam Tramways Co Ltd. A further steam line, linking Birmingham with Dudley via Smethwick, was opened by the Birmingham & Midland Tramways Ltd. Also in December 1882, the Birmingham Central Tramways Co Ltd was established, and over the next four years was to introduce services over a number of routes which were all built to the 3ft 6in gauge. The first, to Nechells, opened on 11 November 1884, and this was the company's one horse-tram route; the remainder were all steam operated. These lines included Perry Barr (opened on 25 November 1884), Sparkbrook (11 May 1885), Lozells (1 October 1885) and Small Heath (16 January 1886). The company was granted a 21-year lease over all these lines from 1 January 1886.

The deathknell for the standard-gauge tramways in the city came with the renewal of the Birmingham Tramway & Omnibus Co's lease in 1885 which included a clause stipulating that the track must be relaid to 3ft 6in. This work was undertaken, but the leases passed to the Birmingham Central company in January 1886. With this transfer the former company sold the sections of track it owned outside the city to Birmingham Central, and this company came to own all tramways in the district, with the exception of those operated by the Birmingham & Aston and Birmingham Midland companies. As an experiment, the Colmore Row-Hockley Brook route was converted to cable operation on 24 March 1888, but, despite an extension the following year to New Inns, this new service was not a success. On 29 September 1896 the City of Birmingham Tramways Co Ltd took over Birmingham Central; the last phase of company-operated trams in the city was about to begin.

In March 1899 the Corporation decided that it would exercise the right to take over the operation of the tramways upon the expiry of the leases. Despite this decision it allowed the City of Birmingham company to start work on the electrification of the system with the conversion of the Bristol Road route. The first section of the newly electrified line was opened on 14 May 1901 when the route was extended to Selly Oak. The following month British Electric Traction acquired a major stake in the City of Birmingham company, but the gradual shift away from company operation was taking place. Under the Birmingham & Midland Tramways Act of 1902, the

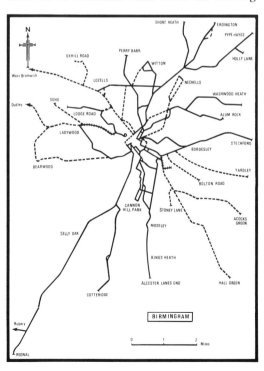

Birmingham & Midland company, one of the other two remaining company operators, was empowered to electrify its line and to build a branch to Bearwood. This work was completed in 1904-05. The section within Birmingham passed to the Corporation on the expiry of the lease in 1906, but from that date joint running ensured that Birmingham & Midland cars could continue to reach the centre.

In 1903 the Corporation obtained an Act which empowered it to operate tramcars, and in January 1904 the lease of the Birmingham & Aston company expired and the first Corporation-operated route, from Steelhouse Lane to Aston Brook Street, commenced. This was extended in June 1904 to Aston Cross. In 1904 BET built a line in Yardley, then outside the city boundary, which was linked with the Coventry Road route. With the agreement of the Corporation the Coventry Road route was electrified and through services to Yardley commenced on 23 February 1905. Also outside the then city boundary, the Urban District Council of Kings Norton & Northfield built a line linked to the Bristol Road route and reached an agreement for the City of Birmingham company to operate it until the expiry of the Bristol Road lease. The new route opened during 1904.

The transfer of operation from company to Corporation seems to have been much smoother in Birmingham than in a number of other cities, with the Corporation, for example, being granted access to the company's main depot/workshop at Kyotts Lake Road before the physical transfer. The actual take-over was sanctioned by the Birmingham Corporation Act of 1905, which also allowed for the construction of a number of new lines. Thus a number of new Corporation routes started operation during 1906: Edmund Street to Lodge Road (14 April); Navigation Street to Ladywood (17 October); and High Street to Bordesley Green (24 November). The majority of the City of Birmingham leases expired on 31 December 1906 and the last steam trams in the city operated on that day. The following day, 1 January 1907, new Corporation-operated electric services started to, inter alia, Stratford Road, Nechells, New Town Row, Alum Rock and Bolton Road. The City of Birmingham company continued to operate on those lines outside the city boundary, with the result that the route to Yardley was jointly operated. Further extensions soon followed, such as that to Alcester Lanes End on 12 January 1907, to Erdington on 22 April 1907 (although there remained a dispute with the company over operating through Aston) and to Washwood Heath on 2 May 1907.

On 30 June 1911 the final company leases in the city expired and the Corporation took over the operation of the Bristol Road, Pershore Road and Handsworth services. The situation was further complicated by an Act of 1911 which saw Birmingham expand in November 1911 to include the formerly independent areas of Aston, Erdington, Handsworth and Yardley as well as part of Kings Norton & Northfield. The company retained a number of operating rights in these areas, and, prior to the enlargement of the city, discussions were held with the company over these rights. The idea that the Corporation should acquire the company foundered initially since the Corporation was not empowered to purchase tramways outside the city. However, this position changed in November when the city's boundaries were altered. On 28 November 1911 an agreement was reached whereby the Corporation acquired the company, and City of Birmingham operations ceased with effect from 31 December 1911.

The acquisition heralded a period of considerable investment in the tramways as the Corporation sought to consolidate the ex-company routes. Apart from the modernisation of many of the older cars, a total of 125 brand-new trams entered service in the period up to the outbreak of World War 1, and numerous extensions were built. These included Stockland Green (12 June 1912), Villa Cross (20 November 1912), Oxhill Road (20 December 1912) and Soho Road (8 January 1913). 1913 also saw the launch of the first Corporation motorbus service when on 19 July a

route linking Selly Oak with Rednal was inaugurated. Powers to operate buses had existed since 1903 but they were only enshrined into general powers in 1914.

The early 1920s witnessed further investment in the tramways, with some 39 miles of track being reconstructed; over the decade some 250 new tramcars were acquired and others were modernised in a programme that eventually saw the majority of the fleet fully-enclosed. Unlike most of the other 3ft 6in-gauge tramway systems, such as Halifax, where the Ministry of Transport was unwilling to sanction fully enclosed trams, Birmingham lacked the exposed locations that were considered unsuitable for fully-enclosed narrow-gauge trams (with the exception of Cape Hill, Smethwick, on route No 87 to Dudley on which balcony cars only could be operated). The vehicle acquisitions allowed for numerous extensions during the period. The first postwar extension, to Salford Bridge (to serve the increasingly important factory at Fort Dunlop), was opened on 13 May 1920, and this was followed by an extension to the Warwick Road route to Westley Road (9 October 1922), Northfield (1 October 1923), Longbridge (17 December 1923), Rednal (replacing the bus service on 14 April 1924; the loop at Rednal was completed on 5 April 1925), Alum Rock extended to Pelham Road (14 October 1925), Bordesley Green extended to Eastfield Road (4 November 1925), Rubery (8 February 1926), Short Heath (23 June 1926), Pype Hayes Park (20 February 1927), an extension along Stratford Road (2 April 1928) and Stechford (on 26 August 1928). Many of these extensions were constructed on central reservations, of which Birmingham was an early exponent and which might have allowed for a further development of the tramways in Birmingham had it not been constrained by its narrow gauge.

The 1920s were also a significant decade for the extension of operations outside the city area. On 26 May 1923, alternate services to Darlaston were extended to Bilston; the following year, on the expiry of the South Staffordshire company's lease on the lines in West Bromwich, Birmingham took over these operations as well as the Great Bridge to Dudley service; and new through services from Colmore Row to Dudley station and Wednesbury were introduced. On 1 April 1928 the Corporation took over sole operation of the previously joint line from along Dudley Road into Dudley.

Although the 1920s were basically a decade of tramway investment, the period did also witness the first casualty amongst the electric tramway

routes. In 1922 it was decided to convert the Nechells route to trolleybus operation, and on 14 August 1922 the trams were withdrawn and replaced by buses. The buses ran until 27 November 1922 when the new trolleybus service was introduced. The Nechells conversion was significant as being the first tram-to-trolleybus conversion in the country.

1930 was a watershed year for Birmingham's tramway system. Not only had the two experimental cars, Nos 842 and 843, been introduced, but the tramway system had grown substantially over the past 10 years, while the increasing cost of maintenance and the improving economics of bus operation were beginning to undermine the tramway system. The extension to Stechford in 1928 was to prove the last substantial line to be constructed in Birmingham, although the branch into Fort Dunlop was to follow (on 13 February 1930) and the diversion of the route through Erdington (on 25 September 1938) was the last major infrastructure change. The first indication that the future of the tramway was in doubt came with the decision not to reconstruct the Bolton Road route which was, therefore, converted to bus operation on 5 February 1930. This was followed on 10 August 1930 by the conversion of the Hagley Road route to Bearwood.

Although the first two conversions had been to motorbus, the decision to replace the initial batch of trolleybuses for the Nechells route in 1932 gave this form of transport a second wind,

and the next conversion, of the Coventry Road route, on 7 January 1934, was to trolleybuses. This was, however, to be the last such conversion; the next 20 years were to witness the complete domination of transport in the city by the motorbus. Three years later, on 6 January 1937, the Stratford Road group of routes (to Stoney Lane, Hall Green and Acocks Green) were converted to bus operation.

The next stage in the conversion policy was influenced by West Bromwich, which decided that it wished to replace the trams in the borough with buses operating on the joint services. This led to the abandonment of the Soho Road group of routes (Oxhill Road and West Bromwich) on 2 April 1939, quickly followed on 1 October 1939 by the conversion of the Dudley Road group of services again when those local authorities outside the city (Smethwick and Dudley) decided to abandon the sections of tram track in their areas. This left the Lodge Road and Ladywood services (along with Rosebery Street depot) as effectively the only tram routes serving the west of the city. The planned abandonment of these routes was cancelled due to the war.

Inevitably, Birmingham suffered severely during the war, and a number of depots were hit. The most severe damage occurred in April 1941 when Miller Street depot was hit. A total of 18 cars were destroyed, with a further four lost at Washwood Heath. Yet only one significant section of line closed during the war, the link from

Aston towards Witton in 1941. And the war did ensure that the trams survived longer than initially expected — although the reprieve was destined to be relatively short-lived.

In 1945, the Birmingham system saw the trams concentrated on routes in the north and south of the city, including the superb reserved track sections along the Bristol Road and other lines. Although the track on the Lodge Road route was suspect, that elsewhere was in reasonable condition. Over 500 cars remained in service of which about half had been built in the interwar period. Since 1930, however, there had been little investment in the fleet, and it came as no surprise that the policy of tramway abandonment was quickly resumed after the war. 1945 saw the scrapping of many of the older trams that had been retained since the prewar closures as 'spares', and in early 1946 the Corporation applied to the Ministry of War Transport for permission to convert the Lodge Road, Ladywood and Stechford services. Although permission was initially refused for the last, sanction was given to the first two. The introduction of buses to the previously tram only depot at Washwood Heath in August 1946 was an indication of things to come. The Lodge Road service was converted on 30 March 1947 and that to Ladywood on 31 August 1947. Rosebery Street depot also ceased to house trams on the latter date, and the closure also enabled the section of track along Dudley Road, retained in 1939 for depot workings, to be abandoned.

The Stechford services were the next routes to be converted to bus operation. The last trams operated on 3 October 1948. The routes had originally been scheduled for closure in 1940, but this had been postponed due to the war. The next abandonment, on 2 October 1949, saw trams withdrawn from the Moseley Road group of services to Moseley itself, Kings Heath, Alcester Lanes End and Cannon Hill Park. The closure also marked the end of Moseley Road depot as a tram shed, the withdrawal of the last open balcony four-wheel trams, and the demise of the unusual air-oil brake that was fitted to many of Birmingham's vehicles. The next closure, which saw the withdrawal of trams from the Witton and Perry Barr routes, occurred on 1 January 1950. It also marked the end of Witton depot as a running shed, although it was retained for the storage and scrapping of withdrawn cars, and as a base for PW use until late 1952. 1 October 1950 saw trams withdrawn from the Lozells and Saltley/Washwood Heath/Alum Rock routes, as well as the conversion of Washwood Heath depot to buses only.

By now the tram system had declined to two main corridors – the Bristol Road and the Lichfield Road. But the trams were destined to receive a short reprieve as the Corporation's attention was turned to the trolleybus system. Always destined to play a subsidiary role, little had been invested in the trolleybuses since the conversion of the Coventry Road routes in 1934, and by the early 1950s the equipment needed replacement. The decision was made to convert the routes to bus operation and on 1 October 1951 the last trolleybus operated along the Coventry Road.

With the trolleybuses dealt with, attention could again turn to the trams. On 6 July 1952 trams were withdrawn from the Bristol Road group of routes (Cotteridge, Rubery, Rednal, etc). The penultimate closure saw the withdrawal of the last air-braked trams as well as the closure of the depots at Selly Oak and Cotteridge. This left Miller Street as the last operational depot, housing some 50 trams for the remaining services. The end came on 4 July 1953, when the final service trams were withdrawn from the services to Short Heath, Erdington and Pype Hayes Park. 1920-built Brush car No 616 acted as the last tram, although with its crudely painted slogans it looked poor in comparison with many of the last trams in other cities. After closure, the final cars were disposed of with almost indecent haste. The last passenger car to be scrapped, No 597, disappeared in early August 1953, leaving by 8 August only railgrinder No 8 (ex-No 226) to be scrapped. Of the fleet only No 395, preserved in the Birmingham Science Museum, exists to remind locals of 80 years of tramway operation in the city.

Birmingham Closures

30 March 1947	Lodge Road
31 August 1947	Ladywood
3 October 1948	Stechford routes
2 October 1949	Moseley routes
1 January 1950	Witton
1 January 1950	Perry Barr
1 October 1950	Saltley
1 October 1950	Lozells
6 July 1952	Bristol Road routes
6 July 1952	Pershore Road routes
4 July 1953	Short Heath
4 July 1953	Pype Hayes
4 July 1953	Erdington

Last tram: No 616

Birmingham

Fleet Numbers	Date	Trucks/Bogies	Body	Withdrawn
3/8/9/13/5/7-9[1]	1904	Brill 21E	ERTCW	1945-49
49/53/5/9/61/3/4/7[2]	1905	Brill 21E	United Car Co	1946-47
73/87/9/97/9/104/9/11/3/6/25/137/42/4/60/70/2/16/7/83/207/10[3]	1906	Originally M&G — retrucked 1929 to Peckham P35 except Nos 89/125 on Brush	UEC	1945 (1939)
222/44/8/54-6/9/60/2[4]	1906	Brill 21E	Dick Kerr	1945-47
301/2/4-6/8-22/325-34/6/7/9-45/347/9-59/61/3-83/385-9/91/93-400[5]	1911-12	UEC Preston 7ft 6in	UEC	1947-50 (except No 341 1952)
401-38/40-50[6]	1912	M&G 7ft 6in — No 413 later received Peckham P22	UEC	1947-49
451-2[7]	1903 (acquired)	Brush Type D	City of Birmingham	1949
512-24/6-37/9-63/5/6/9-73/576-81/3-6[8]	1913	M&G 'Burnley'-type bogies. Nos 569-73/6-8/580/1/4-6 received EMB bogies from damaged trams 1942-43. Ditto 579/83 in 1948	UEC	1950-53
587-636[9]	1920	Brush 'Burnley'-type bogies. 1923 No 630 received EMB 'Burnley'-type — later fitted as standard on 732-61	Brush	1949-53
637-61[10]	1923	EMB 'Burnley'-type	Midland RCC	1952-53
662/4-8/70/2-9/682-4/6-96/8/700/1[11]	1924-25	EMB 'Burnley'-type	Brush	1952-53
704-6/9/10/2/3/715-7/9/21/2/5/726/8-31[12]	1925	EMB 'Burnley'-type	Brush	1953
732-61[13]	1926-27	EMB 'Burnley'-type	Brush	1952
762-84/6-811[14]	1928-29	EMB 'Burnley'-type	Brush	1952
812-20/22-41[15]	1928-29	M&T 'Burnley'-type	Short Bros (Brush underframe)	1952
842[16]	1929	EE 'Burnley'-type (lightweight)	Short Bros	1952
843[17]	1930	M&T 'Burnley'-type	Brush	1952

1 Batch 1-20, originally open top, top-covers fitted 1904-07. Platform vestibules added 1924-29. Remainder of class withdrawn 1941 following bomb damage.

2 Batch 21-70 — top-covers fitted 1911-25. Platform vestibules added 1923-28.

3 Batch 71-220. Top-covered from new. Platform vestibules added 1923. All withdrawn by 1939. These 22 retained as spares but scrapped in 1945.

4 Batch 221-70. Top-covers fitted 1911-25. Platform vestibules fitted 1923-28.

5 Batch 301-400. Nos 342/7 experimental top-deck vestibules 1921. All new trams from No 637 so fitted and Nos 512-636 converted. Nos 303/7/24/38/46/8/360/2/84/90/2 damaged during World War 2 and scrapped 1945. No 395 preserved. Nos 361/7/8/75/9 converted to SD in 1917 and reconverted 1923.

6 1915 No 431's top deck to No 329. No 431 used as Committee Car — back to double-deck 1923. No 439 withdrawn 1941 and scrapped 1945.

7 Ex-City of Birmingham Tramways Co built 1903. Were CBT 178/80 respectively. Top deck and vestibules added 1926.

8 Nos 525/38/64/7/8/74/5/82 damaged World War 2 and scrapped 1945. 1951 — EMB bogies from No 585 transferred to No 551.

9 Last open-canopied trams bought. Top vestibules added 1927-31. No 616 was the official last tram and No 597 the last tram broken up.

10 'Midland' cars — only tram bodies constructed by this firm in Birmingham. First fully-enclosed trams from new.

11 Nos 663/9/70/80/1/597/9 destroyed in air raid 1941.

12 Nos 702/3/7/8/11/4/8/20/3/4/7 damaged during World War 2 and scrapped in 1945. No 729 exchanged bogies with No 551 in 1953.

13 No 757 converted to cleaners' room at Selly Oak depot in 1951. First class of air-braked tram.

14 No 785 destroyed 1941.

15 First tram bodies produced by Short Bros. No 821 overturned 1941 and scrapped 1945. Bogies retained as spares.

16 Ventilation modified 1929. 1950 received trucks ex-No 821 and new controllers.

17 Frames of both floors required strengthening. Route number boxes later modified.

Situated on the northernmost fringe of the Lancashire textile region, Blackburn could lay claim to being the first electric tramway operator in north Lancashire as well as being the penultimate operator of 4ft 0in gauge tramcars in Britain. It was also typical of the many small town systems that had grown up in the industrial north during the early years of tramway development which remained relatively unchanged throughout their history.

The first tramway in the town was the line linking it with its southern neighbour Darwen. This line, operated by the Blackburn & Over Darwen Tramways Co, was the first tramway in Britain authorised to be operated solely by steam. The Blackburn & Over Darwen Tramways Act received the Royal Assent on 15 August 1879, and the line opened some 18 months later on 16 April 1881, using the 4ft 0in gauge. Further lines followed, all on the 4ft 0in gauge, with the opening of the first line of the Blackburn Corporation Tramways Co Ltd on 28 May 1887. This company operated a number of steam and horse routes, along the Preston New Road and Witton Stocks by horse and from Blackburn to Church by steam. The second company was the first to be taken over by the Corporation, on 24 August 1898, and the work commenced immediately to convert the steam and horse routes to electric traction. Before the first of these routes was finally converted, the Blackburn & Over Darwen

company was taken over on 1 January 1899, and from that date the line south of the borough boundary became the responsibility of Darwen Corporation.

The first electric trams ran on 20 March 1899 with the conversion of the Billinge End route along the Preston New Road. To operate the new services, eight open-top cars were delivered from Milnes. These were numbered 28-35; unusually, Blackburn did not start a new numbering system with its first electric trams, but continued on from those numbers (Nos 1-27) already allocated to the steam-tram trailers and horse-cars. The electric system was soon extended to Witton (along the Preston Old Road) on 31 March 1899 and work proceeded on the other routes. In late 1900 the route to Intack was converted, although steam trams continued to operate until 9 June 1900. The last steam tram ran to Darwen on 16 October 1900, on which date Darwen inaugurated its electric services over the southern part thus breaching temporarily the through service, and Blackburn's new electric service started on 1 December 1900.

The conversion continued with the first electric car operating to the Cemetery on 4 July 1901, and on 9 July 1901 the last non-electric services were operated with the conversion of the Intack-Church section. A further 40 open-top trams were delivered from Milnes during 1901 and these, combined with the earlier delivery, were to form the backbone of the fleet for almost 50 years. On 14 May 1902 the Cemetery route was extended northwards to Wilpshire; and August of the same year saw the line eastwards extended to Church. 1903 was to witness the final two extensions to the system with the opening of the lines to Audley, which was predominantly single track, and the line from Witton Stocks to Cherry Tree. The Blackburn system was now complete except for the introduction in 1907 of the through service to Accrington. Initially this route used only Blackburn cars and it was not until 1917 that the first Accrington cars appeared in Blackburn. 1907-08 also witnessed the final additions to the fleet, with the acquisition of 13 single-deck cars. The majority (Nos 76-87) were built by UEC, but the last, No 88, was actually constructed by Blackburn Corporation itself – the only tram built by the department.

The next two decades were to be a period of little change for Blackburn's trams. No new extensions were constructed, although many of the double-deck tramcars were rebuilt between 1920 and 1935. The rebuilding programme did not include all the trams, and a number of open-

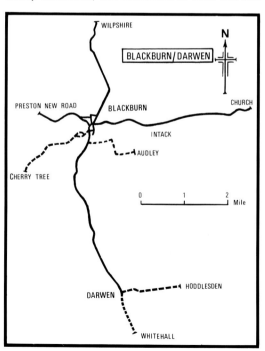

top cars remained in the postwar era. The late 1920s did, however, witness the first portents of the tramways' future demise. Although Blackburn was a relatively late operator of buses – its first routes to Little Harwood, Hensley Road and Whitekirk not being introduced until 1929 – the effects of the post-World War 1 depression in the textile industry was having serious repercussions to the economics of tramway operation. Neighbouring Accrington, despite the acquisition of new tramcars as late as 1926, decided to abandon its tramcars shortly thereafter, the through service ceasing in 1931, although Blackburn was to continue to operate to the borough boundary at Church for a further 17 years. By the mid-1930s the position in Blackburn was equally uncertain, with many of the trams reaching the end of their economic life. The late 1930s witnessed two closures in Blackburn with the conversion to bus operation of the route to Audley on 13 February 1935 and that to Cherry Tree on 31 March 1939. These closures meant the end of the single-deck trams. It is certain that World War 2 ensured that Blackburn's trams had a longer life than could earlier have been expected.

The Blackburn system by 1939 had contracted to effectively four routes: north to Wilpshire; south to Darwen; east to Church; and, west to Preston New Road. To operate the services there were some 48 tramcars, dating from 1899 and 1901, although the majority of these had had topcovers fitted during the rebuilding programme. All the tramcars were housed in the single depot

at Intack on the route to Church. One of the most notable features of the Blackburn system was the complex one-way system in the town centre which affected the Wilpshire and Preston New Road routes in particular. There were few material changes during the war, although the through service to Darwen was threatened on more than one occasion by Darwen's desire to rid itself of the last tram route in the borough. Darwen's entreaties to the Ministry of War Transport for permission to convert the line were

Below left:
Although the through tram services to Darwen were abandoned with the withdrawal of Darwen's last tram route on 5 October 1946, Blackburn's trams continued to reach the borough boundary for a further three years. Seen at the Darwen Road terminus on 2 October 1948 is Blackburn tram No 42. This car was one of a batch of 40 delivered from Milnes in 1900 (Nos 36-75) which considerably modified through their life and which continued to give service until the final withdrawal of Blackburn's trams in 1949.

Below:
At the terminus of the Church route the conductor changes the trolley-pole of Blackburn tram No 69. Until 1931 it was possible to travel beyond this terminus on the through tram route to Accrington. The section from Intack to Church was abandoned in January 1949, whilst the remaining section of the route from Blackburn to Intack (where the depot was located) was withdrawn in July 1949, thus bringing to an end the story of narrow-gauge trams in Lancashire.

rejected, and therefore the through service, along with the remainder of Blackburn's tram routes, soldiered on into the postwar era. That Blackburn was not immediately contemplating the conversion of its trams is evinced by the re-laying of the Wilpshire route during 1944.

On the cessation of hostilities, the Corporation announced that the policy of tramway conversion would be renewed. The first route scheduled for conversion was that to Preston New Road. This route was finally converted, after several delays, on 5 January 1946, although some football specials operated over part of the route later than this date. The last car from the Preston New Road terminus was No 42. This closure allowed for the withdrawal of the first of the original cars, Nos 28-35, which remained open-top throughout their career; the survivors were to soldier on for a further two years. 1946 also saw the final demise of the through tram service to Darwen, when the section from the borough boundary to Darwen was finally converted on 5 October. During the last few months of operation, Darwen's fleet had proved insufficient to maintain its share of the service and Blackburn had lent cars to Darwen to assist until the final closure. As with the earlier closure of the through service to Accrington, Blackburn continued to operate its section of the tram route, although the track and overhead inside Darwen were quickly removed.

There was now a gap of some 14 months before the next closure. On 21 December 1947 the trams operated for the last time on the route to Wilpshire — buses took over the service the following day. The next closure, on 16 January 1949, saw the Church service curtailed to Intack. This curtailment had been first threatened in 1946. There was little point in converting the whole of the route at this stage since the track and overhead would have to be retained for access to the depot at Intack. Again there was to be a delay before the next closure. On 2 July 1949 trams operated on the route to the Darwen boundary for the last time. This left one route still operational, that to Intack, and this was to last for two months. The final rites, with car No 74 suitably decorated, took place on 3 September

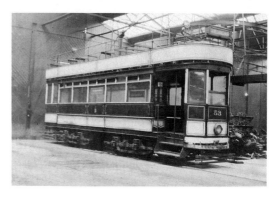

Above:
Although the majority of the 1900 Milnes-built cars were eventually rebuilt fully enclosed, eight remained open-top throughout their career. One of these eight, No 53, is seen inside Intack depot on 2 October 1948. On a subsequent visit, in April 1949, the photographer saw No 53 partly dismantled outside the depot.

1949. None of Blackburn's fleet of tramcars was preserved.

With Blackburn's closure, so ended the story of the non-standard gauge tram in Lancashire. Although the larger systems had all been constructed to standard gauge, the 4ft 0in gauge dominated the smaller systems to the north of Manchester. After 1949 there remained only one 4ft 0in operator – Bradford – in Britain, and even over the Pennines the gauge did not have long to live.

Blackburn Closures	
5 January 1946	Blackburn to Preston New Road (football trams ran slightly longer)
21 December 1947	Blackburn to Wilpshire
16 January 1949	Intack to Church
2 July 1949	Blackburn to Darwen Boundary
3 September 1949	Blackburn to Intack
Last tram: No 74	

Blackburn

Fleet Numbers	Date	Trucks/Bogies	Body	Withdrawn
28-35[1]	1899	Brill 22E	Milnes	1945-47
36-75[2]	1900	Peckham 14B bogies	Milnes	1949

1 Rebuilt with end canopies 1920-23.
2 Nos 45/9/61 received top-covers in 1907, and No 62 in 1912. Remainder of class (except Nos 36/47/51/3-5/9/66) top-covered 1923-35. The exceptions remained open-top until withdrawal.

There are few greater ironies in the history of public transport in Great Britain than the fact that conventional street tramways in England started in Blackpool and, after years of growth and subsequent decline, Blackpool remains alone as the last operator of conventional tramcars in the country.

By the early 1880s, electric traction was becoming more widely appreciated. Amongst the earliest promoters of electric transport was Michael Holroyd Smith, of Halifax, who produced a demonstration line. The Corporation of Blackpool, a town which was growing rapidly as a coastal holiday resort, was suitably impressed and determined to establish a tramway along the promenade as an amenity for visitors. In January 1885 the Blackpool Electric Tramway Co was formed, with Holroyd Smith's involvement, and the first track was laid on 13 March 1885. The two-mile line, linking Cocker Street with Dean Street, was jointly built by the Corporation and the company, and adopted the conduit principle for the power. After initially failing its inspection

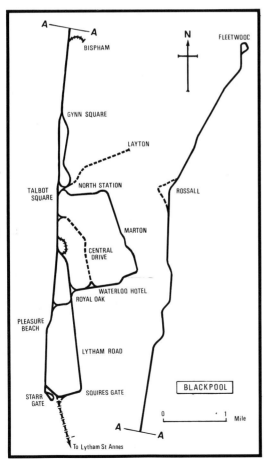

and the temporary provision of a horse-tram service, the new electric services were officially launched on 29 September 1885. The company ran the service until 1892, when the Corporation took over.

The conduit system, never wholly successful (partly as a result of sand being blown into the groove), was overhauled by the Corporation in 1894 and was extended in September 1895 to South Shore station where, eventually, a connection was made with the tramways that served Lytham St Annes. A further extension to the conduit system was opened on 7 August 1897 along Station Road, from South Shore station, to join the Promenade route at Victoria Pier. 1897 was, however, to be a watershed year as it was decided that year to replace the conduit system with overhead. The initial application to convert was refused by the Board of Trade, but permission was eventually granted on 10 June 1898.

1898 also saw three other important events. The first, in July, was the opening of the Blackpool & Fleetwood Tramroad Co's line from North station to Fleetwood. No direct connection was made with the Corporation-owned lines, although the section from North station to Gynn Square was constructed by the Corporation. Also in 1898, the first of the unique 'Dreadnought' trams was built. The first of the type were built for use on the conduit track, but the final event of 1898, the start of the conversion, soon rendered the conduit equipment redundant. The first trials of the new overhead system were undertaken in June 1899 and the last conduit cars ran at the end of that month. Between 1896 and 1899 the North Promenade was built, and in 1900 the existing tramway was cut back from Cocker Street to Church Street and connected with a new extension northwards to Gynn Square. The opening of this section, on 24 May 1900, heralded a period of dramatic growth for the tramways. On 23 May 1901 the Marton route, including Central Drive, was opened. This was followed on 18 June 1902 by the route to Layton from Talbot Square and on 1 August 1902 by the link between the Marton and Lytham Road routes along Waterloo Road. The electrification of Lytham Road in May 1903 by the Blackpool, St Annes & Lytham Tramways Co Ltd (eventually taken over by the respective councils) enabled through services between the towns to operate after a period of dispute.

After the expansion of the early years of the 20th century there was little further development until after World War 1. On 1 January 1920 the line of the Blackpool & Fleetwood Tramroad Co

Right:
Seen at Little Bispham on 9 September 1948, No 246 was one of a batch of 13 'Luxury Dreadnoughts' delivered to Blackpool from English Electric in 1934. Originally open-top, the cars were fully enclosed during 1941-42. The entire class was to survive until 1968 when they were renumbered 700-712, and all remain in service (except No 705), with No 706 having been reconverted to open-top condition in 1980.

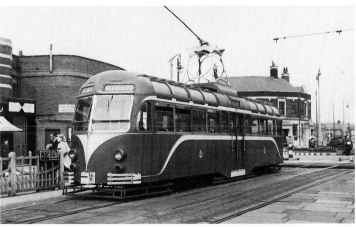

Below right:
During the 1930s, Blackpool tramways underwent a considerable modernisation as streamlined designs, both double- and single-deck, were introduced. Amongst these acquisitions were 20 cars, Nos 284-303, built by Brush in 1937. The last of the batch, No 303, is seen at Cleveleys on 9 May 1948. These cars were destined to be the last tramcars manufactured by Brush. Ironically, No 303 was the first of the class to be withdrawn, in 1962, although a number of others of the class remain in service. One of the type, No 298, is currently undergoing restoration.

was acquired for £280,000 and connections were installed between the Corporation and ex-company lines. Also, work started on the creation of Rigby Road depot and workshop in the immediate postwar years. This was important because by the early 1920s the condition of the tramway, and in particular the age of the tram fleet, was giving serious cause for concern. As a result, in 1923 the first of the immortal 'Standard' cars emerged from the new workshops. Over the next decade almost 50 of these classic tramcars were to emerge from either Rigby Road or from the works of Hurst Nelson. The last significant development of the 1920s was the completion of the extension to Starr Gate and the associated link to Squires Gate, which were completed on 2 October 1926 but not used in public service until 1927.

By the early 1930s the tramcar was in retreat in many towns and cities throughout Britain, and it is probable that a similar fate would have befallen the trams in Blackpool but for the inspired

appointment of Walter Luff as the new General Manager in 1933. Whilst Luff was only the second choice — the original selection had declined to take up the post — he led the revolution which ensured the survival of the tram in the town. On his appointment he was faced by stagnating passenger figures, little investment and growing demands for the replacement of the 'town' trams (to Marton and Layton) by buses. On 20 February 1933 he presented a five-year plan for the development of public transport in the town and, following earlier consultations with the local firm of English Electric, he simultaneously unveiled proposals for a brand-new type of car. The plan Luff advocated was to modernise the Promenade route but only to undertake routine maintenance on the remainder whilst the future of the 'town' service was considered. To emphasise that the new regime was a complete break with the past he introduced a new green and cream livery to replace the earlier red and ivory. The new policy was adopted by the council, and the first of the

new English Electric cars, No 200, was officially launched in June 1933. The effect was dramatic; further batches of the revolutionary new cars were ordered, including replacements for both the 'Dreadnoughts' and toastracks, and over the next two years English Electric delivered some 83 new cars. This enabled the withdrawal of many, but not all (the opportunity being taken to increase the strength of the fleet), of the older cars. After public pressure, one of the 'Dreadnought' cars, No 59, was preserved although, until it passed to the Tramway Museum Society, its existence was always tenuous. No 59 thus became the first electric tramcar to be preserved.

Part of Luff's responsibilities included the restoration of the department's finances. Although buses had been first operated in Blackpool in 1921 and by 1933 some 50 buses were in service, these were operated at a loss. In an effort to improve the overall finances it was decided to introduce buses on the Layton and Central Drive routes in place of the existing trams. The conversion of these routes was effected from 19 October 1936. Earlier proposals to introduce trolleybuses — powers were obtained in 1934 — came to nothing. Further adverse changes occurred beyond Blackpool's control when the blue trams of Lytham St Annes were withdrawn on 28 April 1937. This also meant the breaching of the tracks at Squires Gate and the end of the circular tram

tours. The proposal that Blackpool should take over the tramway south of Starr Gate and operate it as part of the Promenade service also failed.

The original 1933 five-year plan envisaged closer examination of the 'town' routes'; such was the success of the new cars that agreement was readily given to the re-laying of the Lytham Road route in 1936 and of the Marton route, although this latter work was postponed by the outbreak of World War 2. Other significant track work at this time included the laying of the turning circles at Pleasure Beach, Starr Gate and Little Bispham.

The outbreak of World War 2 led to a number of significant changes, apart from the delay to the re-laying of the Marton route. In September 1939 Marton depot was requisitioned,, and this led to severe storage problems. Bispham depot was reopened for operational cars and a number of older cars were scrapped — even No 59 barely escaped the carnage (being used as a tool store at Copse Road depot). Passenger traffic grew rapidly and the fleet was not capable of handling this growth without modification. The most recent cars, Nos 10-21, had been delivered with canvas sun roofs and half height windows, but were still required to operate in all weather conditions. Such was their unpopularity — they were nicknamed 'cattle trucks' — that permanent roofs were fitted; similar rebuilding work also affected

the open-top double-deck cars built by English Electric in the 1930s. In 1941 a proposal was produced to extend the Squires Gate tramway to the Vickers' factory at Common Edge Road, but nothing was progressed.

· By 1945 Blackpool had a fleet of some 200 cars, of which the majority had been built either under Luff's management or in the preceding decade. Much of the trackwork was in reasonable condition and even the delayed re-laying of the Marton route was agreed in January 1947. The tramcar seemed secure in the town. Of course, there still remained the problem of the town routes, but the introduction of No 10 to the Marton route in January 1948, the first modern car to

Above:
The last trams delivered to Blackpool prior to the outbreak of World War 2 were 12 cars, Nos 10-21, built by English Electric as 'Sun Saloons'. The cars were fully enclosed in 1942, and between 1949 and 1951 were converted to Crompton Parkinson VAMBAC. No 11 is seen at Talbot Square on 9 September 1948 prior to this later modification. When fitted with the VAMBAC control system, the 12 cars became particularly associated with the Marton route, and all were withdrawn between 1958 and 1962 as Blackpool's tramway system contracted. Purchased for preservation, No 11 spent some time associated with the ill-fated Hayling Island project before passing for continued preservation and restoration to the East Anglian Transport Museum at Carlton Colville.

operate the service, seemed to indicate a positive future. Over the next four years all 12 of the batch were rebogied and fitted with VAMBAC control. Just as the last of the converted cars

Left:
The Blackpool 'Standards', built between 1922 and 1929, were the last traditional tramcars to operate in England. After their final withdrawal, in 1966, Blackpool relied on the streamlined designs dating from the 1930s. 'Standard' No 51 is seen at Royal Oak on 17 April 1949. Six of the 'Standard' cars have been preserved: two at Crich; one at the East Anglian Transport Museum; and three in the USA. A seventh, No 158, was also acquired by the National Tramway Museum, but only as a source of spares.

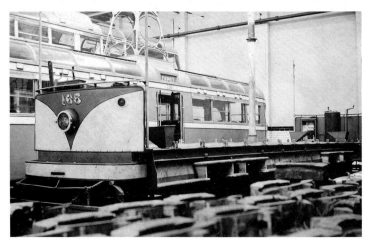

Left:
Former toastrack car No 165 was one of a batch of six built in 1927 at Rigby Road works. All were last used in passenger service in 1939, but all survived World War 2 and were eventually converted for alternative uses. No 165 is seen in store at Rigby Road on 16 April 1949; two years later No 165 and sister car No 166 were converted into mobile studios for use by television companies. After withdrawal from this work, No 166 was eventually preserved and is now on display at the National Tramway Museum.

were entering service, the first of 25 'Coronation' cars, built by Charles Roberts, was being introduced. Unfortunately, these cars, the last new power cars to be bought for 30 years, were to prove a disappointment. The arrival of these new cars allowed for the withdrawal of certain earlier cars, including some of the 'Standards' for storage, in Blundell Street depot.

In 1954 Walter Luff retired and was replaced by Joseph Franklin. In many ways the new manager faced many of the same problems that had faced his predecessor — with one significant difference. Prior to the purchase of the 'Coronation' cars the Corporation, fearing the Nationalisation of the transport department, had transferred the reserves to the Corporation's general funds. This meant that the new cars were funded by borrowing, which added considerable interest charges to the department and reduced the viability of the tramways. Despite this, there remained no real threat to the remaining system and the late 1950s witnessed a number of developments that seemed to bode well for the future. In 1957 the lines to Squires Gate were uncovered and a circular tour service along the routes was operated for the first time in 20 years. In 1958 the important junction at Royal Oak was relaid and the same year witnessed the first experiments in trailer operation when the twin-car set, Nos 275/276, was introduced on 9 April. 1959 saw the introduction of the first new illuminated car for more than 20 years, the 'Blackpool Belle' (based upon the remains of toastrack No 163) replacing the 'Progress' car which had been withdrawn the previous year. 1960 saw the introduction of 10 trailer cars, which were hauled by Nos 272-81, which had been rebuilt from 1935 cars for the purpose. The period also saw the first operation of double-deck cars through to Fleetwood.

However, there were indications that things were under review. Two damaged cars, Nos 10 and 41, were not rebuilt after accident damage, even though work had started on them, and on 8 October 1960 it was announced that the Lytham Road trams would be withdrawn at the end of the 1961 season. The cost of re-laying the route could not be justified. The last car over the route, No 268, operated on 29 October 1961. This closure adversely affected the finances of the Marton route, since the circular tours could no longer be run. Thus the Marton route, along with the depot, was the next casualty, being closed on 28 October 1962. 1961/62 saw the launch of further new illuminated cars, 'Tramnik One' and the 'Western Train', but it also witnessed the withdrawal of two earlier illuminated cars, the 'Gondola' and the 'Lifeboat', as well as the final operation of the 'Pantograph' cars. With the closure of the Marton route, the VAMBAC control cars, Nos 10-21, were withdrawn, although one, No 11, passed to preservation. After a period at Hayling Island, No 11 eventually went to the East East Anglian Transport Museum.

1963 was an equally depressing year. The last of the street tramways, Dickson Road, was converted to bus operation on 27 October, and during the winter of 1963/64 no trams operated. There were now serious doubts as to the long-term future of the Promenade route itself. Copse Road depot, in Fleetwood, was closed in 1963, and this was followed in 1964 by Bispham, leaving all trams based at Rigby Road or Blundell Street. By 1964 the 'Coronation' cars were starting to give serious concern, and 12 of them were fitted with Z4 controllers in place of their original VAMBAC control. 1966 was to see the final withdrawal of the 'Standard' cars after many months of rumour. A number passed into preservation:

Nos 40 and 49 at the National Tramway Museum; Nos 48/144/147 in the United States; and, No 159 at Carlton Colville. No 158 was acquired by the Tramway Museum Society as a source of spares and eventually dismantled.

1968 saw the renumbering of the tramcar fleet — the first such major exercise in 80 years of operation. The surviving single-deck cars were numbered in the 600 series and the double-deckers in the 700 series. Works cars were renumbered into the 750 series. The renumbering marked another watershed in the history of Blackpool's tramways as it marked another period of refurbishment, not as dramatic as that of the 1930s, but just as important in ensuring the survival of the tramways into their second century.

Although 1968 was the year of the withdrawal of the first 'Coronation' car, it also saw the rebuilding of No 618 with tapered ends and the experimental conversion of No 638 for OMO operation. The development of the OMO trams was essential in reducing the operating costs of the tramway, in particular during the winter season, just as new methods of track maintenance were a vital part of making repairs cost effective. In 1971 the Government agreed to part-fund the building of OMO trams and the programme was well under way by 1972. The first of the new

OMO cars, converted from the 1930s railcoaches, appeared in April 1972 and a total of 13 were eventually completed by 1976. The new OMO cars appeared in a new, and somewhat garish, livery of crimson and yellow although this was subsequently changed to red and cream.

In 1973 Stuart Pillar was appointed Chief Engineer and the following year, on the retirement of Joseph Franklin, Derek Hyde became General Manager. Both were committed to the maintenance of the tramway and in this they were aided by the creation of the new Lancashire County Council in April 1974, since this body agreed to part-fund major track work. New methods of track maintenance, such as that developed by Thermit Welding, and the removal of the

Below:
One of the most famous aspects of Blackpool's tramway operation were the numerous illuminated cars converted. Amongst the cars so treated were two 'Standard' cars Nos 158 and 159, which emerged in their new guise in 1959. One of the two is seen on 16 July 1960; they were to survive in this guise until withdrawal in 1966. No 158 went to Crich as a source of spares and was eventually dismantled in 1978, whilst No 159 was preserved at the East Anglian Transport Museum where it continues to give rides to the general public in a restored condition. *Roy Marshall*

required check rail (thus releasing rail for reuse), allowed for considerable improvement in the running lines. During the mid-1970s, experiments were undertaken using pantographs, although these were not wholly successful but, at the same time, work was progressing on the building of a new double-deck car. This appeared for the first time in 1979 and was followed three years later by a second. Although based round two of the 1930s double-deck cars which had been withdrawn earlier, both incorporated major advances in suspension and control equipment. Two years later the first of the 'Centenary' class, No 641, appeared, built in conjunction between East Lancashire Coachbuilders and the Corporation and this was followed by six similar cars (Nos 642-647) and by an experimental GEC-sponsored car (No 651). This car was subsequently modified and renumbered 648.

Apart from these changes, all bar one of the 'Coronation' class was withdrawn by 1975 and a number of the trailer cars were also disposed of. Double-deck car No 706 reverted to its original open-top condition in 1985, in time for the centenary celebrations, and the arrival of the new 'Centenary' class allowed for the gradual withdrawal of some of the OMO cars which, by the late 1980s, were beginning to show their age. One of these was rebuilt as a mock toastrack car and renumbered 619 during 1989. In terms of infrastructure, the most dramatic alteration was the closure of Blundell Street depot in 1982 and its subsequent demolition.

In the space of 20 years Blackpool's tramcars had regained their confidence. Little could have demonstrated this better than the massive centenary celebrations of 1985 and the regular operation in the 1980s of preserved tramcars. Uncertainty remains, however, with the effects of bus Deregulation and Privatisation still uncertain. In a curious reversion to the original condition, the Corporation retains ownership of the track, whilst operation has passed to a limited liability company, albeit (at the moment) Corporation owned. Whilst Blackpool's trams have set out well on their second century, nothing is guaranteed for the future.

Inevitably, Blackpool's tramcar fleet is well represented amongst the ranks of preserved trams. Apart from those already mentioned, the National Tramway Museum at Crich houses 'Pantograph' car No 167, Toastrack car No 166, one of the original conduit cars, and two ex-Blackpool & Fleetwood cars (No 2 of 1898 and No 40 of 1914). The North of England Open Air Museum at Beamish has recently completed the restoration of 'Marton Box' car No 31, which dated originally from 1901 and which had been used as an overhead car from 1934 until withdrawal in 1982. Of the single-deck boats built in the 1930s, two are preserved in the United States and one is on loan to the Heaton Park tramway in Manchester. Finally, one of the Brush-built cars, No 298 (post-1968 No 635) is currently being restored to original condition for ultimate display at the National Tramway Museum. Three of the 'Coronation' cars survive: one at the West Yorkshire Transport Museum in Bradford (close to where it was built at Horbury), a second is at Burtonwood, whilst the third is still based in Blackpool.

Blackpool Closures

29 October 1961	Station Road/Lytham Road
28 October 1962	Marton
27 October 1963	North Station/Dickson Road

Blackpool

Fleet Numbers	Date	Trucks/Bogies	Body	Withdrawn
28/34-43/45/47-9/ 51/53/99/100/ 142-160/177[1]	1922-29	Hurst Nelson (Nos 34, 43, 53, 99, 100) Preston bogies, McGuire type rest. Nos 43/53 received Preston bogies 1927-28	Blackpool CT	1945-66 (Nos 33, 46, 50 withdrawn 1940)
161-6[2]	1927	Preston McGuire	Blackpool CT	1941 — last used 1939
167-76[3]	1928	Preston McGuire 1950-53 Nos 168-75 gained EE bogies from 10-21 batch	EE	1950-61
200-2[4]	1933	EE 4ft 0in bogies	EE	1962-63
203-24[5]	1934	EE 4ft 0in bogies. No 208 tested with M&T 6ft 0in bogies 1946-47	EE	1961-65 (except 224)
225-36[6]	1934	EE 4ft 0in bogies	EE	1963 onwards (600/2/4-7 still in service)

Blackpool

Fleet Numbers	Date	Trucks/Bogies	Body	Withdrawn
237-49[7]	1934	EE 4ft 9in bogies	EE	All in service except 705 withdrawn 1980
250-63[8]	1934-35	EE 4ft 9in bogies	EE	All in service except 714/25 withdrawn 1981
264-83[9]	1935	EE 4ft 0in bogies	EE	(1958-75)
284-303[10]	1937	EMB Hornless 4ft 3in bogies	Brush	1962 (303), 1966 (301), 1969 (628), 1971 (624), 1972 (629), 1974 (635), 1980 (638). Nos 621-3/5-7/30-4/6/7 still in service
10-21[11]	1939	EE 4ft 0in bogies — 1949-51 converted to M&T HS44 resilient wheel bogies	EE	1958-62
304-28[12]	1952-53	M&T HS44 6ft 0in bogies	Roberts	1963-75
275/6[13]	1958	EE 4ft 0in	EE/BCT	—
T1-T10[14]	1960-61	M&T 5ft 6in	MCCW	1972 Nos 688-90, rest in service
272-4/7-81[15]	1960-61	EE 4ft 0in bogies	EE/BCT	—
1-13[16]	1972-76	EE 4ft 0in bogies	EE/BCT	1984 onwards
761[17]	1979	Blackpool CT bogies	EE/Metal Sections	—
762[18]	1982	Blackpool CT bogies	EE/Metal Sections	—
641-47	1984-88	Blackpool CT bogies	East Lancs	—
651[19]	1985	M&T (ex-'Coronation')	East Lancs	—

1 Blackpool 'Standard'. No 143 to works car No 3 1957, renumbered 753 1972. Nos 40/8/9/144/147/158/9 preserved. No 158 acquired only as spares and scrapped 1978.

2 Toastrack. No 161 watercar No 7 — scrapped 1960. Nos 162/4 scrapped 1954. No 163 basis of Blackpool Belle 1959, renumbered 731 1968, preserved Oregon 1982. Nos 165/6 television trams 1951, No 165 scrapped, No 166 preserved at Crich and restored.

3 'Pantograph' or 'Pullman'. Converted to trolleypole 1933. 1950 — No 176 used for tests, scrapped 1954. Nos 167/70 to PW 1954/62, No 167 to TMS 1962 and restored. No 174 converted to Santa Fe trailer 1962 — renumbered 734 1968. No 168, Tramnik 1 1961, renumbered 732. 1968. No 170 to HMS Blackpool 1965, renumbered 736 1968.

4 No 200 was prototype rail coach, Nos 201 onwards were 2ft longer.

5 No 224 rebuilt 1961, renumbered 610 1968, later rebuilt as OMO 3. No 209 underframes to Santa Fe locomotive 1962, renumbered 733 1968. No 220, rebuilt as OMO 4 1972. No 221, PW5 1965, remotored 1967, rebuilt OMO 5 1972. No 222 underframes to Hovertram 1963, renumbered 735 1968.

6 'Boat' open-top single-deckers 229/31/2/4 withdrawn 1963, remainder renumbered 600-7. No 601 withdrawn 1970 — to California. No 603 withdrawn 1975, to San Francisco 1985. No 600 loaned to Heaton Park 1985. No 607 loaned to Crich 1985 and returned to Blackpool in 1987.

7 No 237 originally No 226, renumbered 1934. 'Luxury Dreadnoughts' originally open-top, covers fitted 1941-42. renumbered 700-12 1968. No 706 withdrawn 1980, reinstated 1985 on conversion to open-top.

8 'Balloons'. Renumbered 713-26 1968. Nos 714/25 used as basis of 762/1 respectively.

9 Nos 272-81 rebuilt to tow trailers 1958-61 (see below). Nos 264-71/82/3 renumbered 611-20 1968. No 618 rebuilt with tapered ends 1968. Nos 611-20 rebuilt as OMO 12, 8-11, 1, 6, 13, 7 and 2 respectively 1970-75.

10 Nos 284-300/2 renumbered 621-38 1968. Nos 638 used for OMO tests 1969/70. Nos 624/8 to works cars — renumbered 748/751 1973. No 635 preserved. Brush's last trams.

11 'Sun Saloons'. Rebuilt 1942. 1949-51 converted to Crompton Parkinson VAMBAC. No 11 preserved at EATM.

12 'Coronation'. VAMBAC control. Nos 306/10/8-28 converted to Z4 1964-70. Nos 304-12/4-28 renumbered 641-64 1968. Nos 641/60/3 preserved.

13 No 276 motored/275 de-motored trailer as twin-set. 1961 No 275 re-motored with T5. 276 coupled with T6. Permanent coupling 1965/69 when No 2 end controls moved to trailers. Renumbered 675/6 1968.

14 Trailer cars. Renumbered 681-90 1968. Nos 689/90 to GEC 1981, preserved WYTM 1984 but scrapped 1989.

15 Rebuilt form 272-4/7-81 above. Renumbered 672-4/7-80/71 1968. Nos 272-4/7/81 permanently coupled to T2-4/7/1. When 688-90 withdrawn, 678-80 operated singly. No 678 used for pantograph tests 1975-76.

16 OMO cars. Rebuilt from 616/20/610, 220/1, 617/9/2/3/4/5/1/8 respectively.

17 Rebuild of 725.

18 Rebuild of 714.

19 Subsequently renumbered 648 in 1990.

With links into the tramways of Bury and of South Lancashire Tramways Co, the tramways of Bolton formed an integral part of the standard gauge tramway network that was built to serve the area. However, by 1945 the Bolton trams, following the closure of the adjacent tramway systems, had become isolated.

In 1878 Bolton Corporation and the local boards of Astley Bridge (an area eventually incorporated with Bolton in 1897), Farnworth and Kearsley obtained orders to allow for the construction of 14½ miles of standard-gauge tramway. The services, which were leased out to E. Holden & Co, were inaugurated on 1 September 1880 from Bolton to Moses Gate (Farnworth), to Halliwell and to Dunscar Bridge (via Astley Bridge). By 1882 further extensions saw horse-tram operation on routes to Daubhill station and Lostock Junction Lane. Further acts of 1891 and 1897 allowed for the construction of a further 16 miles of tramway. In June 1899, E. Holden & Co sold out to Bolton Corporation, which, through the transaction, acquired 48 horse-trams and some 350 horses.

The Corporation acted quickly to electrify its new acquisition. On 9 December 1899 the first electric trams operated on routes to Great Lever, Toothill Bridge and Tonge Moor. These were followed on 2 January by electric services on the three original routes of 1880 (with the conse-

quent withdrawal of the last of the horse-trams), and also to Daubhill station, Doffcocker, Lostock Junction Lane and Blackshaw. On 19 May 1900 the Lostock Junction Lane tramway was extended to Horwich (where the Lancashire & Yorkshire Railway has its main workshops). However, the Corporation had moved too quickly in seeking to convert the horse-tramways — rather than re-laying the horse track with heavier electric tramway track, the conversion saw the reuse of the lighter section track and this caused problems which required almost immediate action.

Outside the borough, Farnworth UDC electrified the route from Moses Gate to Black Horse. The first services, operated by Bolton Corporation, starting on 13 April 1900. Progressively, over the next two years, this tramway was extended by both Farnworth and Kearsley to the Manchester boundary, along with a branch to Walkden, and from 1 June 1902 Farnworth's trams replaced those of Bolton on the Moses Gate to Black Horse section. Farnworth continued to operate its own trams for four years, until 1 April 1906, when their tracks were leased to South Lancashire Tramways for a 21-year period. Through services from Bolton started from 14 June 1909.

Back in Bolton proper, 21 December 1900 saw the Blackshaw Lane route extended to Deane. The next extension, on 18 March 1905, saw the

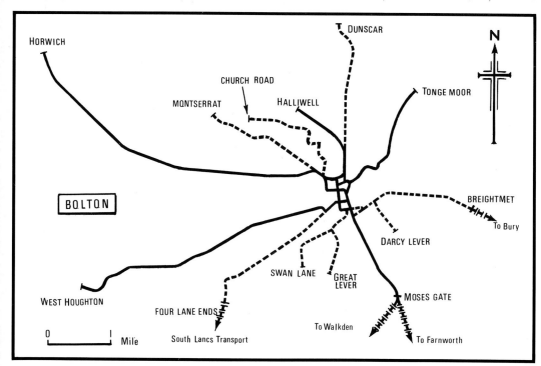

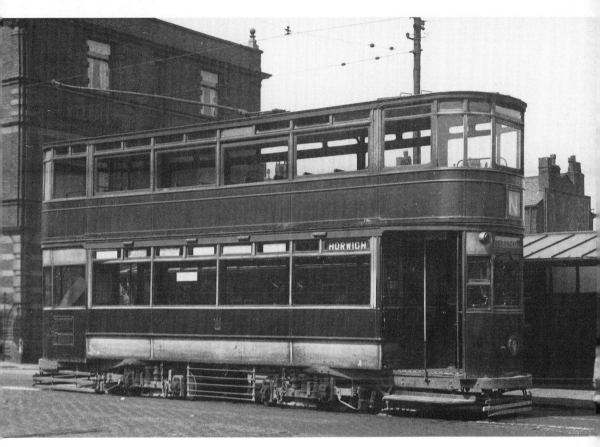

Bolton No 447, seen here awaiting departure on the long route to Horwich, was one of a batch of 12 fully-enclosed trams bought from English Electric in 1927, the last new trams to be bought by Bolton. Bolton used route letters rather than numbers (the route to Horwich being given route letter 'N') and early in 1941 several short-workings on the remaining tram routes were given new identification by using letters previously used on now-closed routes. *Author's collection*

Toothill Bridge route extended to Breightmet, with a further extension, through Radcliffe UDC, to meet up with the trams of Bury Corporation on 20 May 1907. A through service between Bury and Bolton was started. On 6 May 1910 trams replaced buses (which Bolton had first operated in 1904) on the route to Darcy Lever, and this was followed on 4 May 1911 to Brownlow Fold. Bolton was not to operate buses again until 1923. The pre-World War 1 period did, however, witness the first abandonment when the Victoria Road loop was closed in Horwich.

After World War 1 the Bolton tramway system was extended further by a series of primarily sin-

gle-track sections with passing loops. The first, on 8 June 1923, was an extension of the Doff-cocker route to Montserrat, and this was followed on 26 October 1923 by the route to Swan Lane. On 11 April 1924 the Brownlow Fold route was extended to Smithills (Church Road) and, finally, on 19 December 1924 the Deane route was extended to Westhoughton. The Westhoughton line was destined to be the final new tramway constructed in the area, but Bolton's trams were to play a more significant role on the tramways of Farnworth UDC in the near future. However, despite the building of the new tramways, an ill-omen for the future had already appeared — on 29 December 1923 buses had been introduced to the Darcy Lever route, a short branch which was operated by single-deck trams. Inevitably closure was to follow in 1928 — the first route abandonment.

In 1927 South Lancashire Tramways renewed its lease on the tramways owned by Farnworth UDC. However, SLT was now moving to abandon its tramway operations and Bolton Corporation came to operate the trams to both Farnworth and Walkden under SLT's auspices — as SLT remained responsible to Farnworth UDC under the terms of its lease. On 17 December 1933 the through trams to Leigh, via Four Lane Ends, operated jointly with SLT ceased in favour of trolleybuses. Bolton Corporation trams did, however, continue to serve the route to the boundary at Four Lane Ends until abandonment on 28 March 1936.

The 1930s witnessed an almost constant reduction in the size of the Bolton tramway system. On 1 March 1933 the route to Smithills was abandoned. This was followed on 22 January 1934 by the cessation of the through service to Bury and the closure of the route to Breightmet. Apart from the Four Lane Ends closure, 1936 also saw the withdrawal of the route to Great Lever on 1 May. Then, just over a year later, on 4 October

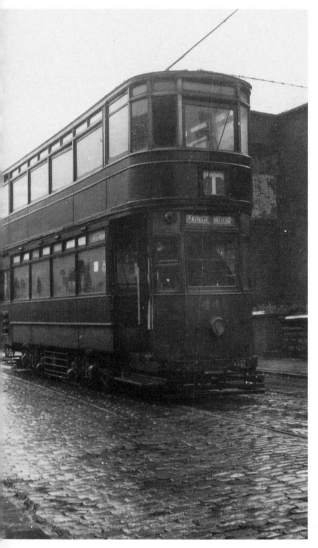

1937, the route to Dunscar was closed, followed by that to Montserrat on 31 December 1938. The final prewar closure, that to Halliwell, occurred on 13 August 1939. However, this last route was to receive a reprieve as tram services were restored on 1 April 1940 as a measure to save fuel.

Over the prewar decade, Bolton's tramway system had more than halved in size and only 78 trams remained in service by 1940. In that year the remaining trams (which included six of the eight ex-SLT trams acquired in 1934) were renumbered in the 308-450 series. Although the trams may have received a short-term reprieve, little was done to ensure their survival. Maintenance, especially of track, was limited, although four trams were acquired from Bury Corporation in 1943 to supplement services. By the end of the war the state of the track on certain sections was giving serious cause for concern and on 3 October 1944 the Ministry of War Transport inspected, and condemned, the tracks in Farnworth and Walkden. Barely a month later, on 12 November 1944, the last trams operated on these routes, although the track within the borough to Moses Gate was retained for football specials and Sundays for a further year or so. The closure of these two routes led to a great deal of criticism in the pages of *Modern Tramway*, not over the closure itself but over the reasons why the tram track had been allowed to deteriorate in the first place. Given the somewhat unusual operations in the Farnworth area — Bolton Corporation operating over tracks leased by SLT (which had long ceased to operate trams) but owned by Farnworth UDC — it is easy to see why nobody took the responsibility.

Peace came to Europe in May 1945, by which time Bolton's trams were limited to four routes — Halliwell, Horwich, Westhoughton, and Tonge Moor — in addition to the periodic services to Moses Gate. Almost immediately, in June 1945, 67 new buses were ordered and the tram replacement programme was resumed. The first casualty was the reprieved route to Halliwell, which operated for the last time on 5 August 1945. During the 1945-46 football season specials continued to serve Burnden Park, but when, in September

Left:
Sister car No 445 is pictured on route T to Tonge Moor. The Tonge Moor route was destined to be Bolton's last service, being converted to bus operation on 29 March 1947, when another of the type, No 440, was suitably decorated to mark the occasion. *F. N. T. Lloyd-Jones*

1946, the service was due to be reinstated, it was found that another Corporation department had lifted a short section of track and this was never replaced.

The next service to be withdrawn was the long route out to Horwich. This closed on 6 October 1946, with 1923 English Electric car No 422 operating the final service. Subsequent to this closure, 12 of the newest trams were transferred to the Tonge Moor route. A month later, on 3 November 1946, the extension from Deane to Westhoughton was closed, being followed on 8 December 1946 by the centre to Deane section. During December 1946 serious consideration was given to a more widespread introduction of trolleybuses to the town. Bolton already had some limited experience of this form of transport since, in addition to the SLT trolleybus services in Farnworth, through SLT trolleybuses operated from Leigh to Bolton (on the line of one of the earlier through tram services) and Bolton Corporation owned four trolleybuses for use on this section, although these were painted in SLT livery. It was decided, however, that the motorbus would replace the final trams.

The final closure came on 29 March 1947 when the Tonge Moor route was converted. The last car, suitably decorated, was 1927-built English Electric car No 440. This was, however, not to be the end of the Bolton tram story. As elsewhere, numerous bodies were sold after withdrawal for conversion into farm buildings, sheds and the like. From the many bodies disposed of in this fashion, one, No 66, built originally by the Electric Railway & Tramway Carriage Works Co in 1901, has been restored completely and has operated regularly in Blackpool.

Bolton Closures

12 November 1944	Farnworth
12 November 1944	Walkden (football specials to Burnden Park, or Sunday services to Moses Gate until 28 September 1946)
5 August 1945	Halliwell
6 October 1946	Horwich
3 November 1946	Outer part of Westhoughton (beyond Deane)
8 December 1946	Inner part of Westhoughton (inside Deane)
29 March 1947	Tonge Moor

Last tram: No 440 (decorated)

Bolton

Fleet Numbers	Date	Trucks/Bogies	Body	Withdrawn
308-10/2/3/5/9/20/3/4/7/30[1]	1899	Brill 21E	ERTCW	By 1947
331[2]	1943 (acquired)	Mountain & Gibson 21EM, retrucked Brill 21E 1943	Milnes	By 1947
334-7/9/40[3]	1933 (acquired)	Burnley EMB bogies	EE/Milnes	By 1947
341-5[4]	1900	Brill 21E	ERTCW	By 1947
360/5-8/74/6-9/380[5]	1901-02	Brill 22E	ERTCW	By 1947
397-403	1910	Brill 22E	UEC	By 1947
404-6	1928	Brush 22E	EE	1945-47
407-12	1912	Brill 21E	UEC	1945-47
413-20	1921	Brill 21E	EE	1945-47
421-30	1923	Brill 21E	EE	1945-47
439-50	1927	Brush 22E	EE	1945-47
451-3[6]	1943 (acquired)	EE 'Burnley'-type bogies	EE	1945-47

Note: All surviving trams renumbered 308-450 from 8-150 respectively in 1940

1 Originally open-top. Nos 8-10 new EE bodies 1926. Nos 12/4/9/20/4/7/30 enclosed top-covers 1924-27. Nos 15/23 balcony top-covers by 1914.
2 Ex-Bury CT, new 1903, rebuilt fully-enclosed 1926.
3 Batch 333-40 ex-South Lancashire Tramways (44/5/7/8/50/4/5/8). Nos 44/5 EE from 1927, others SLT rebuilds (1923-25) of ex-Farnworth UDC from 1901-02.
4 Batch 41-8. Balcony top-covers fitted by 1914.
5 Batch 60-81, balcony top-covers fitted by 1914. No 66 preserved.
6 Ex-Bury, new 1925. Were Bury 55/6/8 respectively.

Whilst Bradford is traditionally better known as Britain's leading exponent of trolleybus operation, the city also played a significant part in the history of tramway operation in Britain and survived to become the last 4ft 0in-gauge system. Unlike South Lancashire, where there was a chain of standard gauge systems stretching from the Mersey to the Pennines, the northern West Riding saw no such consistency. Each of the four main systems selected a different gauge: Halifax 3ft 6in; Bradford 4ft 0in; Huddersfield 4ft 7¾in; and, Leeds — 4ft 8½in. This, without a doubt, affected the development of the tramcar in the region despite efforts to get round the problem. In the worst case, from Huddersfield to Bradford, intending through passengers were faced by trams of three different gauges in a journey of around 10 miles.

During the 19th century, Bradford grew rapidly and was at the forefront of many of the important developments in urban life. In 1881 the Corporation obtained powers for the construction of a tramway along Manningham Lane to Victor Road. Although built by the Corporation, the new service, which started on 1 February 1882, was leased out to the Bradford Tramways & Omnibus Co. This first route was operated by horse-trams, but Bradford, with its centre surrounded by numerous hills, was ill-designed for horse-trams and the next route, up Leeds Road, opened on 8 August 1882, was operated by steam-trams. Further routes, to Four Lane Ends, Allerton, Bankfoot and Tong Cemetery, soon followed. All these routes were leased to the Bradford Tramways & Omnibus Co, except that to Bankfoot which was leased to the Bradford & Shelf Tramways Co.

In 1885 Michael Holroyd Smith, a native of Halifax, had been the promoter of the new conduit electric tramway in Blackpool and Bradford Corporation, who had built the first municipally owned electric power station in 1889, were keen to see if the new power supply could be harnessed to the tramcar. In March 1892 an experimental overhead electric tram service was operated up Cheapside under aegis of Holroyd Smith. The experiment seems to have impressed the Corporation since powers were obtained to operate electric trams directly. The first two routes — to Bolton Junction and Great Horton — were opened on 30 July 1898 and 27 August 1898 respectively. Over the next few years numerous extensions were built and 1902-3 witnessed the operation of the last horse- and steam-trams.

An extension was constructed in 1899 to Eccleshill (from Bolton Junction), and an alternative route to Horton, via Park Avenue, was also opened that year. 1900 saw the electric tramcars reach Thornton, Lidget Green and Duckworth Lane, followed in 1901 by the routes to Queensbury, Idle and Thackley. On 1 February 1902 the Corporation took over the remaining steam-tram operated routes and converted all, bar the Shelf route (which was converted in 1903), to electric traction. 31 January 1902 had also seen the last horse trams operated, on the route to Lister Park and Heaton. This meant new electric services on the routes to Heaton, Allerton and Little Horton. In 1904 the system was further extended by the acquisition of the Mid Yorkshire Tramways Co (which had built two routes in Shipley to 4ft 0in gauge in 1902 and 1903) and by a line in Thackley linking the two operations. Further extensions followed, such as that to Bowling Old Lane in 1904 and to Nab Wood in 1905, and 1907 was to witness the introduction of the through tram service to Leeds despite the difference in gauge.

A number of cars from each undertaking were modified so that the gauge could be altered on specially-tapered track installed for that purpose in Stanningley. Although the service was a success, and although discussions were held with other local operators (such as Halifax in 1913), the Leeds-Bradford service was destined to be the only example in Britain of a through service over tracks of differing gauges. The service lasted until 25 March 1918 when the strains of wartime operation had made the maintenance of the special trucks difficult. The tapered tracks were to remain visible for more than 20 years after this —

44

On 6 November 1948 Bradford tram No 52, one of the Thornbury-built trams of 1922, heads up Morley Street on route No 2 to Horton Bank Top. On the right, West Yorkshire Road Car Co No 308, a Bristol G05G dating from 1935, can be seen departing from Chester Street bus station. Horton Bank Top, where Bradford had a depot, was a short working on the much longer route to Queensbury. The terminus at Queensbury, which was one of three points where Bradford's trams met those of Halifax, was the highest tram terminus in Britain.

a monument to one of the more bizarre aspects of Britain's tramway history.

Further extensions continued to be built: Wibsey in 1907; Wyke to Bailiff Bridge in 1913; and Nab Wood to Bingley and Crossflatts in 1914. This last extension, opened on 13 October, was destined to be the last major extension to Bradford's tramway system. By that date Bradford (in conjunction with Leeds) had introduced trolleybuses to the streets of Britain, and, whilst Leeds' trolleybus installation was destined to be short-lived, that in Bradford was eventually to become the dominant form of transport in the city. Initially, however, the trolleybus was perceived as a feeder to the tramway. The first trolleybus route, introduced in June 1911, linked two tram routes at Dudley Hill and Laisterdyke.

As elsewhere, World War 1 was a period of strain upon the maintenance of the system, but the early 1920s were to witness a considerable investment in both new cars and in trackwork. Between 1918 and 1931 around 150 new tramcars were built, many in the Corporation's own workshops at Thornbury, and all, bar one, were of the standard double-deck, open-balcony four-wheel type that dominated Bradford's tramway history. The exception, the unique No 1, was a dramatic departure from the norm when it was completed in 1926; it was a bogie single-deck car and appeared in a distinct livery. The car was an attempt by Bradford Corporation to get round the Ministry of Transport's restrictions that limited the city to open-balcony double-deck cars because of the narrow gauge. Whilst No 1 was a considerable success, its speed and length made it unsuitable for much of the system and so this

bold attempt to modernise the system came to nothing. No 1 was eventually withdrawn in 1931.

The 1920s also saw several improvements to the system's infrastructure. The important junction in Forster Square was completely relaid in 1922; three sections of reserved track were also constructed (along Thornton Road, Halifax Road and Huddersfield Road); and other sections were relaid. However, as early as 1925 the Council contemplated the conversion of the Bolton Road routes to trolleybus, but this was not progressed due to public opposition.

1926 was a turning point. Not only did it see the introduction of No 1, but it also witnessed the appearance of the first motorbuses in the city and was the year in which the tramcar fleet reached its maximum size (251 cars in total). From this point the decline of the tramcar was destined to commence. The first tram-to-trolleybus conversion occurred on 11 November 1928 when the Greengates route was converted. This was quickly followed by the route to Allerton on 29 November 1929, and the following year the Corporation obtained powers to replace all the

Left:
On 6 November 1948 Bradford No 35 is seen heading towards Odsal. Again a Bradford-built car on English Electric truck, No 35 was renumbered 135 later in 1948, a move intended to avoid duplicating the number of a new AEC Regent III delivered as part of a batch that entered service in 1949-50. The Odsal route, with its wartime extension over part of the closed Shelf route to Horsfall Playing Fields, was destined to become the last Bradford tram route to close.

trams with trolleybuses. Construction of new tramcars ceased in 1931 and the 1930s witnessed an almost continuous decline in the tram mostly, but not exclusively, in favour of trolleybuses.

Trams were replaced on the routes to Saltaire and Thackley on 31 March 1930, to Bolton and Idle on 22 March 1931 and on 8 November 1932 the section of line beyond Wyke to Bailiff Bridge was reduced to peak hours only. 19 March 1933 saw the first tram-to-bus conversion when the long route out to Drighlington was converted. Generally speaking, during this period those routes within the city were converted to trolleybus (the exceptions being the routes to Heaton and Undercliffe which were both converted to bus on 7 April 1935) and those which included sections outside the city to bus (the exception to this being the long route out from Saltaire to Bingley and Crossflatts which was converted to trolleybus operation on 7 May 1939). The route to Eccleshill, the last tram route to run up Bolton Road (scene of one of the pioneering routes in 1898), was converted to trolleybus operation on 1 June 1934, to be followed the same year by the routes to Thornton (21 November) and Lidget Green (12 December). Apart from the Heaton and Undercliffe closures, 1935 also saw the conversion to bus operation of the routes to Shelf

(20 February) and Birkenshaw (30 October). There was only one closure in 1936, the route to Baildon Bridge being abandoned in favour of West Yorkshire Road Car Co buses on 4 February. Apart from the Crossflatts conversion in 1939 already mentioned, there remained only one further prewar conversion when, on 6 July 1938, the routes to Dudley Hill and Tong Cemetery were converted to trolleybuses. Access to the depot at Bowling was, however, retained since the majority of the trams were scrapped in the PW yard there.

By 1939, Bradford had dramatically reduced its tramcar fleet with only 135 cars still in service by the end of March of that year, with a further 20 to be withdrawn with the conversion of the Crossflatts route. The outbreak of war, however, led to a dramatic reversal of the tramcars' fortunes initially. Trams were reintroduced to the Undercliffe route on 11 September 1939 after a gap of four years, and were extended from Odsal to Horsfall Playing Fields on the former route to Shelf. Although these were significant developments, the problems of lack of maintenance on a system that was already in decline led to pressure for further conversions. On 19 October 1942 the short section of track beyond Thornbury to Stanningley was converted to bus operation, although a request to convert the Wibsey route in the same year on the grounds that the track was unsafe was rejected by the Ministry of War Transport. 1942 also witnessed the sale of 10 cars to Sheffield where they were regauged and fully enclosed for service as replacements for cars damaged in the blitz. Finally, 1942 saw the introduction of the light blue and primrose livery in place of the earlier dark blue and white. This livery was to remain standard in Bradford until the Corporation's buses were taken over by West Yorkshire PTE in 1974.

By 1944 the situation was needing resolution. Early in that year the manager, C. R. Tattam, produced a report which advocated that the prewar policy of conversion be confirmed. This was duly agreed and the first conversion in favour of buses, of the line to Wyke and Bailiff Bridge, occurred on 11 June 1944. Shortly afterwards Col Trench of the Ministry of War Transport visited the city and agreed to the Corporation's request that further closures be sanctioned due to the state of the track and equipment. The next closure were the routes to Little Horton and Wibsey, which were replaced by buses on 8 January 1945. The period did, however, see some track work, including the re-laying of certain sections (Barkerend Road, Manchester Road and Great Horton Road), which helped to extend the life of those routes by some years.

Bradford thus entered the postwar era with a fleet of just less than 100 trams operating over some six radial routes, the longest of which was that to Queensbury. Its policy was to replace the trams as quickly as possible, although the prewar emphasis on trolleybuses gave way during this period (with two exceptions) to the motorbus. Indeed there were grave doubts at the time as to the future of the trolleybus system.

The first postwar abandonment was that of the short route to Bowling Old Lane, which was converted to bus operation on 13 December 1947. It was followed on 18 July 1948 by the conversion of the route to Undercliffe to bus for the second time. There was to be no second reprieve! Although traction columns were acquired to convert this route to trolleybus operation, the columns were eventually used elsewhere and Undercliffe was destined to remain a bus route.

April 1949 was to witness the final tram being repainted in Thornbury works but three months later, on 23 July 1949, the trams were withdrawn from the Bradford Moor route in favour of a temporary bus service, which was itself replaced by a trolleybus service later in the year. 1949 was also to witness the demise of the highest tram route

in Britain when the Queensbury and Horton Bank Top routes were converted to bus operation of 5 November with No 149 being the last car from Queensbury. Queensbury was one of three points where Bradford's trams had met the 3ft 6in gauge trams of Halifax. Also closed to trams at this date was Horton Bank Top depot which was Britain's highest tram shed. The Queensbury closure left only two routes: Thornbury and Horsfall Playing Fields. As before the war, trams were taken to Bowling depot yard for scrapping, and during 1949 a short section of track was laid into it for the purpose.

The next closure was the route to Thornbury which was again converted to bus operation temporarily on 4 March 1950, pending conversion to a trolleybus service. The overhead for the trolleybus service was already extant — indeed had been so for more than 30 years to give the trolleybuses access to Thornbury depot and works — and the depot at Thornbury was retained for trams until the final closure. At 31 March 1950 the Bradford tramcar fleet had shrunk to 28 and the end was not far off. The last route, ironically the restored remnant of the Shelf route to Horsfall Playing Fields, was converted to bus operation on 6 May 1950 with No 104 as the official last car. With Bradford's closure came the official end for the 4ft 0in gauge tram in Britain.

But this was not quite the end of the story. Although no Bradford car was preserved when the system was closed, No 104 passed to Odsal Stadium where it was converted into a scoreboard. After three years, the car was rescued and

---

Bradford Closures

11 June 1944	Wyke and Bailiff Bridge
8 January 1945	Little Horton and Wibsey
13 December 1947	Bowling Old Lane
18 July 1948	Undercliffe (had been reopened 11 September 1939)
23 July 1949	Bradford Moor
5 November 1949	Queensbury and Horton Bank Top
4 March 1950	Thornbury (Stanningley closed 1942)
6 May 1950	Horsfall Playing Fields (had reopened during World War 2 — Shelf route closed 20 February 1935)

Last tram: No 104

was carefully restored by local enthusiasts. A truck was acquired from Sheffield (not from one of the ex-Bradford cars, which had then all been withdrawn bar No 330, but from No 358) and on 23 July 1958 the fully-restored car was operated in the precincts of Thornbury Works. Over the following few years No 104 made regular excursions over this section of track. These excursions, however, ceased in the early 1960s, and with the withdrawal of the trolleybuses the overhead disappeared. No 104 remained in storage at Thornbury until it was moved to the Bradford Industrial Museum in the mid-1970s where it is now displayed with one of Bradford's trolleybuses. No 104 has an important place in Britain's tramway history as the first tramcar to rise, phoenix-like, from a derelict condition. A second Bradford tram, No 251, survives at Crich in the guise of Sheffield railgrinder No 330.

Above:
Bradford Moor and Thornbury were the termini for two routes that ran east out of the city towards Leeds. Route No 30, along Leeds Old Road, terminated at the former, whilst route 9, along Leeds Road and past the main depot/workshops at Thornbury, terminated at the latter. Prior to 1942 the Thornbury route ran on further into Stanningley, where an end-on connection was made with the trams of Leeds: it was along this route that the unique dual-gauge through service was operated. Traditionally, the Bradford Moor route had been linked with those heading out along Manningham Lane towards Bingley and Crossflatts, but this linkage had ceased prior to World War 2 when the latter routes were converted to trolleybus operation. Car No 53, another product of Thornbury, dating from 1928, waits at Bradford Moor on 6 November 1948. The Bradford Moor route was converted to trolleybus operation in July 1949 thereby restoring the through services to Bingley.

Bradford

Fleet Numbers	Date	Trucks/Bogies	Body	Withdrawn
17/9, 20/3/4/6-31/3/4/7/9/40/2-5/7-53/5-7/61/71-3/5/7/9-81/3/6/88-90/2-5/7/9, 102-5/8/9/11/119/30/78/81/189/95/6[1]	1921-30	EE	Bradford CT	1945-50
213/8/20-32[2]	1921	Brill 21E	EE/EE-rebodied BCT	1945-50
233/5/6/8/9-241/4/5/7-50/252-6/8[3]	1919-20	Brill 21E	EE/EE-rebodied BCT	1945-50

1 17/9/20/3/7-9, 34/5/7/40/2-5/8/9 renumbered 117/9, etc, 1948. No 104 Bradford's last tram, was restored after period at Odsal Stadium. Now preserved in Bradford Industrial Museum.

2 Batch 213-32. Nos 214-7/9 not rebodied and sold to Sheffield 1942. Nos 213/8/21-3/5-32 rebodied with BCT-built bodies of Nos 2, 3, 125, 69, 63, 205, 4, 14, 74, 82, 5, 6 and 164 respectively 1935-39.

3 Batch 233-55. Nos 234/6-8/42/3/6/251/6-8 not rebodied. Nos 237/42/3/251/7 to Sheffield 1942. Nos 233/5/9-41/4/5/7-50/2-5 rebodied with BCT-built bodies off Nos 7, 87, 158, 8, 58, 12, 13, 70, 21, 60, 41, 33, 15, 16 and 54 respectively 1935-39. No 234 withdrawn 1944. No 246 withdrawn 1942, truck to snowplough S4.

48

With some 19 trams operating over three standard-gauge routes in 1945, Bury's tramway system was but a fraction of its maximum size. At its peak it had been possible to travel by through tram to Rochdale, Bolton or Middleton (with connections onwards to Manchester), but closures during the 1930s had isolated the system.

In 1880 the Manchester Bury Rochdale & Oldham Steam Tramways Co had obtained powers for the construction and operation of a number of routes. This company, which eventually became the second biggest steam-tram operator in Britain, built and operated a network of standard- and narrow-gauge tramways in Bury, Oldham and Rochdale. Despite its name, it never actually operated trams in Manchester, and that part of the title was dropped in 1888. In Bury the company built a number of lines. These included routes to Tottington, Limefield, Heywood and Rochdale, and from Heywood to Hopwood, on the 3ft 6in gauge; and one, from Bury to Whitefield (where the horse-trams of Manchester were met) on the standard gauge. Although initially horse-operated, steam-trams were introduced in 1886.

In November 1899 a Tramways Committee was appointed by Bury Council and the following November a bill was deposited to allow for the takeover and reconstruction of the ex-company lines in Bury, Tottington and Unsworth as well as the building of new lines in Bolton Road, Bell Lane, Rochdale Old Road and Dumers Lane. Although there was opposition, the bill was passed. In order to reduce the level of capital expenditure (the saving was estimated at £186,000) a number of sections were built using interlaced track to avoid the necessity of acquiring property for road widening. Work started on 7 March 1903 on the conversion and the ex-nar-

row-gauge routes were converted to standard gauge as this work progressed. The new electrified services were opened to Fairfield on 3 June 1903, to Heap Bridge on 19 April 1904 and to Walmersley Road on 20 May 1904. To house the trams a new depot was constructed in Rochdale Road.

With the municipalisation of the old company system, the routes in Heywood were left without a service temporarily, and Heywood Corporation stepped in to provide a steam-tram service from the Bury boundary at Heaps Bridge through to the Rochdale boundary near Sudden, as well as the branch to Hopwood. The services to Rochdale were withdrawn on 10 June 1904 (those to Bury having been withdrawn earlier upon the electrification of the line to Heaps Bridge in April 1904). Initial investigations by the Corporation to provide a bus service in place of the trams proved that this option was impractical, and on 31 October 1904 the decision was taken to acquire a number of the company's redundant locomotives and trailers. These were delivered in November and December from Rochdale and on 20 December Heywood Corporation inaugurated its steam-tram service. It could, therefore, lay claim to being the last municipality to introduce steam-trams! Steam-trams started to operate on the Hopwood branch two days later. Due to a disagreement with Rochdale, the steam-trams of Heywood and the electric trams of Rochdale were separated by 1 mile at Sudden. It was not until April 1905 that Rochdale's trams finally met up with those of Heywood. By now, the costs involved in the steam-tram operation were becoming apparent, as were the paucity of the receipts. It was, therefore, with much relief that Heywood negotiated a deal with Bury for the electrification of the lines in the district in August 1905. On 21 August Bury started the reconstruction of the line at Heaps Bridge and from that date the steam-tram service was curtailed to the Summit in Heywood. On 15 September 1905 the steam-trams operated for the last time west of Heywood and on 20 September 1905 the last steam-trams operated. This brought to the end Heywood's short career as a tramway operator. The conversion work was completed in February 1906 and, after an inspection, services commenced on 1 March. Initially, there were no through trams, passengers being expected to change tram in Heywood. Through services commenced on 1 August 1909.

The through service to Rochdale commenced after that to Bolton. As with Heywood, Bury operated the trams on behalf of Radcliffe Urban Dis-

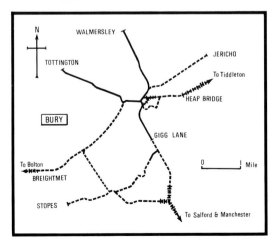

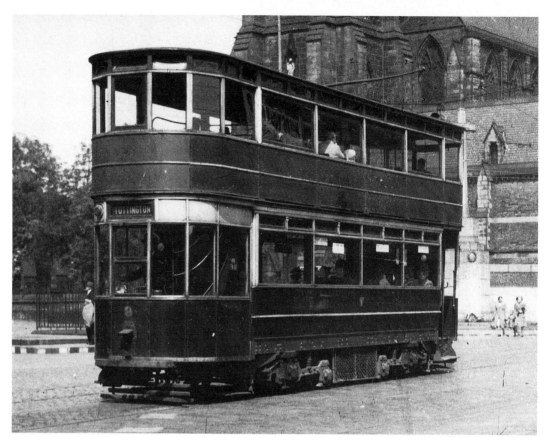

Above:
With the church of St Mary in the background, Bury car No 9 is seen heading towards Tottington. Typical of the majority of Bury's postwar fleet in being fitted with English Electric Burnley-type bogies, No 9 was one of a batch of 14 delivered in 1903, albeit subsequently modernised, with which electric tramcar services were initiated. Apart from the bogie trams, Bury also possessed two four-wheel cars for use, primarily, on the shuttle to Starkies. *Author's collection*

trict Council and on 18 March 1905 the trams of Bolton were extended to the boundary at Breightmet. A new through service was introduced on 20 May 1907. The next two decades saw few new developments except for the acquisition of new trams and the reconstruction of some of the older ones. The last new trams, Nos 55-60, were acquired from English Electric in 1925 and the original batch of cars, Nos 1-14, were rebuilt as fully enclosed on English Electric trucks at about the same time. Four other cars were also rebuilt at this time: Nos 15 and 21 along with two others. The latter two cars were renumbered 30/38 and in 1930 No 30 was fitted with a new EMB truck. This was the last significant development to a Bury tram since the tide was soon to turn against the tramcar in the town. Already, by 1925, there were some 30 motorbuses in service and the neighbouring operators were also gradually converting their systems.

Before the programme of abandonment started, however, there was to be one final extension to the local tramway scene. On 9 August 1925 the tramways of the Middleton Electric Traction Co Ltd were taken over by Manchester, Oldham and Rochdale Corporations. From the terminus of the Hopwood branch to Middleton was some two miles, and as part of the reconstruction of the former company's lines a new route was opened along Hollins Lane and Heywood New Road linking the two systems. This new route, opened on 19 May 1928, enabled a through Bury-Middleton service to operate. The lease on the Hopwood branch passed from Bury to Manchester and Manchester Corporation allocated the service from Heywood to Manchester route No 18. Although Bury did not participate on the through service to Manchester it did operate to Middleton, with the retrucked No 30 as the usual tram.

The 1930s witnessed an almost unrelenting decline in the Bury tramway system. The through service to Rochdale was withdrawn on 3 July 1932, although peak-hour cars continued to operate to Heywood until 18 February 1933. The last Bury car ran to Middleton on 19 February 1933, although Manchester continued to operate route No 18 until it was abandoned on 1 May 1934. The last Bury car to Heywood operated on the same day. Earlier in 1934, on 22 January, the through service to Bolton was withdrawn and by 1938, when there were some 71 buses in service, trams had been withdrawn from all the routes except those to Tottington and Walmersley. The onset of World War 2 gave the trams of Bury an unexpected reprieve.

With much of the tramway system only recently abandoned, Bury was able to reintroduce a tramway service along the Manchester Road as far as Starkies (adjacent to the football ground at Gigg Lane) as a wartime measure on 30 September 1939. At the start of the war, the Bury fleet numbered some 20 trams, the majority of which were bogie cars. This number was reduced by four through the sale in 1943 of three bogie cars (Nos 55/56/58) and one four-wheel car (No 21) to Bolton. The other two four-wheel cars, Nos 30/38, were primarily used on the shuttle service to Starkies, leaving the bogie cars, Nos 1-14, to operate the Tottington and Walmersley route. No 30 had been modernised in 1930 and, prior to the service's withdrawal, had been Bury's usual contribution to the route to Middleton. The only other major wartime change was the appointment of R. Le Fevre as Manager to succeed C. P. Paige, who had moved to Oldham.

With the restoration of peacetime conditions, the Corporation was in a position to recommence its policy of withdrawing the trams. The shuttle service to Starkies was soon reduced to a Saturdays-only service using only one tram, and it was finally withdrawn on 6 July 1946. The withdrawal of the service allowed for the final withdrawal of the two four-wheel cars, and No 30 was eventually sold to Sunderland in 1947. As No 85 it became the last tram to be acquired by Sunderland and was to operate for a further seven years before withdrawal for the second time in March 1954 — thereby outliving its home town's tram system by some five years.

Also in 1946, it was announced that the final trams in Bury would be withdrawn within two years. In the event the forecast was to prove optimistic, but a two-route system, operated by 14 elderly bogie cars, was never going to be secure. The first closure occurred on 15 February 1948 when the route out to Tottington was converted to bus operation. This was followed, almost exactly a year later, on 13 February 1949, by the withdrawal of the last route to Walmersley. The official last tram was one of the bogie cars, No 13.

The Bury tramway system, although relatively small, had several interesting features. One of these was the amount of interlaced track used on the main routes — a reflection of the narrow streets through which the trams had to operate — including an unusual slip crossover in one of the sections of interlaced track. Of the Bury fleet none now survive.

Bury Closures

6 July 1946	Starkies (wartime re-introduction, service originally abandoned 1939. Latterly Saturdays-only)
15 February 1948	Tottington
13 February 1949	Walmersley

Last tram: No 13

Bury

Fleet Numbers	Date	Trucks/Bogies	Body	Withdrawn
1-14[1]	1903	McGuire No 3 Maximum Traction bogies, replaced by EE Burnley-type bogies 1925-26	G. F. Milnes	By 1949
30 (ii)[2]	1905	M&G 21EM, retrucked EMB 1930	G. F. Milnes	1947
38 (ii)[3]	1905	M&G 21EM	G. F. Milnes	By 1949
57/9/60[4]	1925	EE 'Burnley'-type bogies	EE	By 1949

1 Originally open-top, rebuilt fully-enclosed 1925-26.
2 Originally balcony-top, rebuilt fully-enclosed 1925-26. Sold to Sunderland (No 85) 1947.
3 Balcony-top rebuilt fully-enclosed 1925-26.
4 Fully-enclosed from new. Batch 55-60, Nos 55/6/8 sold to Bolton (Nos 451-3) 1943.

One of four tramways systems to remain in the Principality after the end of World War 2, Cardiff's main claim to fame is that it saw the only new trolleybus installation to be established during the period of hostilities (and the penultimate to open in Great Britain). Cardiff was also the first Welsh tramway to succumb after 1945.

The origins of the Cardiff tramways lay in two company-owned horse-tramways totalling some six route miles. The Cardiff Tramways Co, whose services started in 1872, operated over five routes — to Canton, Clarence Road, Bute Docks, Roath and Cathays — whilst the Cardiff District & Penarth Harbour Co operated the sixth route, from Adamsdown to Grangetown. Already, one factor that was to play a considerable part in Cardiff's transport history was in play — the number of low railway bridges which meant that until the bridges were raised (or the roads lowered) Cardiff was forced to reply upon single-deck vehicles on a number of routes. Whilst this may not have been a significant problem in the horse-tram era, with electrification and the growth of traffic the inability to operate double-deck trams was a serious impediment to development of the tramway system.

In 1898 Cardiff Corporation promoted a Bill to take over the operation of the company tramways and to allow for the electrification and extension of the system. Initial thoughts were that the conduit system would be adopted, but by the time work started, conventional overhead was utilised. Although the takeover of the company horse-trams was not effective until 1 January 1902, the Corporation started on the extension of the tramways in 1900 and a number of sections, for example that along Wood Street, were constructed during this period. Pending electrifica-

tion these new sections were operated by horse-trams. Following the takeover, the Corporation moved quickly to reconstruct the track and to erect the overhead, with the result that the first electric tram routes were opened on 1 May 1902 when the official party travelled over the Canton and Cathedral Road routes. Public services started the next day.

Further conversions were opened rapidly, such as that to Newport Road on 3 May 1902 and Cathays and Bute Street on 13 June 1902. These were followed by the progressive conversion of the ex-Cardiff District & Penarth Harbour Co route from Grangetown to Splott, which was completed on 24 April 1904. This was followed by two further extensions, to the Canton and Cathays routes, which were opened on 25 November 1904.

By now the vehicle fleet had expanded to a total of 131, including 30 single-deckers, and the next 15 years were to witness little change to the system. No new extensions were built and no new vehicles were acquired. Indeed, such was the complete lack of investment during the period that the tramways became increasingly unpopular and the track increasingly uncomfortable to ride upon. It seemed that there were only two real options for Cardiff's trams — either abandonment or renewal.

However, in 1920 a new manager, R. L. Horsfield from Walsall, was appointed, and under his aegis the tramway system was upgraded. Five extensions were built, including a virtual doubling of the size of Clare Road depot, and the tram fleet was almost completely replaced. Immediately on his appointment he launched a policy of refurbishing the existing tramcar fleet: over the next two years, two-thirds of the 130 trams were modernised. Due to the low bridges on several routes this modernisation did not see the fleet top-covered, but elsewhere steps were being taken that would enable fully-enclosed trams to operate later. It was not practical to lower the roads beneath the bridges since this would increase the likelihood of flooding, but, in co-operation with Brush, No 101 was constructed utilising small diameter wheels and motors, which, in conjunction with low headroom body, allowed for a fully-enclosed tram. Such was the success of this new tram when it was delivered in 1923 that a further 25 were immediately ordered from Brush and a further 55 during the next two years. In 1926-27, 31 new single-deck trams were bought, and this saw the total fleet increased to 137 of which 112 had been built over the previous five years. The remainder were modernised

N

GABALFA (WHITCHURCH ROAD)

ROATH PARK

CATHEDRAL ROAD

PENGAM
(NEWPORT
ROAD)

CANTON
(VICTORIA PARK)

3

1

2

CARDIFF

SPLOTT

GRANGETOWN CLARENCE RD   PIER HEAD

Scale   0   1 Mile

1 — St Mary St
2 — Adamsdown
3 — Salisbury Road

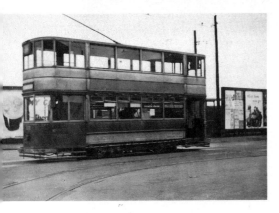

Above:
Typical of the majority of Cardiff's tram fleet after the modernisation of the 1920s, No 112 is seen at Roath depot on 31 July 1948.

trams, some of which were to give a further 20 years service.

The Cardiff Corporation Act of 1920 allowed for a number of tramway extensions, as well as allowing powers to operate motorbuses and, as a consequence, the first buses were acquired that year. On 4 June 1924 the first of the newly-authorised extensions, the Duke Street link, was opened. On 20 August 1927 the Newport Road route was extended by 480yd over track previously used only to give access to Roath depot. On 16 June 1928 the Whitchurch Road route was extended to Gabalfa, followed on 6 August 1928 by an extension along Cathedral Road. Although a certain amount of progress was still to take place, this marked the final extension to the tramway as R. L. Horsfield had departed in September 1928 to become manager at Leeds, and had been replaced at Cardiff by William Forbes from Aberdeen, a manager perceived to be pro-bus.

The problem of the low bridges remained. Although the Moira Terrace-Adam Street bridge was raised to allow for the operation of double-deck trams, it was another bridge, that on Salisbury Road, that led to the first tramway abandonment on 4 April 1930. As elsewhere in Britain, Cardiff in the early 1930s witnessed severe economic depression with the consequence that receipts fell and frequency of service was reduced. In 1934 the Cardiff Corporation Act for the first time gave the Corporation powers to operate trolleybuses. Increased pressure upon finances led to a decline in track maintenance, and in 1936 the deterioration of track on the Splott and Grangetown routes led to discussion over their future. Forbes advocated their replace-

ment by bus, and on 11 October 1936 the trams were withdrawn. Although track was lifted to Splott and Grangetown, that in Adamsdown was retained for diversions. This closure meant that all 31 of the single-deck trams, then only 10 years old, were withdrawn and stored and offered for sale.

The next threatened closures occurred the following year, in 1937, when Forbes advocated the replacement of the Wood Street and Clarence Road routes by motorbuses. This advice was rejected by the City Council in favour of a study into the comparative figures between bus and trolleybus. In May 1939 the City Council resolved to adopt trolleybuses. However, before the decision could be implemented, World War 2 broke out. Nevertheless, determined to proceed with the introduction of trolleybuses, the Corporation obtained the Cardiff Corporation (Trolley Vehicles) Order Confirmation Act in 1940. In the same year William Forbes died in office and was replaced by W. V. Evans from Rotherham. Work progressed slowly on the introduction of trolleybuses and on 1 March 1942 the first five vehicles were delivered. This enabled the partial conversion of the Clarence Road route, the trams being progressively withdrawn as further trolleybuses became available.

The end of World War 2 saw Cardiff operating a fleet of some 89 trams (including eight of the modernised trams dating originally from 1902) and 10 trolleybuses, in addition to motorbuses. The policy was still to convert to trolleybus operation, and the next section to come under scrutiny was that along Bute Street to the Pier Head. The track on this section had seriously deteriorated and the Corporation was faced by either immediate renewal of the track or replacement. Although suitable single-deck trolleybuses to operate the service were part of an order for 75 vehicles placed in 1945, such were the constraints on delivery that it seemed unlikely that Cardiff would receive the new vehicles until 1948-49. As a consequence, the Pier Head route was converted to bus operation. The last trams on service 16 and the workmen's specials operated on 27 April 1946. To facilitate conversion of the route to trolleybus operation (which occurred on 17 August 1947), a number of second-hand trolleybuses were acquired from Pontypridd.

By the late 1940s the increased availability of new trolleybuses allowed for the rapid withdrawal of the remaining trams. The first route to succumb was that from Canton (Victoria Park) to St Mary Street on 6 June 1948. This was followed,

Although no passenger tram survives from Cardiff, the collection of the National Tramway Museum at Crich does include the single-deck water car, No 131, which was originally built by Brush in 1905. The car is currently in store at Clay Cross.

barely a month later on 4 July, by the route from Canton to Queen Street. The final closure of 1948, on 17 October, saw trams withdrawn from the Newport Road route. This left only two routes — Roath Park and Whitchurch Road — in operation. However, before the next closure, the two routes were to be diverted away from Queen Street, which closed on 12 July 1949, to run instead via Adamsdown. This track, which had not seen significant usage for more than a decade, remained in reasonable condition and showed that the trams were still capable of adequate performance if properly maintained. The next closure was not long in coming. On 5 December 1949 the Roath Park route was converted, whilst the last route, to Whitchurch Road, was converted on 19 February 1950. The last service car was No 112. The following day No 11, suitably decorated, operated all day as the city bade farewell to its faithful servants of more than 48 years.

Cardiff Closures

27 April 1946	16 — Hayes Bridge to Pier Head
6 June 1948	5 — Victoria Park to Pier Head
6 June 1948	5A — Victoria Park to St Mary Street
4 July 1948	8 — Newport Road to Cathedral Road
17 October 1948	2 — Newport Road to Pier Head
5 December 1949	4 — Roath Park to St Mary Street
19 February 1950	1 — Whitchurch Road to St Mary Street

Last tram: No 11

Cardiff

Fleet Numbers	Date	Trucks/Bogies	Body	Withdrawn
1-4/7-9/11/4/6-21/5-8/31/3/5-40/55-60/62-71/ 3-5/77-83/5-9/91-8/100-14	1923-25	Peckham Pendulum	Brush	1947-50
22/3/9/30/2/4/84/90[1]	1902	Brill 22E bogies	Brush	1947
131[2]	1905	Brill 21E	Dick Kerr	1950

1   Original open-top trams which had been reconditioned after 1920.
2   Covered water tram, now preserved at Crich (in store at Clay Cross).

The Lancashire town of Darwen, along with its northern neighbour Blackburn, kept the 4ft 0in gauge alive west of the Pennines into the postwar era. In Darwen's case this was despite the endeavours of the Corporation, a paradoxical position inasmuch as Darwen operated perhaps the most modern trams (bar Bradford's unique No 1) ever to operate on Britain's 4ft 0in-gauge tramways.

The Blackburn & Over Darwen Tramways Act was passed on 15 August 1879. This was the first tramways act to allow the operator to run steam-trams; prior to this date the 1870 Tramways Act had effectively limited street tramway operators to horse power and it was only in 1879 that the Board of Trade were empowered to allow mechanical operation of street tramways. After a period of construction the tramway, linking the two towns, was opened on 13 April 1881. The company's franchise would run until 1900, but Darwen Corporation bought its section of line in January 1899 and an Act of 9 August 1899 allowed the Corporation to convert the route to electric traction. The new electric services were inaugurated on 16 October 1900. The final extension, from Darwen eastwards to Hoddlesden, was opened on 11 October 1901. Darwen's network represented a total of almost 4½ route miles and just over 7 track miles.

Although the system was small, the Corporation continued to ensure that replacement vehi-cles were acquired, in contrast to the policy of many other small operators. New trams were placed in service in 1921 and 1924, and further 'new' vehicles also appeared in the late 1920s and early 1930s. These were rebuilds from earlier trams and from parts acquired from neighbour-ing Rawtenstall. But already the writing was on the wall for the tramways. In 1925 the Corpora-tion proposed a southern extension and an Act allowing for the construction was passed in 1926. The extension was, however, never built and, more significantly, the 1926 Act also allowed the Corporation to operate motorbuses for the first time. These were introduced on 23 September 1926.

In 1930 the lightly-trafficked route to Hoddles-den was reduced in frequency, with buses provid-ing most of the services. Despite this, however, the route was not finally withdrawn until 13 October 1937. In the meantime the Corpora-tion had acquired the two English Electric fully-enclosed streamlined trams, Nos 23 and 24.

Although the new trams were barely three years old, the next tramway withdrawal occurred in 1939. The route from Circus southwards to Whitehall (where it terminated just five miles north of Bolton terminus at Dunscar) was closed in January 1939. Fuel restrictions caused by the outbreak of World War 2 led to its temporary reintroduction in September 1939, but this reprieve was destined to be short-lived and the line closed finally on 31 March 1940. Having closed this section, Darwen Corporation was eager to close the final route from Circus north-wards to the boundary at Earcroft (and thence to Blackburn). An application to close the route in April 1940 was rejected by the Ministry of Trans-port despite the poor condition of the track.

A further request to close the route from 30 September 1941 was also rejected. Moreover, by this time, one of the remaining 10 trams had been seriously damaged in an accident and two others (Nos 8 and 10) had been withdrawn. A new car, No 10, was, therefore, constructed from the lower deck of No 17 (the car involved in the accident) and the top deck of No 8. Even with the 'new' No 10, by early 1945 Darwen's operational fleet was reduced to just five trams, including the

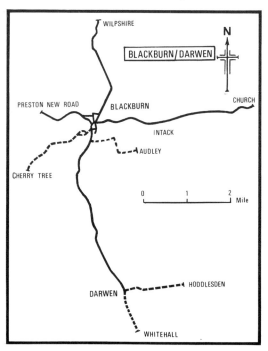

WILPSHIRE

N

BLACKBURN / DARWEN

PRESTON NEW ROAD

BLACKBURN

CHURCH

INTACK

AUDLEY

CHERRY TREE

0   1   2
|——————|——————| Mile

HODDLESDEN

DARWEN

WHITEHALL

Darwen Closure

5 October 1946	Circus to Blackburn Boundary

Last tram: No 3

Above:
Strictly speaking the newest tram ever to operate on the 4ft 0in gauge, nominally dating from 1941, Darwen No 10's origins were, however, much more complex. The car was constructed from the top deck of No 8 (which had been withdrawn) and the lower deck of No 17 (which had overturned). Even this was not the full story as Nos 8 and 17 were themselves earlier reconstructions (in 1925-29) of trams whose origins lay back with the original open-top cars supplied by Milnes in the early 1900s!
Author's collection

plemented by additional Blackburn trams. The problem was increased yet further by the withdrawal in 1945 and eventual sale of the modern trams to the Llandudno & Colwyn Bay Electric Railway in August 1946.

With just three operational tramcars, Darwen soldiered on past yet another proposed closure date (31 March 1946) until 5 October 1946, when No 3, suitably decorated, became Darwen's last tram. Blackburn's trams continued to serve the route, to the borough boundary until July 1949, whilst the two streamlined trams, after being regauged, gave their new owners almost a further decade of service.

two modern streamliners, and the service between Blackburn and Darwen had to be sup-

Darwen

Fleet Numbers	Date	Trucks/Bogies	Body	Withdrawn
3/7[1]	1925-29	'Burnley'-type bogies	Darwen CT	1946
10[2]	1941	'Burnley'-type bogies	Brush	1946
23/4[3]	1936	EE Maximum Traction bogies	EE	1945

1 Constructed using lower saloons from earlier trams combined with new Brush tops.
2 In 1941 new car No 10 built from the lower deck of No 17 (which had overturned) and top deck of No 8. At this point No 8 and previous No 10 withdrawn. These trams were 1925-29 rebuilds similar to Nos 3/7.
3 Centre-entrance streamlined cars; sold to Llandudno, regauged and renumbered 24/23.

One of the most curious of all British tramway survivors is that of the horse-tramway along the Promenade at Douglas on the Isle of Man. In addition to being the only surviving horse-tramway in Britain, the line can also claim to be the oldest surviving tramway in the British Isles.

The first section of the Douglas horse-tramway was opened on 7 August 1876 by Thomas Lightfoot, an Act from the Manx parliament Tynwald having been obtained the previous year, and by the end of that year some two miles, constructed to the Manx 'standard' gauge of 3ft 0in, was in operation. Lightfoot's involvement was, however, destined to be relatively short-lived, and in 1884 the line was acquired by Isle of Man Tramways Ltd. 1890 witnessed the extension of the line from Burnt Mill Hill, where a new depot had been opened four years earlier, to Derby Castle. A further sale, in 1894, saw the line sold to the Isle of Man Tramways & Electric Power Co Ltd, the same company which owned the Manx Electric and the Snaefell Mountain lines. In addition to the horse-tramway, the company also built a cable line to Upper Douglas, which was opened in August 1896 as part of a deal to prevent the municipal takeover of the tramway. Between 1894 and 1896 a new depot was constructed at Derby Castle to replace that built at Burnt Mill Hill.

The Isle of Man Tramways & Electric Power Co Ltd was an ambitious company, which envisaged the construction of an electric tramway from the sea front at Douglas right the way through to Ramsey. In furtherance of this aim, the company promoted the electrification of the horse-tramway, but its proposals were rejected. As with all the other holdings in the company, the collapse of Alexander Bruce's empire led to the disposal of the line. Douglas Corporation exercised its option to buy both the horse-tramway and the cable line, and municipal operation commenced in January 1902. 1902 was also to witness the extension of the tramway a short distance onto Victoria Pier. The early years of the 20th century witnessed further efforts to electrify the line, although, as before, these came to nothing. The rejection came too late for one local entrepreneur, however, who managed to produce a postcard ostensibly showing electric cars operating along the line!

The first part of the cable tramway was destined to be closed very early under the municipal ownership, although the final section was not completely abandoned until 19 August 1929. All the cable cars were disposed of by that date, although the bodies of two cars (Nos 73/73) were subsequently recovered with the intention that the best parts from both be used in the reconstruction of one cable car. The restored car has been used on several occasions over the horse-tramway.

The first Corporation-owned motorbuses had operated just prior to the outbreak of World War 1, and proposals were made that the horse-tramway be replaced by buses. As the tramway was increasingly seen as primarily a tourist attraction — and as it made a profit — these suggestions were not proceeded with. The interwar years were a period of relative stability for the tramway, although 1935 saw the introduction of the last new trams, Nos 48-50. It operated only during the summer season and normally ceased operation at about the end of September. Services were, therefore, suspended on 30 September 1939. It was, however, destined to be a further seven years before the horse-trams were to run again.

The official reopening took place on 22 May 1946. There was a fleet of some 40 single- and double-deck tramcars available, but all the pre-war horses had been disposed of. To operate the new service the Corporation acquired 42 horses from Ireland (well down on the 135 owned in 1935), setting a pattern that was to be repeated for the next two decades. Despite the newly introduced service, there were pressures for the tramway to be abandoned. In November 1947, however, the council voted by 21-1 to retain the trams. The number of trams was, nonetheless, to be reduced as the increasing cost of maintenance and the declining levels of traffic became apparent. In 1949 all the remaining double-deck trams, with the exception of No 14, were withdrawn, to be followed three years later by the withdrawal of toastracks Nos 9, 19, 20, 23-5 and 30. The sole remaining double-deck tram, No 14, was passed to the Museum of British Transport at Clapham in 1955 and was to leave the Isle of Man for two decades.

The newly-restored tramway was financially successful throughout the late 1940s and 1950s, making a peak profit in 1955 of £6,377. The Douglas Corporation buses, however, were not so successful, and the profit from the trams was used to offset part of the losses made by the bus operations. And by the late 1950s even the profit on the trams was beginning to decline, falling to £1,794 in 1959 and a small loss in 1960. Fares, which were regulated by a statute of 1895, could only be increased with the permission of Tynwald, and this permission was now regularly sought and granted. By the early 1960s proposals

Above:
The horse-trams of Douglas Corporation and the electric trams of the Manx Electric Railway meet at only one point — Derby Castle. On 23 August 1964, 1913-vintage horse-tram No 1 is seen departing from Derby Castle, with Milnes-built No 27 having just arrived. At the terminus of the Manx Electric Railway is another Milnes-built car, this time crossbench trailer No 42 waiting to be hauled northwards. *L. Sandler*

for the abandonment of the tramway again surfaced but were, as before, rejected. In 1968, after two decades of buying horses from Ireland, the Corporation acquired its first horses from England. Thereafter, horses were acquired from both England and Ireland until the costs of acquiring them increased to such a level that breeding on the island itself became the preferred option. In 1969, the Duke of Edinburgh drove No 44 during a royal tour of the island; this car was to become effectively the island's royal tram when in August 1972 Queen Elizabeth II travelled on it. This was, apparently, the first occasion on which the Queen had ever travelled on a tramcar.

The royal visit of 1972 led to an interesting problem. During the visit it emerged that the armorial bearings used by Douglas Corporation had never been officially sanctioned by the College of Arms and that the existing arms were unlikely to be accepted. The Corporation was, therefore, potentially faced by a bill not just to register the arms but also the costs of having the new arms adopted for use. Rather than undertake this, the existing bearings were redesignated the Corporate Common Seal of the Borough.

The early 1970s witnessed the continued decline in the finances of the Corporation's transport department, with a then record overall loss of £13,170 being recorded in 1974. The tramcar fleet inevitably suffered; by that year cars Nos 11, 26, 31-4 and 37 were not used, although Nos 48-50 were overhauled. 1976 was the centenary of the horse-tramway and it was celebrated in style with a cavalcade on 9 August when the existing

fleet was joined by double-deck car No 14 (which was returned to the island specially and subsequently remained there on loan from the Science Museum) and by the restored cable-car. 1976 was also to see, after an earlier effort proved unsuccessful, the merger of the Corporation bus services with those of the Isle of Man Road Services. This left the Corporation to operate the tramcars alone.

The gradual decline in the size of the fleet continued in 1978 with the withdrawal of Nos 11, 22, 41 and 47. On withdrawal these were stored at the Corporation's farm. This left a total of 25 cars available for service. At the same time No 33 was rebuilt with bulkheads, completing the conversion of the batch of six, Nos 32-7 — a conversion programme which had started in 1908! 1979 saw further modifications, with the rebuilding of cars Nos 48-50 from convertible to all-weather cars so that a five-minute frequency service could be operated in wet weather. The cars were not, however, destined to remain long in this condition, being sold the following year to the Manx Electric Railway for use as shelters. Only No 49 was used in this guise, at Douglas, and Nos 48 and 50 were dismantled in 1982. The same year, on 27 May, No 49 was moved to Ramsey to form an exhibit in the tramway museum in the town.

In early 1983, Sealink borrowed No 1 and brought it to the mainland where, after a repaint at Lancaster City Transport, it was used for promotion prior to returning to the island on 12 March 1983. This year also saw the dismantling of No 10 and the transfer of two of the cars withdrawn earlier, Nos 11 and 47, to the museum at Ramsey. The continuing parlous state of the operation was revealed by the fact that in 1984 the tramway carried 0.5 million passengers but still lost £18,000. During this period, the Corporation was achieving considerable success with the use of No 14 for private hire work and in 1985 it was decided to rebuild one of the original double-deck cars, No 18, to its original form. Prior to the work being undertaken, dynamometer tests were carried out to prove the suitability of the type. The rebuilt car finally emerged in 1989.

The fleet was further reduced in 1987 with the scrapping of Nos 31 and 41 and the transfer of No 46 to a children's playground. This transfer caused much controversy and the tram was eventually rescued and transferred for preservation to the Wirral on 21 March 1988. Jealous of its uniqueness, Douglas Corporation was reluctant to see the tramcar preserved at a site where it could be operated.

Thus, with a fleet of around 20 cars, Douglas continues to operate horse-trams. The ever increasing costs of maintenance and the increasing age of the vehicles give some cause for concern, but the authorities recognise the uniqueness of the operation and the attraction that the tramway offers to tourists. Without these selling points, it is doubtful whether the tramway would have survived to its half century let alone its centenary.

Douglas

Fleet Numbers	Date	Trucks/Bogies	Body	Withdrawn
1[1]	1913	—	Milnes Voss	—
2-6/8[2]	1876-84	—	Starbuck	1949
9-11[3]	1885-86	—	Starbuck	9-1952; 10-1983; 11-1978
12[4]	1882	—	Milnes	—
14/5[5]	1887 (acquired)	—	Metropolitan	1949
18[6]	1887 (acquired)	—	Metropolitan	—
19/20[7]	1889	—	Milnes	1949
21/2[8]	1890	—	Milnes	22-1978
23-6[9]	1891	—	Milnes	23-5 — 1952, 26 in service
27-9[10]	1892	—	Milnes	—
30/1[11]	1894	—	Milnes	30 — 1952; 31-1987
32-7[12]	1896	—	Milnes	—
38-40[13]	1902	—	Milnes	—
41/2[14]	1905	—	Milnes Voss	41-1978
43/4[15]	1907	—	UEC	—
45-7[16]	1909-11	—	Milnes Voss	47-1978; 46-1987
48-50[17]	1935	—	Vulcan	1980

1 Saloon.
2 Open-top double-deck.
3 Toastracks. No 10 dismantled 1983, No 11 now preserved.
4 Toastrack.
5 Acquired from South Shields Tramway Co. New in 1883. No 14 renumbered from 13 in 1908 and now preserved. Double-deck open-top trams.
6 Acquired from South Shields Tramway Co. New in 1883. Originally open-top double-deck and converted to single-deck in 1903. No 17 withdrawn 1911. No 18 reconverted to double-deck form.
7 Open toastrack.
8 Open toastrack.

9 Open toastrack.
10 Saloons.
11 Open toastracks.
12 Covered toastracks.
13 Open toastracks.
14 Open toastracks.
15 Covered toastracks.
16 Covered toastracks. No 47 now preserved at Ramsey; No 46 now preserved in England.
17 All-weather saloons converted to toastracks. Sold to MER for use as shelters. Nos 48 and 50 dismantled 1982. No 49 now preserved.

The Irish Republic's capital city had the most extensive tramway system in the country and the largest 5ft 3in-gauge system in the British Isles. At its peak it operated more than 300 tramcars over a network of more than 60 route miles that stretched well out into the surrounding country. The system was also peculiar in that modernisation continued well into the mid-1930s, until an abrupt change of policy led to the decision to convert all the tram routes to bus operation.

The development of the tram system in Dublin is particularly complex, involving as it did a number of tramway companies and a variety of gauges. In 1881 three companies came together to form Dublin United Tramways. These three companies were the Dublin Tramways Co, which had acquired in 1871 the rights of the earlier and abortive City of Dublin Co, the North Dublin Street Tramways Co and the Central Tramways Co.

The first of the Dublin Tramways Co's lines, from College Green to Rathgar Road, opened on 1 February 1872, and a second, from Kingsbridge station to Earlsfort Terrace, followed on 3 June 1872. This second line was further extended on 1 October 1872 to Sandymount. Additional routes to Donnybrook, Dollymount and North Quays followed.

The North Dublin Street Tramways Co was established in 1875 and built lines from Nelson Pillar to Phoenix Park, Glasnevin, Grattan Bridge, Drumcondra and Inchicore to College Green.

The third company, the Central Tramways Co, was established in 1878 and built lines from College Green to Palmerston Park via Ranelagh, Ranelagh to Rathmines and Terenure. All these lines were built to the 5ft 3in gauge and were horse-operated.

The Dublin Tramways Co also had powers to build a line south towards Blackrock but these were abandoned and allowed a further company, the Dublin Southern District Tramways, to emerge. This line, from Haddington Road to Blackrock, was opened throughout on 16 June 1879 — the disconnected section from Kingstown to Dalkey, which was built to the 4ft 0in gauge, had opened on 17 March 1879. The intermediate section, from Blackrock to Kingstown, was opened on 9 July 1885 by a further company, the Blackrock & Kingstown Co. This section was built to the 5ft 3in gauge.

In the early 1890s the Dublin Southern District Tramways applied for powers to take over the Blackrock & Kingstown Co, to regauge the Kingstown-Dalkey service and to electrify the through service from Haddington Road to

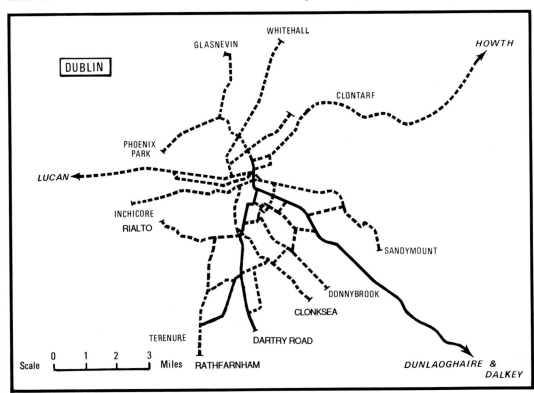

Dalkey. The company had also experimented with steam traction outside the city boundaries, but the reluctance of the city corporation to allow for steam operation within the city meant that both the Dublin Southern and the Dublin United companies used horse-trams only. The first experimental trials of the new electric trams commenced on 30 November 1895 and the public service commenced on 16 May 1896. The new electric trams appeared with the name 'Dublin Electric Tramways' emblazoned on their side.

The operation of electric tramcars by the Dublin Southern District Tramways was relatively short-lived as, on 28 September 1896, a new holding company, Dublin United Tramways (1896) Ltd, was established to take over the assets of both the original DUT and the Dublin Southern. The latter, which was until this point, a subsidiary of the England-based Imperial Tramways Co (which also owned London United Tramways), continued to issue its own annual reports for legal reasons until an Amalgamation Act in 1905. The newly constituted company moved quickly to electrify the horse-tram routes in the city, the first sections opened in 1897 and the final horse-tram reached Nelson Pillar in 1901.

The next significant takeover was of the operations of the Clontarf & Hill of Howth Tramroad Co Ltd. The first proposals to link Dublin with the popular tourist spot of the Hill of Howth by tramway had occurred in 1890, but it was not until later in the same decade that more positive developments took place. In 1898 an Act was passed to enable the construction of a tramway from the DUT terminus at Dollymount through to the Hill of Howth. The act authorised the Clontarf & Hill of Howth Tramroad Co Ltd to build and operate the line. It was to be built to a gauge of 5ft 3in and electric-operated from new. Work proceeded quickly and the line was opened on 26 July 1900. The company operated the line itself for some six years with a joint service with DUT from Nelson Pillar to Howth, but on 15 March 1906 offered the operation of the line to DUT. DUT took over operation of the line from 1 January 1907, although the Clontarf & Hill of Howth Tramroad Co maintained its independent legal existence until the actual closure of the line. DUT inherited the company's tram fleet.

As elsewhere in Ireland, the Easter Rising of 1916 and the resulting civil war had a serious effect upon the tramways in Dublin and this was not assisted by poor labour relations during the period. It is clear, however, that the company continued to perceive the tramcar as the basis of

Above:
Totally-enclosed bogie car No 181 was one of a batch of 12 originally built for the Lucan route (service 25), which closed in May 1940. Upon closure the cars were transferred to the Dalkey service. *R. C. Ludgate*

public transport in the city. A number of pirate bus operators appeared in the early 1920s, and it was to protect its own position that DUT introduced its first bus service on 7 July 1925, from Eden Quay and Killester.

1925 was also to be the year of the final significant extension to the DUT network when, under pressure from the City Commissioners over an extension to the company's lease to the tramways (which was due to expire in 1938), DUT took over the bankrupt Dublin & Lucan Electric Railway. This line, which had originally been authorised in 1880, opened as a 3ft 0in-gauge steam tramway from Dublin to Chapelizod on 1 June 1881 and was extended to Lucan on 20 February 1883. An allied company, the Lucan, Leixlip & Celbridge Steam Tramway, extended the line to Leixlip in 1889. On electrification in 1900 the gauge was increased to 3ft 6in and for the next 25 years the company existed in an inde-

pendent, but increasingly parlous, manner. After the creation of the Irish Free State, and the consequent withdrawal of government subsidies, the company's financial position deteriorated yet further, not aided by competition from pirate bus operators, and on 29 January 1925 it went bankrupt. Earlier efforts to dispose of the line to DUT had come to nought. Following the City Commissioners' pressure, DUT agreed to take over the line and an agreement was signed to that effect on 3 February 1927. Under the terms of the deal Dublin extended DUT's lease until 1966. To incorporate the new route within the DUT system, it had to be reconstructed to the 5ft 3in gauge of the city routes. Work started on the conversion on 2 September 1927. To operate the new service, 10 'Lucan' bogie cars were constructed in DUT's workshops at Inchicore. Two of the bankrupt company's single-deck trailers were sold to the Bessbrook & Newry Tramway. The new DUT services started to Chapelizod on 14 May 1928 and to Lucan on 3 June 1928. The section beyond Lucan to Leixlip was abandoned because of disagreements with Dublin County Council.

Although the Lucan line was the final extension, DUT remained pro-tram. The early 1930s

witnessed the introduction of the 'luxury' bogie cars (which continued to be built until 1936), and the first half of the decade also saw the retrucking and modification to the tramcars inherited from the Clontarf company. Other significant developments at this time included DUT's acquisition, between 1933 and 1935, of the small bus operators in the city. There was also one minor tram abandonment — the first in the city — when in 1932 buses replaced trams on the route from Nelson Pillar to Bath Avenue.

With the new acquisitions the balance of the DUT fleet shifted in favour of the bus, with some 350 buses in service as opposed to 300 trams, and by the late 1930s the works at Inchicore were devoted to the construction of new buses. The first double-deck bus entered service with DUT in November 1937 (the first of more than 150 delivered by the outbreak of World War 2) and the writing was on the wall for the tramway system. On 31 March 1938 the company announced that it intended to convert the entire tramway system over a four year period. The threat to their working conditions led to a threatened confrontation with the trams crews but an agreement, accepted by a staff vote of 1,023 to 654 in early April, paved the way for the first closures. These were

not long in coming. On 16 April 1938 the Bally-bough-Park Street and North Quay services were converted to bus operation. Other routes quickly followed, and, although trolleybuses were seriously considered during this period, the bus was all-conquering. By the outbreak of World War 2 the Dublin system had been reduced substantially although a great deal of disused track and overhead remained. There was press speculation that, in the event of bus services having to be suspended, the trams would be reinstated and that some work to repair the track and overhead had been undertaken in furtherance of this policy. This was, however, officially denied, and the policy of tram replacement was confirmed at the Annual General Meeting of the company. Closures continued with the last tram to Lucan operating on 14 April 1940 (following agreements made in January 1939 and in March 1940) and

the route beyond Dollymount to Howth, the old Clontarf & Hill of Howth route was converted to bus operation on 29 March 1941. This closure had been delayed due to disagreements between DUT and the original company and was only settled by an agreement on 27 January 1941 between the two parties. With the closure of the Howth route the trams inherited from the Clontarf company were all scrapped.

Although the Irish Republic was not directly involved in the war, it could not escape some of the consequences, and by the middle of 1944 the country was suffering an acute power shortage. One of the consequences of this was that the electric trams both in Dublin and on the Hill of Howth were suspended temporarily. Although there were strong rumours that the Dublin system would not restart — after all DUT was undertaking a policy of tramcar replacement — services recommenced on 2 October 1944 on three of the four remaining services. One route, that to Dollymount, was never reintroduced.

On 1 January 1945 the ownership of DUT passed to the nationalised Irish operator CIE. The new company inherited three tramway routes, to Terenure, Dartry Road and Dalkey, operated with some 100 tramcars. Around the city there remained a considerable quantity of disused tram track still visible. Gradually the DUT livery was replaced by the CIE livery of green and cream and service numbers were introduced. These were routes No 15 to Terenure, No 14 to Daltry, No 8 to Dalkey, with short workings Nos 6 and 7 to Blackrock and Dun Laoghaire.

The new owners maintained the previous policy of tramcar abandonment. The first routes to succumb were those to Terenure and Daltry, which were both converted on 31 October 1948. This left the one long route, to Dalkey, with its short workings as the last service. After the closure of the Terenure route a number of the four-wheel cars were transferred to the Dalkey service. The last service was withdrawn on 3 July 1949 when No 252, one of the 'Lucan Bogie' cars, acted as the official last tram.

After closure, a number of the redundant trams were acquired for preservation. These included 'Standard' four-wheel car No 129 and 1906 bogie car No 328. Unfortunately, plans to construct a transport museum to house these cars came to nothing and their storage in the open led to vandalism. Consequently, the trams were eventually dismantled, although other Dublin cars, such as the 1903 Directors' car, do survive in varying states of disrepair. The Director's car is now at the Howth Castle Transport Museum along with bogie car No 253. A second bogie car, No 284, is preserved at Castleruddery, where the intention is to restore it to a condition similar to the lost No 328 as a balcony car. Efforts are also being made to preserve 'Luxury' car No 300.

Dublin Closures

31 October 1948	Terenure
31 October 1948	Dartry Road
3 July 1949	Dalkey

Last tram: No 252

Dublin

Fleet Numbers	Date	Trucks/Bogies	Body	Withdrawn
6/8/10/7/44/6/9/54, 60, 73/87/100/9/29/54/60/74/ 93/4/9/209/15/43/6/59/79/87/91[1]	1922-29	Peckham	DUT	By 1949
9/12/3/22/3/6/31/5/41/3/5/51/6/7/78/96/102-4/23/ 31/2/5/8/40/8/53/67/76/96/7/205/35/42/5/66/8[2]	1931-36	Maley & Taunton 266/8 Brill	DUT	By 1949
70-2/9/81-3/112/3/7/85/214/20/1/8/31/328[3]	1910-24	Peckham or Brill bogies	DUT	By 1949
93/108/59/78/273/80/2/94-300/16/7/26/7/9/30[4]	1931-36	Hurst Nelson	DUT	By 1949
181/4/218/24/52-5/78/84/314[5]	1928-29	Hurst Nelson	DUT	By 1949
Unnumbered[6]	1903	Peckham/replaced with Brierley	DUT	1949

1 'Standard' four-wheelers. No 129 preserved 1949 but eventually scrapped.
2 'Luxury' four-wheelers. No 132 preserved 1949 but scrapped.
3 'Dalkey' bogies. No 328 preserved 1949 but scrapped.
4 'Luxury' bogie cars.
5 'Lucan bogies'. 12 cars built, No 313 scrapped 1942. No 253 preserved at Howth Castle Transport Museum.
6 Directors car. Preserved on withdrawal. Now at Howth Castle Museum.

Left:
After withdrawal in 1949 three Dublin trams, Nos 129, 132 and 328, were preserved. After a period of storage the cars suffered vandalism and were scrapped. The trio is pictured here at Sutton on 14 August 1952. *R. J. S. Wiseman*

The city of Dundee, situated at the mouth of the River Tay, possessed one of the four Scottish tramway systems to survive World War 2 — and the smallest of them. It was also the final 'traditional' tramway system to close when its last cars were replaced by diesel buses in October 1956.

The Dundee Tramways Act of 1872 authorised the construction of a number of tramways. There was, however, a five-year delay between the passing of the Act and the opening of the first tramway on 30 August 1877. This first tramway, from the Old Post Office in Albert Square to Windsor Street, was, like all Dundee's early tramways, built by the Corporation and leased to the Dundee & District Tramways Co Ltd, a company which was granted a 21-year lease on 1 September 1877. Under the aegis of the Dundee Street Tramways, Turnpike Roads and Police Act of 1878, further tramways were built, including lines to West Park Road and to Lochee. Initially, all these lines were horse-operated, but, following from earlier experiments, steam-trams took over on the Lochee route in 1885 and horse-trams were eventually replaced on all routes bar that to West Park Road. Further extensions followed the Dundee Extension & Improvement Act of 1892, and on 31 May 1893 the company's lease was renewed for a further 14 years. However, by the end of the 19th century the Corporation was keen to take over the operation of the trams and introduce electric vehicles. Negotiations started in 1897 with the takeover confirmed by the Dundee Corporation Tramways Act of 1898. Payment for the takeover was to be staged over a nine-year period, culminating in 1907 when the company's original lease was due to expire. The takeover was effected from 1 June 1899 and work started immediately on electrifying the system.

The first of the new electrified services operated on the West Park Road route on 13 July 1900 and this was followed by the Lochee route on 22 October 1900. On 6 March 1901 the route to Maryfield was opened; an alternative alignment to that used by the erstwhile steam-trams was followed leading to the abandonment and lifting of the tracks in Dura Street and Morgan Street. This opening was followed on 11 March 1901 by an extension of the West Park Road route to Ninewells. The line to Balgay Lodge was opened on 30 April 1901 and that to Craigie Terrace on 11 November 1901. The last section to be converted, that to Fairmuir, was electrified on 15 May 1902. The one remaining steam-tram route, to Baxter Park, was abandoned at that time. The former steam-tram locomotives and trailers were disposed of, although four of the former were retained as snow ploughs. The last two steam engines were scrapped in the late 1920s.

The next extension saw the tramway built to the Hilltown district, up Constitution Road. This particularly steeply-graded area had long defeated tramway promoters — such as a scheme in 1890 for a 3ft 6in-gauge cable tramway — but the decision to utilise single-deck combination cars enabled the route to be operated as a conventional tramway. The Hilltown route met the Fairmuir route at Coldside and was opened on 20 November 1902. In 1903 a new depot was constructed at Maryfield, the existing depot at Lochee now being unable to house the expanding tramcar fleet.

The Craigie Terrace route served the eastern side of the city, but beyond the city's boundary there were a number of dormitory settlements. On 27 October 1905 the Dundee, Broughty Ferry & District Tramways Co Ltd opened its route to Monifieth and through services were jointly operated by the Corporation and company. In 1906 it was decided to reconstruct the Baxter Park route, and this new line was opened on 20 August 1906. The following year saw two further extensions: on 5 March the Main Street section in Hilltown was built, thereby enabling the operation of double-deck cars to Hilltown for the first time; and, on 19 December, the Fairmuir route was extended to Downfield. The next extension, to Craig Pier, opened on 12 November 1908 and from that date the Baxter Park service operated through to Craig Pier.

The next development of significance was the introduction of a trolleybus service along the Clepington Road, linking the Maryfield and Downfield routes, which commenced operation, amidst high hopes and great praise, on 3 September 1912. The initial promise, however, led to bit-

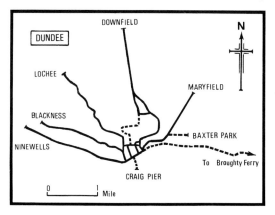

ter disappointment, and the service was withdrawn on 13 May 1914 — the first British trolleybus abandonment. The two trolleybuses, known locally as the 'Stouries' because of their ability to raise dust, were sold to Halifax. In the meantime, on 18 March 1914, the Balgay Road route was extended to Blackness, whilst on 1 November 1915 the Craigie Terrace route was extended to Belsize Road — this did not, however, lead to any additional track being built as the line was simply taken over from the DBFD&Co on a readjustment of the city's boundary. The Dundee system was now at its peak.

On 1 June 1919 the Craig Pier route was abandoned. This line had never been successful. With its closure, the Baxter Park line was linked with Balgay Road. On 21 November 1921 the Corporation introduced its first bus service, to the Castle Green in Broughty Ferry, but was forced to withdraw it following legal action from the DBFD&Co the following July. However, buses were destined to reappear, on 20 September 1922, on a new circular service, and the granting of a Provisional

Order in 1922 allowed the Corporation to operate buses on any route within the city's boundaries. 1922 also witnessed the building of an extension to Maryfield depot. In 1925, powers were obtained for two extensions, but these were never built.

The late 1920s were to be a watershed for Dundee's trams. It would not have been surprising if the system had declined — indeed the Constitution Road route was abandoned on 26 February 1928 as it was considered that the combination cars were now beyond economic repair — but in fact the period witnessed considerable investment in the tramway system. In 1929 a new central depot and workshop was built. A programme of rebuilding the older trams and of doubling the single-track sections was completed in 1932, and 10 new cars, the 'Lochee' trams, were delivered in 1930. These trams were wider than Dundee's normal trams and were generally limited to the Lochee route. In 1933-35 the fleet was completely refitted with Fischer bow collectors. The tram fleet now numbered 60 — as against a peak of 99 — and it was to remain at this size for the next 20 years. On 3 July 1933 the Lindsay Street link was built in the centre; this was destined to be the last new track built.

Not all was positive, however. In addition to the closure of the Constitution Road route, the Corporation's takeover of the DBFD&Co on 5 November 1930 led to the complete closure of the route from Dundee centre to Monifieth on 16 May 1931. The following year the Baxter Park route was abandoned on 2 October, so that a replacement bus service could also serve the new Craigiebank housing estate. Most of the redundant tram track was lifted during 1940-41. At the same time as the number of trams declined, the size of the bus fleet expanded.

In 1945 Dundee's trams were still flourishing. They operated three basic services — from Blackness to Downfield, from Ninewells to Maryfield and from Lochee to the centre — and, although numerically smaller than the bus fleet, their role was still of primary importance. Of the fleet, however, the youngest were 15 years old and some were approaching their 50th birthday. Contemporary reports, despite this, were optimistic as to Dundee's long-term survival, and there were a number of pointers which indicated that tramcars in Dundee did have a future. There was a great deal of work undertaken on the track, such as the modification to the layout in Albert Square in early 1948 and the complete reconstruction of the tracks in the Murraygate in 1950, whilst the trams themselves received attention. A number of cars were fitted with new high-speed motors and one car, No 47, was reconstructed after a serious accident in 1952. Even in the various committees of the Transport Department there was pressure to acquire new — even articulated cars it was rumoured at one stage — or second-hand vehicles, and as late as 1952 a sub-committee was tasked with formulating a policy that made 'the most effective use of the tramway system'.

Apart from the 'politics' of transport operation, there were also a number of other significant developments. In early 1948 the adult ½d fare was abolished — Dundee was the last place in Britain to offer such a fare — whilst in 1950 the Ultimate ticketing system was introduced to replace the existing TIM machines. 1950 also saw the Corporation agree to allow advertisements on the trams, with the consequence that the coat of arms was no longer applied to the front of the cars. In 1953 the livery was simplified by a reduction in the level of lining out.

Despite the general air of optimism, Dundee could not evade the increasing age of its tramcar

fleet. In 1952, Col McCreary, the General Manager of Belfast, was appointed to report on the future of Dundee's trams: inevitably he advocated replacement. Part of the problem was that the majority of Dundee's tramways were built with the minimum spacing (3ft 6in) between the parallel running tracks. This meant that the majority of tramcars then being withdrawn were too wide to operate safely over the Dundee system. With the second-hand market thereby effectively closed, the only real option was to seek new trams, and, in comparison with the cost of buses, the prices quoted were prohibitive. The first postwar closure saw the cessation of regular services from the Moncur Crescent line on 26 April 1953 when all cars were routed via the Hilltown line. This track was, however, retained for use by football specials (a special siding had been laid in 1908 for such a purpose) and for emergencies. In late 1954, the new General Manager, W. L. Russell (who had replaced the pro-tram Robert Taylor the previous year) produced a confidential report which advocated the replacement of the tramcars. On 6 January 1955 it was decided to withdraw experimentally for 12 months the Blackness-Downfield route and to acquire 25 new buses for the purpose. If the experimental closure was not a success then the buses would be transferred to alternative routes and new trams acquired. In pursuit of the policy, the last

Below:
Photographed on 3 June 1954, Walter Young-designed tram No 55 had just re-entered service after a full overhaul which had included having two new high-speed motors fitted (acquired second-hand from Sunderland). Seen outside Maryfield depot, it was the decision to suspend temporarily the Maryfield-Blackness service in 1955 that marked the start of the demise of Dundee's tramway system.

Blackness-Downfield trams ran on 26 November 1955. Twenty-five trams (Nos 1-18, 29, 51-56) were withdrawn and scrapped. Although the track and overhead was retained, the disposal of the trams made the 'experimental' closure all but certain to be confirmed. On 5 July 1956 the Council voted to make the closure permanent and to acquire 30 ex-London Transport buses so that final closure could be expedited. The final Dundee trams operated on 20 October 1956; there was no official ceremony, although the citizens of Dundee ensured that the passing of the trams was marked. 'Lochee' car No 25 was the last tram in service. With Dundee's closure the last 'small town' system closed, and with the withdrawal of the Ninewells route the last British street tramway formed of single track with passing loops also disappeared.

Following closure, a number of trams made their way from Lochee to Maryfield depot for scrapping. The last of these 'ghost' trams, No 21, ran on 25 October 1956. All of Dundee's postwar trams were scrapped; local enthusiasts were offered two (one of the 'Lochee' cars and one of the single-deck works cars) on the proviso that alternative accommodation be found. Unfortunately, no other premises could be located and the trams were, therefore, scrapped. There are, however, a number of reminders of Dundee's trams: the National Tramway Museum is now the home to a fully restored steam trailer (No 21), and two others also survive; the relaid track in Murraygate is now protected by a preservation order; and, it is believed, the body from one of the ex-Paisley cars acquired in 1915 has been located.

Dundee Closures

26 November 1955	Blackness to Downfield (initially service suspended for a year, but confirmed during 1956)
20 October 1956	Maryfield to Ninewells
20 October 1956	Lochee

Last tram: No 25

Dundee

Fleet Numbers	Date	Trucks/Bogies	Body	Withdrawn
1-10[1]	1900	EMB flexible axle (originally Brill 21E)	Dick Kerr	1955
11-8[2]	1902	Peckham P35, retrucked from Brill 21E 1928-29	Milnes	1955
19-28[3]	1930	EMB flexible axle	Brush	1956
29[4]	1925	Peckham P35	Dundee CT	1955
30-3[5]	1926	Peckham P35	Dundee CT	1956
34-40[6]	1921	EMB flexible, retrucked from Brill 21E 1932	Hurst Nelson	1956
41-6[7]	1920	EMB flexible, retrucked from Brill 21E 1932	Hurst Nelson	1956
47-50[8]	1916	EMB flexible, retrucked from Brill 21E 1932	Hurst Nelson	1956
51[9]	1921	Peckham P35, Brill 21E until 1932	Hurst Nelson	1955
52[10]	1908	EMB Hornless, Brill 21E until 1933	Milnes Voss	1952
53-6[11]	1923-25	EMB Hornless/Brill 21E until 1930 then EMB flexible until 1933	Dundee CT	1955
57[12]	1907	Brill 21E	Brush	1947
58/9[13]	1908	Brill 21E	Milnes Voss	1947
60[14]	1907	Brill 21E	Brush	1947
RW1/2[15]	Converted 1935	Brill 21E	Brush	1956

1 Originally open-top. Top-covered 1907-10. Completely rebuilt 1931.

2 Originally open-top, numbered 41-8. Top-covered 1906-07; Nos 44-6 received new Hurst Nelson covers 1916. All rebuilt 1928-29. Renumbered 11-18 1927.

3 'Lochee' cars, were slightly wider than normal. Last trams bought.

4 Originally No 95, renumbered 81 1928 and 29 in 1936.

5 Originally Nos 96-9, renumbered 82-5 in 1928 and 30-3 in 1936.

6 Originally 83-9, renumbered 47-53 1928 and 34-40 in 1936. Rebuilt 1932.

7 Originally numbered 67/8, 79-82. Renumbered 1928. Rebuilt 1932.

8 Originally numbered 75-78. Nos 77/8 renumbered 73/4 1927. Nos 73-6 renumbered 47-50 1936. Rebuilt 1932.

9 Originally 90, renumbered 54 in 1928 and 51 in 1936. Rebuilt 1932.

10 Top-covered from new. Originally 61 of batch 61-6. Renumbered 1936.

11 Originally Nos 91-4, renumbered 77-80 in 1928 and 53-6 in 1936.

12 Top-covered from new. Originally 55, renumbered 57 in 1936. Batch 55-60.

13 Batch 61-6. Originally 62-3 renumbered 58/9 1936.

14 Batch 55-60. Top-covered from new.

15 Converted from 56/7 (i) new in 1907.

Although the Scottish capital city of Edinburgh had the country's second biggest tramway system, with some 400 trams at its peak, the city's tramway history was highly complex.

In 1870, two bills were proposed for the construction of tramways in the city. Of these only one, that of Edinburgh Street Tramways Co, became an Act (in 1871). This empowered the company to build and operate by horse power a number of routes in Edinburgh, Leith and Portobello. The first section of the new tramway, from Bernard Street in Leith to Haymarket in Edinburgh, opened on 6 November 1871. The next section, along Newington Road, opened on 29 May 1872, and a third, from the West End to Grange Road, opened on 11 November 1872. A further Act, in 1873, allowed for further extensions and also for more time to build some of those lines authorised under the 1871 Act. Additional extensions were opened in 1873 and 1874, culminating with the Portobello-Waterloo Place route on 12 May 1875. A total of some 13.5 route miles was now in operation.

Proposals made in 1876 for an extension to Musselburgh came to nothing, but the year did witness the first experiments with steam power. Additional trials were undertaken in 1877 and 1880, but it was not until 23 April 1881 that regular steam-tram services were introduced. Unfortunately, due to the number of complaints received, the steam-tram services were destined to be short-lived and were withdrawn on 27 October 1882. Further extensions were authorised in 1881, and these were opened over the next two years.

In the late 1880s a new company — the Edinburgh Northern Tramways Co — appeared on the scene and quickly opened two routes: Hanover Street to Goldencare on 28 January 1888; and Frederick Street to Comely Bank. With the Edinburgh Northern Tramways Co the cable-tramway reached Edinburgh, and it was this form of transport that was to play an important role over the next three decades. One factor in the interest shown in the cable-tram was that it had greater potential over the steeply-graded routes than the horse-tram with none of the problems associated with the steam-trams. By the end of the 1880s, Edinburgh Corporation was keen to see the extension of the cable network and it hoped that, in conjunction with neighbouring Leith Corporation, the tramways could be taken over by the local authorities and leased out to a company that was prepared to invest in cable routes.

This apparently attractive scenario failed when Leith Corporation decided to maintain its links with the Edinburgh Street Tramways Co. Not to be defeated, however, Edinburgh Corporation assumed ownership of the tracks within the city

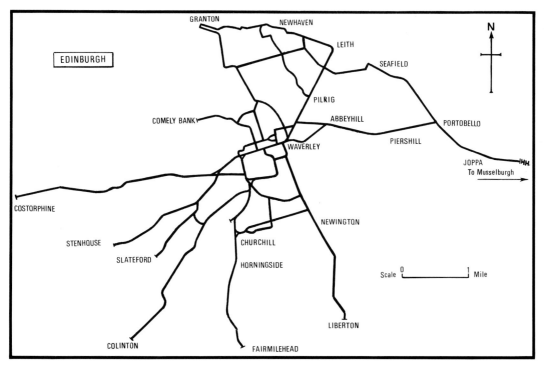

on 9 December 1893 and proceeded to lease them to the Edinburgh & District Tramways Co Ltd, a subsidiary of Dick Kerr, who had agreed to install the equipment to operate cable trams. Initially, whilst the changeover was effected, the new company continued to operate horse-trams over the lines it inherited, the new cable lines being inaugurated in 1897. On 1 July, in the same year, the Edinburgh & District Co inherited the two lines of the Edinburgh Northern Co on the expiry of the latter's lease, and the following year, with the incorporation of Portobello into the city, the Edinburgh Street Tramway Co's line in Portobello was also taken over.

Meanwhile in Leith, outside the control of Edinburgh, the Edinburgh Street Tramways Co continued to operate until, on 23 October 1904, Leith Corporation took over the lines and proceeded to electrify them. The first electric service, from Leith Walk to Stanley Road via Pilrig, opened on 18 May 1905, quickly followed by the Granton circle. The last horse-tram, from Tollcross to Colinton Road, operated on 24 August 1907. Also outside the city, the Musselburgh & District Electric Light & Traction Co Ltd opened an electric tramway from Levenhall to Joppa via

Musselburgh on 12 December 1904. This wa extended to Port Seton in 1909.

The first electrically-operated route in Edin burgh itself was to open the following year, 1910 when the Corporation-built line from Ardmillar Terrace to Slateford was inaugurated on 8 June The line was leased to the Edinburgh & Distric Co and was operated by a number of cable car converted for the purpose. Time was, however running out for the Edinburgh & District Cc since its lease expired on 30 June 1919 and the Corporation took over all operations the follow ing day.

On takeover, Edinburgh inherited some 200 cable cars and the four electric trams converted in 1910. A further 37 electric cars were inherited on 20 November 1920 when Leith Corporatior was incorporated into Edinburgh. Work started on the conversion of the cable tramways to elec tric operation. The first of the converted lines from Leith via the Grange to Nether Liberton and Churchill, was inaugurated on 20 June 1922 and further conversions followed swiftly, including Princes Street in October 1922. To operate the new electric services the majority of the inherited cable cars were converted and a number of nev trams were also acquired. The last cable route, to Portobello, was converted on 23 June 1923. Through running over the Musselburgh lines was also introduced, and, although the company's trams were withdrawn on 28 February 1928, Edinburgh Corporation subsequently acquired the section of track from Joppa to Levenhall for continued operation. Initially this was during 1928-31 as simply an operator but eventually the track was acquired by the Corporation and was subsequently reconstructed.

Further extensions followed, such as that to Comely Bank on 18 November 1923 and that to Liberton on 28 April 1924. By this date the Corporation operated trams over some 36 route miles and buses over an additional 35. Although the first Corporation-owned buses had run for a short period in 1914, it was only in 1919 that a significant effort was made. It is clear, however, that trams were still considered to form the backbone of the city's public transport. Under the Edinburgh Corporation (Tramways, etc) Confirmation Act of 1924 further lines were authorised, although not all were actually constructed. On 26 October 1924, the Seafield-Kings Road extension, authorised in 1920, opened, whilst those along George Street and Melville Drive followed on 19 July 1925. Also in 1925, experiments were undertaken using Fischer bow collectors, but, as with a later experiment in 1933 with a pantograph, the traditional trolley-pole was retained. On 21 March 1926 an extension to Clinton was opened and further routes were again authorised in 1927. In November 1928, Stuart Pilcher, manager since the Corporation's Transport Department was established and the guiding hand in the conversion from cable to electric traction, moved to become general manager at Manchester. He was succeeded by his deputy F. A. Fitzpayne.

The new management made it clear that the policy of developing the tramway would continue. Further route extensions were opened, such as that to Stenhouse on 20 July 1930 and to the Costorphine route to North Gyle. At the same time, it was becoming increasingly necessary to replace many of the cars converted from cable to electric traction. Certain cars had been rebuilt between 1926 and 1930 reusing parts from the older cars, but under Fitzpayne a new semi-streamlined design was to emerge which was to form the basic pattern for all subsequent cars built for Edinburgh either by outside contractors or in Edinburgh's own workshops at Shrubhill. The prototype car, No 180, emerged in 1932, whilst a second, with a domed roof, No 69, appeared two years later.

Left:
In 1934 Edinburgh produced its prototype 'domed roof' car, No 69, and over the next 16 years built more than 80 of the type. The last six, including No 169 seen here at Colinton on 20 November 1954, were built in 1950 and had barely six years of service before the system closed. One of the postwar cars, No 35, was selected for preservation and was displayed for many years at Shrubhill works, the works which had manufactured all the class. The Colinton route was to operate for a further year, before being converted on 23 October 1955.

Fitzpayne's tenure was, however, destined to be relatively short, as he died on 3 March 1935. He was succeeded by Robert McLeod from Aberdeen. Further powers to extend the system had already been obtained, in 1934 and again in 1936, and work started in 1935 on the extension to Fairmilehead, which was opened on 19 April 1936. This was followed on 14 February 1937 by a further extension of the Costorphine route to Maybury. Despite additional powers being obtained, this line was to prove the final extension to the Edinburgh system.

Under the 1936 Act, an extension to the Stenhouse route was authorised. Although traction columns were installed, the route was never completed. Even more tragic was the case of the proposed route to Crewe Toll, authorised in 1934. On 6 January 1938 it was agreed to proceed with the construction of the line, but further disputes led to the actual construction being delayed until early 1939. When the outbreak of war occurred in September of that year, the work was suspended, and despite efforts after 1945 it was never completed. The track and traction columns were finally recovered between 1950 and 1953, by which stage the tide had turned against the whole Edinburgh system.

World War 2 had little effect on the Edinburgh system except for the universal problems of fuel supplies and maintenance: it was widely considered to be amongst the most secure in Britain in 1945. The system entered the postwar era at its peak and with expectations that the delayed extensions would be completed. There remained a number of ex-cable cars in service, but the continuation of the prewar building programme and the purchase of 11 surplus trams from Manchester, ironically cars designed by the erstwhile Edinburgh manager Stuart Pilcher, seemed to bode well for the future. The last of the ex-cable cars were withdrawn in 1947. There were, however, indications that all was not well. In 1946, amongst the recommendations of the Edinburgh Accident Prevention Council was one to withdraw the trams; although nothing happened at this time the recommendation was symptomatic of the tram's increasing unpopularity in official circles.

More significantly, Robert McLeod, like his predecessor, died in office in 1948 and was replaced by W. M. Little, his assistant. Although having a background with tramway operators, Little was not a 'tram man' like those who went before him. Over the next two years there were few changes; on 17 October 1949 routes Nos 7/11/28 were extended from Stanley Road to Craighall Road,

but this was countered by the replacement, on 26 March 1950, by buses of route No 18. This route, linking Liberton with Waverley station, was poorly patronised and the closure did not lead to any reduction in the track mileage. However, 1950 was to witness the fateful decision to start the complete abandonment programme. In June of that year Little prepared a report advocating the replacement of a quarter of the system. After much debate, the policy was adopted by the council on 2 November 1950. Whilst the actual scheme was developed, work still continued on the system: the track in Princes Street was relaid; a new mercury arc rectifier was installed in Portobello depot in 1951; and the last new tram, No 225, emerged from Shrubhill works during August 1950. The plan for the partial replacement was unveiled on 18 September 1951 and formally approved on 27 September 1951. Contemporary investigations reported that those living in the city preferred the trams but that those in the suburbs wanted buses. As elsewhere, the abandonment policy became a political issue and several renowned proponents of abandonment lost their council seats — and yet the abandonment scheme commenced.

The first route to be abandoned, route No 24 from Waverley to Comely Bank, was replaced by buses on 1 June 1952. Hardly had the final tram on the route operated when, on 15 July 1952, it was announced that the policy was now one of complete abandonment. This new policy was confirmed, again amidst controversy, by the council on 25 September 1952.

On 24 August 1952, route No 25 had been extended from Drum Brae to Maybury, whilst at the same time No 26 was curtailed from Drum Brae to the Zoo. On 14 December 1952 route No 2, from Stenhouse to Granton, was replaced by buses. This was followed on 29 March 1953 by the conversion of route No 3 from Stenhouse to Newington. The same month also witnessed the start of the dismantling of the Comely Bank and part of the George Street routes. This latter work was widely regarded as leading to future inconvenience as the track in question was parallel to the Princes Street track, a line that was regularly closed for royal or civic processions.

After these initial closures, 60 surplus cars were sold for scrap to Connells of Coatbridge. The doomed cars were driven to the Maybury terminus under their own power and then winched on to a lorry. The first two cars so dealt with were Nos 270 and 340 on 16 March 1953. Maley & Taunton trucks were transferred to the cars selected for early withdrawal in place of the Peckham-type truck upon which Edinburgh had standardised.

On 3 May 1953 buses replaced the trams on the route from Piershill to Slateford. At the same time Gorgie depot, situated on the rump of the route to Stenhouse, was cleared of its last trams. This closure was, in theory, the completion of the original 25% abandonment policy, and there was a gap of more than a year before the next abandonment. In the meantime, on 31 January 1954, there were a number of significant service alterations. Route No 10 was diverted to run via Junction Street and Ferry Road, whilst route No 16 was diverted to run along Bernard Street (in place of route No 10) but was reduced to a part-day service only. At the same time route No 20 became peak hours only and route No 27 was withdrawn on Sundays and in the evenings. Finally, routes Nos 25 and 28 were also curtailed, but public pressure led to these services being restored on 10 May 1954.

The first of several withdrawals in 1954 occurred on 28 March 1954 when route No 1, from Liberton to Costorphine, was converted. On 6 June 1954 route No 27 was curtailed at Craiglockhart station but was extended back to Happy Valley on 17 October 1954. The remaining routes serving Costorphine (Nos 12/25/26) were converted on 11 July 1954. The track continued

Below:
Seen at Levenhall in 1947, No 401 was one of 11 ex-Manchester 'Pilcher' cars acquired between 1946 and 1948. This particular car was fitted experimentally with standard Edinburgh motor equipment. The 'Pilcher' cars were to survive in Edinburgh until 1954, the route to Levenhall itself closing on 14 November of that year.

to be used for a while by trams making their one-way journey to the scrapyard, but even this soon finished. On 19 September 1954, route No 15, from Fairmilehead to Portobello, was converted, to be followed on 31 October by route No 5, Piershill to Morningside station. The last closures of 1954 occurred on 14 November when routes Nos 20 and 21, from the Post Office to Joppa and Levenhall respectively, were replaced. As the section to Levenhall was outside the city's boundary, Edinburgh had no powers to operate replacement buses over this section, which was, consequently, abandoned. Also closed to trams at this stage was Portobello depot. When it came to remove the final cars, it was discovered that of the two alternative routes, one had lost its overhead and the other some sections of track. Thus, the last cars from the depot suffered the additional indignity of being towed away.

1955 saw four routes converted. The first to succumb, on 3 April, was route No 8 from Granton to Newington station. This was followed on 7 August 1955 by the conversion of route No 27, from Granton Road station to Craiglockhart. Finally, on 23 October, went routes Nos 9 and 10, from Colinton to Granton and Leith respectively. 1956, the last year of Edinburgh's trams, saw more than 120 cars, mostly of the semi-streamlined type built after 1932, operating over 10 routes. With the end approaching rapidly, the standard of track maintenance declined. Such was the state of the track in Princes Street that certain eastbound cars were diverted onto the remaining section of the George Street route from March 1956, and there were a number of other minor service alterations. March also witnessed the first abandonment of the year, when on the 11th of the month routes Nos 7 and 17 (Stanley Road to Liberton and Granton to Newington station) were converted. Complaints over the withdrawal of the No 17 led to the temporary appearance of an unnumbered rush hours-only service to Leith docks. On 5 May Leith depot was closed and its remaining trams transferred to the two remaining depots at Shrubhill and Tollcross. Later the same month, on the 27th, routes No 6, the Marchmont circle, and No 19, Tollcross to Craigentinny, were converted. On 1 June four of the remaining routes (Nos 11/13/14/28) were diverted to run along York Place rather than Princes Street and the track and overhead was removed on the latter street from the Post Office to St Andrew Street. Two of these routes, Nos 13 and 14, were destined to have a short life thereafter, being converted to bus operation on 17 June. No more than four routes now remained.

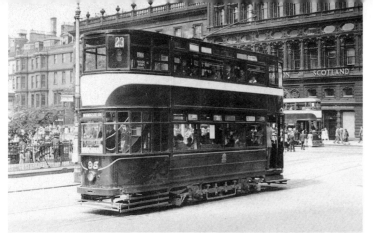

The next two routes to be converted, No 11 (Stanley Road and Granton to Fairmilehead) and No 16 (Stanley Road and Granton to Braids), were replaced by buses on 12 September 1956. Although by late 1956 Britain was in the grip of the Suez crisis and concern over supplies of oil (fears which led to delayed conversions elsewhere), there was to be no last-minute reprieve for Edinburgh's trams. As announced earlier in the year the last two routes, Nos 23 (Granton Road station to Morningside) and No 28 (Stanley Road to Braids), were withdrawn on 16 November 1956. There was the traditional farewell, with councillors and invited guests on board car No 217. To mark the closure No 172 was repainted in a special white livery recording the demise of the tramway, operating in this livery over the week before closure.

After closure, work proceeded rapidly on dismantling. Cars were despatched from Shrubhill depot on a daily basis to the scrapyard, although one, No 35, was retained for display in the Trans-

Edinburgh Closures

Date	Route
26 March 1950	18 – Liberton to Waverley station (via Newington, Tollcross and West End — no track abandoned)
1 June 1952	24 – Waverley to Comely Bank
14 December 1952	2 – Stenhouse to Granton (via Leith)
29 March 1953	3 – Stenhouse to Newington
3 May 1953	4 – Piershill to Slateford
28 March 1954	1 – Costorphine to Liberton
11 July 1954	12 – Costorphine/Zoo Park to Joppa
11 July 1954	25 – Costorphine/Zoo Park to Portobello
11 July 1954	26 – Costorphine/Zoo Park to Piershill
19 September 1954	15 – Fairmilehead to Portobello (Kings Road)
31 October 1954	5 – Piershill to Morningside
14 November 1954	20 – General Post Office to Joppa
14 November 1954	21 – General Post Office to Levenhall
3 April 1955	8 – Granton to Newington station (via Broughton Street)
7 August 1955	27 – Granton Road station to Craiglockhart (via The Mound)
23 October 1955	9 – Colinton to Granton
23 October 1955	10 – Colinton to Leith
11 March 1956	7 – Stanley Road to Liberton
11 March 1956	17 – Granton to Newington station (via Bernard Street)
27 May 1956	6 – Marchmont Circle
27 May 1956	19 – Tollcross to Craigentinny
17 June 1956	13/14 – Granton and Churchill Circle
12 September 1956	11 – Stanley Road and Granton to Braids
12 September 1956	16 – Stanley Road and Granton to Fairmilehead
16 November 1956	23 – Granton Road station to Morningside
16 November 1956	28 – Stanley Road to Braids

Last tram: No 217

port Department's museum at Shrubhill. It rested in the museum for more than 25 years before being removed and sent to Blackpool as part of the fleet of trams operating in that town for the tramway centenary. After a number of years in Blackpool, No 35 is now on loan to the National Tramway Museum. Subsequently, the body of one of the ex-cable cars converted to electric traction has been discovered and, it is hoped, will be restored.

Edinburgh

Fleet Numbers	Date	Trucks/Bogies	Body	Withdrawn
11-18[1]	1935	Peckham P22	Hurst Nelson	1956
19-24	1935	Peckham P22	EE	1956
25-30	1935	M&T, to Peckham P22 c1953	Metro Cammell	1956
31/3/4/6/8/42-4/6/53/7/8/60/1/4/5/8/70/4/5/7-81/4-6/9/94/100/1/4/6/7/9/113-19/38-44/6-9/51-6/8/9/61-3/6-8/74-9/181-5/7/8/91-4/6-8/200/1/3/5-8[2]	1924-34	Peckham P22	Edinburgh CT	1950-56
32/5(ii)/7(ii)/9-41/45/8(ii)/9(ii)/50(ii)/51/2/4-6/9, 62/3/6/7/69/71/2/3(ii)/6/82/3/8/91/103/5/111/2/20/37/45/50/7/160/4/5/9(ii)/72(ii)/173/89/90/5/9/202/204/9/10(ii)/1-6/217(ii)/8/9(ii)/20-3/224(ii)/5(ii)/6/7/228(ii)/9/30/2-8/243/7/8/69[3]	1934-50	Peckham P22	Edinburgh CT	1954-56
87/90/2/3/5-9/102/8/10/70/1/270-311[4]	1923	Peckham P22	Leeds Forge	1953-55
121-36[5]	1922	Peckham P22	Hurst Nelson	1949-52
180[6]	1932	EMB truck ex-177 converted 1932 to M&T (ex-264)	Edinburgh CT	1956
231/9/40	1934	M&T, to Peckham P22 c1953	Hurst Nelson	1956
241/2/4-6/9/60/5	1933-34	M&T, 242/60/5 received Peckham P22 c1953	Metro Cammell	1950-55
250-9	1932-33	M&T (256 EE FL32, to M&T 1934) all bar 255, received P22 c1953	Pickering	1952-56
261/4/6/8[7]	1929-33	Peckham P22	Edinburgh CT	1954-55
262/3/7	1934	M&T, to P22 c1953	EE	1955-56
312-31[8]	1924	Peckham P22	EE	1952-55
332-370[9]	1925-30	Peckham P22	Edinburgh CT	1953-56
401-11[10]	1946-48 (acquired)	Peckham P35	Manchester CT	1954

Ex-Cable Cars

210/7/9/24/5/8[11]	1903	Peckham P22	Dick Kerr	1946-47
73/172[12]	1906	Peckham P22	Edinburgh & District	1945-47
37/48[13]	1907	Peckham P22	Edinburgh & District	1946-47
35/49/50/169[14]	1908	Peckham P22	Edinburgh & District	1947

1 Nos 11/2/6 had Maley & Taunton trucks 1948-53.
2 A number of cars incorporated top covers from withdrawn ex-cable cars. All eventually fully-enclosed. Nos 61/75/8/84/6/138/51/82/4 renumbered from 19, 3, 24, 6, 7, 29, 28, 18 and 20 in 1935.
3 No 69 prototype in December 1934. Straight-sided cars with domed-roof developed from experimental car No 180. No 225(ii) was Edinburgh's last new tram in August 1950. No 172 painted special white livery to mark closure in 1956. No 35 preserved.
4 Top-covered, later fully enclosed.
5 Top-covered, later fully enclosed.
6 Experimental straight-sided car.

7 No 266 renumbered from 371 in 1932.
8 Originally top-covered, later fully enclosed.
9 Early cars were top-covered and later fully enclosed. Later cars fully enclosed from new.
10 Ex-Manchester 'Pilcher' cars dating from 1930-32. Were Manchester 173, 676, 195, 225, 558, 217, 389, 231, 242, 381, 349 respectively.
11 Originally open-top. Converted to electric power 1923.
12 Originally open-top. Renumbered from 27 and 25 respectively 1933. Converted to electric traction 1923.
13 Converted 1923.
14 Converted 1923.

One of the most remarkable postwar tramway survivals and the last surviving horse-tramway — apart from Douglas — was the short line linking Fintona Junction with Fintona proper. Whilst there were a number of similar lines elsewhere, such as the Caledonian Railway's line at Inchture, all had succumbed relatively early.

The origins of the Fintona tramway lay with the Londonderry & Enniskillen Railway. This railway obtained its Act of Incorporation in July 1845 and the first section, from Londonderry to Strabane, was completed in October of that year. The success of the line was not as great as the promoters had hoped and an attempt was made to abandon the line beyond Strabane. This, however, failed; and further sections were opened progressively to Newtonstewart on 9 May 1852, to Omagh on 13 September 1852, and to Fintona on 15 June 1853. For just under a year the terminus of the line was at Fintona, but the construction of a junction three-quarters of a mile from Fintona — the future Fintona Junction — for the further section to Dromore Road meant that for the next 100 years Fintona was destined to be served by a short branch. The section from Fintona Junction to Dromore Road opened on 16 January 1854 and the final section to Enniskillen on 19 August 1854. The line adopted the Irish standard gauge of 5ft 3in. To operate the branch passenger services, Board of Trade permission was obtained to use a horse, although steam was used for freight.

In 1859 the Londonderry & Enniskillen Railway was leased to the Dundalk & Enniskillen, which in turn passed the lease on to its successor the Northern Railway of Ireland, in 1875, and then on to the Great Northern Railway (Ireland) when that was established in 1876. The Londonderry & Enniskillen Railway retained a nominal independent existence until 1883.

In 1877 it was decided that the Fintona branch required a new tram and one was ordered from the Metropolitan Co. For various reasons, however, the new car, originally numbered 74, was not delivered until 1883. It was a double-deck car, with an enclosed lower deck partitioned to provide first and second class with an open upper deck for third class. Originally finished in varnished mahogany, the tram was subsequently renumbered 381. Powered by one horse, the car took 10min from Junction to Fintona and 15min in the reverse direction.

Once established, No 381 was to remain at Fintona for more than 70 years. In order to supplement the service, a second car (No 416) was built at Dundalk in 1913, but this was destroyed by fire before it could be delivered to Fintona. This left No 381 to operate the service with no possible replacement. This was to be of significance only once during the line's history. On 17 January 1953 the car was seriously damaged when the horse pulling it bolted. It remained in service for a short time before being despatched to Dundalk for repair. In its absence, luggage and parcels were carried in an open wagon whilst passengers were, officially, supposed to walk.

As with the other railways in both Ulster and the Republic, the postwar era was one of declining fortunes and, along with the rest of the assets of the GNR(I) (such as the Hill of Howth line), the Fintona tramway was transferred to the new Great Northern Railway Board on 1 September 1953. This Board, jointly controlled by the Governments of Northern Ireland and the Irish Republic, was an uneasy marriage from the start given the dire necessity for modernisation and rationalisation. Matters came to a head when, in 1956, the Northern Minister of Commerce unilaterally announced the closure of some 115 miles of ex-GNR(I) track in Ulster. The sections included the lines from Enniskillen to Omagh and, with it, the branch to Fintona. The proposals, rejected by the Republic's government, were referred to the Transport Tribunals in Dublin and Belfast. Despite all the contrary evidence, the Northern Tribunal agreed to the closures, whilst that in the Republic rejected them. Despite this, the Northern Minister of Commerce confirmed, on 5 June 1957, that the services would be withdrawn at the end of September. The lines, includ-

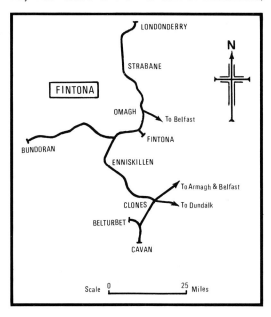

ng the Fintona branch, saw passenger services or the last time on 30 September 1957. With the Fintona closure, Northern Ireland lost its final tramway — in a somewhat bizarre twist of fate the horse-tram had outlasted the electric tramcar in the province. South of the border, the Board rapidly proceeded to obtain the closure of the rump of the affected lines, some 84 route miles, and passenger services on these route were withdrawn on 13 October 1957.

After the withdrawal of the Fintona service, No 381 was attached to a steam locomotive and hauled to Belfast — the longest journey it had ever made — for display in the Belfast Museum of Transport.

Fintona Closure

30 September 1957 Fintona Junction to
Fintona Town

Fintona

Fleet Numbers	Date	Trucks/Bogies	Body	Withdrawn
381[1]	1883	—	GNR(I)	1957

[1] Horse-tram, now preserved.

If any British tramway could be said to have been forced into abandonment that tramway is Gateshead. Throughout the 1940s the operating company was locked into controversy with the town's northern neighbour, across the River Tyne, over the future of public transport provision in the area.

The first Act allowing for the construction of trams in Gateshead and district received the Royal Assent on 12 August 1880. This allowed for the construction of a number of routes using the 3ft 6in gauge. This Act, which established the Gateshead & District Tramways Co, was, however, not progressed with, and on 24 July 1882 a second Act received the Royal Assent. This was a less ambitious Act, since it excluded sections outside the Gateshead area. It was significant, nonetheless, in that the proposed gauge was increased to 4ft 8½in. In December 1882 a prospectus for shares in the company was issued and work on building the tramway went ahead. Three routes — from Gateshead to Heworth, Low Fell and Teams — were constructed. On 22 October 1883 the first of the steam engines was delivered, and in the same month public services were started. The company's lease was extended by seven years in 1892 and in 1897 the controlling interest in the company was acquired by British Electric Traction. The writing was on the wall for the steam trams.

Under the Gateshead & District Tramways Act of 1899, Gateshead Corporation was empowered to purchase the company in 1922. The same Act also allowed for the building of 6½ miles of new track and the conversion of the existing network to electric operation. Work started on the conver-

sion on 12 June 1900 and steam operation ceased on 8 May 1901 when the electric services (to Low Fell etc) were inaugurated. Extensions to the system — to Wrekenton and Dunston — followed in 1903. Due to a number of low railway bridges, almost half of the new trams delivered in 1901 to operate the electric services were single-deck: throughout its history the Gateshead & District Co always operated numerous single-deck trams.

On 2 July 1909 a further Act empowered the company to build three extensions (on the Wrekenton, Low Fell and Bensham routes), all of which were opened in October 1910. Ironically, in the light of future controversy, the Act also empowered the company to operate both buses and trolleybuses. On 25 June 1912 Gateshead officially launched a 'Pay As You Enter' scheme on its trams — the first such experiment in Britain. It was, however, deemed to be unpopular and was quickly abandoned.

In August 1921 Gateshead Corporation decided not to exercise its option under the 1899 Act to purchase the company. With this threat of compulsory purchase removed the company was free to modernise. Modernisation work included the acquisition of new trams and the construction of the Jackson Street link in the town centre, thereby allowing double-deck trams to operate on the Saltwell Park route. More significantly, in pursuit of the Newcastle-Upon-Tyne Corporation Act of 1920, it proved possible to construct a tramway across the High Level bridge to link the two tramway operators. Earlier schemes had failed over the rights of the North Eastern Railway to collect tolls, but an agreement of October 1921 finally cleared this obstacle. Work started on construction in July 1922 and the new through services were launched on 12 January 1923.

Such was the success of the new through services that in 1924 powers were obtained to build a new bridge — eventually named after King George V — which was opened on 10 October 1928, thereby providing a second direct tramway link. This was, however, destined to be the last extension to Gateshead's tramway system. The 1930s, a period of economic depression, saw few changes to public transport south of the Tyne. Conversely, Newcastle-upon-Tyne obtained powers to convert its system to trolleybus operation and commenced this conversion in 1935. Although there was no immediate pressure for conversion in Gateshead, the company obtained new powers to operate trolleybuses through the 1938 Gateshead & District Tramways & Trolley Vehicles Act.

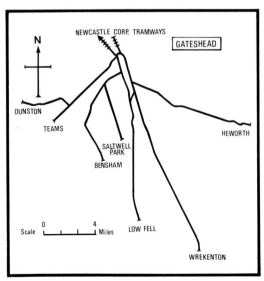

The war left Gateshead's trams in reasonably good condition, although consideration to trolleybus conversion was given in 1944. It was, however, rejected because of the low capacity of the single-deck trolleybuses that Gateshead would be forced to use as a consequence of the low railway bridges. In February 1945 it was reported that Newcastle Corporation's application for a provisional licence to operate trolleybuses to Gateshead was still outstanding; whilst three months later, Newcastle's Bill to convert the remaining tram routes to trolleybus operation was opposed by, inter alia, the Gateshead company. This Bill was eventually passed in late 1945.

Although under considerable pressure to accede to the conversion of its system, pursuant to the powers in the 1938 Act, Gateshead continued to maintain its tramway. In 1947-48, certain of the routes, such as that to Saltwell Park, saw the track relaid, whilst additional second-hand trams were acquired from Oldham and, ironically, Newcastle. The railway bridge at West Street was raised in June 1948, permitting the operation of double-deck buses over the route.

North of the Tyne, however, progress continued to be made on the conversion process. This, inevitably, had an impact upon the through services over the river. In May 1948, Newcastle's trams to Gosforth were replaced by a new trolleybus service, and the through services from Low Fell to Gosforth and Chillingham Road to Heworth were discontinued. Saltwell Park and Low Fell cars now terminated at Central station, whilst those from Heworth stopped at Barras Bridge (Museum), the same terminus as those operating on the Wrekenton service for which there had, as yet, been no change.

By the late 1940s a further complication had entered into the equation — the threat of nationalisation by the postwar Labour government. There was little incentive to invest in new public transport facilities if the state was to be the only beneficiary. To forestall this possibility, the company was again offered to Gateshead Corporation. As in 1936, the last occasion on which Gateshead had an option to acquire the trams, the local authority rejected the proposal.

The last Newcastle trams operated on 4 March 1950, leaving Gateshead as the only operator of trams across the Tyne. By now it was accepted that tramway abandonment was inevitable. In furtherance of this, the company obtained a new Act in 1950, the Gateshead & District Tramways Act, which again allowed for the conversion of the trams, but this time by buses rather than by trolleybuses. The first routes to close, Wrekenton and Heworth, had already ceased except for occasional and rush-hour services in March of that year following an agreement with the council. These closures were followed on 3 March 1951 by the conversion of the Saltwell Park and Bensham routes. After these closures, all remaining double-deck trams were withdrawn, the last in service being Nos 60 and 62. This was followed a month later by the route to Low Fell and by that to Teams on 14 July 1951. The one remaining route, to Dunston, was converted on 4 August 1951, with a single-deck car No 16 being the official last tram to operate on Tyneside. The 1950 Act had allowed for a two-year conversion period; the company had achieved total abandonment in half that time.

After closure, 19 of the single-deck trams were sold to the Grimsby & Immingham Electric Rail-

Left:
Seen at Newcastle Central station on 29 May 1950, Gateshead No 71 was one of six second-hand trams acquired from Oldham in 1946. Originally built by English Electric in 1924, No 71 was numbered 18 in the Oldham fleet. By this date Newcastle trams had ceased to operate completely, but Gateshead kept the cross-Tyne services operating for a further year.

Below left:
Relations between the Gateshead & District Tramways Co and Newcastle Corporation were not totally amicable during the late 1940s, in particular over the disagreement regarding the possible replacement of Gateshead's trams by trolleybuses. Nevertheless, Gateshead did take the opportunity of the gradual decline in Newcastle's tram fleet to strengthen its own. No 73, seen here on the Dunston route on 20 March 1949, was one of five single-deck cars acquired from Newcastle in 1948. These five were destined to be the last 'new' tramcars to be acquired by Gateshead.

way, where the majority were to give a further decade's service. Upon withdrawal from Grimsby, two of the cars were preserved: No 10 is now on display at Beamish, whilst No 5 forms part of the National Tramway Museum collection. A third Gateshead tram, No 52, originally built in 1901 and rebuilt in 1920, was bought by William Southern and presented to the National Tramway Museum in 1960.

Whilst this completes the story of the 'original' Gateshead tramway system, mention should be made of the very successful tramway built to serve the National Garden Festival, which was held in the town in 1990. For the first time in almost 40 years it was possible to ride on a traditional Tyneside tramcar within sight of the river. Although attempts to use one of the ex-Gateshead cars were unsuccessful, Newcastle No 102 performed well throughout the summer over the ¼-mile route.

Gateshead Closures

17 April 1948	Low Fell to Gosforth — cars now terminated at Central station
5 March 1950	Wrekenton and Heworth (both routes remained open at peak hours until overhead removed, September 1950 on route to Wrekenton)
3 March 1951	Saltwell Park
3 March 1951	Bensham
7 April 1951	Low Fell
14 July 1951	Teams
4 August 1951	Dunston

Last tram: No 16

Left:
Seen on 20 March 1949, Gateshead No 42 was one of an older generation of second-hand trams, being acquired from Sheffield Corporation during the mid-1920s. Originally built as an open-top car by Cravens, the top-cover had been fitted in Sheffield, whilst the lower-deck vestibules were added by Gateshead in 1926.

Gateshead

Fleet Numbers	Date	Trucks/Bogies	Body	Withdrawn
1-20[1]	1920-28	Brill 39E 1-11/4/6-8/20, Brill 22E 12/3/5/9	Brush 1/20, Gateshead 2-19	1947-51
21-3/6-8/32/4/ 9-41/3/44/51[2]	1901	Brill 21E	ERTCW	1947-51
24/5/33/6/7[3]	c1925 (acquired)	Brill 21E	Milnes	1950-51
29/30/8[4]	1922-24 (acquired)	Brill 21E	Liverpool CT	1950-51
31/5/42[5]	c1925 (acquired)	Brill 21E	Cravens	1947-51
45[6]	1901	Brill 21E	ERTCW	1947
46-50[7]	1902	Originally Milnes; retrucked to Brill 22E from batch 11-20 1921-25	Milnes	1947
52[8]	1901	Brill 21E	ERTCW	1947
53[9]	1907	Brill 22E bogies	Gateshead	1947
54/5[10]	1913	Brill 39E bogies	Gateshead	1947
56-60[11]	1921	Brill 39E bogies	Brush	1951
61-7[12]	1923	Brill 21E	Brush	1951
65/68-72[13]	1947 (acquired)	Brill 21E	EE	1951
73-7[14]	1948 (acquired)	Peckham P25 bogies	Hurst Nelson	1951

1 All bar Nos 13/5 built with vestibules. Nos 13/5 vestibuled 1926/27. Nos 1/3-11/6-8/20 to Grimsby & Immingham. No 4 was damaged on delivery and did not enter service. Nos 5/10 preserved.

2 Batch 21-45. Originally open-top, rebuilt 1924-25 to balcony-top and lower-deck vestibules. No 51 numbered 45 until 1925.

3 Originally Sheffield CT-built 1899. Were Sheffield CT 16/35/7/8/74 (order unknown). Top-covers fitted in Sheffield; vestibuled in Gateshead 1926. No 33 preserved at Crich as Sheffield No 74.

4 Originally Liverpool Nos 479-81, built 1899 and sold to Tynemouth & District. c1925 top-covers and vestibules added by Gateshead.

5 Ex-Sheffield 176/82/6 (order unknown), new 1901. Top-covers fitted Sheffield; vestibuled in Gateshead 1926.

6 Originally open-top No 25, Converted to single-deck 1923. Renumbered 45 1925.

7 Single deck; fitted with vestibule 1931-32.

8 Originally single-deck car No 7. Renumbered 52 in 1928 after rebuilding in 1920. Preserved.

9 Rebuilt 1926.

10 Rebuilt 1926.

11 To Grimsby & Immingham.

12 Unmodified during life. Last new trams bought.

13 Ex-Oldham Nos 24, 122/5/8, 18 and 17 respectively. New 1924-25.

14 Ex-Newcastle CT Nos 80, 43, 54, 88 and 52 respectively. New 1901. Rebuilt by NCT as single-deckers 1930-33.

Situated on the northern coast of County Antrim, the Giant's Causeway is one of Ireland's most peculiar geological structures and one of the most popular tourist attractions in the country. It was also, until 1949, the destination of one of the oldest tramways in the British Isles.

After earlier proposals to link the steam railway at Portrush with Bushmills and run to the Giant's Causeway had failed, two brothers, Anthony and William Atcheson Traill, took over the scheme. Two Bills were introduced to Parliament in 1880, although, due to opposition, the section from Bushmills to the Giant's Causeway was subsequently deleted. The amended Bill received the Royal Assent on 28 August 1880. Initial problems regarding the raising of finance were solved through the brothers' contacts at Trinity College, Dublin. The first sod was cut near Portrush on 21 September 1881.

By the early 1880s, interest in electricity as a means of power was growing, and there were a number of innovators who took developments further. At Cragside in Northumberland, the arms manufacturer Armstrong had harnessed water power to produce electricity, whilst Magnus Volk at Brighton had shown the potential of electricity as a means of propulsion. It was always the intention that the Giant's Causeway Tramway would be electrically-powered as the Siemens company was appointed Technical Engineers in late 1881 in order to undertake a series of tests. Initially, a two-rail scheme was adopted, but this proved inadequate to power the vehicles due to excessive current leakage. The adoption of a third-rail improved the situation, but it was only the adoption of porcelain insulators that ensured sufficient current to operate the vehicles. Moreover, as the line was intended to operate through the streets of Portrush, where third-rail operation

would have been impossible, the company also had to acquire steam locomotives for this section.

By the end of 1882 construction of the section from Portrush to Bushmills was completed. The line was opened to the public on 29 January 1883, but it was not until the official opening of the line, on 28 September 1883, that the hydro-electric station (situated at Walkmills, south of Bushmills) was operational. From Bushmills the passengers were carried to the Giant's Causeway by means of horse-drawn buses. In 1885 the Board of Directors agreed to proceed with the extension from Bushmills to Giant's Causeway, and this was completed in 1887 and opened to the public on 1 July of that year. In 1889 the existing underground power cables from the power station were replaced by overhead lines.

Although the adoption of the third-rail had not been without controversy, the Directors, in particular W. A. Traill, had always been able to deflect this criticism. However, in 1895 a serious accident occurred, which saw a cyclist killed through falling onto the third-rail. The subsequent inquiry by the Board of Trade condemned the company's operating practices and recommended that the third-rail be replaced with conventional overhead. The company obtained the necessary permission in 1896 and the conversion was completed on 26 July 1899, including the former steam-operated section through Portrush. Despite the conversion, occasional use of steam power continued through to the mid-1920s. The two locomotives were finally sold off in 1931.

Throughout its existence, the Giant's Causeway Tramway had problems with its hydro-electric power station. During the summer, when power requirements were at a maximum, the river flow was often inadequate; and this was compounded by the conflicting needs of tramway

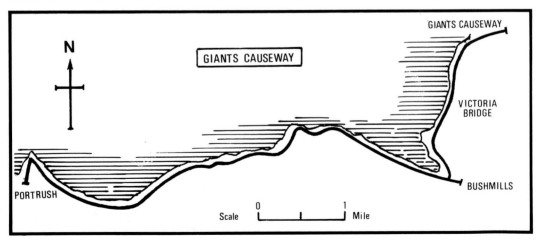

Above:
Now preserved at the Howth Castle Transport Museum, near Dublin, Giants Causeway No 9 dated originally from 1909 and was substantially rebuilt in 1945. It is pictured here hauling two well-filled trailers, the illustration showing to good effect the car's Peckham Cantilever truck. *F. N. T. Lloyd-Jones*

and fishermen, for whom the river was a popular salmon-fishing spot. To obviate these problems, the tramway built, at various times, a number of auxiliary power stations at Portrush. The first of these, gas-powered, lasted from 1911 until 1917, and an oil-fired generator was installed in 1924-25.

By the outbreak of World War 1 passenger figures reached 155,000. Inevitably, war led to a dramatic decline which was compounded by the problem of unrestrained bus competition after 1919. The tramway responded by radically reducing fares; this had the result of seeing off the bus operators at the expense of the company's finances. Recession towards the end of the 1920s also had an effect, and all services were suspended during the winters of 1927-28 and 1928-29. On 6 July 1933 W. A. Traill died: he had been the tramway's guiding light for 50 years. Despite this loss the tramway was, however, determined to soldier on. Indicative of this was the acquisition and regauging to the tramway's 3ft 0in-gauge of one of the recently-withdrawn trams from Dunfermline in 1937.

By 1940 passenger figures had dropped to 63,000. The outbreak of war did, however, bring dramatic changes to the tramway. There were several important military bases established in the region and so from 1940 until 1947 winter services were again run, this time at the request of the military. The tramway suffered only slightly during the war — one major incident being the 'self-inflicted' loss of ¼-mile of overhead brought down by a drifting barrage balloon!

1945 opened with a serious snowfall, which saw services suspended for a 10-day period until 30 January and the freezing-up of the water supply to the power station. Also during 1945, the overhead was extended to the one road at Bushmills depot that had been previously accessible only through fly-shunting. In early 1946 the generator at Walkmills was given a thorough overhaul, but by this time the reduction in traffic caused by the loss of the military custom was starting to have an effect. In September 1947 the Board decided to continue running a winter service through to 1948, even though the results from the previous winter had been poor. However, despite this decision, services were suspended on 27 December 1947. Services did not resume fully until 1 May 1948.

Despite the problems, there remained little intention of closure. Indeed, during 1947, the general manager visited the threatened Bessbrook & Newry tramway with a view to acquiring further rolling stock, whilst during the winter of 1947-48 car No 20 was fully overhauled and certain improvements were made to the depot at Portrush.

In early 1948 the Ulster Transport Authority was created, and the Board decided to offer the tramway to the new authority in order to avoid the cost of road reinstatement should the tramway close. The offer was rejected. Then, in September 1948, the retiring engineer, Chambers, produced a gloomy report on the physical state of the tramway. He commented that the track required a great deal of attention and that the Jubilee bridge, over the River Bush, would soon be unfit for use. In the same month, a new

manager was appointed and immediate work was undertaken on track relaying. Next, in early 1949, the decking of the Jubilee bridge was replaced. The work, which left the company with an overdraft of £650, allowed the trams to operate through the 1949 season, until they were again suspended for the winter on 30 September 1949. They were destined never to run again.

In late 1949 the Directors decided that, in the light of the continued rejection of their offer by the UTA and the decline in the company's financial position, there was no option but to wind up the undertaking. A public announcement to that effect was made in November 1949. An immediate public outcry was the result, with efforts being made through, inter alia, the magazine *Modern Tramway* to save this historic line. At a Board meeting in August 1950 it was estimated that the total cost of restoring the line to public

Below:
Car No 23 along with enclosed trailer No 1 and an unidentified toastrack trailer are seen negotiating 'the Curve' in Portrush en route for the Giant's Causeway on a very wet day in September 1947.
R. C. Ludgate collection

service was of the order of £15,000. Interested bodies, including local authorities, met the Northern Ireland government on 22 September to press the case for assistance. There was to be no reprieve and the company proceeded to obtain an Abandonment Order. Although the Order was not made effective until September 1951, due to significant opposition, the final death knell for the tramway occurred at a public auction in Belfast on 15 March 1951 when the track, vehicles and assets of the tramway were disposed of. These disposals were followed by the sale of the land. The final meeting of the tramway's creditors took place on 2 September 1958.

Although none of the Giant's Causeway cars was immediately saved for preservation, three have subsequently been preserved: No 2 is displayed at the Ulster Folk and Transport Museum at Cultra; No 5 at the Belfast Transport Museum; and, No 9 at the Howth Castle Transport Museum.

Forty years after the closure of the Giant's Causeway Tramway, it is salutory to compare the failure of the preservation attempt with that which saw the revival of the Talyllyn Railway. The Giant's Causeway remains one of Northern Ireland's most popular tourist attractions — indeed, there is now talk of re-creating the tramway. Truly the wheel turns full circle.

Giant's Causeway

Fleet Numbers	Date	Trucks/Bogies	Body	Withdrawn
1/2/10[1]	1883	-	Midland C&W	1949
3/4[2]	1883	-	Midland C&W	1945/49
5-7[3]	1883	-	Midland C&W	1949
9[4]	1909	Peckham Cantilever	?	1949
11/3/5/6[5]	1888-91 (converted)	-	?	1949
19[6]	1897	-	?	1949
20/21[7]	1899	Peckham Cantilever	?	1949
22[8]	1902	Peckham	?	1949
23[9]	1908	UEC	?	1949
24[10]	1937 (acquired)	UEC Peckham P22	UEC	1949

1 Trailer saloons. No 2 preserved.
2 Trailer open cars with longitudinal seating. No 3 withdrawn 1945, parts used in rebuilding of No 9.
3 Trailer open cars/toastrack. No 5 preserved.
4 Saloon power car. Rebuilt 1945. No 9 preserved.
5 Trailer open cars/toastrack. Rebuilt from goods wagons.
6 Trailer open car/toastrack.
7 Toastrack power cars.
8 Toastrack power car.
9 Toastrack power car.
10 Ex-Dunfermline No 34 new 1918. A total of two cars were bought but only one entered service. Originally double-deck and open-top; cut down to single-deck and a shortened truck in Ireland.

Postwar, with the largest surviving tramway system, the acquisition of numerous new and second-hand cars and the building of several postwar extensions, Glasgow was widely regarded as the tram's most secure haven in Britain. However, the last of the familiar and popular 'caurs' had disappeared by 1962 — and this was the last complete system to close in the British Isles.

The distinctiveness of the fleet was compounded by the somewhat peculiar choice of gauge — 4ft 7¾in — which Glasgow shared alone with Huddersfield, and which was a consequence of the desire to run railway wagons over the tramway track, and of the differing wheel profiles adopted by both railways and tramways.

The first tram routes in Glasgow were built by the Corporation, with work commencing on the first section on 22 September 1871. As elsewhere, the new lines were leased out, in this case to the Glasgow Tramways & Omnibus Co, for a 21-year period from July 1871. The first section was opened on 19 August 1872 and was expanded considerably over the next two decades. All the routes were horse-operated. On 12 November 1891 the Corporation decided that it wished to take over the actual operations, but negotiations with the company were to prove fruitless and it was not until 30 June 1894 that the last company-operated horse-car ran. The first Corporation services, still horse-powered, ran the following day.

By its Act of 1891 the Corporation was empowered to use any form of mechanical power on its tramways, and so during 1896 a number of tours to inspect electric tramways were undertaken. The decision was made to adopt this method of propulsion. The first section of line, from Springburn to Mitchell Street, opened on 13 October

1898, with a total of 21 single-deck cars (Nos 665-685) and two double-deck cars (Nos 686 and 687) to provide the service. Although the former cars were relatively short-lived (one, No 672, however, remains in preservation), the two double-deck cars were forerunners of one of the most successful designs of British tramcar — the Glasgow 'Standards' — which through various phases and rebuilds were still to be vitally important almost to the closure of the system. Around 1,000 of the type were built, making it the second most numerous type of tramcar in Britain after London's 'E/1'. All but 80 were built in the Corporation's own workshops. The growth of the tramway system was rapid so that by the outbreak of war in 1914 there were some 851 trams operating over 197 miles of track.

After the war, the expansion of the tramways continued with the acquisition of the Airdrie & Coatbridge Tramways Trust on 31 December 1921. The Trust, which had inherited the tramways of the Airdrie & Coatbridge Tramways Co in September 1920, had a fleet of 15 cars, which were renumbered 1073-87 by Glasgow. They were, however, destined to be short-lived, being withdrawn between 1925 and 1934. The second acquisition, on 1 August 1923, saw the Corporation take over the Paisley & District Tramways Co. This brought Corporation-owned tramcars to the Paisley, Renfrew and Barrhead area. The company possessed 73 tramcars, of which 72 were renumbered 1001-72 by Glasgow. The exception, a single-deck tramcar bought from Sheffield in 1920, was not renumbered by either Paisley & District or Glasgow and was disposed of in 1928. Of the Paisley cars, the majority were withdrawn by 1939, but almost half sur-

Left:
Second only to the 'E/1' cars in terms of numbers, the Glasgow 'Standard' cars totalled some 1,000 built over a near 30-year period. No 63, seen outside Newlands depot on 19 June 1949, was a comparative late arrival, being introduced to service in May 1921. Although by this date the majority of Glasgow's trams were painted in standard livery of green, orange and cream, a number retained their earlier route colours, such as the red worn by No 63, until the 1950s. Glasgow was the last British operator to perpetuate this method of differentiating routes.

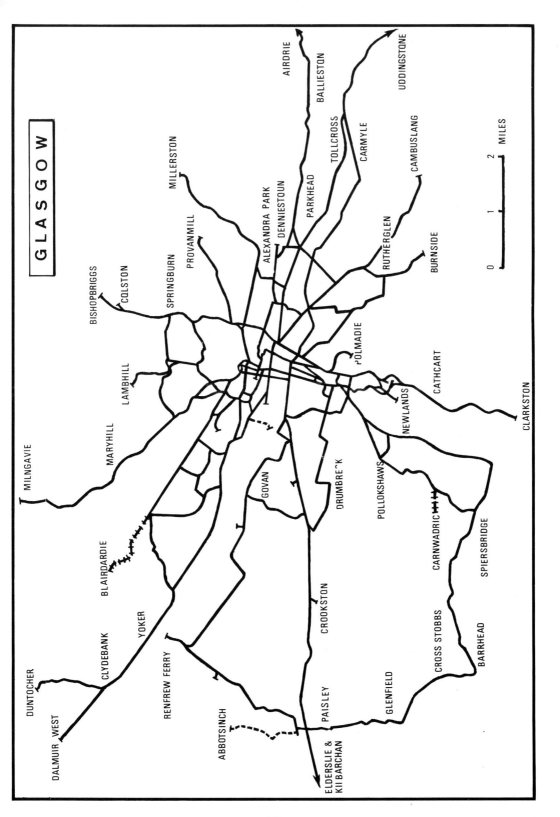

GLASGOW

MILES

0 1 2

DUNTOCHER
DALMUIR WEST
CLYDEBANK
YOKER
RENFREW FERRY
ABBOTSINCH
ELDERSLIE &
KILBARCHAN
PAISLEY
GLENFIELD
CROSS STOBBS
BARRHEAD
SPIERSBRIDGE
CARNWADRIC
CROOKSTON
DRUMBRE°K
POLLOKSHAWS
GOVAN
BLAIRDARDIE
MILNGAVIE
MARYHILL
LAMBHILL
BISHOPBRIGGS
COLSTON
SPRINGBURN
PROVANMILL
MILLERSTON
ALEXANDRA PARK
DENNIESTOUN
PARKHEAD
TOLLCROSS
CARMYLE
BALLIESTON
AIRDRIE
UDDINGSTONE
CAMBUSLANG
RUTHERGLEN
BURNSIDE
P°OLMADIE
CATHCART
NEWLANDS
CLARKSTON

87

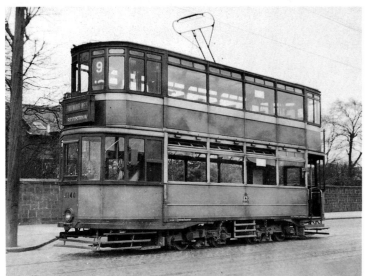

vived into the postwar era. Some of these survivals were cut-down to single-deck cars for use on the Duntocher route and, although scheduled for withdrawal in c1939, the majority soldiered on until the route closed. A number of the ex-Paisley cars survived until 1960, including No 68 which is now preserved in its original open-top form at the National Tramway Museum.

1921 was also to see the first consideration of the possible operation of buses and trolleybuses in the city. An extensive network of routes, primarily to act as feeders to the successful tramway system, was promoted. Although the first bus route, from Monteith Row to Maryhill, was inaugurated on 8 December 1924, it was not until the late 1920s that bus operation commenced seriously. It was, however, to be a further two decades before trolleybuses were to appear on the city's streets. The 1920s were to witness the continuing modernisation of the tramways, with the rebuilding of the 'Standard' cars and the introduction, in 1927, of the famous 'Kilmarnock' bogie cars. The period also saw the first tramway abandonment, when in the mid-1920s the service was withdrawn from the Carlton Place route. The track was to remain on this section for a further 30 years, until removal in the mid-1950s, in the expectation of the replacement of the suspension bridge — a replacement which would have allowed the trams to cross the river at that point. In 1927 there were some 1,100 tramcars in service operating over 129.5 route miles. Of this total, almost one-third of the mileage lay outside the city boundaries. The extensive mileage outside the city was later to prove one of the system's Achilles heels.

1927 was, to some extent, a watershed year. A new manager, Lachlan MacKinnon, succeeded the influential James Dalrymple, whose departure had been precipitated by trouble following the 1926 General Strike. It was also the year in which the Fischer bow collector, later to be fitted as standard to all Glasgow trams, made its first appearance in the city. Then, in 1930 the Glasgow Corporation Act gave a monopoly of bus operation within the existing city boundaries. The Act was, however, not extended to cover those areas, like Drumchapel, which were subsequently added to the city. On 1 May 1932 the first significant tramway abandonment took place with the withdrawal of the service from Paisley to Kilbarchan. The only other withdrawal prior to 1939 was that to Abbotsinch, also in Paisley, which was closed on 26 March 1933. Also in 1933, the Corporation obtained trolleybus powers under the Glasgow Corporation Provisional Order, with the aim of replacing trams on those routes where the cost of track replacement was prohibitive. Fears over job losses at the Permanent Way Department, however, led to no conversions at this date. The Corporation had also sought powers in 1933 to build bus and trolleybus bodies at Coplawhill, but this application was rejected. One consequence of this, along with the forthcoming Empire Exhibition (due to be held at Bellahouston Park in 1938), was the introduction of the 'Coronation' class in 1937. Originally 600 cars were scheduled in the programme, but when hostilities caused the suspension of the building programme in 1940 only some 152 had been built. Meanwhile, in 1935 MacKinnon had retired. He had been succeeded by John Wilson, who was in turn succeeded by Robert F. Smith in 1937.

In general the 1930s were a period of consolidation, there being a number of positive developments, such as the extension to Milngavie, which opened in 1934 and which gave the city its longest tram route (almost 23 miles long from Milngavie to Renfrew Ferry). The 'Coronation' programme should have enabled the withdrawal of many of the older 'Standard' cars, the condition of which was starting to give cause for concern, but the curtailment of the programme meant that Glasgow entered the 1940s with a relatively aged tram fleet. The late 1930s did, however, see the construction of four experimental cars, Nos 1001-1004. These cars were an attempt to provide the same level of comfort and style as the 'Coronation' cars, which had proved prohibitively expensive to build, at a lower cost. One of the 'Kilmarnock' bogie cars, No 1100, was also used as a test-bed, being eventually rebuilt during 1940 with tapered ends similar to the 'Coronation' cars. At the same time, considerable investment had gone into the expansion of the bus fleet — indeed more than 350 new buses were placed in service between 1937 and 1940.

Inevitably, the war affected Glasgow — and Clydebank in particular — seriously. During the German air attack on Clydebank in March 1941, 'Standard' car No 6 was destroyed and a replacement car, similar to Nos 1001-1004, was built. From a tramway point of view the war delayed the necessary modernisation of the fleet. Another

event of considerable significance was the appointment in 1943 of Eric Fitzpayne as the new General Manager. He was to hold the post throughout the remaining years of the tramway system; indeed, he also survived to see Glasgow become an all-bus operator.

With the cessation of hostilities the Corporation was able to turn its attention once again to the future. The possibility of trolleybus operation was again discussed and on 10 January 1946 the Corporation approved a scheme for the introduction of trolleybuses. Fitzpayne went to great lengths to emphasise that this did not mean the commencement of a tram abandonment policy but that trolleybuses would enable electrically-powered vehicles to serve economically the newly-built housing estates. Later in 1946 the first contracts were placed, although it was to be

Below:

After the construction of the Mk 1 'Coronations' prior to the outbreak of World War 2, authority was given to the Transport Department to build four experimental trams, Nos 1001-1004. Whilst the bodies were to be completely new, with frames supplied by Pickerings, two of the cars were to be fitted with reconditioned trucks — an exercise to try out the possibility of building a new generation of tramcar at a lower unit cost. The second of the four cars, No 1002 seen here on 23 March 1949 at Millerston, was, however, fitted with a new Maley & Taunton truck. Whilst the experimental cars were destined to remain non-standard, many of the features incorporated were developed into the postwar cars.

a further three years before the trolleybuses were actually introduced.

Parallel with the construction of the trolleybus system, considerable investment also went into the trams. On 6 August 1945 Fitzpayne was authorised to construct a further experimental tram. This vehicle, No 1005, was two years in construction, but when it emerged in late 1947, the result was remarkable. A single-ended car carrying 72 passengers, and representing the most modern tramcar then to enter service, No 1005 also carried a striking, non-standard livery in three shades of blue. Being single-ended the tram was restricted to certain routes. The tram was, however, destined not to be a total success, and gradually many of the non-standard features disappeared, culminating with the car being rebuilt as a two-ended vehicle in 1956.

More significant, in retrospect, than the introduction of No 1005, was the 1946 decision to build more new tramcars. The first of the Mk II 'Coronations', or 'Cunarders' as they became known, No 1293, entered service in 1948. Although similar to the prewar trams, wartime cost inflation led to the 'Cunarders' having a slightly reduced specification. Production of the new trams was slow, and thus it was not until 1952 that the last of 100 entered service. Parallel with this investment in new cars there was also authorisation given in early 1946 to the construction of an extension of the Knightswood service to South Drumry. Work on this extension started in early 1949.

1948 saw the peak number of tramcars in service, with over 1,200 available. However, a fire at Newlands Depot on 11 April 1948 led to the destruction of a number of 'Standard' and Mk I 'Coronation' cars. Although the latter cars were either repaired immediately or, in the case of two officially listed as 'destroyed', rebuilt completely in 1951, the insurance money obtained from damage to a number of the former enabled the Corporation to acquire EMB bogies from Liverpool. These bogies, recovered from trams destroyed in the Green Lane fire of 1947, were used to build eight replacement 'Coronation' cars, Nos 1393-98, 1255 and 1279, in 1954-55. Nos 1393-98 were the last new trams to be built for Glasgow, both 1255 and 1279 being reconstructions of earlier fire-damaged trams. The first postwar abandonment saw trams withdrawn from the Uddington-Broomhouse section of route No 29 on 28 August 1948.

On 23 January 1949 buses replaced trams on part of route No 10, between Townhead and Oatlands, as the trolleybus scheme gradually took effect. In February buses also replaced trams on routes Nos 2 (Provanmill-Polmadie) and 19 (Springburn-Muirend) to facilitate trolleybus construction. With an adjustment to the other local routes, the amount of track closed at this stage was relatively small. Trolleybus services were introduced on 3 April 1949; Glasgow being the last city in Britain to introduce this form of transport. The previous day saw another tramway abandonment, this time part of the former Paisley & District system, when a short section from Glenfield to Cross Stobs (Barrhead) was closed. At the same time route No 14 was extended to serve Barrhead.

On 3 December 1949 the route to Duntocher was converted to bus operation. This abandonment, long foreshadowed, had been strongly opposed. Its reliance, however, on the increasingly aged ex-Paisley cars, which had been cut down for service on the route in the 1920s, meant that its position was always exposed. The citizens of Duntocher were assuaged by the possibility that the extension to Blairdairdie, which had opened earlier in 1949, would later be further extended to Duntocher. In the event this plan came to naught and the Blairdairdie line, which opened on 31 July 1949, was to prove the final extension to the system. Of the single-deck cars two bodies survive — Nos 1016 and 1017 (the latter of which had been used for driver training since the 1920s).

Over the next year the Corporation's efforts were to be devoted towards the extension of the trolleybus system, and there were few developments to the tramway until 21 December 1950, when the Corporation received a report from the Joint Committee of Transport, Highways & Planning. This report advocated the limited replacement of a number of tram routes. Although the report was referred back to the committee, the increasing threat to Glasgow's tramway system was becoming apparent and this spurred the LRTL into the production of a counter-report which advocated the future development of the system. A similar story was to be followed over the next two years, with the trolleybus network being gradually expanded with only minor changes to the tramway system. During this period, on 13 February 1952, the last of the 'Cunarders', No 1392, appeared; and later in the same year Glasgow finally abandoned its traditional route colours. By this date only some 40 cars in fact retained these distinctive bands; until the closure all trams would henceforth be painted in the standard fleet colours of green and orange.

Between 1950 and early 1953 there was only one minor tramway abandonment, when on 15 June 1952 route No 9 was cut back by approximately 1,200yd from Carmyle to Causewayside Street. This closure was followed, later that same year, by an extension, over existing tracks, of route No 31 from Greenview Street to Nether Auldhouse Road. 1953 was, however, to be a year of considerable change. Early that year a subcommittee of the main Transport Committee met to discuss the recommendations of the Inglis Report. This report, which advocated tramway abandonment, was rejected by the sub-committee, a decision later endorsed by the Corporation. Nevertheless, the problem of the increasing age of the tram fleet continued to cause disquiet, and Fitzpayne proposed that 24 of Liverpool's surplus 'Green Goddess' trams be acquired at £500 apiece. This recommendation was agreed and the first of these purchases entered service in October of that year.

On 4 July 1953 the southern part of route No 13 was abandoned in favour of new trolleybus service No 105. The introduction of this new service also led to a number of other service alterations. Route No 5 was cut back from Clarkston to Holmlea Road, the remains of route No 13 were diverted to operate via Hope Street and Argyle Street, and route No 23 was diverted to run along Maryhill Road. These diversions were all a consequence of the Ministry of Transport's reluctance to sanction the operation of trams fitted with bow collectors on roads fitted for trolleybus operation. Despite these alterations, Glasgow remained committed to tramway operation and Fitzpayne restated this commitment at a meeting of the Institute of Transport in Glasgow that year. On 4 October 1953 route No 29 was extended from Anderston Cross to Milngavie and the Spiersbridge short working on route No 14 was extended to a new crossover at Arden to serve a new housing and factory development. By the end of 1953, Glasgow had 1,100 trams in service (of which 258 were of modern design), 835 buses and 74 trolleybuses. Also in late 1953, Renfrew Town Council voted 7-2 in favour of tramway retention within the borough and voted the money for alterations to the track at the Renfrew Ferry terminus. The new arrangements were brought into use on 27 August 1954.

This was to be a year of considerable significance for Glasgow's trams in that the increasing age of the tram fleet led to the first major decisions for abandonment. However, the year started well with the extension, on 7 February, of route No 4 along Renfrew Road to the Paisley North (Sandyford Road) crossover. A few months later the first of Fitzpayne's decisive reports was presented. He reported that 87 older trams had been scrapped and partially replaced by the new 'Cunarders', the replacement 'Coronations' built that year and the acquisition of trams from Liverpool. There remained a further 487 cars which could be considered as life

Left:
Between 1948 and 1952 no less than 100 Mk II 'Coronations' or 'Cunarders' were built, making them the single largest batch of tramcars delivered to a British tramway system after 1945. No 1297 was the sixth of the 'Cunarders' to be put into service, in December 1948, and was barely three months old when seen at the terminus of the Millerston route on 23 March 1949. Two of the 'Cunarders' are preserved, including No 1297 itself at the National Tramway Museum.

Left:

Although the decision was taken by 1953 gradually to run down the Glasgow tramway network, there remained a short-term need to replace the increasingly aged 'Standard' cars and, since authority to build new cars was refused, this could only be achieved by second-hand acquisitions. A total of 46 ex-Liverpool 'Green Goddesses' were therefore acquired in 1953-54. No 1020, seen here at Tollcross on 22 May 1954, was originally Liverpool No 937. The 'Green Goddesses' were not wholly successful in Glasgow, requiring a great deal of remedial work, and their life was destined to be relatively short. All were withdrawn between 1957 and 1960. One, Glasgow No 1055 (Liverpool No 869), was preserved and is now displayed at the National Tramway Museum.

expired, of which 100 needed to be withdrawn quickly. Given that £2,250,000 had been spent over the previous seven years on the power station at Pinkston, the report continued, a conversion programme to trolleybus operation of a number of routes, thus enabling the tram fleet to be reduced to c800, would allow the benefit of this investment to be continued. As part of the continuing investment programme, a further 22 surplus Liverpool trams were acquired, whilst when No 1279 caught fire at Renfrew Ferry on 26 April the car was speedily repaired. The Labour group on the Corporation (the dominant political force) decided to adopt the suggested policy — although, as yet, no definite plans existed.

There followed a number of service alterations. On 22 August the Sunday service on route No 40 was abandoned and this was followed on 10 October by alterations to five routes: No 17 was diverted from Whiteinch to Anniesland; No 21 was withdrawn between High Street and Anniesland; No 23 was cut back from Airdrie to the boundary at Baillieston (leaving only one route to serve Airdrie); No 25 was back to Colston; and No 32 Elderslie-Springburn was altered to run from Crookston-Bishopbriggs. A month later, on 26 November, the Labour group rejected a proposal that 450 trams be replaced by buses in favour of a policy of conversion to both bus and trolleybus. Fitzpayne was instructed to select the most appropriate routes. Finally in 1954, on 3

December, the extension to Pinkston power station was officially opened; it remained the one municipally-owned power station in the British Isles.

In early 1955 Fitzpayne provided his list of service cuts. He envisaged a programme over five years to eliminate 10 routes and 300 old cars — the remaining 150 cars had already succumbed with the introduction of the ex-Liverpool cars. Of the 10 routes, eight were to be converted to bus and two to trolleybus. The report was accepted on 14 April 1955, and the process of conversion gradually got under way. On 7 August 1955 the section of track between Shawfield and Rutherglen saw tram services suspended whilst trolleybus overhead was erected, and later in the same year authorisation was given for the acquisition of more new buses and trolleybuses.

A further indication that all was not well with the tramway system came on 2 February 1956 when the Corporation decided to abandon sections outside the city boundary. This plan, expected to save £80,000 per annum, envisaged 24 miles of track being abandoned in areas like Paisley and Airdrie. The Corporation was to cease operating the routes outside the city completely, leaving other bus companies to provide the replacement services. Inevitably, there was much opposition since these changes represented a significant reduction in the quality of public transport. Two months later, on 17 April 1956, the Glasgow Passenger Transport Joint Committee agreed on a programme of suburban electrification. Later in the same month route No 1 (Dalmarnock-Dalmuir West) was curtailed to Dalmuir during weekday peaks. On 29 September 1956 Langside depot was closed to trams and the fleet had been reduced to less than 1,000, although there were still almost 600 'Standard' cars in service. A proposal, however, for the complete scrapping of the tram system was rejected by the Council by 50 votes to 20 — it still looked like trams had a future in the city, despite the adoption of a programme to abandon 10 routes.

On 29 September the first of the out-of-city route abandonments occurred, when route No 14 was curtailed from Cross Stobs to Arden. This was followed on 3 November with the withdrawal of route No 15 beyond Baillieston to Airdrie (with the closure of Coatbridge depot), route No 29 withdrawn from Maryhill Park to Milngavie and route No 17 curtailed from Cambuslang to Farme Cross. The withdrawals were not popular; on 6 December 1956 Airdrie Council voted to ask for the trams to be reintroduced, but this was impractical due to the commencement of track recovery. Also withdrawn at this stage were weekday services on route No 40. The withdrawal of the Paisley routes was delayed due to the Suez crisis.

In addition to the reprieve for the Paisley routes, the Suez crisis also led to the temporary reintroduction of all-night tram services on a number of routes (these had been originally abandoned in the early 1950s). It also meant that the Corporation was unable to dismantle the old generating equipment at Pinkston power station — the need to alter the power supply to Paisley was one factor in the decision to abandon the routes in the town.

In early 1957 a new crossover was installed at Martin Crescent (Baillieston), which allowed for the slight shortening of routes Nos 15 and 23. On 2 April 1957 it was announced that with the cessation of fuel rationing for public transport that the Paisley routes would be converted in May 1957; the reintroduced all-night tram services had already been withdrawn again on 30 March. On 11 May 1957 the Paisley routes were closed, route Nos 21 and 28 were converted to bus operation and Nos 4 and 27 now terminated at the city boundary. The now-isolated Elderslie depot was closed to trams. This depot had been used for the scrapping of redundant trams (the last dealt with being No 847) and future disposals were handled by contractors, such as McConnell of Coatbridge (which had also disposed of many

of the Edinburgh trams). The last tram in Paisley was 'Coronation' No 1277.

Later in 1957 the first announcements for the possible total abandonment of the system over the long term emerged. A report was submitted to the Transport Committee on 24 June 1957. The report stated that it would cost £11,230,000 to replace the existing tram fleet with new trams, £7,412,000 to replace the system with trolley-buses and £5,539,000 to convert to bus operation. It was, therefore, considered to be uneconomic to renew the tram fleet. The 'Coronation' cars and other modern trams were considered to have a 20-year life and that the final routes would consequently be withdrawn in the 1970s. The process of eliminating the older cars in the fleet continued with the withdrawal of Nos 696 and 697, both of which dated from 1899 and which were the 32nd and 33rd electric tramcars built for the city. On 18 August, route No 23, Baillieston-Gairbaird Avenue, was extended to Maryhill; a month later, however, on 25 September, the Labour group of the council approved in principle the policy of total abandonment. On 17 November 1957 routes Nos 5 and 5A, Holmlea Road-Kelvinside, were converted to bus operation.

The fate of the tramway system was sealed on 6 February 1958 when the city council approved abandonment over a 12-15 year period. Trolley-buses were to be limited to a maximum of 200 vehicles and the primary form of replacement was to be the bus. It was also recommended that Pinkston power station be sold to the South of Scotland Electricity Board for £1,175,000. Although the actual programme of closures was not agreed by the Municipal Transport Committee on 22 April 1958, two further routes had succumbed prior to that date. On 15 March route No 24 was converted to bus operation and on the same day route No 27, Shieldhall-Springburn, was also converted. In the latter case no track was physically abandoned since the route was also served by route No 4.

The next conversion, on 14 June 1958, saw route No 7, Bellahouston-Millerston, converted to trolleybus, whilst on 26 June the Transport Convenor announced that the abandonment programme would probably be accelerated due to the condition of certain trams. *Modern Tramway* commented, ironically, on rumours of a total abandonment that the 'figure of eight years mentioned by an opposition councillor is unlikely to be achieved for reasons of finance'. The magazine's optimism was to prove ill-founded when, on 13 August, it was announced that the abandonment programme would be accelerated yet again, to be completed within five years so as to reduce losses. On 6 September route No 4, Hillington Road-Springburn, was converted to bus operation, and this was followed on 15 November when four routes, Nos 12, 17, 22 and 32, were converted. These closures also marked the end of Govan depot, although it continued for a period to store withdrawn trams. A further significant break with the past occurred on 31 October when Pinkston power station passed to the SSEB.

1959 started with the diversion of routes Nos 3 and 14 due to the repair of Eldon Bridge. This was followed on 28 January by a tragedy when a collision involving No 1145 killed two passengers. The first closure of 1959 saw route No 8, Millerston-Rouken Glen, converted to bus operation on 14 March. At the same time route No 25 was temporarily extended to Giffnock. Two months later, on 2 May, route No 33 was abandoned. At this date Glasgow still had seven depots serving the tram fleet. This figure was reduced by one on 6 June when Possilpark depot closed at the same time as route No 25 Bishopbriggs-Carnwadric/Rouken Glen was converted to bus operation. The section to Carnwadric had opened on 7 November 1948. By now the Glasgow fleet had been reduced to 613, of which 188 were 'Standards'. On 6 September route No 16 was curtailed from Springburn to Keppochhill Road. The last track repairs using Thermit welding occurred at this time; in future all replacement track work was fixed using fishplates to facilitate the later removal of the track. A further, unexpected, withdrawal saw the trams on routes Nos 6 and 9 terminate some 600yd short of the original terminus at Dalmuir West from 7 September, due to the condition of the canal bridge over the Forth & Clyde Canal at Dalmuir. There were to be three further abandonments in 1959: on 31 October routes No 6, Scotstown-Alexandra Park (with peak hours to Riddrie) and No 14, Kelvinside-Arden, were converted to bus; whilst on 5 December route No 31, Lambhill-Merrylee, was abandoned with no replacement.

By now, the withdrawals had started to eat into the ranks of the more modern cars, including the majority of the ex-Liverpool trams, and early 1960 was to see the withdrawal of the first of the postwar 'Cunarders'. There were by early 1960 only some 400 trams in service. On 12 March 1960 two routes, No 1 (Dalmarnock-Dalmuir) and No 30 (Dalmarnock-Blairdairdie), were converted to bus operation. At the same time, Parkhead depot was closed to trams. These routes

were the last to be wholly operated by 'Standard' cars — from now on their operation was severely limited. Three months later, on 4 June, route No 3, Mosspark-Kelvinbridge (Park Road), was converted to bus operation and route No 10, Kelvinside-London Road, was withdrawn but not directly replaced, being covered in part by a strengthened service on route No 9. At this point Newlands depot was closed.

Surprisingly, the next significant event was an extension! With repairs to the bridge at Dalmuir completed, route No 9 was extended to terminate again at Dalmuir West on 1 August 1960. It was not long before the process of abandonment once again got underway, though. On 5 November route No 23, Baillieston-Maryhill, was converted to bus operation and Denniston depot closed. At the same time route No 29, Broomhouse-Tollcross, was curtailed at the eastern end.

By early 1961 the tram fleet had declined to around 300 and only nine 'Standard' cars remained in service. These, and other elderly cars, were to have a temporary reprieve when, on 22 March 1961, a serious fire at Dalmarnock depot destroyed some 50 cars, including four of the 1954-built 'Coronations'. The traffic requirements led to many withdrawn cars, including some scheduled for preservation like No 1088, re-entering service. Ten days prior to the fire, on 11 March, route No 16, Scotstoun-Keppochhill Road, was converted to bus operation. Without the Dalmarnock fire this would have been the end for the 'Standards'. The period also saw the end of the Maryhill-Whiteinch shipyards specials. On 3 June routes Nos 18 (Springburn-Burnside) and 18A (Springburn-Shawfield) were converted to bus operation. At the same time route No 26 was cut back from Burnside to Farme Cross. After these closures all the cars reprieved after the Dalmarnock fire were again withdrawn — this time permanently. Included were the last of the 'Kilmarnock bogies'. By October 1961 the tram fleet had declined to only 188, only three routes remaining from the once great network.

On 10 March 1962 route No 15, Anderston Cross-Baillieston, was converted to bus operation. The last tram from Anderston Cross was 'Coronation' No 1242. At this stage Partick depot closed leaving one depot, Dalmarnock, to serve the remaining routes. On 2 June 1962 the penultimate route — No 26 Clydebank-Dalmarnock — was converted leaving some 60 cars in service. The end was not long in coming. On 1 September 1962 the last service cars operated on route No 9, Auchenshuggle-Dalmuir West. The last service car to Dalmuir West was No 1383 and the last car from Dalmuir West to Yoker, No 1313, carried a notice proclaiming 'The End of the Greatest British tramway'. No 1313 was also the last car to operate to Dalmarnock depot. Yet this was not to be the end of Glasgow's trams, as on the following three days farewell services operated on a shuttle from Anderston Cross to Auchenshuggle. A total of about eight cars were used on this service, the last in public service being No 1174. Following the cessation of the farewell services the closing procession marked the official closure of the system on 4 September. Twenty cars were used, including many that had been progressively restored for ultimate preservation. Even this was not the end of Glasgow's trams as an official last tram operated in Clydebank on 6 September 1962 and the withdrawn trams continued to run until 15 September from Dalmarnock to Coplawhill works for scrapping, the last car to make this journey being No 1165.

Inevitably a large number of Glasgow's trams have survived. On display in Glasgow, originally at Coplawhill and now at Kelvin Hall, are horse-tram No 543, single-deck 'Room & Kitchen' car No 672, 'Standard' cars Nos 779 and 1088, unique single-deck car No 1089, 'Coronation' No 1173 and 'Cunarder' No 1392. At Crich, there are two 'Standards' (Nos 22 and 812), two 'Kilmarnock Bogies' (No 1115 as originally built and the rebuilt No 1100), 'Coronation' No 1282 and 'Cunarder' No 1297. In addition Crich also houses restored Paisley car No 68 (Glasgow No 1068) and Liverpool No 869 (Glasgow No 1055) along with two ex-Glasgow works cars. Elsewhere in Britain, 'Standard' No 585 is on static display at the Science Museum in London and 'Coronation' No 1245 is at the East Anglian Transport Museum. The Summerlee Heritage Park at Coatbridge has recently acquired the bodies of the two ex-Duntocher cars, Nos 1016/7. Two Glasgow trams were exported: 'Standard' No 488 is on display in Paris and 'Coronation' No 1274 is at the Seashore museum in the United States.

Left:
Originally No 11 in the fleet of Paisley & District, No 1011 was acquired by Glasgow in 1923 and was one of 12 of the class to be converted from open-top double-deck to single-deck to operate on the Clydebank-Duntocher route. The Duntocher service was withdrawn on 3 December 1949 and No 1011 did not last much longer, being withdrawn in January 1950.

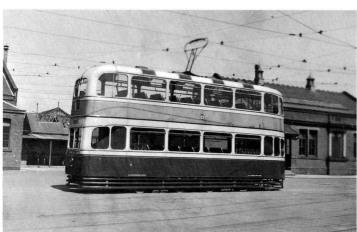

Left:
In the late 1940s Glasgow Corporation built a number of experimental tramcars including one, No 1005, as a single-ended streamlined car. Seen here at Newlands depot on 19 June 1949, No 1005 was finished in a striking and unique livery of two-tone blue and white. This livery was destined to be short-lived but the car remained single-ended until it was converted to a more orthodox style in 1956. Upon its withdrawal one bogie from the tram was retained for display in the Corporation's transport museum.

Glasgow Closures

28 August 1948	29 – Uddingston to Broomhouse
20 February 1949	2 – Polmadie to Provanmill
20 February 1949	19 – Springburn to Netherlee
2 April 1949	28 – Glenfield to Cross Stobs
3 December 1949	28 – Duntocher to Clydebank
15 June 1952	9 – Cut back from Carmyle to Causewayside station
4 July 1953	5 – Clarkston to Holmlea Road
2 August 1953	32 – Cut back from Bishopbriggs to Springburn
7 August 1955	Shawfield to Rutherglen Cross
29 September 1956	14 – Cross Stobs to Arden
3 November 1956	15 – Airdrie to Ballieston
3 November 1956	29 – Milngavie to Maryhill Park
3 November 1956	17 – Eastfield to Cambuslang
11 May 1957	21 – Elderslie
11 May 1957	28 – Renfrew Ferry to Glenfield
11 May 1957	4 – Renfrew to Hillington Road
11 May 1957	27 – Renfrew to Hillington Road (11 May 1957 marked the end of operation in Paisley and those services that operated to Paisley were cut back to the Glasgow boundary at Hillington Road)
16 November 1957	5/5A – Holmlea Road to Kelvinside
15 March 1958	24 – Anniesland to Langside
15 March 1958	27 – Hillington Road to Springburn
14 June 1958	7 – Bellahouston to Millerston
6 September 1958	4 – Hillington Road to Springburn
15 November 1958	12 – Mount Florida to Paisley Road Toll
15 November 1958	17 – Anniesland to Farme Cross
15 November 1958	22 – Crookston to Lambhill
15 November 1958	32 – Crookston to Bishopbriggs
14 March 1959	8 – Millerston to Rouken Glen
2 May 1959	33 – Springburn Circular
6 June 1959	25 – Bishopbriggs to Carnwadric/Rouken Glen
6 September 1959	16 – Cut back from Springburn to Keppochhill Road
31 October 1959	6 – Scotstoun to Alexandra Park
31 October 1959	14 – Kelvingrove to Arden
5 December 1959	31 – Lambhill to Merrylee
12 March 1960	1 – Dalmarnock to Dalmuir
12 March 1960	30 – Dalmarnock to Blairdardie
4 June 1960	3 – Moss Park to Park Road Kelvinbridge
4 June 1960	10 – Kelvinside to London Road
5 November 1960	23 – Ballieston to Maryhill
5 November 1960	29 – Tollcross to Broomhouse
11 March 1961	16 – Scotstoun to Keppochhill Road
3 June 1961	18 – Springburn to Burnside
3 June 1961	18A – Springburn to Shawfield
21 October 1961	29 – Maryhill to Tollcross
21 October 1961	26 – Cut back from Farme Cross to Dalmarnock
10 March 1962	15 – Anderston Cross to Baillieston
2 June 1962	26 – Clydebank to Dalmarnock
4 September 1962	9 – Dalmuir West to Auchenshuggle

Openings

7 November 1948	Carnwardric
31 July 1949	Blairdardie

Glasgow

Fleet Numbers	Date	Trucks/Bogies	Body	Withdrawn
1-5/7-14/6-141/144-50/2-345/347-95/7-678/ 80-737/9-44/6-8/51-761/3-82/4/6-94/796-820/ 2-35/7-868/70-86/8-93/5/97-901/3-6/8-11/ 914-22/27-31/4-6/938-48/50/1/4-6/958-65/ 7-70/3/4/7/980-1000/39/40/1050/1/88[1]	1899-1924	Brill 21E	Glasgow CT (901-80 Gloucester R&CW)	1946-62
143/679[2]	Rebuilt 1944 and 1943 respectively	Brill 21E	Glasgow CT	1959/58 respectively
821/36/923/6/75[3]	1939 (rebuilt)	Brill 21E	Glasgow CT	1950
1009/11-3/5-9/1022-4[4]	1923 (acquired)	Brush 'A-A' 6ft 6in	BEC	1949-51 (No 1017 retained for driver training)
1053-72[5]	1923 (acquired)	Fitted with Brill 21E 1924 and Brush/GCT 21E 1930	53-62 Brush, 63-72 Hurst Nelson	1951-53 (except No 1068 1960)
1089[6]	1925-26	Brill 77E1	Glasgow CT	1961
142, 1090-1140[7]	1927-29	142, 1090 Hurst Nelson, Maximum Traction. 1091-1140 Kilmarnock Engineering Co	142 and 1090 GCT, 1091-1120 Hurst Nelson, 1121-30 Pickering, 1131-40 Brush	1959-61 except: 1945 (142), 1954 (1109), 1952 (1128), 1962 (1100)
1141[8]	1936	EMB Lightweight bogies	Glasgow CT	1961
1142[9]	1937	M&T	Glasgow CT	1960
1143-1292[10]	1936-41	EMB Lightweight bogies	Glasgow CT	1959-62
1001-4[11]	1939-40	1001/2 M&T, 1003/4 EMB	GCT/Pickering	1959
6[12]	1941-42	Brush/GCT 21E	Glasgow CT	1959
1005[13]	1946-48	M&T HS44 bogies	Glasgow CT	1962
1293-1392[14]	1948-52	M&T bogies	Glasgow CT	1960-62
1393-8/1255/79[15]	1954	EMB bogies (ex-Liverpool)	Glasgow CT	1961-62
1006-16/8-38/1041-9/52-6[16]	1953-54 (acquired)	1006-16/8-30 M&T, 1031-8/41-9/ 52-6 EMB	Liverpool CT	1957-60

1 Glasgow 'Standard' cars. Much rebuilt over time, second most numerous class of British tram. Nos 27, 334, 409, 643 rebuilt after 1945. Nos 22, 488, 585, 779, 812 and 1088 preserved.
2 Rebuilt 'Standards'.
3 Single-deck rebuilds of 'Standard' cars.
4 Ex-Paisley & District Nos 9, 11 etc. New 1904. Originally open-top double-deck rebuilt to single-deck for use on Duntocher route 1924-25. Nos 1016/1017 preserved.
5 Ex-Paisley Nos 53-72 new in 1912-19. Rebuilt 1924 and 1930. No 1068 preserved.
6 Designed as high-speed bogie car — body altered 1932. Ran on Duntocher route 1932-49, stored 1949-51 then on John Brown works services till 1960. Restored again after Dalmarnock fire. Now preserved.
7 'Kilmarnock' bogies. No 1100 rebuilt 1941. Nos 1100 and 1115 preserved.
8 Experimental saloon car, rebuilt 1948 after Newlands fire.
9 Special livery to mark 1937 Coronation. Slight damage 1940 led to rebuild. Resilient wheels fitted 1945-52.
10 'Coronation' class. No 1168 rebuilt after fire November 1938. No 1275 rebuilt after Blitz. No 1220 rebuilt after fire 1942. No 1163 rebuilt top-deck 1941. No 1178 rebuilt 1944. Nos 1148/1239 rebuilt 1951 after

damage in Newlands fire. Nos 1153/6/1204/7/8/10/4/6/27/129/ 33/44/51 destroyed in Dalmarnock fire. Nos 1173/1245/74/82 preserved. No 1147 last tram scrapped.
11 Experimental 4-wheel cars. Nos 1001/3 received reconditioned trucks from Nos 97 and 413 respectively.
12 'Standard' No 6 destroyed in Blitz 13 March 1941. New car built as per 1001-4. Damaged Newlands fire 1948, rebuilt 1951.
13 Experimental single-ended car. Delivered in special blue livery, VAMBAC control, 1949 to standard livery. 1951 standard electrical equipment. 1956 converted to double-ended. One bogie retained for museum.
14 'Coronation II' or 'Cunarders'. Nos 1293, 1300-3/9/10/3/21/4- 6/2/7/44-7/53/4/7/65/8-70/6/6-8/91 destroyed Dalmarnock. Nos 1297 and 1392 preserved.
15 Replacement 'Coronation' cars paid for out of insurance following Newlands fire. 1961 certain cars re-equipped with standard Glasgow trucks. Nos 1393/5-7 destroyed Dalmarnock.
16 Ex-Liverpool streamliners built 1936-7. Were LCT 942/34/38/35/30/31/23/928/32/40/21/22/26/37/36/18/39/927/925/9 41/924/933/29/19/899/901/881/885/902/891/880/883/878/886/ 903/874/877/875/871/887/893/897/884/890/869 and 904 respectively. No 1055 (LCT 869) preserved.

Although appearing to the casual viewer a perfectly conventional electric tramway with overhead, and being generally regarded by enthusiasts as a cable tramway, the Great Orme Tramway is in fact neither of these. Wales's only surviving tramway is in effect a long funicular where both cars are permanently affixed to the same cable and the rising car is assisted up the hill by the descent of its twin.

During the late 19th century, prompted by the growing prosperity of the town, there were many proposals for the development of the Great Orme peak. The Great Orme is a limestone peninsula situated to the west of Llandudno. The peninsula is surrounded by the sea on three sides and the fourth side links it to the mainland. It was up this slope that the initial proposals were made for the construction of a funicular. It was generally regarded that the overall length of the line would be dangerous for a funicular built in one long stretch. Despite the doubts, however, the original Bill, the Great Orme Tramways Act of 1898, allowed for the construction of a single section and empowered the Great Orme Tramway Co to raise £25,000 in capital. Prior to the construction it was decided that two sections would be built on a gauge of 3ft 6in.

By 1900 all the necessary land had been bought and by October 1900 the company announced that the scheme would proceed. In March 1901 £21,000 of the authorised capital had been raised and construction started the following month. Although there were a number of problems to be overcome, the first test runs on the lower section were made on 23 May 1902 and, after an inspection on 30 July 1902, public services on the lower section started the next day. Work continued on the upper section and this was officially examined on 8 May 1903 and again, after certain changes, on 7 July 1903. Without any public ceremony, the upper section opened to the public on 8 July 1903. The lower section to Halfway measures some 872yd and the upper section, from Halfway to the Summit,

827yd. The average gradient for the lower section is 1 in 6.5 and that of the upper section 1 in 15.5. Apart from a minor alteration in the location of the lower terminus in Llandudno during 1903-04, the Great Orme Tramway was to have 30 years of relative success — a success rudely shattered by a fatal accident.

In 1932 one of the lower section cars ran away and two people were killed. The Inspector's report, issued in 1933, was highly critical of the tramway, highlighting the lack of an emergency brake and the inadequate nature of the drawbar that linked the tram to the cable. In February 1933 the Board held its Annual General Meeting at which it was reported that the tramway did not possess a reserve fund and that the insurance cover was inadequate to cover the claims resulting from the accident. The lack of proper cover led to the Sheriff taking possession of the line on 7 June 1933, and at an emergency meeting of the Board held the same day it was decided to make a petition to the High Court to seek the compulsory winding-up of the company. This Order was made six weeks later on 24 July. This might have sounded the death knell for the tramway, but the creditors, at the creditors' meeting held on 25 August 1933, decided that their best option was to continue with brake tests (to provide an emergency braking system for the trams) and to endeavour to sell the tramway as a going concern.

After the successful conclusion of these tests, the tramway reopened on 17 May 1934 and was sold to a syndicate in December of that year. The syndicate created the Great Orme Railway Ltd in March 1935.

In 1947 Llandudno Council decided to exercise its option, enshrined under the 1898 Act, to purchase the tramway. After a disagreement over price, the council exercised its powers of compulsory purchase in November 1948, backdated to 31 March 1948, and the transfer took effect from 1 January 1949. The Great Orme Railway Ltd, with its primary purpose now out of its control, was wound up in 1950.

Under council ownership a certain number of changes were made. A second overhead wire was added to the upper section in 1949. Much more significant was the changeover from steam to electric power at the winding house at Halfway. It was estimated that the ending of the annual use of 250 tons of coke could save £1,400 per annum and, as a result, in 1956 a contract was placed with English Electric for the provision of electric power. 1957 was to prove the last season that steam was used.

98

In 1962 all four of the trams were repainted in bright blue livery. The livery was again changed in 1967 when the blue was changed to royal blue. This livery was to last a further 10 years until 1977 when a new livery of trafalgar blue was adopted, coinciding with the alteration of the side lettering along the cars to read 'Great Orme Tramway' — between 1934 and 1977 the lettering had read 'Great Orme Tramways'. Other cosmetic changes were made, such as the construction of a brick waiting shelter at Halfway in 1965. The tramway remained a popular tourist attraction.

By the late 1980s, however, not all was right. Pressures on local government finance meant that the tramway was beginning to look careworn

Below:
With Llandudno Bay as a backdrop, lower section car No 4 heads up Old Road towards Halfway with a full load on 12 August 1953. *H. C. Casserley*

and there were increasing rumours that Llandudno was seek to dispose of it. For a while it seemed that Bolton Tramways Ltd, which had previously restored Bolton No 66, would take over the operations, but eventually, in early 1990, it was announced that operation and maintenance would pass to the Direct Services Department of Llandudno Council.

Immediately work started on restoring the tramway. Track was relaid and new radio communication equipment was installed. This equipment allowed for the removal of the overhead since the overhead was only ever provided to allow for communication. (It is intended that certain sections of the overhead will remain, but this will be for cosmetic, rather than practical, purposes.) With the major investment going into the tramway, Great Orme, Wales's only surviving tramway, can look forward to its centenary with confidence. During 1991 operation of the tram changed to one-man control with dead-man (vigilance) control. Early 1992 witnessed the strange sight of the two upper section cars being taken into Llandudno for major overhual — the first time Nos 6/7 had been away from their section since the line opened. It also appears likely that all the overhead will be restored, although purely for cosmetic reasons.

Great Orme

Fleet Numbers	Date	Trucks/Bogies	Body	Withdrawn
1	1902	Hurst Nelson	Hurst Nelson	—
2	1903	Hurst Nelson	Hurst Nelson	—

Lower section.
Upper section.

The electric tramway from Grimsby to Immingham, the last complete tramway to close in England, was unusual for a number of reasons. Firstly, it was the only tramway to be operated after 1945 by one of the main line railways (with the slightly atypical exception of the Ryde Pier Tramway); secondly, because it was railway-owned, it underwent an even more convoluted closure procedure than the majority of other tramways; and, finally, it was effectively an inter-urban tramway possessing some of the longest tramcars ever to operate in Britain.

By the end of the 19th century, the Great Central Railway had come to dominate railway transport in north Lincolnshire. However, it still lacked access to a deep water port through which it could ship out the coal mined at the Midlands pits that the Great Central Railway served. It therefore decided to construct a completely new dock complex at Immingham, some six miles north of Grimsby. As the docks would be a completely 'green field' development, the pool of labour from which the dock employees would be drawn were situated in Grimsby and there would need to be some form of transport linking the new docks with this source of labour.

The actual construction of the dock facility was governed by the Humber Commercial Railway & Dock Act of 1904. The Great Central Railway, realising the need for transport links, obtained a Light Railway Order on 15 January 1906 for the Grimsby District Light Railway. Initial thoughts were that the light railway would operate as two sections — one, which would be electrified, from Alexandra Dock in Grimsby along Corporation Road to Pyewipe and from there steam-operated to Immingham. Work commenced in late 1906 on the actual construction, but before this was completed the decision was made in 1909 that the line would be electrified throughout. Parallel with the eventual Grimsby & Immingham Electric Railway, there was also constructed a steam-operated freight line, and it was over this that the first passenger services — a steam rail-motor — operated between 3 January 1910 and 14 May 1912. This freight line remains in use to this day as part of the complex of lines serving the Grimsby and Immingham area.

In March 1910 the contract for the new trams was let to the Brush company and the first eight cars were delivered in late 1911 (Brush having stored them until then). 1910 also witnessed the completion of the street section (along Corporation Road) and the opening of the first phase of the docks. The line was completed throughout to Immingham Halt in mid-1911 and was inspected on 22 November 1911. Public services were started on 15 May 1912, the day after the last temporary rail-motor services had operated. As the line was built by the Great Central Railway to carry dockers to the Great Central-owned docks at Immingham, the number of fare-paying passengers (as opposed to those carried free as part of their employment) was relatively small. This was not, necessarily, a problem when the whole operation was owned by one company as was the case with the Great Central and later with the LNER. However, after 1948, with the nationalisation of both the railways and the docks, the railways found the subsidy paid to the docks for the carriage of dockworkers free of charge an increasing burden, and this was a major contributory factor in the line's eventual closure.

At Immingham Halt the tramway stopped before the actual docks complex, and so in 1911 the Great Central obtained a further Act allowing for two extensions. One, which was built, took the tramway into the actual docks, while the second, towards Immingham village, was only constructed in part (along Queens Road) and never used regularly. The docks extension opened on 17 November 1913 and the abortive Queens Road route was inspected two years later on 20 July 1915.

In 1923 the Great Central Railway, along with the Grimsby & Immingham Electric Railway, passed to the newly-formed London & North Eastern Railway. The Grimsby & Immingham was one of two electric tramways that the LNER inherited, the second being the Cruden Bay line in Scotland. To the casual viewer, the most significant change after 1923 was that the trams appeared in the LNER teak livery, rather than the reddish brown that the Great Central had adopted. The 1920s were a period of little change for the line. At the Grimsby end, Corporation Bridge was rebuilt between 1925 and 1928, as had been long expected, but the tentative

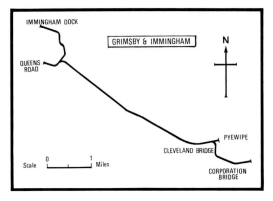

IMMINGHAM DOCK

GRIMSBY & IMMINGHAM   N

QUEENS ROAD

PYEWIPE

CLEVELAND BRIDGE

Scale 0   1 Miles

CORPORATION BRIDGE

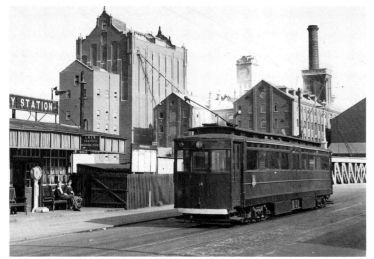

scheme to link the line with Grimsby's electric tramcars came to nought as Grimsby's policy was to abandon the tramways it had inherited from the Great Grimsby Street Tramways Co in 1925. The powers to build the link line lapsed in 1931. Between 1927 and 1930 the LNER operated a local service over the street section, as a means of combating bus competition, but this was not a great success.

The 1930s were to witness the first substantial changes to the composition of the fleet with the withdrawal of the four shorter vehicles (Nos 5-8). Whilst the ultimate fate of three of the cars is uncertain, the fourth (No 5) became a works car, in which guise it survived until being replaced by one of the ex-Gateshead cars in 1955. World War 2 was to see a number of significant developments. Firstly, Grimsby Corporation bought a large area of land between the tramway and the coast, upon which a major industrial estate was constructed. This had the effect of stimulating yet further the passenger demands made upon the tramway, and was a further bone of contention later in the tramway's history when the companies which had established themselves along the line were unwilling to contribute to the operating costs of the service. Also during the war, the irrelevant section of track in Queens Road was dewired. The points at Immingham Halt leading to the section were removed in 1945 and the route's traction colums were recovered in 1947.

On 1 January 1948 the LNER was nationalised. Again the most immediate change was the appearance of a new livery, with some of the trams reappearing in brown. By the late 1940s, there were, however, indications that all was not well with the tramway. As elsewhere, wartime

conditions had led to a decline in maintenance, in particular the street section was causing grave concern, and the increasing traffic loads required additional cars. In 1948 and 1949 there were talks between British Railways and the Corporation over the future of the street tramway, and in early 1949 Grimsby's Highway Committee sent a deputation to the Railway Executive seeking the street tramways curtailment 'in the interests of the safety of traffic and pedestrians'. The talks failed as British Railways were only prepared to countenance abandonment if the Corporation agreed to fund the reinstatement work. With closure no longer an immediate option, the street tramway section was relaid in part.

The question of additional rolling stock was also partially solved by the acquisition, in early 1948, of three single-deck cars from Newcastle. These cars were, however, destined to have a relatively short life in Grimsby, being replaced in the early 1950s by the second-hand cars acquired from Gateshead. In 1951 there were two significant changes to the fleet. Firstly, the Railway Executive decreed that all electric vehicles were to be painted in green, and this led to the Grimsby cars appearing in their fourth livery. Secondly, the opportunity was taken with the abandonment of Gateshead's trams to acquire a number of their single-deck cars. A total of 19 cars were acquired; of the 19, 17 eventually entered service (at least two in their original Gateshead livery of red and cream), one (Gateshead No 4) was destroyed in an accident on delivery (the crane lifting the car's body off the railway truck, on which the body had been delivered, collapsed on top of the car) and one (Gateshead No 17) was converted into a breakdown car in place of the remaining original short car. The arrival of the Gateshead cars allowed for the withdrawal of the ex-Newcastle cars and the first of the original Grimsby long cars.

For the next few years little changed on the tramway, but in February 1955 the Clerk to Grimsby Rural District Council told members of the Town Council that 1955 was one of the years in which the council was empowered to acquire the street tramway. On 20 June 1955 British Railways notified the Council that the street tramway was available, free of charge, for replacement by Corporation buses. The offer was accepted and six second-hand buses were acquired. Despite considerable opposition the street tramway section was closed on 30 June 1956. Services now ran from Pyewipe, where a connection was made with the replacement buses, to Immingham. No trams were withdrawn at this stage since the peak period still required a total of 19 cars. Despite this curtailment, investment continued to go into the tramway, with heating being installed in certain of the cars in 1957 and the rebuilding of two cars (Nos 1 and 14) after a fatal collision in January 1958. In 1957 the power station at Immingham, which had powered the tramway from the start, was reduced to stand-by status, and normal power was obtained from the commercial supply. The power station was finally closed in 1958.

Also, in 1958, the question of the cost of operating the line arose. As a result of the line's history a large proportion of the passengers travelled free, and the losses incurred by British Railways in operating the line were increasing. A request for financial support from the local industries that made use of the line failed and British Railways applied for closure of the line in July 1958. At the subsequent inquiry British Railways reported that revenue from the line totalled £23,000 as opposed to direct operating costs of £72,000. There was, however, strong opposition, much of it the result of the County Council's refusal to build a direct road between the two points. The inadequacy of alternative transport links led all the involved local authorities, in particular Grimsby Town Council, to come out against closure. At the Transport Users Consultative Committee meeting, held at Grimsby on 24 April 1959, a compromise was reached, whereby the docks would be served by buses using the indirect road, supplemented by the trams at peak hours. This new arrangement came

Below:
Grimsby & Immingham No 29, ex-Gateshead No 1 dating from 1923, is pictured outside Pyewipe depot. *J. W. C. Halliday*

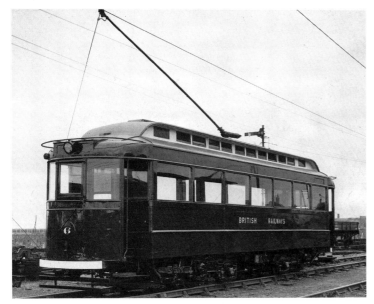

into effect on 28 September 1959, thereby reducing the number of trams required to a maximum of 10.

Inevitably, gradual improvements were made to the condition of the road (although no direct road has even in 1991 been built), and patronage of the tramway continued to decline. It came as little surprise, therefore, that British Railways announced closure for a second time on 29 December 1960, going one stage further on this occasion by stating that even if permission were refused, the electric cars would be withdrawn and replaced by a new diesel service. Grimsby Corporation, worried by the possible impact of the proposed diesel service on its own bus services, this time agreed to support the closure. At the meeting of the TUCC held in Grimsby on 21/22 February 1961 there were only 10 objectors, and, inevitably, consent was given to closure. British Railways announced that the last day of operation would be 1 July 1961 — the first day upon which the TUCC had allowed clo-

sure — and closure took place as scheduled. The official last car was one of the original ex-Great Central trams, No 4.

Of the trams, one of the original Great Central cars (No 14) was acquired on behalf of the national collection. Two other cars (ex-Gateshead Nos 5 and 10) were also preserved and have now been restored to their original condition. The remaining trams were all dismantled by 1963.

Grimsby & Immingham Closures

30 June 1956	Cleveland Bridge to Corporation Bridge
1 July 1961	Cleveland Bridge to Immingham (Queen's Road, Immingham, lifted in 1955)

Last tram: No 4

Grimsby & Immingham

Fleet Numbers	Date	Trucks/Bogies	Body	Withdrawn
1-5/9-16[1]	1911-15	Brush	Great Central Railway/Brush	1952-61 (6-8 withdrawn 1931)
6-8[2]	1948 (acquired)	Peckham P25	Hurst Nelson	1954
17-33[3]	1951-52 (acquired)	Brill 39E	Brush/Gateshead	1961
DE320224[4]	1951 (acquired)	Brill 39E	Gateshead	1961

1 No 5 used as repair car. Nos 15/6 rebuilt 1951-52.
2 Ex-Newcastle Nos 29, 42, 77 respectively. New 1902 and rebuilt 1930-33.
3 Ex-Gateshead Nos 57, 18, 9, 5, 56, 7, 20, 3, 6, 10, 16, 58, 1, 8, 11, 60 and 59. New 1921-28.
4 Ex-Gateshead No 17. New 1925. Gateshead No 4 was also acquired but was destroyed in transit.

Situated on a rocky promontory northeast of Dublin, the Hill of Howth tramway was destined to be Ireland's last tramway when it closed in 1959 — a closure which had been threatened for more than 30 years.

Although commercial development had seen a harbour built at Howth as early as 1807 and the building of the Dublin & Drogheda Railway branch to Howth West Pier in May 1847, the Howth peninsula remained essentially an attraction for visitors to its 560ft-high summit. From 1867 a horse-bus service linked the summit with the branch line and in 1894 the Clontarf & Hill of Howth Tramway Co announced that it was seeking powers to construct a number of tramways, including a line to Howth Summit. After several years of dispute with the Great Northern Railway (Ireland), which had taken over the Dublin & Drogheda Railway and which had developed its own scheme for a line, the Clontarf & Hill of Howth company eventually got an Order enabling it to construct a route from Dollymount to Howth East Pier. This route was ultimately operated by Dublin United Tramways.

Having thwarted the efforts of the Clontarf & Hill of Howth Co, the GNR(I) then sought its own powers to construct a tramway. The Great Northern Railway (Ireland) Act of 1897 enabled the company to build a tramway of some 5½ miles in length of the gauge of 5ft 3in. A further Act of 1900 allowed for a slight deviation over the actual alignment, but despite this construction was still further delayed due to arguments over land ownership.

The official opening of the section from Sutton to Summit took place on 17 June 1901 and was followed on 1 August 1901 by the remaining section from Summit to Howth. To operate the new service, eight cars with Brill 22E trucks were acquired from Brush. These were followed, in 1902, by two further cars, Nos 9 and 10, built by G. F. Milnes on Peckham trucks. The final tram

acquired, No 11, was built between 1905 and 1908 and was used solely for works purposes. It was rebuilt at various times during its career. The depot and power generating station was constructed at Sutton.

The tramway had cost some £113,000 to construct, and whilst it regularly made an operating profit this was never enough to cover the interest on the capital costs, with the consequence that the tramway never made money. This was primarily the result of the failure of the Howth peninsula to develop commercially except as a tourist attraction. Inevitably, therefore, harsh economic reality decreed that the line was kept under almost constant scrutiny and in the years prior to the outbreak of World War 2 the tramway was subject to no less than six reports on its future. Initially, ideas of replacing the tramway with buses was rejected on the grounds that the roads (with gradients of up to 1:8½) were unsuitable for bus operation. Then, by the early 1930s, when bus technology had improved, the GNR(I) had become sufficiently impecunious to be unable to afford to buy replacement buses. Efforts were made to improve the tramway's financial position (for example, the unsuccessful testing of a railbus over the line in 1934) but, with the support of a number of the GNR(I)'s senior personnel, the tramway continued to battle on in its traditional form. However, efforts to reduce expenditure by lowering the pay of the staff led to a strike in 1933. This was one of only a few occasions when the service was actually suspended — the next, between June and September 1944 — was the result of an acute coal shortage in the Irish Republic and led to the temporary replacement of the trams by buses. It was an unfortunate omen of what was to follow.

By the early 1950s the railways of Ireland were finding the financial situation an ever-increasing strain. On 1 September 1953 the governments in both Northern Ireland and the Irish Republic took over the GNR(I) and replaced it with the Great Northern Railway Board. Amongst the first acts of the new administration was the posting on 28 January 1954 of notices stating that the tramway would close on 31 March 1954. There was a storm of protest, and the state of the road was again to come to the tramway's rescue. The Irish government's Department of Industry & Commerce agreed to underwrite the losses that the tramway was making for at least two years whilst the road was improved. In early 1957 the first trials with replacement buses were undertaken. It was, however, to be a further two years before the final withdrawal of the trams.

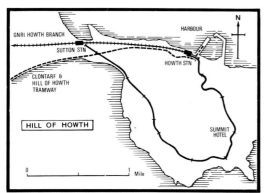

Above:
Cars Nos 4 and 7 are seen at Howth Summit. Both are in the GNR(I) livery of blue and ivory. No 4 is now preserved in Belfast. *R. C. Ludgate*

1957 did witness, though, the first casualty amongst the tram fleet when No 8 was withdrawn due to body rot. It was not, however, scrapped until after the line's closure. On 30 September 1958 the Great Northern Railway Board was dissolved and its assets were split between Coras Iompair Eireann in the south and the Ulster Transport Authority in the north. Paradoxically, the Hill of Howth tramway passed to the control of the Road Passenger Section of CIE. On 14 May 1959 CIE announced that the Howth tramway would close with effect from 31 May 1959. After an eventful evening, No 9 operated the final service — slightly curtailed due to vandalism which had seen a fishplate removed on a sharp curve — before returning to Sutton depot to await its fate. Almost immediately, work started on the dismantling of the line, initially with the assistance of tram No 11, and the first track was lifted in November 1959. Work on demolition was completed in January 1960.

Inevitably, the closure of the Hill of Howth tramway had stimulated a great deal of interest (not all of it positive — as witnessed by various acts of vandalism during the last day) and it was inevitable that many of the trams would be saved for preservation. No 2 was exported to the Orange Empire Trolley Museum in California,

where, regauged to 4ft 8½in, it has operated. No 4 is preserved in the Belfast Transport Museum in the company of the surviving Belfast trams. No 9, after an initial period of storage in Dublin, was passed to the Transport Museum Society of Ireland. No 10 was acquired by the Tramway Museum Society at Crich and was regauged to 4ft 8½in. After restoration, keeping the mahogany livery that Nos 9 and 10 retained virtually throughout their operational life (in contrast to the remainder of the fleet that were painted Oxford blue and cream after 1929), No 10 was one of the most impressive exhibits at the Blackpool Centenary celebrations in 1985. A

Hill of Howth Closure

31 May 1959	Sutton station to Howth station
Last tram: No 9	

further two trams, Nos 3 and 11, were stored at the St James' Gate Brewery in Dublin until 1965 when, unfortunately, they were scrapped. No 6 was scrapped, although the truck frames were retained and used in the restoration of Manchester single-deck tram No 765.

The depot at Sutton, which had been modified in 1951 as part of a possible programme to maintain the newly-introduced GNR(I) railbuses there, continued to be used after the tramway's closure, although only for storage of surplus steam locomotives and departmental use.

Hill of Howth

Fleet Numbers	Date	Trucks/Bogies	Body	Withdrawn
1-8[1]	1901	Brill 22E Maximum Traction	Brush	1957-59
9/10[2]	1902	Peckham 14 D-5 Maximum Traction	G. F. Milnes	1959
11[3]	1905-08	Brill 22E	GNR(I)	1959

1 No 2 preserved in USA, now regauged to 4ft 8½in. No 4 preserved in Belfast. Bogies from No 6 used in restoration of Manchester No 765. No 3 stored until 1965 and then scrapped.
2 No 9 preserved in Dublin. No 10 preserved by TMS and regauged to 4ft 8½in.
3 Works car. Stored until 1965 then scrapped.

The city of Kingston-upon-Hull was the last tramway operator in either the East or North Riding of Yorkshire. It was one of a number of systems that had witnessed a major contraction prior to the outbreak of World War 2 but which survived, just, into the postwar era.

The first trams to operate in Hull appeared on 9 January 1875 when horse-trams were introduced on the Beverley Road route. Further extensions to the horse-tram network saw routes established along Spring Bank, to the Pier, along Hessle Road, Anlaby Road and Holderness Road over the next few years. There followed, on 22 May 1889, the introduction of steam-trams along Great Union Street and Hedon Road to serve Marfleet.

All the original tram operations, both horse and steam, were company-owned, but in 1896 Hull Corporation gained parliamentary powers to borrow £350,000 and to construct an electric tramway system. On 15 October 1896 the horse-trams of the Hull Street Tramway Co were acquired and work started to convert the routes to electric traction. The new electric services along Anlaby Road and Hessle Road were inaugurated on 5 July 1899, and later the same year the steam-trams of the Drypool & Marfleet Street Tramway Co were purchased. 1899 also witnessed the final horse-tram; the final steam-tram operated less than two years later in January 1901. The initial electric track was unusual (Doncaster Corporation being probably the only other example) in having a central groove rather than the more normal off-centre one.

Over the next quarter of a century the electric tramway system expanded to a total of some 21 route miles. The final extension (to Cottingham Road) was opened in 1927. Apart from the diversion of the track over the new North Bridge in 1931, this extension was the last positive development to Hull's tramway system. The first abandonment, to the Pier, occurred on 5 January 1931, but a much more significant event was the signing of the co-ordination agreement with East Yorkshire Motor Services in 1934. This agreement led to the withdrawal of a number of routes and extensions, including the recently-opened Cottingham Road line, two of which (along Anlaby Road and Hessle Road) were well provided with reserved track.

Initially the bus (which had first appeared in Hull in 1909) was used for the replacement services, and a proposal to introduce trolleybuses, made in 1929, was rejected. A later proposal to introduce trolleybuses was, however, passed and the first trolleybuses were introduced on 23 July 1937. At the outbreak of World War 2 three routes remained served by trams: H, along Holderness Road; A, along Anlaby Road; and D, along Hessle Road. As a port city, Hull, was a major target for the Luftwaffe and during the war serious damage was sustained on several occasions. In one attack alone, in 1941, 43 buses were destroyed. Although withdrawal of tram services

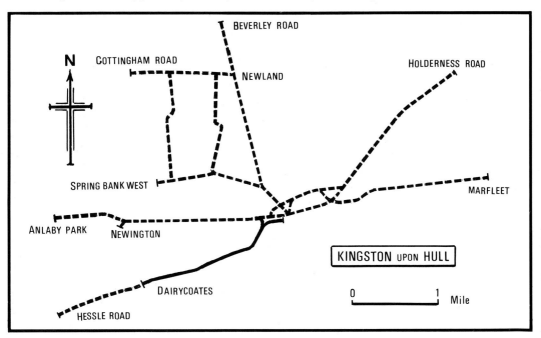

Left:
Hull No 103, built by Milnes in 1903, underwent many changes during its 42-year life with Hull. Originally delivered as an open-top tram, it, along with the rest of the batch, had been fully enclosed during the 1930s. Withdrawn between 1942 and 1945, many of the batch, but not No 103, were to get a second life for a few years in Leeds. *Author's collection*

during the war was not common, two of Hull's did, in fact, succumb: Holderness Road on 17 February 1940 and Anlaby Road on 5 September 1942. As a result, 32 trams were made surplus and these were sold to Leeds. Both routes were replaced by extensions to the trolleybus network.

By the end of World War 2, one route and some dozen trams remained operating out of Liverpool Street depot and works. But Hull's trams survived into the postwar era by barely a month. The final tram, No 169 suitably decorated, ran on the Hessle Road route on 30 June 1945. After closure a further 10 trams were sold to Leeds.

Fortunately, two ex-Hull cars survive: No 96, a 1901 car converted into a snowplough in 1933 and sold to Leeds in 1945, is now operating on the Heaton Park tramway in Manchester, albeit as a single-decker; whilst No 132, one of a batch of 14 built in 1909/10 and also sold to Leeds, is now preserved in its home town. The National Tramway Museum also owns an unrestored Hull tram body.

Below:
Hull No 142 was one of a batch of 24 cars produced by Brush in 1912. All bar five were fully enclosed between 1921 and 1935. No 142 passed to Leeds in 1945 (as No 478) and was finally withdrawn in 1951. *G. E. Baddeley*

Hull Closure

30 June 1945	Osborne Street to Dairycoates

Last tram: No 169

Hull

Fleet Numbers	Date	Trucks/Bogies	Body	Withdrawn
103/5/11/3[1]	1903	Brill 21E	Milnes	1945
117/9[2]	1909	M&G 21EM. 117 received Brill 21E and 120 a Peckham P22 in 1930s	UEC	1945
123[3]	1909-10	M&G 21EM retrucked to Peckham P22 1933-35	Hull CT	1945
139/42/6/8/51/160[4]	1912	M&G 21EM: Retrucked 1933-35: Peckham P22 138-40/50/3/9/60; Brill 21E 142/7/52/5/6/8	Brush	1945
169/70/3/5/6[5]	1915	Brill 21E; all later retrucked, 163/4/73/4 on Peckham P22	Brush	1945

1 Batch 102-16. Delivered as open-top, top covers fitted before entering service. Fully-enclosed 1920-31. Nos 104/5/9/11/13-6 to Leeds 1942-45.
2 Batch 117-22. Balconies enclosed 1916-19. Fully-enclosed 1933-35. No 117 to Leeds 1945.
3 Batch 123-36. Fully-enclosed 1920-31. Nos 124-36 to Leeds 1942. No 123 to Leeds 1945. No 132 preserved.
4 Batch 137-60. Balconies enclosed 1916. Nos 138-40/2/4/6-56/8-60 fully-enclosed 1921-35. Nos 138-40/2/7/50/2-6/8-60 to Leeds 1942-45.
5 Batch 161-80. Nos 163/4/9/70/3-6/8 fully-enclosed 1921-35. Nos 163/4/73/4 to Leeds 1942/45.

Of the four main operators in the West Yorkshire area, only Leeds adopted the standard gauge for its tramway system – although this did not preclude through running to its neighbour Bradford – and appropriately Leeds was the last operator in the area to close. It was also the penultimate city system in England. Arguably, with its development of its single-deck cars in the early 1950s and with its planned programme of subways, Leeds could have been the city to have bucked the abandonment trend, but political factors led to the ultimate demise of the trams in 1959.

Under the Leeds Tramway Order of 1871, William and Daniel Busby were granted powers to build and operate five routes. The first of these, to Headingley, was opened on 16 September 1871 and subsequently extended. In 1872 the powers were transferred to the Leeds Tramway Co and further routes were opened to Kirkstall (on 1 April 1872) and to Hunslet, Marsh Lane and Chapeltown (all during 1874). These early routes were all horse-tram operated, but on 25 October 1877 the first experiments with steam traction were undertaken. Such was the success

that steam was soon introduced to the Headingley and Wortley routes (the latter only opening in July 1878 at the same time as the line to Meanwood). Further lines were opened in 1890 to Roundhay and to Beckett Street. During 1890 Leeds Corporation was approached by a representative of the American Thomson-Houston Co who offered to take over the Roundhay service and operate it with electricity. The offer was accepted and the new service was started on 29 October 1891 – the first line in the British Isles to be powered by conventional overhead.

In February 1894 Leeds Corporation took over the operation of the tramways and progressively replaced the horse-trams and steam-trams. This work also included the takeover and modernisation of the Roundhay route and the first of the new electric services, linking Kirkstall with Roundhay, was inaugurated in 1897. Work proceeded rapidly on the conversion of the system so that the last horse-tram (along Kirkstall Road) operated in October 1901 and the last steam-tram (to Stanningley) in April 1902. Electric lines opened during this period included Harehills on

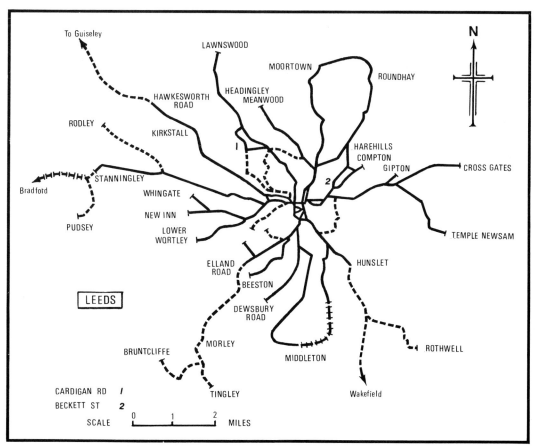

Left:
Leeds No 20, seen here in City Square on 18 September 1948, was one of a batch of 75 cars delivered from Brush in 1926-27 and fitted with EMB Pivotal trucks. These trucks were not wholly successful, and a number of these 'Chamberlain' cars were fitted with replacement Peckham P35 trucks after 1946. Generally those cars, such as No 20, which retained their original trucks, were the first to be withdrawn during the early 1950s.

2 June 1900, Beeston and Hyde Park (via Woodhouse Street) on 18 March 1901, Whingate and New Inn on 10 January 1902 and Stanningley on 2 April 1902. In 1904 trams from the West Riding company started to operate a through service from Wakefield via Hunslet. Over the next few years expansion was rapid so that by 1908 some 282 tramcars were in service. In 1907 the unique through service to Bradford, involving the change of gauge in Stanningley, was introduced. Already, however, the first motorbus services had been introduced (in 1905). Along with Bradford, Leeds introduced the first trolleybus services to Britain – the first route, from Aire Street to New Farnley, being opened in June 1911, further extensions outside the city boundary to Otley following as a feeder to the tram service. Leeds was not to persist with the experiment, unlike Bradford, and the trolleybuses were progressively replaced by buses between 1926 and 1928.

The tramways continued to expand, with many of the new extensions outside the city's boundaries. For example, on 26 May 1909 the Horsforth route was extended to Yeadon (later this route was further extended to Guiseley) and on 5 July 1911 the Elland Road route was extended to Morley. Other extensions were built in the actual city, such as that from West Park to Lawnswood on 8 April 1913 and the Halton branch on 10 May 1915. After World War 1, the tramways continued to expand, although the lack of wartime maintenance had led to the end of the through service to Bradford in 1918, as the growth of suburban council housing estates required new services. On 21 May 1922 the Harehills route was extended to Oakwood, and from there it was further extended on 29 July 1923 to Roundhay to form a circular route. On 10 November a branch

off the Dewsbury Road route was opened to Middleton Arms – the first stage of a second circular route. April 1924 saw the opening, in two stages, of the Temple Newsam line. The period also, however, saw the first abandonment when the Whitehall Road route, which was paralleled by the first trolleybus service, was closed on 15 June 1922. The early 1920s also saw the first developments in the use of motorbuses on services to the suburbs and eventually as trolleybus replacements.

The 1930s were to be years of considerable change in Leeds, which saw developments both positive and negative for the tramcars. Much of this reflected the pro-tram views of the new General Manager, W. Vane Morland, who was appointed in succession to R. L. Horsfield in 1932. The positive aspects included the transfer of certain street sections to reserved track – such as that from West Park to Lawnswood in 1938 and the Halton route in 1936 – the continuing construction of new routes (such as that to Gipton on 11 September 1936), the gradual conversion of the overhead to allow for the use of bow collectors, and the construction of many new tramcars, including the 'Horsfields' and the 'Middleton Bogies'. In addition, numerous extensions were authorised and, without the outbreak of war, would have been constructed. As it was, certain track work was undertaken during the war. This allowed for the opening of the Balm Road-Belle Isle section on 22 July 1940 and the completion of the doubling of the Compton Road route in 1942.

On the negative side, 1932 witnessed the decision to withdraw all tramway routes outside the city's boundaries and all those routes served by predominantly single-track sections. The first section to go, the routes beyond Thwaite Gate (Hunslet) to Rothwell and Wakefield (thus ending the West Riding service) were withdrawn on 31 May 1932. If it had not been for the existence of a depot at Thwaite Gate and the problems of turning buses at that location, the route to Hunslet would also have succumbed at this date. As it was, the Hunslet route was destined to last for a further 27 years. On 30 January 1934 trams were diverted away from the single-track lines along Belle Vue Road and Woodhouse Street. Later in 1934, on 16 October, the routes beyond Hawksworth to Yeadon and Guiseley were abandoned. The following year saw the services to Morley cut back to the borough boundary on 22 January. A year later, on 26 March 1936, the Accommodation Road route was abandoned. This

was followed on 1 May 1937 by the Domestic Street section. The last two prewar closures, to Rodley and the Stanningley-Pudsey section, occurred on 17 May 1938 and 3 December 1938 respectively. A number of single-track sections remained, but these were closed quickly after the cessation of hostilities.

The closures in the 1930s dramatically improved the financial position of the tramcars, with the result that there were no increases in fares between 1928 and 1944, whilst Vane Morland's judicious fleet acquisitions, including three ex-LPTB 'HR/2s' in 1939, helped to modernise the fleet. The Leeds tramways were not severely affected by the war, although the urgent need for tramcars gave a temporary reprieve to many trams that would otherwise have been replaced. Certain track work was continued and the fleet was further strengthened by the acquisition of the first batches of ex-Hull cars in 1942. A further second-hand car was acquired from Sunderland. This tram, Sunderland No 85, was eventually destined to form the basis of single-deck tram No 600.

In 1945 Leeds had a fleet of more than 450 cars operating over some 52 route miles. It was, like many other cities, faced by the twin problems of postwar reconstruction and lack of resources. Prior to the outbreak of World War 2 the city authorities had already started to address the problem of congestion with, for example, the opening of a major new thoroughfare, the Headrow, in 1933, and the first proposals for tramway subways in 1938-39. It is clear that the authorities in Leeds remained pro-tram; an exhibition held in early 1943 demonstrated a number of proposed extensions, and when the Reconstruction Committee was established in January 1944, public transport was to have a pivotal role. In his two reports to the Committee, produced in April and June 1944, Vane Morland looked to the future of the tramway system. Whilst he accepted that a number of on-street sections would disappear, he envisaged that the central area would be served by tram subways. Initially these were to be con-

Left:
Just prior to the outbreak of World War 2, Leeds acquired three ex-LPTB 'HR/2' trams, Nos 1881, 1883 and 1886. They were renumbered 277-79 by Leeds. Here the last of the three is seen on 17 July 1949 on route 6 to Meanwood. The tram is seen here in its prewar livery of pale blue; No 279 was to retain this livery until mid-1953 when it was repainted in the postwar red livery — as such it was the last tram to run in the prewar colours.
V. C. Jones/Ian Allan Library

Above:
Prior to its acquisition of 90 surplus 'Feltham' trams from London, Leeds tested ex-LPTB No 2099 in 1949 in its original London Transport livery and retaining its LPTB number. It is seen here in Kirkstall Road depot in August 1950 prior to its repainting as Leeds No 501. At least one enthusiast was reported to have amended his log-book to include all the numbers between 500 and 2100 on seeing No 2099 in operation in Leeds!

Above:
Very few tramway extensions were constructed in Britain in the postwar era. One of the most significant was the completion of the Middleton-Belle Isle section to form a circular route. The work in progress in track-laying is seen here in May 1949; the line opened throughout on 28 August 1949 and was to close finally a decade later.

structed on the cut-and-cover principle, but following discussions with the Civil Engineers Department, deep level tubes were settled upon. In November 1944 the City Council went public with the subway proposals. In the event, little was achieved and over the next seven years the tramways gradually drifted to the point where abandonment became the inevitable policy.

The initial enthusiasm for the tramway subways were tempered by the need for reconditioning the existing tramways, the general air of austerity and the increasingly dire financial position of the transport department. The average age of the tramcar fleet was 19 years in 1945 – a position not helped by the acquisition of the elderly trams from Hull in 1942 and a further batch of 10 in 1945, although this did allow for the scrapping of a number of the older cars in October 1945 at Torre Road. Before real progress could be made with the reconstruction, Leeds was hit by a major transport strike. This occurred between 25 September and 3 October 1945. As with earlier transport strikes, services were operated temporarily by members of the public – although this was to be last occasion when such strike-breaking occurred on a British tramway. Also in October, the Labour Party achieved power at the local elections; at this stage the party was pro-tram, but by the early 1950s, with the worsening economic state of the tramways, the policy abruptly changed.

1946 marked the real postwar era in Leeds. On 24 February the first postwar extension, from Balm Road to Belle Isle, was opened. This was a continuation of a scheme started before the war

Left:
The last of the three railcoaches, No 602, entered service on 1 June 1953. Arguably, with its VAMBAC control equipment, No 602 was the most modern first-generation tram to operate in Britain. By the date of its introduction, however, the decision to abandon the Leeds system had already been taken and No 602, with its sisters, was destined to have a relatively short life. Seen here at Temple Newsam in April 1954, No 602 retains the special purple and cream livery in which she was completed, a livery adopted to mark the Coronation of 1953. No 602 is now preserved at the National Tramway Museum.

and which had been temporarily suspended in 1940. This opening was countered by the first postwar closures, when, on 24 August, the single-track section along Beckett Street was converted to avoid the cost of re-laying to double-track. The equipment recovered was used in the construction of the next extension. A short section of track was retained to form a terminal stub at Harehills and the Dewsbury Road-Harehills service was diverted to run to Gipton. Also closed at this time was the route to Lower Wortley. 1946 also saw the conversion of the small depot at Hunslet for buses. The following year saw two further closures: the disused link along West Street and St Pauls Street in the centre and, more significantly, the line along Victoria Road and Cardigan Road on 8 December 1947. A short stub from City Square into Infirmary Street was retained, although this too was progressively removed. The final closure in the period up to 1950 was the line from Kirkstall Abbey to Hawksworth Road which closed on 7 December 1949 to avoid the cost of track replacement. Earlier in the year the tram depot at Bramley was closed for conversion into a bus depot; four depots were retained for use by the trams: Chapeltown, Headingley, Torre Road and Swinegate (where the sidings underneath the railway arches were restored for use).

So far, all these closures had been foreshadowed in the Vane Morland plans of 1944-45, and there were other, more positive, developments. Following a trial, almost 100 of the ill-fated 'Pivotal' cars had their trucks replaced by conventional Peckham-type P35 trucks, manufactured under licence in Leeds between 1944 and 1952. After testing one of the Manchester 'Pilcher' cars, a total of seven were acquired. These were followed by the appearance, on 15 September 1948, of No 276, the prototype for a postwar fleet but which became the last new double-deck tram built for Leeds. In 1949, 37 surplus trams were acquired from Southampton, although only 11 entered service; and then, again after a trial (involving LPTB No 2099), the decision was made to acquire the 92 remaining 'Feltham' trams. In the event only 90 were delivered (two were destroyed by fire in London and replaced by LPTB No 1, which became Leeds No 301) and were progressively introduced to service until 1956 (bar seven, which never operated in Leeds). In 1951 certain of the 'Felthams' were tested with pantographs, but the experiment was deemed not to be a success and the cars were fitted with bow collectors. 1949 also saw the final extensions to the tramway system with the completion, in two stages, of the Middleton line. The first stage, opened on 6 March, linked Belle Isle with Middleton Road, and the final opening, from Belle Isle Top to Middleton, occurred on 28 August. By this date Vane Morland was due to retire; his successor, A.B. Findlay from Glasgow, was appointed in December. Findlay was, like his predecessor, pro-tram and his first report to the Transport Committee, in March 1950, saw a long-term future for the tram system. In May 1950, partly as a mark of the new regime, the blue livery on the trams was replaced by red. Blue trams, predomi-

nantly those due for early withdrawal, were still seen until October 1953.

By the early 1950s, the financial position of the transport department was becoming dire. The election of a new Conservative council in 1951 led to a review of transport provision. This resulted in the withdrawal of one short section of track in Stanningley in January 1953, although there was no threat to the actual system. On 19 March 1951 the department was authorised to construct two single-deck trams, eventually Nos 601-02, and the local firm of Chas. H. Roe won the contract. These were destined to be the only tramcars built by the company. The two cars were officially launched on 1 June 1953, and were specially painted in a purple livery to mark the Coronation of Queen Elizabeth II. No 602, with its all-electric control equipment, was the most modern tramcar to operate in Britain, but both were destined to become white elephants since three months earlier, on 6 March 1953, the

Labour Party had adopted a policy of tramway abandonment as one means by which the ever-increasing losses of the transport department could be stemmed. The writing was on the wall for the Leeds system when, in May 1953, the Labour Party took power.

On 14 June 1953, at the first meeting of the new Transport Committee, the new ruling group wasted no time in putting its policy into practice when it was proposed that the Kirkstall and Stanningley routes, the two biggest loss makers, be converted to bus operation. The policy was adopted, although not without controversy both political and within the department. On 3 October 1953 the Stanningley route, No 14, was converted, even though the overhead had only been recently renewed. A total of 24 trams, mainly unmodernised 'Pivotals', were withdrawn, and the overhead was quickly recovered for reuse elsewhere. A month later, on 3 November, came the widely expected announcement that the

Left:
Between 1942 and 1945 Leeds acquired no fewer than 42 trams second-hand from Hull. No 472, seen here outside Swinegate depot on 18 September 1948, was originally Hull No 138 and was one of those cars sold in 1942. The Hull cars were destined to have a relatively short life in Leeds, all being withdrawn between 1949 and 1951, except for No 476, which had succumbed earlier. One of the cars, No 446 (ex-Hull No 132), was preserved and is now displayed in its home town.

entire system would be abandoned. As in certain other towns, the argument over the policy descended into a personality clash; in Leeds, this was between Councillor Rafferty, the Labour leader of the Transport Committee, and Councillor Mather, his Conservative opponent, who was staunchly pro-tram. It is clear, also, that the senior members of the transport department staff were hopeful that the abandonment policy would be reversed.

The first withdrawal after this occurred on 3 April 1954 when the trams on the routes to Kirkstall Abbey and Compton Road were replaced. The tracks were, however, retained to Kirkstall Works. At this juncture the last of the unmodernised 'Pivotal' cars were withdrawn – the retrucked cars were to last a further two years – along with the last of the 'Pilchers'. Later the same year, on 4 August, the rebuilt Sunderland single-decker No 288 emerged as the third of the single-deckers, No 600, after a reconstruction taking almost five years. Acquired as a test-bed for the introduction of single-deck cars in the proposed subways, No 600 was destined, along with Nos 601-02, to eke out a twilight existence on the shuttle service to Hunslet. 1954 also saw the last trams at Headingley depot and the start of a two-year scheme to re-lay the track along the York Road. Even with the end of the trams in prospect, the need to maintain the infrastructure was paramount.

The first casualty of 1955 was the route to Gipton which was withdrawn on 24 April 1955. At the same time Chapeltown depot was closed, and the Dewsbury Road service, which had been linked to Gipton, was rerouted to serve Harehills and Chapeltown. This was followed on 25 June by the withdrawal of the tramcars to Meanwood and Elland Road. This latter line, the rump of the earlier route to Morley, also served the football

ground and the yard at Low Fields Road, and the track was retained to serve the latter site for a further three years. The final closure of 1955, on 19 November, saw the last cars operate to Beeston. Concurrently, the depot at Torre Road was closed and all remaining cars were transferred to Swinegate. The withdrawals at this stage included the three modern four-wheel cars, Nos 272-74, which were built in the 1930s and nicknamed the 'Lance Corporals'. By January 1956, the tramcar fleet had been reduced to about 267 trams and the withdrawal process rapidly reduced that total further.

On 3 March 1956 the trams were withdrawn from the prestigious route No 1 from the City Square to Lawnswood via Headingley. This closure was followed on 21 July when the trams ceased to operate to Whingate and New Inn. These were the last routes to be served on the west of the city, and with their withdrawal trams ceased to run along the important thoroughfare Boar Lane. Apart from access to the main workshops at Kirkstall, all trams had ceased to run through City Square. However, the system was due to receive an unexpected reprieve in the autumn of 1956 when the Suez crisis led to a cessation of tramway scrapping and even the reintroduction, from 8 December 1956 to 16 March 1957, of the football specials to Elland Road. This respite was to be purely temporary and in April 1957 it was announced that the final closure would be accelerated to the financial year 1959-60.

The first closure (apart from the withdrawal of the football specials) after the Suez crisis occurred on 28 September 1957, when the trams were withdrawn from the Moortown (via Chapeltown)-Dewsbury Road service. This closure allowed for the withdrawal, inter alia, of the three ex-LPTB 'HR/2s', ex-LPTB No 301 and the remaining 'Middleton Bogies'. The trams withdrawn at this stage, along with others already surplus to requirements, were sold for scrap to Cohens and were taken over the still extant track to Low Fields Road for scrapping. After this batch of vehicles was disposed of the track along Elland Road was closed on 26 October 1957 and all subsequent disposals were by road. The final closure of 1957, in November, saw the link to Kirkstall

Below:
In 1948 Leeds No 328, one of a batch built in 1913-14 at Kirkstall Works, was restored to original livery and condition and renumbered No 309 for use in a film. Seen here in Kirkstall Road depot on 2 April 1949, No 309 was to survive in this modified condition for a further two years. Unfortunately, despite the increased interest in tramcar preservation by 1951, No 309 was scrapped.

works removed. In the future, all minor work would be undertaken at Swinegate, with any trucks requiring repair transferred to the works by road.

1958 saw few alterations and the trams entered 1959 serving four main routes: along the York Road (to Temple Newsam and Cross Gates), to Moortown (via Roundhay), the Middleton loop and the shuttle to Hunslet. To provide the service, there were some 120 trams, of which some 70 were the 'Horsfields' and the rest the remaining 'Felthams'. Due to the length of the 'Felthams', they had been restricted in Leeds to a

Below:
One of a series of tickets produced by Leeds City Transport to mark the end of tramway operation in the city on 7 November 1959. The reverse of the ticket included a brief account of the city's tramway history. *Author's Collection*

LEEDS CITY TRANSPORT DEPARTMENT
CROSS GATES, HALTON & TEMPLE NEWSAM TRAM SERVICES
THIS TICKET WAS ISSUED ON THE LAST DAY
OF OPERATION, SATURDAY NOVEMBER 7th
1959, TO MARK THE CLOSING DOWN OF THE
TRAMWAY SYSTEM IN LEEDS.
Fare 6d.
19062

Leeds Closures

24 August 1946	11 – Nippet Lane-Beckett Street, Stanley Road and Harehills Road (Harehills Road terminus remained in use until 1957)
24 August 1946	19 – Crown to Lower Wortley
3 December 1949	4 – Kirkstall Abbey to Hawksworth Road (route 4 continued to serve Kirkstall Abbey)
7 December 1947	27 – Victoria Road and Cardigan Road
2 January 1953	14 – Half Mile Lane to Stanningley
3 October 1953	14 – White Horse to Stanningley
3 April 1954	4 – City Square to Kirkstall Abbey (trams continued to use the route to Kirkstall Works until 7 November 1957)
3 April 1954	10 – York Road to Compton
24 April 1955	11 – Corn Exchange to Gipton
25 June 1955	8 – City to Elland Road/Lowfields Road (service temporarily reinstituted to Elland Road during Suez crisis; track to Lowfields Road retained for access to scrapyard)
25 June 1955	6 – City to Meanwood
19 November 1955	5 – City to Beeston
3 March 1956	1 – City Square to Lawnswood
21 July 1956	16 – Briggate to Whingate and New Inn
28 September 1957	2 – City to Moortown (via Chapeltown)
28 September 1957	9 – City to Dewsbury Road
28 March 1959	3 – Briggate to Moortown (via Harehills)
28 March 1959	12 – City to Middleton (via Moor Road)
28 March 1959	26 – City to Middleton (via Belle Isle)
18 April 1959	25 – Swinegate to Hunslet
7 November 1959	17 – City to Harehills Lane
7 November 1959	18 – City to Cross Gates
7 November 1959	20 – City to Halton
7 November 1959	22 – City to Temple Newsam

Last tram: No 160

certain number of routes, such as those along the York Road. The first closure of 1959, on 28 March, was in many ways the most significant. It saw the last trams withdrawn from the Middleton loop and from the Moortown service. The last trams were, therefore, withdrawn from the important city centre streets of Briggate and Vicar Lane. Less than a month later, on 18 April, the trams operated to Hunslet for the last time. A total of 47 cars were left to operate the remaining services through the summer. Finally, the end came on 7 November, when the final trams served the York Road routes. The official last car was No 160.

Several Leeds trams have survived into preservation. The National Tramway Museum plays host to 'Horsfield' No 180, 'Convert' No 345, 'Beeston Air Brake' No 399 (recently fully-restored), ex-LPTB No 301 (now restored to its London Transport livery) and two of the single-deckers (Nos 600 and 602) as well as works car No 2. Two of the ex-LPTB 'Feltham' cars survive, one at the London Transport Museum and one in the United States. A third was also preserved, but along with a second 'Horsfield' No 160 (nominally reserved for the city museum) and the third single-decker No 601, were eventually scrapped after vandalism during storage at the Middleton Railway. One of the ex-Hull cars, No 446, was also preserved and is now displayed in Hull in its home town guise of No 132. The Hull works car No 96, also acquired in 1945, is now operational at Heaton Park.

Openings:
The link from Belle Isle to Middleton (to complete the circular) was authorised in 1945 and work was resumed in 1948. Middleton Road to Belle Isle (Ring Road) opened on 6 March 1949 and from Belle Isle Top to Middleton (Lingwell Road) on 28 August 1949.

Leeds

Fleet Numbers	Date	Trucks/Bogies	Body	Withdrawn
1-75[1]	1926-27	EMB Pivotal (1-4, 6-10/2, 34/8/9/44/9/51-7/9/60/2/4/5/ 67/8/71-4 received Peckham P35 1946-49)	Brush	1951-56
76-103/5-50[2]	1926-27	EMB Pivotal (76-84/7-96/9-103/5-16/120/2-6/28/30-2/ 4-43/145/7/9 received Peckham P35 1945-52)	EE	1952-56 (104 withdrawn 1942)
151-4[3]	1930	Peckham P35 151/2/4, EMB Flexible 153	Leeds CT	1959
155-254[4]	1931-32	Peckham P35 (174 EMB Hornless 1950-54; 204 M&T Hornless 1945-51)	Brush	1956-59
255-71[5]	1933-35	M&T Swing Link bogies	Brush (255-63) EE (264-71)	1956-57
272-4[6]	1935	M&T Swing Link	Leeds CT	1955
277-9[7]	1939 (acquired)	EMB Heavyweight	EE	1957
283-96 (i)[8]	1910-13	Brill 21E	Leeds CT	1945
275-6[9]	1908	Brill 21E	Leeds CT	1949 (342), 1951 (349)
280-7 (ii)[10]	1946-48 (acquired)	Peckham P35 (281 received EMB Hornless 1950)	Manchester CT	1952-54
297-329[11]	1913-14	Brill 21E	Leeds CT	1945-51
276 (ii)[12]	1948	Peckham P35	Leeds CT	1957
290-300 (ii)[13]	1949 (acquired)	Peckham P35	Southampton CT	1952-53
301[14]	1951 (acquired)	EMB Heavyweight	LCC	1957
330-9[15]	1914-15	Hurst Nelson	Leeds CT	1945-51
340-56/8/60[16]	1919-22	Hurst Nelson 21E (346/7/9/50/4-6/8 converted to Peckham P22)	Leeds CT	1948-50
357/9/61-9[17]	1921-23	Peckham P22	Leeds CT	1949-51
370-5[18]	1923-24	Peckham P22	Leeds CT	1949-52
376-88/90-2/ 399/401/2[19]	1924-28	Peckham P22	Leeds CT	1949-54
389[20]	1925	Brush	Leeds CT	1951
393-8/400/3-10[21]	1925-28	EMB Pivotal	Leeds CT	1951-55
411-45[22]	1926-28	EMB Pivotal (420/3/33/4/39 received Peckham P35 1945-49)	Leeds CT	1951-56
446-87[23]	1942-45 (acquired)	Peckham P22: 446-58/460-3/8/72/4/5/9/81/2/486/7 Brill 21E: 459/64-7/469-71/6-8/80/3-5. Cravens: 473	Hull CT/Milnes/ Brush/EE	1949-51 (except 471 withdrawn 1946)
501-50 (501 to Leeds 1949 as 2099 and ran with that number for a time)[24]	1949-51 (acquired)	EMB Maximum Traction	Union Construction & Finance Co	1957-59 (except 507 withdrawn 1952 after an accident)
551-90[25]	1951 (acquired)	EE Maximum Traction	Union Construction & Finance Co)	1956-59
104[26]	1943	Peckham P35	Leeds CT	1957
115A, 117A, 118A, 120A, 122A, 123A[27]	1908	Brill 21E	Leeds CT	1945

Leeds

Fleet Numbers	Date	Trucks/Bogies	Body	Withdrawn
600[28]	1954	EMB Heavyweight	Leeds CT (1949-54)	1957
601/2[29]	1953	EMB Lightweight (601) M&T PCC (602)	Roe	1957

1 'Chamberlain' cars. Nos 1 and 9 swapped numbers November 1959. No 57 renumbered 64 December 1955 and 141 January 1956. Nos 80/96 swapped numbers September 1955. No 81 renumbered 142 January 1956.

2 No 102 renumbered 112 November 1955. No 112 renumbered 102 November 1955 and 115 February 1956. No 115 renumbered 102 February 1956. Nos 135/47 swapped numbers December 1955. No 141 renumbered 64 January 1956. No 142 renumbered 135 December 1955. No 83 withdrawn November 1955 and converted to snowplough No 7, withdrawn 1959.

3 Original 'Horsfields'.

4 'Horsfields' or 'Showboats'. Nos 180/9 swapped numbers April 1958. Nos 212/42 swapped numbers December 1957. Nos 219/21 swapped numbers December 1957. No 180 (i) now preserved at Crich. Nos160/202 both preserved but subsequently scrapped.

5 'Middleton Bogies'.

6 'Lance Corporals'.

7 Ex-LPTB HR/2s 1881/3/6, new 1931.

8 –

9 Originally from batch 115-26 — renumbered 115A-126A in 1927. Nos 119A/124A rebuilt 1938-39 and renumbered 275/6, renumbered 342/9 1948.

10 Ex-Manchester CT 'Pilcher' cars, new 1930-32. No 287 retained Manchester number until renumbered 280 in 1948. Nos 281-6 were MCT 104, 272, 266, 144, 263, 370.

11 No 321 renumbered 337 1948. No 328 restored as 309 for filming in 1948 and scrapped 1951.

12 Prototype of new class (rest never built): Leeds' last new double-deck tram.

13 Ex-Southampton CT built 1930. Were originally SCT 108/9/7/6/5/ 104, 50, 35, 32, 25, 23 respectively. Another 11 were bought which did not enter service, last of these scrapped 1958, outliving those in service.

14 Acquired in lieu of 'Felthams' Nos 2144/62. Ex-LCC No 1 built 1933. Now preserved at Crich.

15 Nos 332/9 rebuilt fully-enclosed c1938 and 1942. No 332 renumbered 338 1948.

16 All bar No 342 rebuilt as fully-enclosed 1935. No 345 withdrawn 1948 and used as joiners shop, now preserved.

17 All rebuilt fully-enclosed 1935. No 359 withdrawn 1951 and converted to decorated car, scrapped 1956

18 Fitted with air brakes 1926. First trams in Leeds totally-enclosed from new.

19 Received air brakes 1925-28. 'Beeston Air Brakes'. No 399 used as works shunter, now preserved.

20 –

21 No 393 exchanged trucks with 401 in 1927. No 396 acquired EMB Hornless truck 1950 and later Peckham P35. No 408 received P35 1949.

22 'Chamberlains'. No 420 withdrawn 1953, became snowplough No 2 withdrawn 1959.

23 Ex-Hull CT, were respectively Hull Nos 132, 127, 130, 26, 136, 126, 129, 124, 128, 133, 125, 131, 135, 115, 134, 150, 159, 153, 147, 156, 155, 109, 174, 152, 116, 114, 138, 154, 163, 164, 158, 104, 142, 140, 105, 139, 123, 113, 111, 117, 160 and 173. No 446 (HCT 132) now preserved.

24 Ex-MET 'Felthams' built 1930-31. Were ex-LPTB Nos 2099/97/77/ 82/69/2066/70/73/78/74, 2105, 2085, 2100/15, 2093/80, 2118, 2087/84/2081/72, 2108, 2096/76/83/85/75, 2086, 2116, 2071, 2106/4, 2092, 2102/19/10, 2089/94/68, 2114/07, 2098/95/90, 2111/01/12/03/17, and 2079 respectively. Nos 505/20 swapped numbers August 1957. Nos 511/19 swapped numbers August 1957. Nos 517/54 swapped numbers February 1959. Nos 524/65 swapped numbers November 1958. No 527 renumbered 528 July 1957 then 539 August 1957. No 528 renumbered 527 July 1957. No 539 renumbered 528 August 1957. Nos 501/26 preserved.

25 Ex-LUT 'Felthams' built 1930-31. Were LPTB Nos 2139/64/50/38/31/ 52/2120/21/37/48/25/61/40/23/26/34/2136/27/32/41/55/28/24/29/5 6/51/2145/42/46/49/43/33/60/35/59/57/2147/53/54/58. Nos 571/2/5-8/84 never entered service. No 582 was last Leeds tram to enter service 31 July 1956. Nos 557/64 swapped numbers February 1959. Nos 561/87 swapped numbers February 1959. No 554 (ex-517) preserved but scrapped 1968.

26 'Austerity' replacement car, renumbered 275 (ii) in 1948.

27 Batch 115-26: see Nos 275-6 (i) above.

28 Originally Sunderland No 85, bought 1944, never operated. Renumbered 288 November 1948, rebuilt 1949-54. Now preserved at Crich.

29 Charles H. Roe's only tram bodies. No 602 had VAMBAC all-electric control and was painted purple to mark the Coronation. No 601 preserved but scrapped. No 602 preserved at Crich.

Left:
With bodywork by Brush the 'Pivotal' cars were introduced in 1926-27. Seen here at the Cross Gates terminus on 21 August 1949, No 57 was one of the type which received replacement P35 trucks in the late 1940s.

By the end of World War 2 there remained only one tramway operator in the East Midlands area — the City of Leicester. With a fleet of 178 standardised four-wheel double-deck tramcars at its peak and with some 11 routes radiating out from the centre, Leicester was one of the most successful medium-sized British tramways.

The first tramcars — horse-operated — were introduced to Leicester in 1874 by the Leicester Tramways Co. Following an Act of Parliament in 1902 the local authority took over the horse-trams in that year and proceeded to convert the lines to electric traction. The new services were officially inaugurated on 18 May 1904 when the official party travelled from Abbey Park Road (where the main depot and workshops were situated) to Stoneygate. On the same day the routes to Clarendon Park (via London Road), Belgrave and the Melbourne Road circular were also introduced. Later the same year the lines to Narborough Road, Western Park, Fosse Road, Aylestone, Humberstone, East Park Road and Groby Road were also opened.

Unusually, therefore, the Leicester tramway system was substantially completed from an early date — the advantage of a relatively compact city. The Melton Road route followed on 8 June 1905. There followed a 10-year period of stability before the link to Fosse Road via King Richard's Road was opened on 20 September 1915. The line to Welford Road opened on 20 September 1922 and the final two extensions — Blackbird Road and Coleman Road — opened in June 1924 and March 1927 respectively.

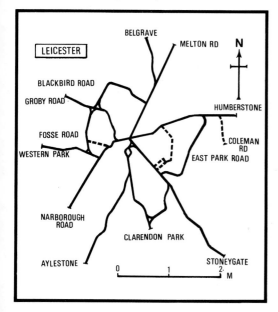

To operate the system Leicester had a fleet of 178 four-wheel tramcars built over a 17-year period from 1903 to 1920. The majority had been originally open-top, but, as elsewhere, modernisation meant that by the outbreak of World War 2 the majority of the fleet had been substantially rebuilt. The process of reconstruction continued well after the first abandonment (in 1933) until 1937.

Motorbuses first appeared in Leicester in the early 1920s to operate supplementary routes, but in contrast to the rest of the East Midlands where the process of tramcar abandonment was rapid (and often involved trolleybuses), the tramcar continued to dominate public transport in Leicester until the postwar era. Prior to 1939, three sections of line had been abandoned: Melbourne Road (13 December 1933); Coleman Road (23 October 1938); and King Richard's Road (2 April 1939). Upon the closure of the last of these the Fosse Road route reverted to using the track in Fosse Road Central, a section of track that had lain out of use from the opening of the King Richard's Road stretch in 1915. The prewar closures allowed for the reduction of the fleet by some 19 trams.

For Leicester's tramways the major turning point came with the publication in 1938 of a report that argued for the conversion of the trams to either trolleybuses or motorbuses, and if it had not been for World War 2 the closure process would have been much more rapid. As it was, the first stage of the final abandonment came on 2 May 1945 when the Welford Road route was converted to bus operation and the steady procession of trams to Eldin's scrapyard at Groby commenced.

There followed a two-year lull before the next closure, Aylestone, on 5 January 1947. This was followed six months later, on 15 July 1947, by the Fosse Road route. Amongst tramcars consigned to the Blaby scrapyard at this stage was No 76, which after resale (less its truck) from the scrapyard to a private owner was eventually rescued for preservation and can now be seen fully restored at the National Tramway Museum.

Right:
Leicester's first batch of tramcars were all supplied by the Electric Railway & Tramway Carriage Works between 1903 and 1905. Originally all open-top, the majority were eventually fully enclosed. No 80, sister car to the preserved No 76, is seen at the Clock Tower on 16 December 1948. By this date the trackwork had been simplified at this pivotal point of the Leicester network, but prior to 1947 the Clock Tower boasted a full 'Grand Union' junction.

The next closures, on 21 November 1948, saw the demise of the Narborough Road and Western Park routes. Early 1949 saw the pace of abandonment accelerated with three routes closed: Groby Road (23 January 1949); and Clarendon Park and Blackbird Road (13 March 1949). The closure of the Blackbird Road route allowed for the recovery of the track from the Blackbird Road reservation, and this was laid to the rear of the main depot at Abbey Park Road to facilitate the scrapping of the trams.

The next two routes to be withdrawn were East Park Road on 15 May 1949. Three routes now remained in operation, requiring a total of some 36 trams. The penultimate stage in the conversion process, on 9 October 1949, witnessed the withdrawal of the Belgrave and Stoneygate

Leicester Closures

Date	Route
2 May 1945	Welford Road
5 January 1947	Aylestone
15 July 1947	Fosse Road
21 November 1948	Narborough Road
21 November 1948	Western Park
23 January 1949	Groby Road
13 March 1949	Clarendon Park
13 March 1949	Blackbird Road
15 May 1949	East Park Road
3 July 1949	Melton Road
9 October 1949	Stoneygate
9 October 1949	Belgrave
9 November 1949	Humberstone

Last tram: No 58

routes, whilst barely a month later — on 9 November — the last route, to Humberstone, succumbed. The final tram, No 58, was suitably decorated to mark the demise, after 75 years, of the tramcar in Leicester.

With Leicester perished the tram in the East Midlands. Leicester's was a compact system, but, despite this, it could lay claim to have possessed one of the most complex pieces of tram track in Britain at the Clock Tower in the city centre. 'Grand Union' junctions were not all that common in Britain, and that in Leicester was even more complex, incorporating, as it did, cross-overs as well. It was only in 1947 that the 'Grand Union' was rationalised and even well into 1949 it remained an important junction.

Although Leicester's trams have long departed from their native city, the survival of No 76, now restored into its open balcony condition, in its maroon and cream livery, is a graphic reminder of Leicester's neat system. More recently, a second body has been recovered and the intention is that this will be restored for display in Leicester itself.

Above:
Also seen at the Stoneygate terminus on 16 December 1948, No 159 was one of a batch of 10 balcony-top cars built by Brush in 1914. As with the majority of Leicester's tram fleet, these 10 trams were also rebuilt fully enclosed.

Leicester

Fleet Numbers	Date	Trucks/Bogies	Body	Withdrawn
1-9/11/3-8/20-3/25-8/30-3/35-43/ 45-7/50-52/54-87/89-97/9[1]	1903-05	Brill 21E	ERTCW	1945-49 (10/2/9/24/9/34/44/8/9/ 53/88/98/withdrawn 1933-39)
101-21[2]	1905	Brill 21E	UEC	1945-49
100/23-7/9-40[3]	1905	Brill 21E	UEC	1945-49 (122/8 withdrawn 1933-39)
141-50[4]	1913	Brill 21E	UEC	1945-49
151-60[5]	1914	Brill 21E	Brush	1945-49
161-66[6]	1920	Preston Standard 21E	Leicester CT	1945-49
167-71/3/4/7/8[7]	1920	Preston Standard 21E	EE	1945-49 (172/5/6 withdrawn 1939)
179-81[8]	1904/05	Brill 21E	ERTCW (179) UEC (180/1)	1945-49

Note: In September 1947 Nos 108 and 116 exchanged numbers and No 108 (ii) scrapped. December 1947 162 renumbered 20 and scrapped, No 20 renumbered 8 and scrapped, No 8 renumbered 162. September 1948 No 115 scrapped and 177 renumbered 115. No 115 (ii) scrapped October 1948.

1　Open-top. All fitted with balcony tops 1912-27, all bar Nos 12/24/9/44, fully-enclosed 1924-34. No 76 preserved.
2　Balcony-top, rebuilt fully-enclosed 1924-34.
3　Open-top, balcony tops fitted 1912-27. All bar Nos 122/8 rebuilt fully-enclosed 1924-34. 1912 No 137 (i) renumbered 100 and No 141 (i) renumbered 137 (ii).
4　Balcony-top, rebuilt fully-enclosed 1924-34.
5　Balcony-top, rebuilt fully-enclosed 1924-34.
6　Balcony-top, rebuilt fully-enclosed 1924-34.
7　Balcony-top, rebuilt fully-enclosed 1924-34.
8　Water cars/grinders. Were Nos 100/142/3 until 1912 then Nos 151-3 until 1920.

With its tightly-knit network of routes, a high proportion of its track on segregated rights of way, and with a large number of trams built in the decade prior to World War 2, Liverpool might have been considered to have offered the greatest opportunity for the development of a modern tramway system in Britain. Indeed, plans for such a development did exist, but the growing antipathy towards the tramcar in Britain and the Corporation's desire to provide the cheapest possible fares led to the demise of one of the most progressive tramway operators in the country.

Although the first tramway in the city, an experimental route along Prescot Road, operated in 1861, this was short-lived and it was not until December 1869 that the Liverpool Tramways Co opened its first horse-tramway from the city southwards to Dingle. The network of horse-tram routes expanded rapidly and in 1879 the company merged with the Liverpool Omnibus Co as the Liverpool United Tramway & Omnibus Co. By 1896 a total of 267 horse-trams were in operation in the city, along with some 100 horse-buses. In that year the company was taken over by Liverpool Corporation and work started on the electrification of the routes.

The first electric tramway, that linking the city to Dingle via Park Road was opened on 16 November 1898 and the next route, from Princes Park, was opened on 15 January 1899. Extensions rapidly followed, including the Pier Head loops in July 1900, so that by 27 August 1902 the last horse-bus was operated. The final horse-trams were withdrawn on 25 August 1903 when they ceased to run over the section from Linacre Road (on the borough boundary) to Litherland Canal

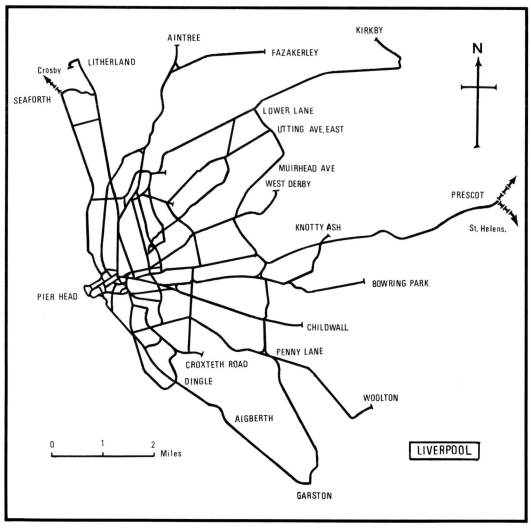

Left:
Dating originally from 1929, Liverpool No 5 was one of several of its type to be retrucked with EMB Hornless trucks immediately prior to World War 2. It is seen here, on 24 July 1949, in the wartime livery of olive green. The postwar livery was a much brighter green.

The next few years witnessed further extensions to the tramway system, although much greater work went into the modernisation of the tram fleet through the provision of top covers. 1911 saw the Corporation take over the Woolton Omnibus Co, and the first Corporation-operated motorbus service was instituted as a tram feeder at Calderstones to Woolton. In 1913 service numbers were introduced for the first time; at this date there were some 35 services. In 1915 the first section of reserved track, to Bowring Park, was built. Ironically, this was to prove to be one of the city's last tram routes 40 years later.

The 1920s saw the continued modernisation of the tramcar fleet and the opening of several extensions, many of which were built on reserved track. Extensions were built, for example, to the Walton Hall Avenue route as far as Stopgate Lane, to Mill Street, a connecting route along Great Crosshall Street in the centre to relieve congestion, and along Mather Avenue to Allerton (bringing the Allerton and Garston termini within 600yd of each other). In 1932 the Corporation decided to retain and modernise the tramways. As a mark of the new era the existing red livery was replaced by green.

In 1934 Walter Marks was appointed manager. This was of considerable significance in that Marks became a confirmed exponent of tramway development in Liverpool; indeed, until he felt compelled to resign as a result of Liverpool's abandonment policy, he was president of the Light Railway Transport League. On his appointment Marks prepared a report on the future of the tramway system and his detailed analysis convinced the council that the tramways should continue to form the backbone of the city's transport network. With this agreed, a policy of extensions (the majority on reservations) and new vehicle acquisitions was started. Amongst the new sections of reserved track opened were Childwall (1936), Utting Avenue East, Townsend Avenue and Edge Lane Drive (all 1937), Muirhead Avenue East (1938) and Allerton-Garston (1939). In 1938 the first part of the East Lancs Road route was opened and over the next five years the route was progressively extended to Kirkby. The final stretch, opened on 12 April 1944, was used

bridge. The Liverpool system was unusual in that the first trams included some trams and trailers manufactured in Hamburg in Germany. One of these trailers (No 429) was to survive until the early 1950s when it was acquired for preservation, but lack of storage facilities and vandalism led to it being dismantled. Other unusual features included the provision of first-class trams on certain routes: painted a distinct livery, the final first-class trams were withdrawn as late as 1923.

In 1902 Liverpool's trams met those of the New St Helens & District Tramways Co at Knotty Ash and a through service between the two towns was instituted for a short period on 18 May 1903. When the through service was abandoned, passengers had to change at Knotty Ash. In 1921 St Helens Corporation took over the bulk of the company's lines, with Liverpool inheriting the section to Prescot. Following refurbishment, a new through service ran for a short period after 1928.

only at peak hours and was destined to be the last significant addition to the network.

To operate the new routes and to replace many of the older cars, over 300 new trams were built between 1934 and 1940. Although the first, the bogie cars of batch 818-867, were relatively conventional in design, the period witnessed the introduction of streamlined bogie cars, nicknamed 'Green Goddesses', and the similar four-wheelers, nicknamed the 'Baby Grands'.

Thus, by the end of World War 2, Liverpool had potenitally one of the most modern of British tramways but it was severely run-down. About a third of the system's route mileage was on private reservations and a similar proportion of the tram-car fleet was less than 10 years old. As in many other cities, wartime damage was looked upon as an ideal opportunity to reconstruct the city and the thoughts of Marks were turned towards the part that public transport would play in the 'new' Liverpool. As a professional Marks examined the pros and cons of public transport provision in a series of reports produced in 1944 and 1945. Recognising that congestion would become a

Below:
The four-wheel version of the 'Green Goddesses' were the streamlined 'Baby Grands', which also dated from the late 1930s. One of the type, No 227, is seen at the Pier Head terminus of route 14. It was one of this type, No 293, that became Liverpool's official last tram in 1957. No 245 is now preserved in its home town, and a second 'Baby Grand', No 293, is preserved in the United States of America.

serious problem, he foresaw that the choice would fall between bus and light rapid transit on reserved track. Given Liverpool's existing investment in such track, this policy need not have led to the demise of the trams, but in October 1945 the Transport Committee voted to replace the trams with buses since the latter offered the possibility of cheaper fares. The policy was confirmed by the full council in November 1945. A local group, the Liverpool Tramway Passengers' Association, was formed on 10 November 1945 to reverse the policy, but achieved little.

With the closure policy now adopted, Marks was instructed to prepare a scheme for complete abandonment. This took until 1947 to complete and the final plan envisaged the last tramcars being withdrawn by 31 March 1958. Although the policy was now one of abandonment, the major priority after 1945 was to get the system fully operational again. Thus certain track (eg Mather Avenue) was relaid, a number of services which had been temporarily withdrawn as a wartime measure were reintroduced and all trams with open lower decks were fitted with vestibules. In early 1946 a new paint style was adopted and this was further modified in 1947 by the addition of a cream band. Fate was, however, to step in and cause disaster. On 7 November 1947 a total of 66 trams were destroyed when the depot at Green Lane went up in flames. The cars lost included many of the most recent trams, and although no services were withdrawn as a consequence the opportunity was taken to reduce frequencies on

Below:
To mark the demise of the tramcar, Liverpool produced a series of traditional Bell Punch-style tickets. Pictured on the reverse was a horse tram and a 'Baby Grand'. *Author's Collection*

the tram routes. Offers of replacement trams from other operators were declined.

The first conversion took place on 12/13 June 1948 when outer circular routes Nos 26 and 27 were converted. A month later Marks retired, to be replaced as manager by W. M. Hall. This was followed on 11/12 December 1948 by the conversion of route No 3 from Walton to Dingle. In addition to the main closure, the single-track sections in St Annes Street and Norton Street were closed, requiring the diversion of routes Nos 23, 24 and 28. The first of many closures in 1949 saw the conversion of route No 43, from Pier Head to Utting Avenue on 15/16 January 1949. The track from Everton Valley to Utting Avenue was however retained for service No 37, but was singled later in the year. As the trams were still expected to last for nearly another 10 years, there remained a pressing need to undertake track replacement on those routes destined to last longer, and a request was made for a grant of £67,500 towards track replacement. This request was accepted but only on the basis that the tramway's life would be extended for a further five years (to 1963). Following a deputation from the city, even this proviso was rescinded and some of the track relaid as a consequence saw only two to three years of use.

1949 was to witness the withdrawal of a further 13 services. Route No 15 from Pier Head to Croxteth was converted on 14/15 May; this was followed on by the conversion on 21/22 May of route No 12 from Castle Street to West Derby. A month later, on 25/26 June, route No 10 from Castle Street to Prescot was converted. This had originally been scheduled for April but had been postponed due to local opposition. On 13/14 August two routes, Nos 1 (Pier Head to Garston) and 20 (Aigburth Vale to Aintree), were converted. The weekend of 14-16 October saw the first of the 'area' conversions when five routes serving the Woolton area were converted. A sixth route, No 4A serving Childwall, was to survive to become the last conversion of 1949 when it succumbed on 11/12 December. This date also marked the closure of Prince Alfred Road depot.

November was to witness the demise of two peak-hours only services, when routes Nos 7 and 32 were converted over the first weekend of the month. With the closures of 1949 many of the older cars in the fleet were withdrawn, including the last of the 'Bellamy' roof type. Despite pressure for preservation none was to survive at this stage. Not all was negative, however, as 21 November 1949 saw the extension of routes Nos 30 and 31 from Walton to Aintree and the period 1950-53 saw 146 trams refurbished and further cars retrucked as well as the construction of new track arrangements at three roundabouts.

The extension of routes Nos 30 and 31 to Aintree was, however, destined to be short-lived. On 23 September 1950 routes Nos 30 and 46 were replaced by buses (along with peak hours only service No 34) and route No 25 was diverted. On the same day route No 31 again terminated at Walton. On 3 December four routes, Nos 16, 23, 24 and 28 serving Bootle and Litherland, were converted to bus operation. Peak hours only service No 22A was also coverted at this stage. These were followed by the conversion of route No 17 from Pier Head to Seaforth, via Great Howard Street, on 30 December 1950. These closures allowed for the closure of Litherland depot. The last trams in Bootle were to operate some two months later. On 10 February 1951 routes Nos 36 and 37, from Seaforth to Lower Lane and Utting Avenue East respectively, operated for the last time. The same day saw the withdrawal of routes Nos 18 and 18A from Seaforth to Breck Road and Grant Gardens (peak hours only) respectively. This left only one tram route operating in Bootle,

route No 35, and this was destined to run only for a further four days, being converted to bus operation on 15 February. The departure of the last tram in Bootle, No 990, was marked by the presence of the Lord Mayor of Liverpool and the Mayor of Bootle on board. The closure of the Bootle services enabled the north loop at Pier Head to be abandoned. Proposals made at this time for the acceleration of the closure process were rejected; indeed, the almost leisurely way in which Liverpool's tramway system was converted over almost a decade is one of the more peculiar aspects of the city's transport history.

1951 saw some four services converted to bus operation. The first of the year's abandonments occurred on 4/5 August when two routes, Nos 21 (Aigburth Vale-Aintree) and 22 (Pier Head to Fazakerley), were converted. These were followed by the conversion of route No 45, Pier Head-Garston, on 8/9 September. This closure allowed for trams to be withdrawn from Castle Street and for the closure in the same month of Dingle depot. The last closure of 1951, on 10/11 November, saw trams withdrawn from route No 2, from Pier Head to Aintree. By the end of 1951, there remained some 350 trams in service operating over 15 basic services. Of these services, only three were street-only, the remainder being carried for some length on reserved track, and the next closure, on 5/6 January 1952, was to witness the conversion of two of these remaining routes: No 25 Aigburth Vale to Walton and No 31 Pier Head to Walton. These closures allowed for the withdrawal of the last hand-braked four-wheel trams.

A further four services were to be converted during 1952. On 21/22 June 1952 route No 10C, Pier Head-Longview Lane, was converted and route No 10B, Pier Head-Page Moss Avenue, was reduced in frequency. The later service was, however, to continue operating for a further three years until March 1955. The next closures, on 6/7 September 1952, saw trams withdrawn from route No 49, Penny Lane-Muirhead Avenue East, and from two peak-hours-only services, No 42 (South Bank Road-Penny Lane) and No 48 (Penny Lane-Gillmoss). These withdrawals allowed for the withdrawal of all remaining standard four-wheel cars, although four were converted into snowploughs and renumbered SP1-4 (originally Nos 30, 703, 684 and 646 respectively). Not all the events of 1952 were, however, negative as on 6 October 1952 route No 19A was extended from Lower Lane to Croxteth Brook, along the track to Kirkby, to serve a new housing estate that had grown up in the area. The route was further extended on 17 May 1953 to Southdene and at the same time route No 44 was extended to Croxteth Brook. Route No 44 was further extended, on 7 December 1953, to Southdene; this was the last service extension in the city.

The next closures were amongst the most controversial. On 6/7 June 1953 trams were withdrawn from routes Nos 8 and 33 (Pier Head to Garston). Opposition to the closure surfaced in the Traffic Commissioners hearing into the proposed closure when a ratepayer objected to the abandonment of track that had been only recently relaid. The Corporation, however, argued that the losses on the two routes more than outweighed the interest charges on the section of track relaid and eventually the Corporation's view prevailed. With the closure of the Garston routes, Garston depot ceased to house trams. The closure of route No 8 also marked the end of the long reserved track section along Mather Avenue, the last car to operate along this section of track being No 979. Following the closure, 24 surplus 'Green Goddess' bogie trams were sold to Glasgow and all remaining Liverpool services were now operated by modern trams. The next closure in 1953, on 4/5 July, saw the conversion of the last all-street track route, No 11, from North John Street to Green Lane. By October the tramcar fleet had shrunk to only 219 cars. This number was soon to be reduced yet further by accident when, on 1 March 1954, seven cars (Nos 829, 835, 844, 847, 965, 983 and 985) were either destroyed or scrapped and a further nine cars seriously damaged by a fire in Walton depot. As a result of the fire a number of older cars (such as Nos 760, 762 and 764-66) which had been withdrawn, were temporarily reprieved.

The only closures of 1954 occurred a month later on 2-4 April 1954, when three routes, Nos 29 (Pier Head-Lower Lane), 29A (Pier Head-Muirhead Avenue East) and 47 (South Bank Road-Muirhead Avenue East), were converted. These closures allowed for the final trams to be withdrawn from the ill-fated Green Lane depot (which had effectively been a shell since the fire in 1947) and for normal service trams to cease using the central loop at the Pier Head. The track was, however, retained for emergency use. Following on, a further batch of 22 of the 'Green Goddesses' were despatched to Glasgow. 1955 was to witness the end of four routes. The first two to succumb were the now reduced frequency route No 10B and the peak-hours-only route No 41 (South Bank Road-Page Moss Avenue), which were converted on 4-7 March. All pre-streamlined

cars, including those reprieved after the Walton fire, were withdrawn, although one, No 762, was to survive in use at one of the municipal parks. The other two routes which were converted on 5/6 November were Nos 13 (Pier Head-Lower Lane) and 14 (Pier Head to Utting Avenue East). By the end of 1955 only some 118 trams remained in service on four basic services.

There was again a year's gap before the next two routes to close. In the interim, the Corporation applied for licences to convert the remaining routes. However, the Suez crisis developed and there was considerable pressure to prevent these conversions. There was to be no last-minute reprieve, and routes Nos 19 and 44 were converted on 3/4 November 1956. The withdrawal of these services, which linked the Pier Head with Kirkby and Southdene, allowed for the closure of Walton depot — the remaining two routes were both served from Edge Lane — and the withdrawal of the remaining bogie trams. After withdrawal, these trams were taken to the Kirkby

Trading Estate where they were stored awaiting possible purchase. Unfortunately, none was to materialise and they were eventually scrapped. The Corporation now possessed a fleet of about 70 four-wheel cars to operate the two remaining services. It had been policy for several years to achieve final closure by the end of the 1957-58 financial year.

The final two services, Nos 6A (to Bowring Park) and 40 (to Page Moss Avenue) were finally converted on 14 September 1957. A procession of 13 of the remaining four-wheel cars was run to Pier Head to mark the end of tramway operation in the city. The official last car, No 293, was repainted in a special cream livery with green and silver bands. This was not quite the end of the operation of Liverpool's trams, since the 'Green Goddesses' sold to Glasgow continued to give service in their adopted home for a further few years. Of the Liverpool fleet two of the four-wheelers, Nos 245 and 293 survive; the former has stayed in Liverpool whilst the latter was exported to the United States of America. One of the 'Green Goddesses', No 869, was preserved after withdrawal from Glasgow and has now been restored to Liverpool livery for display at the National Tramway Museum. Although none of the earlier schemes to preserve older Liverpool trams was to prove ultimately successful, the 1931-built car No 762, which languished at a municipal park for more than 20 years, was rescued for preservation in 1977 and is currently undergoing restoration.

Liverpool Closures

Date	Route
12/13 June 1948	26 — Outer Circular from South Castle Street via Everton Valley and Oakfield Road
12/13 June 1948	27 — Outer Circular from South Castle Street via Park Pale and Lodge Lane
11/12 December 1948	3 — Walton to Dingle (via Cazneau Street, Lime Street and Park Road)
15/16 January 1949	43 — Pier Head to Utting Avenue (via Dale Street and Everton Valley)
14/15 May 1949	15 — Pier Head to Croxteth Road (via Church Street and Princes Road)
21/22 May 1949	12 — Castle Street to West Derby (via Church Street)
25/26 June 1949	10 — Castle Street to Prescot (via Prescot Road)
13/14 August 1949	1 — Pier Head to Garston (via Church Street, Park Road and Aigburth)
13/14 August 1949	20 — Aigburth Vale to Aintree (via Park Road, Whitechapel and Scotland Road)
14/16 October 1949	5A — Pier Head to Penny Lane
15/16 October 1949	4 — Pier Head to Penny Lane (via Dale Street and Wavertree Road) (returning as 5)
15/16 October 1949	4W — Castle Street to Woolton (via Dale Street and Wavertree Road)
15/16 October 1949	5 — Pier Head to Penny Lane (via Church Street, Myrtle Street and Smithdown Road)
15/16 October 1949	5W — Castle Street to Woolton (via Church Street, Myrtle Street and Smithdown Road)
5/7 November 1949	7 — Old Haymarket to Penny Lane (via London Road and Smithdown Road) (peak-hours only)
	32 — Castle Street to Penny Lane (via Park Lane and Smithdown Road) (peak-hours only)
11/12 December 1949	4A — Pier Head to Childwall (via Church Street and Wavertree Road) (unnumbered from 16 October 1948)
2/3 September 1950	30 — Pier Head to Walton (via Dale Street and Netherfield Road)
	46 — Penny Lane to Walton (via Smithdown Road and Netherfield Road, returning via St Domingo Road)
2/4 September 1950	34 — Seaforth to Long Lane (via Everton Valley and Sheil Road) (peak-hours only)
2/4 September 1950	38 — Seaforth to Penny Lane (via St Domingo Road and Smithdown Road) (peak-hours only)
2 December 1950	22A — Pier Head to Fazakerley (via Vauxhall Road) (peak-hours only)
2/3 December 1950	16 — Pier Head to Litherland (via Vauxhall Road)
2/3 December 1950	23 — Lime Street to Seaforth (via Scotland Street and Strand Road)
2/3 December 1950	24 — Lime Street to Seaforth (via Cazneau Street and Knowsley Road)
2/3 December 1950	28 — Lime Street to Litherland (via Cazneau Street and Stanley Road)
30/31 December 1950	17 — Pier Head to Seaforth (via Great Howard Street)
10/11 February 1951	18 — Breck Road to Seaforth (via Breckfield Road North and Sandhills Lane)
10/11 February 1951	18A — Grant Gardens to Seaforth (via St Domingo Road and Sandhills Lane) (peak-hours only)

10/11 February 1951	36 — Seaforth to Lower Lane (via Melrose Road and Walton Hall Avenue) (peak-hours only)
10/11 February 1951	37 — Seaforth to Utting Avenue East (via Everton Valley) (peak-hours only)
15/16 February 1951	35 — Seaforth to Fazakerley (via Melrose Road) (peak-hours only)
4/5 August 1951	21 — Aigburth Vale to Aintree (via Mill Street, Whitechapel and Scotland Road)
4/5 August 1951	22 — Pier Head to Fazakerley (via Scotland Road)
8/9 September 1951	45 — Pier Head to Garston (via Church Street and Mill Street) (returning as 8)
10/11 November 1951	2 — Pier Head to Aintree (Black Bull) (peak-hours only)
4/7 January 1952	(94) — Dingle to Kirkby (tram service unnumbered)
5/6 January 1952	25 — Aigburth Vale to Walton (via Princes Road and St Domingo Road, returning via Netherfield Road)
5/6 January 1952	31 — Pier Head to Walton (via Church Street and St Domingo Road)
21/22 June 1952	10C — Pier Head to Longview Lane (via Dale Street)
5/8 September 1952	42 — South Bank Road (Edge Lane) to Penny Lane (via Mill Street) (peak-hours only)
5/8 September 1952	48 — Penny Lane to Gillmoss (via Muirhead Avenue East) (peak-hours only) also Woolton to Muirhead Avenue East (peak-hours only)
6/7 September 1952	49 — Penny Lane to Muirhead Avenue East (via Mill Lane and St Oswald Street)
6/7 June 1953	8 — Pier Head to Allerton and Garston (via Church Street, Myrtle Street, Smithdown Road and Mather Avenue) (returning as 1 or 45)
6/7 June 1953	33 — Pier Head to Garston (via Princes Road and Aigburth Road)
4/5 July 1953	11 — North John Street to Green Lane (via Church Street and West Derby Road, returning via Dale Street)
2/5 April 1954	47 — South Bank Road (Edge Lane) to Muirhead Avenue East (peak-hours only)
3/4 April 1954	29 — Pier Head to Lower Lane (via Dale Street and Muirhead Avenue) East
3/4 April 1954	29A — Pier Head to Muirhead Avenue East (via Dale Street)
4/7 March 1955	41 — South Bank Road (Edge Lane) to Page Moss Avenue (via St Oswald Street) (peak-hours only)
5/7 March 1955	10B — Pier Head to Page Moss Avenue (via Dale Street)
5/6 November 1956	6 — Pier Head to Broad Green
5/6 November 1955	13 — Pier Head to Lower Lane (via Dale Street and Townsend Avenue)
5/6 November 1955	14 — Pier Head to Utting Avenue East (via Church Street and Townsend Avenue)
3/4 November 1956	19 — Pier Head to Kirkby (via Church Street, Robson Street and Walton Hall Avenue)
3/4 November 1956	19A — Pier Head to Lower Lane (via as 19)
3/4 November 1956	44 — Pier Head to

Liverpool

Fleet Numbers	Date	Trucks/Bogies	Body	Withdrawn
1/5-18/20-32/34-6/8-43/5-58/ 60-102/104-24/6-31/133-5/7-44/ 146/7/9[1]	1921-32	All originally Brill 21E (except 1/5/6/12/35/38/51-4/62/3/71/81/4/ 5/87-9/91/2/4/5/7/-9/101/104/5/7/9/ 11/2/4/5/20/3/126/8/39/44/6/7/9 on LCT 8ft 6in trucks and 130/42 on Peckham Pendulum). The following were retrucked with EMB Hornless trucks in 1938-39: 5/28/31/5/8/54/ 81/7-9/91/5-8/101/5/14/26/128/31. Nos 130/42 retrucked to Brill 21E. 64/131/40 retrucked from Brill 21E to LCT 8ft 6in	Liverpool CT	1946-51
151-70/2-88[2]	1937	EMB Lightweight	Liverpool CT	1947-56. No 171 withdrawn after fire 1942
201-24/6/7/9-98[3]	1937-40	EMB 9ft 0in Hornless truck	Liverpool CT	1945-57. Nos 225/8 withdrawn after fire and war damage 1942
299-300[4]	1942	EMB Flexible 9ft 0in	Liverpool CT	1947-57
301-7/9-36/8-44/348/53/6/8/9/63/ 367/8/72/3/6/8/380/2/3/5-7/9/391/3/ 400/7/10/415/20/9/32/40/441/5/50/ 1/4/9/462/9/71[5]	1921-33	All LCT 8ft 6in except 303/4/6/11/ 2/4/21/2/5/6/330/2/3/5/9/48/58/76/ 378/87/450. The following had EMB Hornless trucks fitted 1938-39: 317/ 8/28/34/6/340/2/3/67/82, 407/51/9/ 469. 323/68 had their Brill 21E trucks replaced by LCT.	Liverpool CT	1947-52
502/6/7/13[6]	1908	Brill 21E	Liverpool CT	1947-52
539/40/4/6[7]	1910	Brill 21E	Liverpool CT	1949-50
553/5/8[8]	1911	Brill 21E	Liverpool CT	1946-53
564-6[9]	1912	Brill 21E	LCT	1946-53
571/5/7-83[10]	1913	Brill 21E	LCT	1946-59
584-96[11]	1914	Brill 21E (584 originally fitted with Peckham RE1)	LCT	1946-51
597-9[12]	1915	Brill 21E (597 originally fitted with a Peckham truck)	LCT	1947-49
600/14/8/21/5[13]	1919	Brill 21E (600 originally fitted with Brill Radiax)	600 LCT rest EE	1947-49

Liverpool

Fleet Numbers	Date	Trucks/Bogies	Body	Withdrawn
601-5/27-30[14]	1920	Brill 21E	LCT 601-5, rest EE	1946-50
607/8/34-6[15]	1921	Brill 21E	LCT	1946-50
637-60[16]	1924	Brill 21E	LCT	1947-52
661-3[17]	1924	LCT 8ft 6in (originally LCT radial 10ft 0in)	LCT	1949-51
664-73[18]	1924-25	LCT Radial (664-71 had LCT 8ft 6in standard trucks fitted)	LCT	1947-51
674-84/95[19]	1925	Brill 21E	LCT	1951-52
685-94/6[20]	1926	LCT 8ft 6in (originally fitted with LCT radial 10ft 0in)	LCT	1947-51
697-708[21]	1926	Brill 21E	LCT	1948-51
709-732[22]	1926-27	709-20 LCT 8ft 6in, 721-32 EMB 9ft 0in, all originally LCT radial	LCT	1947-52
733-44	1926	LCT Standard	LCT	1946-50
745-56	1926-27	EMB 9ft 0in Hornless (originally EE Kilmarnock 10ft 0in radial)	LCT	1949-52
758-69[23]	1931-32	EE Equal wheel bogie. 759-62/4-7/9 rebogied to EMB Lightweight 1937-44	Liverpool CT	1947-55
770-2/4-81[24]	1933	EMB JB bogies	Liverpool CT	1951-53. 773 withdrawn 1943 after bomb damage in 1941
782-5/7-817[25]	1933-35	EMB JB bogies except 809 EMB Lightweight; 815 re-equipped with EMB Lightweight in 1948	Liverpool CT	1946-53 786 withdrawn after bomb damage 1941
818-53/5-67[26]	1935-36	818-42/66 EMB JB; 843-65/7 EMB Lightweight, 866/7/70 rebogied 1948-50	Liverpool CT	1945-55. 854 withdrawn 1944 after overturning 1943
868-913[27]	1936	868-78/80 EMB JB, 879/81-913 EMB Lightweight	Liverpool CT	1945-56
914-42/4-92[28]	1936-37	914-7/43-52/5/7 Lightweight; 918-42 M&T; 953/4/6/8-92 EMB JB. 955 rebogied to EMB JB in 1954; 961/3/7 rebogied to Lightweight 1954	Liverpool CT	1946-56: 943 withdrawn 1943

1 Nos 1/6/8/12/117/126/7/42/9 were renumbered from 168/51/54/55/79/170/86/99/64 in 1937. Nos 52/74/8/126/39 were destroyed in Green Lane fire 1947. No 157 damaged but repaired. No 61 renumbered 599 in 1948. No 30 became SP1 in 1952, withdrawn 1956.

2 Nos 159/63/73 destroyed by Green Lane fire. No 157 damaged but repaired.

3 Nos 233/4/56/82/90/2/4/5 destroyed by Green Lane fire, the fire started in No 295. 1957 No 293 received truck from No 247 and became official last tram. Nos 245/93 preserved.

4 Last new trams. No 300 destroyed in Green Lane fire.

5 Nos 302-7/10-2/4/6-20/4/6/8-33/335/9 renumbered from 208/09/12/14/15/17/19/21/30/36/192, 252/3/63/65/68/71/75/76/80/281/87/88/91/97/33 in 1937. Nos 316-8/29/34/6/40/67/82/5/6, 407/20/45 destroyed in Green Lane fire 1947.

6 Nos 506/13 used as snowploughs post-1942, 503 snowplough 1943 and 507 snowplough 1946. No 506 destroyed in Green Lane fire. Batch 501-19.

7 Nos 539/40/6 used as snowploughs post-1942. Batch 532-46.

8 Nos 553/8 used as snowploughs post-1942. No 558 used as cloakroom 1940-46. No 558 sold to LRTL Museum Committee 1951 but scrapped 1955.

9 Nos 565/6 converted to snowploughs 1942 and 1946 respectively.

10 Batch 571-83. Rebuilt to single staircases from twin staircases.

11 Batch 584-96. Originally twin staircases but converted to single staircases.

12 No 597 converted to snowplough 1942, destroyed in Green Lane fire 1947.

13 Batch 600/9-26/32.

14 Batch 601-5/27-31/3.

15 Batch 606-8/34-6. No 606 withdrawn 1940.

16 Nos 640/1/9/55/7 destroyed in Green Lane fire. 646 renumbered SP4 1952, withdrawn 1957.

17 –

18 Nos 665/70 destroyed in Green lane fire 1947.

19 No 684 renumbered SP3 1952 and withdrawn 1957.

20 Nos 686/91/2 destroyed in Green Lane fire.

21 No 703 renumbered SP2 1952, withdrawn 1957.

22 Nos 711/3/7/28 destroyed in Green Lane fire.

23 No 762 lower deck to Parks Department and preserved in 1977.

24 First cars in green livery. No 780 withdrawn in 1950 after overturning at Kirkby on 6 December 1950.

25 'Cabin' class. No 795 destroyed by fire in 1935 and rebuilt.

26 'Marks' bogie cars. Nos 829/35/44/7 destroyed in Walton depot fire 1 March 1954.

27 'Bogie Streamliners'. Nos 876/82/8/92/4-6/8/908/12 were destroyed by Green Lane depot fire 1947. No 887 was damaged but repaired. Nos 869/71/4/5/7/8/80/1/3-7/890/1/3/7/9/901-4 sold to Glasgow 1954. No 869 (Glasgow 1055) preserved.

28 'Bogie Streamliners', Nos 915/59/60/80/7/91 destroyed in Green Lane depot fire 1947. Nos 918/9/21-42 sold to Glasgow.

Overall note: EMB JB ('Johannesburg') was Liverpool's designation of the EMB Heavyweight bogie.

Right:
1927-built No 729 passes Liverpool Exchange station on route 17 to Seaforth on 24 July 1949. This was one of 24 cars built by Liverpool Corporation between 1926 and 1927, Nos 709-732, that were originally fitted with Liverpool Radial trucks but were subsequently retrucked with either Liverpool 8ft 6in or EMB 9ft 0in trucks.

Although the 3ft 6in gauge trams had dominated certain parts of Britain, most notably in the West Midlands and the West Country, the last conventional system of this gauge to close was the remarkable and much-mourned Llandudno & Colwyn Bay Electric Railway in North Wales.

At the end of the 19th century the twin seaside resorts of Llandudno and Colwyn Bay experienced rapid growth and this stimulated a number of proposals for improved transport. Amongst proposed links were a number of tramways — including the schemes that eventually led to the Great Orme Tramway and the line between Llandudno and its neighbour — but it was only with the Llandudno & Colwyn Bay Light Railway Order of 2 June 1899 that real progress came to be made. This Order confirmed the powers of the Llandudno & Colwyn Bay Light Railway to construct a line between the two towns. Although the original powers allowed for the construction of a much longer route, part of these were transferred to the Rhyl & Prestatyn Light Railway, which was never built.

The Order specified a certain time-scale for the construction of the line, but, as with so many other schemes, financial problems led to delays. Thus by 26 September 1903, when the Llandudno & Colwyn Bay Light Railway (Deviation) Order was confirmed, little had been achieved. This Order allowed for a ½-mile deviation from the original route and also for an extension to the original time-scale. Contracts were let in 1904 which stipulated that the line be completed by 1 May 1905, but by that date again there had been little progress. The continuing financial problems of the original company led to the creation of a new company, the Llandudno & Colwyn Bay Electric Traction Co, but this too failed, and a third company, the Llandudno & District Electric Tramway Construction Co Ltd, was established in July 1907. Despite these problems, construction had in fact been proceeding, such that in early 1907 it proved possible for the company to borrow two tramcars for trial purposes.

The new line was inspected by the Board of Trade on 26 September 1907 and public services started in a limited fashion on 19 October of that year. The full service, however, did not commence until November 1907. The line was extended from the car sheds at Rhos-on-Sea to Colwyn Bay (Station Road) on 7 June 1908. On 21 April 1909 the company changed its name to the Llandudno & Colwyn Bay Electric Railway Ltd, a title it was to retain for the next 50 years.

Although the tramway was now substantially complete, further powers were obtained for extensions in 1907 and 1912, but, apart from one stretch, none were constructed. This final stretch, from Colwyn Bay (Station Road) to Old Colwyn (Queens Hotel) was opened on 26 March 1915 and was the final extension to the tramway. Two years later, however, a first contraction occurred when the short stretch of track to West Shore in Llandudno was abandoned and the track and overhead recovered. This stretch of line was part of the original proposed route beyond Llandudno to serve Deganwy station, which had never been completed. A further wartime innovation was the granting of Board of Trade permission for the use of double-deck trams. It was to be a further 20 years before the company made use of this provision.

The interwar years witnessed both development to the tramway and the first intimation that the tramway's future was not secure. In 1920 four new single-deck trams (Nos 19-22) were acquired from English Electric. From 1912 until 1931 the company undertook the doubling of most of the route, with the exception of three short sections of single track and one section of interlaced track. One of the longest sections of single track to remain was that from Greenfield Road in Colwyn Bay to the Queens Hotel in Old Colwyn, with the exception of part of the route along Abergele Road. By the late 1920s bus competition was beginning to pose a serious threat to the tramway, with a number of new operators, both independent and municipal, appearing. The company itself obtained powers to operate buses, but the clause in the original Order, which required the company to reinstate the road on tramway abandonment, was a disincentive to convert to bus operation completely. Nonetheless it was decided in 1929 to abandon the route beyond Greenfield Road, and the section to Queens Hotel was consequently abandoned on 21 September 1930. The replacement buses were run not by the company but by Crosville, an omen for the future. The potential cost of road reinstatement was also a factor in the rejection of

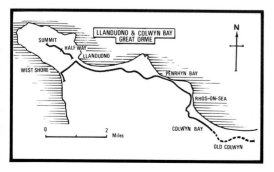

replacing the trams with trolleybuses, an idea seriously considered in 1931.

With the rejection of both buses and trolleybuses, the early 1930s witnessed a considerable change in the composition of the tramway fleet. Between 1932 and 1936 all bar seven of the original tramcar fleet were withdrawn and scrapped. In their place, second-hand single-deck trams were obtained from Accrington in 1932-33 (L&CBER Nos 1-5) and these were followed by 10 second-hand double-deck trams (Nos 6-15) acquired from Bournemouth Corporation. The latter were the first double-deck cars to be operated by the company and initially were limited in terms of operation, although subsequently were able to operate over the entire route with restrictions only in high wind (for which purpose a wind gauge was installed at Penrhyn Bay).

The tramway entered the war years reasonably secure. The majority of the fleet was 'new' and 1938 had witnessed the complete replacement of the overhead. Additionally, the wartime years were to witness an increase in traffic levels due to the transfer to Llandudno and district of a number of Government departments. But one wartime incident bode ill for the future. During 1943 the combination of high tides and gales caused serious damage to the section of track at Penrhyn Bay, and this was a precursor to more serious damage in both 1945 and 1952-53. In October 1945 the sea wall was lost and the track formation was undermined, with the result that the track nearest the sea was declared unsafe and single-line working through this section was instituted. This arrangement lasted for a fortnight whilst the track was repaired. Finally, in 1952-53 the track was undermined and, whilst initial efforts were made to improve the strength of the sea defences at this point, these were to prove too costly and were consequently abandoned. It was decided that the seaward track would have to be abandoned, with the consequence that this

section became single-track for the final three years of the tramway's life.

The final event of 1945 was the loss through fire damage of car No 16 in November of that year. No 16 was one of the four original trams to survive the 1930s, but was destroyed when an axlebox ran hot. This loss was, however, more than made up for by the acquisition in 1946 of ex-Darwen streamlined trams Nos 23 and 24. These cars, which were the most modern to operate on any British 4ft 0in-gauge system, were barely 10 years old when Darwen's trams were withdrawn. After converting the gauge, the new cars were tested by the Ministry of Transport on 14 April 1948. The result of the tests was to be a great disappointment to the company since the Ministry refused to allow the trams to operate the

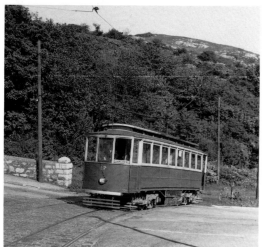

the early 1950s, the costs of operation were increasing rapidly, with the result that by 1953 the company was operating at a loss. The situation worsened in 1954 when it was announced that passenger numbers had fallen by some 47,000 to 2,698,000 during 1953-54, and that revenue had fallen despite an increase in fares from 5 July 1953. The result of this was that the loss had increased from £1,222 to £3,004. The continuing decline in the tramway's financial position led to the Board considering the possibility of tramway abandonment. The threat to the tramway galvanised interest in the line amongst the preservation movement and there were several appeals made through the pages of *Modern Tramway*. At one point efforts were made to obtain shares in the company to prevent any possible closure. However, these efforts failed. In September 1955 the company acquired its first bus, an ex-East Kent Leyland Titan TD5, for crew training purposes, and on 14 September 1955 the formal announcement of closure was made.

The closure was to be delayed for two reasons. Firstly, on 12 October 1955 the North West Area Traffic Commissioners decreed that a joint company/Crosville timetable had to be agreed before the closure could be countenanced, whilst the following month the perennial problem of the liability to restore the roads after tramways abandonment raised its head again. Both these problems were eventually resolved. The final nail in the tramway's coffin was, however, an intervention by the Manchester & North Western Electricity Board (MANWEB).

Historically, the L&CBER had drawn its power from local power stations. On nationalisation of

whole route, limiting them instead to two shuttle services, from Rhos to Colwyn Bay and from Llandudno West Shore to Nant-y-Gamar Road.

Despite this disappointment, work continued to ensure the future of the tramway. 1946-47 had witnessed the re-laying of the track between Colwyn Crescent and Church Road, whilst the company sought to take advantage of tramway closures elsewhere by acquiring second-hand equipment. Enquiries were made to the London Transport Executive (although these came to nought) and, more successfully, to Birmingham, Stockport and Sunderland Corporations. It was the latter source that provided the replacement traction columns used when singling the Penrhyn Bay section. In 1952 the track was relaid in Mostyn Street and additional work was undertaken in 1953 and 1954, including the moving of a crossover in Colwyn Bay.

Although the level of work undertaken might have been indicative of a thriving undertaking, not all was right with the company. Whilst passenger levels were at a historically high level in

Left:
Originally built for the 4ft 0in gauge Darwen system, L&CB No 23 migrated to Wales in 1946. The L&CB's high hopes for the two ex-Darwen cars were dashed by the restrictions imposed on their use. *A. D. Packer*

the power industry these local stations had passed under MANWEB's auspices. Increasingly, these small local stations were uneconomic and MANWEB calculated that eight men were employed solely in providing the power for the tramway. It therefore gave notice that after the existing contract to supply power expired (after the summer of 1956) that it would only continue to supply electricity for a fee of £100 per day. This was a prohibitive amount and led to the Board deciding on a rapid cessation of services. It was agreed that the final day for tramway operation would be 24 March 1956. Further new buses were acquired — a total of six were available for service by the end of March — and the closure went ahead as planned, with ex-Bournemouth car No 8 acting as official last tram. The company continued to run its bus service for a further five years, until it sold out to Crosville.

After closure, all the trams were dismantled at Rhos depot, with the exception of ex-Bournemouth No 6. Bournemouth Corporation had expressed an interest in acquiring a tram for preservation, but it was left to the efforts of a private individual to ensure that this tram was secured. After withdrawal, No 6 was placed on display in the museum of British Transport in Clapham. After this Museum closed it was returned to Bournemouth where it remains to this day, now restored to its original condition of Bournemouth No 85. A second Bournemouth tram is currently being restored as a fictitious L&CB No 7 for local display.

Llandudno & Colwyn Bay Closure

24 March 1956	Llandudno to Colwyn Bay

Last tram: No 6

Llandudno & Colwyn Bay

Fleet Numbers	Date	Trucks/Bogies	Body	Withdrawn
1-5[1]	1932-33 (acquired)	M&G bogies	Brush	1955/56
6-15[2]	1936 (acquired)	Brill 22E bogies	UEC 6, Brush 7-15	1955/56
16-8[3]	1907	M&G bogies	Midland RCC (Shrewsbury)	16 in 1945, 17/8 in 1955
23A[4]	1936 (acquired)	American Brill-type	Brush	1956
19-22	1920	EE (M&G-type)	EE	1955
23-4[5]	1946 (acquired)	EE Maximum Traction	EE	1955/56

1 Ex-Accrington 28-32 built 1920. Nos 2/5 retained original bogies regauged from 4ft 0in to 3ft 6in; Nos 1/3/4 bogies ex-original L&CBER trams.
2 Ex-Bournemouth 85, 115/6/08/03, 95, 128/12/21/14 respectively; No 85 built 1914; remainder 1921-26. No 115 was Bournemouth's last tram. No 6 (85) now preserved.
3 Originally numbered 6, 14 and 11 respectively until c1936.
4 Ex-Bournemouth No 55 (originally ex-Poole), rebuilt to railgrinder in 1921.
5 Originally Darwen CT 24/23 respectively. Streamlined cars built in 1936-37. Regauged from 4ft 0in to 3ft 6in. Into service 1948.

With more than 2,600 trams at its peak, London had by far Britain's biggest tramway system. It could also lay claim to have the largest and last conduit tramway system in Britain and the country's only tram subway. It was amongst the first cities in the country to see tramcars and at its closure inspired one of the most impressive transport films ever made.

The first street tramways in London were three routes opened by the American entrepreneur George Francis Train in 1861, shortly after Train's success in Birkenhead. The three routes (Marble Arch-Porchester Terrace, Victoria Street and Westminster Bridge-Kennington Gate) were not a great success and were all dismantled within months. The capital had to wait a further nine years before trams reappeared. On 2 May 1870 the Metropolitan Street Tramways Company introduced horse-trams to a route from Brixton to Kennington and this was extended on 5 October 1870 to Westminster. A week after the first opening, on 9 May 1870, the North Metropolitan Tramways Co opened a horse-tramway from Whitechapel to Bow, and other routes and operators quickly followed. By 1875 there were more than 50 miles of horse-tramway route in operation through the metropolis and this had increased to 130 route miles by the 1890s. Although most were horse-operated, the North London Tramways Co did use steam between 1885 and 1891. In addition there were also two stretches of cable tramway. The first, constructed to a gauge of 3ft 6in, was opened up Highgate Hill on 29 May 1884 and was the first cable tramway in Europe. The line lasted until 1910. A second, operated by the London Tramways Co, linked Kennington and Streatham between 1892 and 1904.

The first electric street tramcars in London were introduced by London United Tramways on 4 April 1901 on lines from Shepherds Bush to Acton and Kew Bridge. These were extended to Southall and Hounslow at the official opening on 10 July 1901. The first municipal operator of electric tramcars was East Ham, which inaugurated its services on 10 June 1901. The dominant force, however, was destined to be London County Council through its exercising of powers of compulsory purchase. To avoid any disputes over the use of overhead in sensitive areas, the LCC adopted the conduit method. The first section of LCC electrified tramway opened from Westminster to Tooting on 15 March 1903. With further rapid growth, the LCC became the largest single operator of trams in London.

Other tramways followed quickly. The first section of the Metropolitan Electric Tramways Co opened in 1904, for example, and 1906 saw the inauguration of services by Leyton UDC and the South Metropolitan Electric Tramways. 1908 witnessed the first overhead line of the LCC and the completion of the Kingsway subway. One of the essential weaknesses of the tramway system, and of the later trolleybus network, was its failure to penetrate the real centre of London. The majority of city termini were situated on the fringes of the centre due to the reluctance of the city authorities to permit surface fixed transport into the centre. The Kingsway subway was one means of circumventing this, but other proposed subways were never constructed. That the tram was never the same dominant force in London's public transport as it was elsewhere is demonstrated by the fact that in 1911 the trams carried only one-third of the passengers in London and that London General was already operating 1,500 buses.

Indeed, by 1911 the first abandonment had already taken place! The previous year the North End branch of Erith UDC's small system was closed. This was the first of a small number of closures that occurred in the 20 years prior to the establishment of the London Passenger Transport Board. Despite their problems, the trams were widely believed to have a pivotal role in the future of London's transport and during the 1920s the LCC in particular spent a great deal in modernising and extending the fleet and system. During the period 1926-30 the LCC refurbished some 1,400 trams and between 1929-32 built more than 300 new cars, culminating in the unique No 1, a car which was designed to set the standard for future tramway development but which was destined to be the last new tram built for the metropolis. The 'Pullmanisation' of the refurbished trams did have the desired effect of increasing the number of passengers.

On 30 June 1932, the last extension of the LCC system, along Westhorne Avenue, opened as part of a much longer proposed route. Although shown on early LPTB maps as a proposed route, the route was never completed. New trams, the immortal 'Felthams', were also bought for the MET and London United.

Elsewhere, however, the story was not so rosy. In 1921 the LCC had taken over the operation of Leyton's trams when the latter was refused permission to operate buses. Further attempts at co-ordination were blocked by the LGOC, although there were limited successes, such as the introduction of through trams to Croydon in 1926. The most significant reversal in the trams' for-

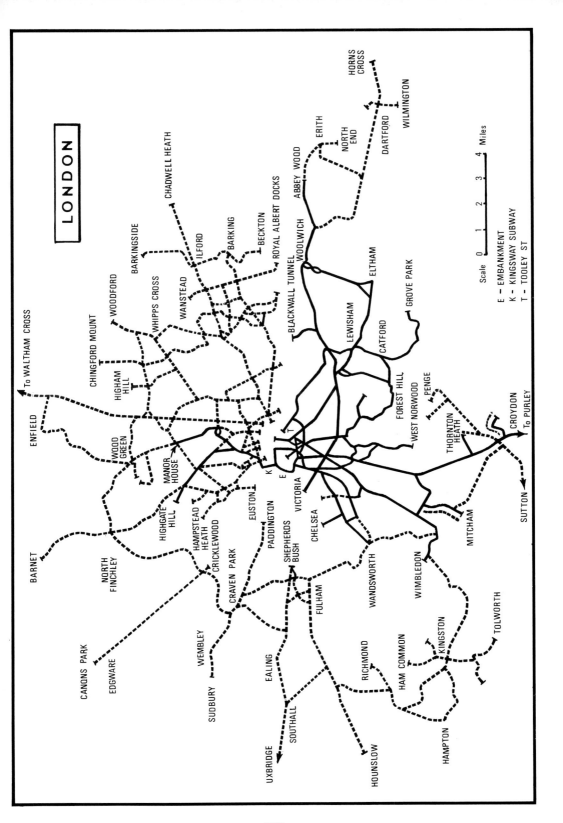

LONDON

To WALTHAM CROSS

E – EMBANKMENT
K – KINGSWAY SUBWAY
T – TOOLEY ST

Scale 0 1 2 3 4 Miles

Left:
**'Feltham' No 2160, seen
outside Telford Avenue depot
on 16 January 1949, was one of
46 of the type built for London
United Tramways, all of which
passed to the LPTB in 1933. Of
the 'Felthams', 90 were
acquired upon withdrawal in
London by Leeds and No 2160
became Leeds No 583. After
conversion work which started
later in 1949, Telford Avenue
depot ceased to house trams
after Stage 3 of Operation
'Tramaway' in April 1951.**

tunes prior to 1933 was the decision of London United Tramways to convert their Kingston area routes to trolleybus operation. LUT's position had been undermined earlier, in 1922, when the LCC had taken over those sections of the former company inside the LCC area. The cost of installing trolleybuses was less than refurbishing the tram network, despite the recent investment in the 'Feltham' cars, and trolleybuses cost less to operate. Thus, in May and June 1931, trolleybuses were introduced over one-third of the LUT network around Twickenham and Kingston.

The evident need for co-ordination led to the creation of the London Passenger Transport Board, chaired by Lord Ashfield, on 1 July 1933. The Board inherited 2,630 trams operating over 326 route miles along with 61 trolleybuses from LUT. It is clear from statements that he made that Lord Ashfield held the increasingly popular view that trams were a serious cause of congestion and the next six years were to witness the gradual demise of much of the London tramway system. In this policy the Board was assisted by a clause in the LPTB Act which allowed for any tram route to be abandoned subject to three months notice to the Highways Authority. Indeed the first abandonments occurred on 7 December 1933. There were, nonetheless, benefits from the new Board, such as the establishment of a link at Abbey Wood between the LCC and Erith tracks.

From this point on, however, the process was one of almost continuous tramway decline. Although the first closures of 1934, Dartford-Wilmington on 19 April and Merton-Summerstown on 16 May, were both to bus, the LPTB clearly saw the trolleybus as the tram's natural

successor. On 31 July 1934 the LPTB's trolleybus Bill received the Royal Assent. This authorised the conversion of 48 route miles. A further Act in 1935 gave powers for the conversion of a further 148 route miles. Clearly the process of conversion was about to commence, but it would not be achieved overnight and the LPTB was to need trams for many more years. In August 1935 the Board announced that a number of the 'E/1' class were to be refurbished in order to extend their lives. In theory a total of 1,000 were originally scheduled, but in the event only 154 were so modernised, including four 'HR/2s' and four ex-Croydon cars. October 1935 witnessed the first LPTB tram to trolleybus conversion and the next four years saw a radical reversal in the relative importance of tram and trolleybus. In 1938 the trolleybus route mileage exceeded that of the tram for the first time and by the following year there remained 1,255 tramcars in service as opposed to 1,444 trolleybuses. Tramcars had been eliminated from many of their traditional haunts, such as Bexley, Erith and Dartford.

Despite the gathering clouds of war, the process of conversion continued into 1939. In March the last trams over ex-MET lines were replaced by trolleybuses, to be followed in June by the trams of Leyton and Walthamstow, and in November the last routes inherited from Ilford were converted. With the conversion policy, the most modern tramcars from those routes closed, such as the 'Felthams', were transferred to depots serving the remaining routes, thereby allowing for the withdrawal of the older trams (like the earlier 'E/1s'). Under the powers of the Emergency Powers (Defence) Act of 1939, control of the LPTB passed to central government. There was to be no immediate cessation in tramway abandonment, as in June 1940 the remaining routes in East and West Ham and in Barking were converted. However, the onset of the Blitz on London and the need to maintain existing services ensured that there would be no further conversions during the war. Inevitably, London's trams (along with the rest of the metropolis) suffered severe wartime damage. For example, in September 1940 some 29 trams were destroyed in Camberwell depot, and in total 73 trams were destroyed as a result of enemy action. Many of the remainder suffered less severe damage, and 48 members of London Transport staff lost their lives whilst at work.

Without a doubt, World War 2 had prolonged the life of London's trams. Apart from the Kingsway subway routes (which had been scheduled for closure), all routes on the north of the Thames had been converted. The powers that the LPTB held allowed for the conversion of the remainder of the system, but the pressure in 1945 was to restore rather than replace. Of the surviving tramway network in 1945, some 75% of the 102 route miles (compared with the trolleybus network of 255 route miles) was conduit and there were around 900 trams remaining —

Below:
Seen here at Purley on 21 July 1948, London No 2048 was one of a batch of 12 'E/1'-type trams delivered to Walthamstow Urban District Council in 1926. Originally built with open platforms, the 12 were eventually fully enclosed. The Walthamstow trams succumbed to trolleybuses at the same time as those of Leyton, and like Leyton's 'E/3s', these 12 cars, along with a further eight built in 1932, migrated southwards.

despite the prewar closures, London was still the second biggest tramway operator in Britain.

Although the first postwar report issued in 1946 stated 'The urgent necessity of replacing trams in South London with a more modern and attractive form of transport', and the announcement on 15 November 1946 that the remaining trams would be replaced by buses rather than trolleybuses, the greater priority was replacing worn-out buses, strengthening existing services and opening new bus routes. Over the next year some £1 million was spent by London Transport in refurbishing the tramway system, Charlton works undertaking much work in strengthening many of the existing trams since the immediate threat of withdrawal had again been lifted.

The 1947 Transport Act, which received the Royal Assent on 6 August 1947, saw the LPTB nationalised as the London Transport Executive from 1 January 1948. The LTE inherited 871 trams operating over the same 102 route miles. The next two years were to witness few dramatic changes. 1 September 1948 saw Purley depot reopened as a works annex (it had been closed previously in June 1945) so that cars could be transferred eventually from Thornton Heath when that depot was temporarily closed to facilitate conversion to a bus garage. July 1949 saw a temporary bridge installed over Deptford Creek, complete with tram tracks, whilst the original bridge was replaced; and in September 1949 the first of the 'Feltham' trams to go to Leeds, No 2099, was despatched northwards to see whether Leeds Corporation was interested in acquiring the rest.

1950 was to be a momentous year for the trams. In January Thornton Heath's allocation of cars was transferred to Purley. On 23 March Bat-

Below:
Just as most of the surviving London trams had 'Last Tram Week' notices placed on their advertising panels, so too did the special tickets produced in July 1952 to mark the closure. Pictured on the reverse were a horse-tram of 1861 and an electric car of 1952. *Author's Collection*

Above left:
London No 182, seen here on Victoria Embankment on 15 July 1949, was one of 50 'E/3'-type trams delivered from English Electric to Leyton Urban District Council in 1930-31. On the abandonment of Leyton's trams in June 1939, the 50 cars, then only eight years old, were transferred to other areas until made surplus to requirements a second time as a result of Operation 'Tramaway'.

Above:
Designed at a prototype for a replacement fleet of double-deck trams, London No 1 was destined to remain unique. Built by London County Council on EMB trucks, No 1 is seen here outside Telford Avenue depot on 21 July 1948. Upon withdrawal in 1951, No 1 was sold to Leeds as a replacement for two 'Felthams' that had been destroyed by fire. As Leeds No 301, No 1 was eventually preserved and is currently displayed at the National Tramway Museum.

tersea Bridge was hit by the collier *John Hopkinson* and severely damaged. This meant that route No 34, which was the only route to use the bridge, now terminated south of the river — thus becoming the first postwar abandonment. By the end of March 1950 the operating stock had been reduced to 830, of which only 713 were available for service. With much of the South Bank area scheduled for use in the 1951 Festival of Britain, the opportunity was taken to alter the tram layout in the region. The new layout, the last significant trackwork undertaken on London's trams, came into effect in two stages on 11 June 1950 and 22 October 1950. The latter stage led to little real benefit as the process of tramway abandonment had, in the intervening period, been resumed.

On 5 July 1950 Lord Latham, chairman of the Executive, announced a £10 million programme for the conversion of London's remaining trams. Codenamed 'Operation Tramaway' the scheme envisaged the complete replacement of London's trams in nine stages over a three-year period. The programme included the conversion of seven depots, the closure of two old ones and the building of two new bus garages. To facilitate the closure procedure a yard at Penhall Road in Charlton was fitted out. Known as the 'Tramatorium', the first car to be disposed of there, No 1322, was burnt in July 1950 to test the local reaction. As if to emphasise that the end was

nigh, the first of the main series of 'Feltham' trams was sent to Leeds in August 1950.

The first stage of 'Tramaway', which took place over the weekend of 30 September/1 October 1950, was essentially a completion of the conversion process in the Wandsworth and Battersea area. At the same time route No 72 was extended from Savoy Street along Southwark Street to replace tram route No 26. This stage saw buses operating along the Embankment for the first time. A total of 94 cars were made surplus after these closures. A reshuffle, which saw a number of 'E/3' cars transferred, allowed for the withdrawal of some 58 old cars (primarily 'E/1s') and the sale of 23 'Felthams' to Leeds. In addition, three cars were converted for staff use at Penhall Road. This closure also saw the first trolleybus abandonment, when route No 612 was converted. The first of these withdrawn cars to be scrapped at Penhall Road, No 1656, was dismantled on 2 October 1950 and the remaining cars followed at a rate of one per day. Between October and January a further nine cars were withdrawn due to accident or fire damage, including two 'Felthams' (Nos 2144 and 2162) destroyed by fire at Brixton depot on 18 October 1950. Destined for Leeds, the two cars were eventually replaced in the contract by No 1.

The weekend of 6/7 January 1951 witnessed stage 2. This stage saw the elimination of trams from Clapham depot and from the routes from the Tooting group of routes. A total of 84 older trams were withdrawn for scrap and a further 19 'Felthams' were despatched to Leeds. An additional five cars were withdrawn between this stage and stage 3, including 'Feltham' No 2139,

damaged in an accident but repaired and sent to Leeds.

The Croydon group of services, stage 3, were converted to bus operation over the weekend of 7/8 April 1951. A total of 55 cars were withdrawn for scrap, although five were eventually restored to service and the remaining 'Felthams' were despatched to Leeds in the company of No 1. This closure meant the end of trams in Croydon and the removal of trams from Brixton Hill, Telford Avenue and Purley depots. Eleven more cars were to succumb between this stage and the next stage.

Stage 4, was atypical in that it took place midweek. It saw the conversion of the Rotherhithe group of services from London Bridge at Waterloo to Deptford and Greenwich. This was the smallest of the planned stages and involved the withdrawal of only 24 cars, on 10/11 July 1951; although it also saw route No 72 cut back from the temporary terminus along Southwark Street at Borough to its original terminus at Savoy Street, with the tracks along Southwark Street now disused. Between this and the next stage a further 11 cars were withdrawn.

Left:
During the 1930s, London Transport undertook a policy of 'rehabilitating' a number of the 'E/1' class in order to prolong their life. This work included the fitting of flush-panels along the lower decks. One of the 'rehab' cars, No 1392, is seen in Mitcham Lane on 16 July 1949. Route No 10, from Southwark Bridge to Streatham and Tooting, was to fall victim to the bus under Stage 2 of Operation 'Tramaway' on 6/7 January 1951.

Left:
Numbering more than 1,000 in total, the 'E/1' type trams built for London County Council were both the biggest single class of tram designed for use in Britain and, arguably, the one perpetuated for the longest. Typical of the majority of the class in their final years, No 1562 is seen outside Telford Avenue depot on 16 January 1949. Only one 'E/1' survives, No 1025 in the London Transport Museum although a second, No 1622, is currently being restored.

Stage 5 involved the conversion of the Dog Kennel Hill group of routes. This section, with its four-track layout up the 1 in 11 gradient of Dog Kennel Hill (installed at the Board of Trade's insistence in 1911 after a tram ran away), meant that the last trams had now served Dulwich. Some 98 cars were withdrawn as a consequence of this closure, although three were subsequently returned to service. The cars withdrawn included many of the 'HR/2s', although those fitted with trolley poles as well as conduit ploughs were transferred to other depots rather than withdrawn. Again a further nine cars were withdrawn between this and the next stage.

Stage 6, over the weekend of 5/6 January 1952, was the largest conversion so far and involved the replacement of more than 100 trams with buses on the Grove Park routes along with routes Nos 48, Southwark-West Norwood, and 78 Victoria-West Norwood. A total of 119 trams were withdrawn, although four were again returned to service. The preserved 'E/1' car, No 1025, which is now on display in the London Transport Museum, was withdrawn at this time. Between stages 6 and 7, an additional five cars were withdrawn. With stage 6, trams ceased to operate to Victoria, Brixton, Catford and Grove Park.

The next stage, 7, on 5/6 April 1952, was to see the closure of the Kingsway subway and bring a final close to the history of London's trams running to areas north of the Thames. Two routes were involved, from Manor House and Highgate Archway through the subway to West Norwood and Forest Hill. The closures also spelt the end for Norwood and Holloway depots and the last

trams to serve West Norwood and Forest Hill. A total of 72 trams were withdrawn for scrap and a further three followed shortly thereafter.

The scene was now set for the last rites. Originally the final closures had been scheduled to form two stages, but in the event they were combined to form one — stage 8. In the three weeks leading up to the conversion, 20 trams were withdrawn so that the maintenance requirements were reduced to an absolute minimum. Stage 8, the conversion of the remaining routes to Abbey Wood, Woolwich and Eltham, was scheduled to take place on the weekend of 5/6 July 1952. During the last week the majority of trams were fitted with posters announcing 'Last Tram Week' and special commemorative tickets were issued. After numerous special tours, the official last tram, No 1951, reached New Cross depot at about 1.15am.

The process of dismantling the trams continued at Charlton for some months longer and it was not until 29 January 1953 that a forlorn No 179 was the last car to be scrapped — a last-minute preservation attempt having failed. Elsewhere, the 'Feltham' cars were destined to have a relatively short life in their new home. Apart from No 1025, a number of other London cars do survive. 'HR/2' No 1858, after many years on display at Chessington Zoo, eventually found a secure home at Carlton Colville. The National Tramway Museum is home to ex-LCC car No 1 (rescued on withdrawal from Leeds), ex-MET No 331 (one of the prototype 'Feltham' cars) and ex-LCC 'B' class open-top car No 106. This car was converted to a snowbroom on withdrawal from passenger ser-

Left:
No 385, seen here outside Telford Avenue depot on 16 January 1949, was one of 25 'E/1'-type trams acquired by Croydon Corporation in 1926-27 and was built by Hurst Nelson. All of the type, except two, survived through to 1952. Four of the cars, but not No 385, were rehabilitated by London Transport during the 1930s.

vice and was restored in London. The group responsible is now undertaking the restoration of a second tram, 'E/1' class No 1622, which was recovered from an orchard in Hampshire. Apart from No 1025, the London Transport Museum also houses ex-West Ham No 290 and one of the production 'Felthams', MET No 355 (LPTB No 2099 — the first 'Feltham' to migrate to Leeds). A second Feltham, No 2085, was exported to the United States after withdrawal in Leeds, whilst a third, No 2138, was rescued by the Middleton Railway in 1960. However, vandalism and the failure to find an alternative home led the group to dismantle the car in 1968. In addition to the actual cars, the wonderful British Transport Films production *The Elephant Will Never Forget* provides an evocative reminder of the biggest tramway system in Britain.

London Closures

| 23 March 1950 | Battersea Bridge to Beaufort Street, Chelsea — route 34 truncated due to collier hitting Battersea Bridge |

Stage 1
30 September/1 October 1950

12 — Wandsworth to Borough (also trolleybus 612)
26 — Clapham Junction to Borough
28 — Clapham Junction to Victoria
31 — Wandsworth to Islington Green
34 — Battersea Bridge to Blackfriars
3 (all night) — Battersea to Blackfriars
26 (all night) — Clapham Junction to Borough

Stage 1 also saw route 72 extended from Savoy Street over Blackfriars Bridge to Borough to cover part of route 26 not covered by replacement buses.

Stage 2
6/7 January 1951

2 — Wimbledon to Embankment (via Westminster)
4 — Wimbledon to Embankment (via Blackfriars)
6 — Southwark Bridge to Clapham and Tooting (peak-hours only)
10 — Southwark Bridge to Streatham and Tooting
8 — Victoria-Clapham-Tooting-Streatham-Victoria
20 — Victoria-Streatham-Tooting-Clapham-Victoria
22 — Savoy Street to Streatham and Tooting (peak-hours only)
1 (all night) — Tooting-Streatham-Embankment-Clapham-Tooting and vice versa

Stage 3
7/8 April 1951

16 — Purley to Embankment (via Westminster)
18 — Purley to Embankment (via Blackfriars)
42 — Thornton Heath to Croydon (the preserve of the former Croydon Corporation cars)

Stage 4
10/11 July 1951

68 — Waterloo station to Greenwich Church
70 — London Bridge to Greenwich Church
72 — Between Borough and Savoy Street

Stage 5
6/7 October 1951

56 — Peckham Rye to Embankment (via Westminster)
84 — Peckham Rye to Embankment (via Blackfriars) (weekdays only)
58 — Blackwall Tunnel

to Victoria
60 — Dulwich Library to Southwark Bridge (weekday peak-hours only)
62 — Forest Hill to Savoy Street (via Westminster) (weekdays only — Saturdays Lewisham to Elephant)
66 — Forest Hill to Victoria (weekdays only)
36 — Woolwich to Greenwich and Catford (special peak-hour journeys)
7 (all night) — Savoy Street to New Cross Gate

Stage 6
5/6 January 1952

48 — West Norwood to Southwark Bridge
52 — Grove Park to Southwark Bridge (weekday peak-hours only)
54 — Grove Park to Victoria
74 — Grove Park to Blackfriars
78 — West Norwood to Victoria (weekdays only)

5 (all night) — Savoy Street to Downham

Stage 7
5/6 April 1952

(Kingsway subway routes)
33 — West Norwood to Manor House
35 — Forest Hill to Highgate Archway
35 (all night) — Bloomsbury to Highgate Archway

Stage 8
5/6 July 1952

38 — Abbey Wood to Embankment (via Westminster)
36 — Abbey Wood to Embankment (via Blackfriars)
40 — Woolwich (Plumstead weekday peaks) to Savoy Street
44 — Woolwich to Eltham (weekdays only)
46 — Woolwich to Southwark Bridge
72 — Woolwich to Savoy Street

Last tram: No 1951

London

Fleet Numbers	Date	Trucks/Bogies	Body	Withdrawn
1[1]	1932	EMB Heavyweight bogie	LCC	1951
2[2]	1933	Heenan & Froude bogie	LCC	1952
81-100[3]	1927-28	Brush Maximum Traction	Brush	1952
101-11/3-22/126-8/32-47/ 149-59[4]	1930	EMB Heavyweight (radial arm type)	Hurst Nelson	1950-52, 112/23-5/9-31/48 withdrawn 1940-45
160[5]	1930	EMB Maximum Traction	Hurst Nelson	1952
161-210[6]	1930-31	EMB Maximum Traction	EE	1951-52
290[7]	1910	Peckham	UEC	1938
295-302/4-12[8]	1928-31	Hurst Nelson bogies	West Ham 295, Brush rest	1952, 303 withdrawn 1940
325-30[9]	1925	Hurst Nelson bogies	Hurst Nelson	1946-50
331-44[10]	1925-29	Hurst Nelson bogies	331-3/44 West Ham, 334-43 Brush	1951-52
375-95/7-9[11]	1927-28	Hurst Nelson bogies	Hurst Nelson	All 1952, bar 376 in 1945, 396 withdrawn 1940

London

Fleet Numbers	Date	Trucks/Bogies	Body	Withdrawn
552-82/4/5-87-96/8-601[12]	1930	Mountain & Gibson Maximum Traction	EE	1950-52, 583/97 withdrawn 1940-45
752-1426/1477-1676/ 1727-1851[13]	1907-22	M&G/Hurst Nelson/ Heenan & Froude	Hurst Nelson/LCC Brush	1938-52
1370[14]	1910 (rebuilt 1933)	Originally Heenan & Froude, later 'E/1'-type bogies	Hurst Nelson	1952
1444[15]	1910 (rebuilt 1932)	As 1370	Hurst Nelson	1951
1854-64/6-80/2/4/5/7/ 8/90-7[16]	1930	EMB Heavyweight bogie (first type)	LCC	1881/3/6 withdrawn 1939, 1865/89/98-2003 wartime losses. Remainder withdrawn 1951-52
1904-66/8-71/4/5/9-81/ 4/6-2003[17]	1930-31	EMB bogies (maximum traction)	LCC	1967/72/3/6/8/82/3/5 wartime losses. Rest withdrawn 1951-52
2042/3/5-50/2/3[18]	1926	Hurst Nelson bogies	Hurst Nelson	2044/51 destroyed World War 2. Remainder withdrawn 1950-52
2054-61[19]	1932	Brush bogies	Brush	1952
2066-108/110-2/4-65[20]	1931	2066-119 EMB, 2120-64 EE, 2165 EE equal wheel later EE Maximum Traction	UCC	2109/13 destroyed World War 2. Rest 1950-52
2167[21]	1929	Brush Maximum Traction	UCC	1949

1 Originally LCC 1, Experimental car. Sold to Leeds (No 301) and now preserved at Crich.

2 'E/1', rebuilt from No 1370 after accident damage.

3 Ex-East Ham Corporation Nos 51-70, similar to 'E/1'-type. Fully enclosed 1937-38.

4 'HR/2' class. Ex-LCC Nos 101-59.

5 'E/3' class. Originally LCC No 160.

6 Ex-Leyton UDC 161-210. 'E/3' class.

7 Ex-West Ham Corporation 102 (batch 101-6 renumbered 1933 289-94). All withdrawn 1937-38. No 290 retained and now preserved in LT Museum.

8 Ex-West Ham Nos 68-85. No 68 (295) West Ham's last new tram and fully enclosed from new. Rest rebuilt fully enclosed.

9 Ex-West Ham Nos 119-24. Enclosed top-covers.

10 Ex-West Ham Nos 125-38. Originally enclosed-top; rebuilt fully enclosed 1931-32.

11 Ex-Croydon Nos 31-55. 'E/1' class; Nos 376/9/80/98 rehabilitated.

12 Ex-LCC 552-601. 'E/1' class. Reused bogies from earlier 'F' & 'G' class single-deck trams.

13 'E/1' class. Britain's most numerous design. Withdrawals started in 1938 and majority of older cars withdrawn by 1940. 146 cars rebuilt

1935-37. 36 cars (including five 'Rehabs') victims of the Blitz. Surviving cars largely withdrawn during Operation 'Tramaway'. No 1025 preserved at London Transport Museum and a second (No 1622) currently undergoing restoration. Space precludes detailed analysis of withdrawal dates.

14 'ME/3' class, rebuilt 1933 from 'M' class No 1446.

15 'ME/3' class, rebuilt 1932 from 'M' class No 1444. No 1441 also rebuilt but destroyed 1944.

16 Class HR/2. Originally LCC 1854-1903. Nos 1881/3/6 sold to Leeds 1939. No 1858 preserved at Carlton Colville.

17 Class 'E/3'. Ex-LCC Nos 1904-2003.

18 Ex-Walthamstow Corporation Nos 53-64. 'E/1' type.

18 Ex-Walthamstow Corporation Nos 39-46. 'E/1' type, fully-enclosed from new.

20 'Feltham' class. Nos 2066-2119 ex-MET 319/21-9/332-75. Nos 2120-65 ex-LUT Nos 351-96. Class sold to Leeds; Nos 2144/62 destroyed prior to delivery to Leeds. Nos 2085/99 preserved.

21 Originally MET No 330. One of experimental 'Felthams'.

With almost 1,000 trams at its peak, Manchester could lay claim to the largest provincial tramway system in England and the third biggest, after London and Glasgow, throughout the United Kingdom. With through running to many of its close neighbours, such as Salford and Stockport, Manchester also played a pivotal role in the provision of transport in the South Lancashire area and, without a doubt, its decision to convert its tramway system, taken in the 1930s, was one factor that influenced many of its neighbours to adopt a similar policy.

In 1875 both Manchester and Salford Corporations obtained powers to build a tramway from Pendleton, through Manchester, to Kersal Bar. This proposed line was leased to the Manchester & Salford Tramways Co from 31 March 1877, but this company's interests were sold to the Manchester Carriage Co on 16 April 1877 before the first trams had operated. The line from Pendleton to Bury New Road in Manchester was opened on 17 May 1877 and the extension to Kersal Bar followed on 30 July in the same year. Additional powers saw a network of lines, owned variously by several local authorities and the company, over the next five years, but in 1880, in pursuance of the Manchester Tramways & Carriage Co Act of that year, the company was merged with the Manchester Suburban Tramways Co to form the Manchester Tramways & Carriage Co. Over the next 20 years the company was to undertake many improvements, such as doubling of certain single-track sections, and extend its operations over further new lines. By the end of the 19th century the company's power was at its peak and it operated more than 500 horse-trams over 143 route miles throughout South Lancashire. However, its period of dominance would soon end.

As with many other cities the opportunity was taken by Manchester to take over the actual operation of the system and electrify it at the end of the company's lease. So far as the Manchester Tramways & Carriage Co was concerned, however, the situation was complicated by the fact that it operated trams over tracks owned by many local authorities and each of these local authorities had the right to take over their sections of track on the completion of each lease — as Salford, Oldham, etc, all did. So far as Manchester was concerned, powers to take over and electrify the lines were enshrined in the 1897 Manchester Corporation Act. Threatened with the loss of its business, the company did its best to respond. It promoted a Bill, subsequently rejected, in 1897 to allow for the conversion of the routes it oper-

ated subject to the agreement of the individual local authorities; it tested a steam tram in 1898; and it launched an experimental electric car based upon a converted Eades patent reversible horse-tram (Eades was employed by the company and his son was appointed, at the age of 20, to a senior position within the Corporation tramways). But to no avail. It was agreed that the Corporation would take over in a piecemeal fashion the system as each route was converted. This meant that during the transition period, Corporation electric cars and company horse-trams could be seen side-by-side.

The first of the new electric services, from Albert Square to Cheetham Hill Road/Hightown, was officially opened on 6 June 1901 — the date on which Manchester's first depot, Queens Road, was also officially inaugurated. These openings were followed on 5 July 1901 by the lines from High Street to Blackley/Queens Park/Moston Lane, on 16 July 1901 by the route from Cheetham Hill Road to Rochdale Road, and on 30 September by the line from Deansgate to Hightown. By the end of the first year some 150 electric cars were in service. Not all of the transition went smoothly, however, as 1901 also witnessed the start of the dispute with Salford over through running, a dispute which was not settled for two years.

Further extensions to the tramway followed quickly; a total of 17 sections were electrified in 1902, including Piccadilly to Denton on 1 June and Exchange/Victoria Street to West Didsbury on 1 December. In December 1902 the second depot, Hyde Road, was opened; the adjacent works were formally opened on 24 October 1905. 1903 saw the settlement of the dispute with Salford, and through running recommenced on 31 May. A total of 12 sections were electrified during that year, including the lines from Piccadilly to Audenshaw/Openshaw/Hollinwood/Newton Heath on 1 April. The previous day had witnessed the final horse-tram operated by the company over the line to Hollinwood. 1904 saw the opening of two routes, whilst 1905 saw two further routes along with the takeover, in conjunction with Salford, of the small Trafford Park undertaking on 31 October.

The next 10 years were to witness the continued expansion of the tramways, with numerous extensions being opened, such as those to Altrincham on 10 May 1907 and the two routes from Piccadilly to Southern Cemetery on 31 May 1911 and 15 June 1913. A third depot, Princess Road, also opened during this period, on 10 July 1909, and by the following year almost 600 trams were

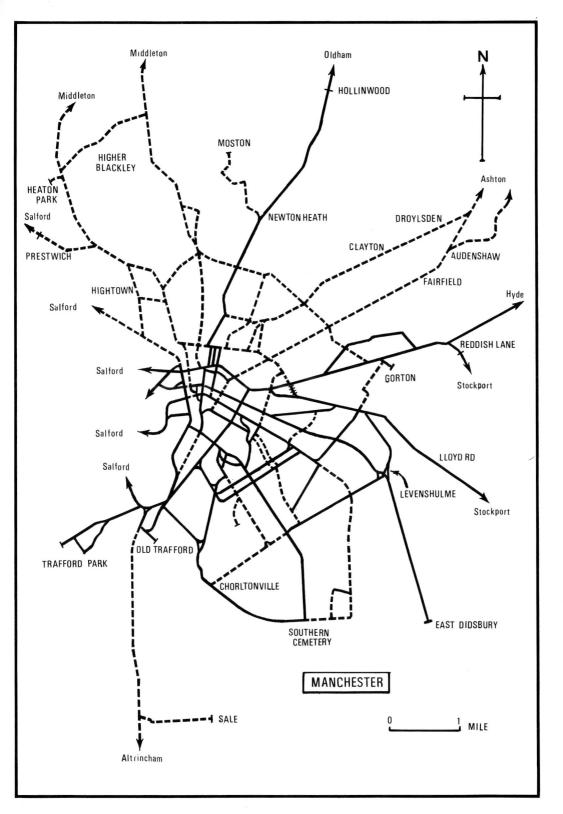

operating over 103 route miles of track. The period also saw the introduction of new through services to Oldham (on 21 January 1907) and Ashton (on 4 March 1907) and the first appearance of buses in July 1906 when the existing horse-buses were replaced on the route from the tram terminus at West Didsbury to Northenden. As elsewhere, the buses were considered, at this date, to be purely feeders to the trams. By 1914, when service numbers were introduced, Manchester had a thriving tramway system, but the first doubts had already emerged as to the long-term future when in the same year the local Watch Committee produced a report on traffic congestion.

World War 1 caused delays to many of the proposed extensions although some minor track alterations were undertaken, as well as a backlog of maintenance. In many ways, World War 1 marked a watershed in the development of public transport in the city as the tide gradually turned against the tram. Many of the planned extensions were never built and the deterioration of the local economy — mainly the result of the gradual decline of the cotton industry — increasingly put the finances of the tramways under strain not just in Manchester, but throughout the region. Initially, however, peace seemed to bring the promise of further tramway development. The city's first fully-enclosed tram, No 208, emerged in December 1919, and the early 1920s saw a number of further innovations. The end of

the lease of the Oldham, Ashton & Hyde Co in 1921 opened the way for new through services to Ashton and Hyde. The takeover of the lines of the erstwhile Middleton Electric Traction Co Ltd (by Manchester, Rochdale and Oldham) on 15 June 1925 enabled a new through service to Rochdale to be introduced from 9 August 1925, whilst the opening on 19 May 1928 of a connection from Middleton, to link up with the Bury trams at Heywood, allowed for a through Manchester-Bury service. 1925-26 saw the opening of Manchester's first reserved track sections, including the Kingsway route to East Didsbury, the last section of which was opened on 13 December 1926. 1928 also saw the opening of Birchfields depot, one of the last purpose-built tram sheds in Britain. By 1930 almost 1,000 trams were operating over 164 route miles, and joint services were operated with no less than seven neighbouring operators. The period also saw an increase in the bus fleet, from 16 vehicles in 1926 to 127 in 1930, and the inauguration of the express cross-city bus services that were an integral part of the department's efforts to thwart the competition in the years before licensing.

On 1 September 1928 the General Manager, Henry Mattinson, died and was eventually replaced by R. Stuart Pilcher from Edinburgh, where his success in modernising the trams may have been a factor in his gaining of the Manchester job. This was a crucial change in that the trams were increasingly threatened by the prob-

Left:
Built in 1929, No 391 was one of 110 replacement bogie cars built by Manchester Corporation Transport Department between 1924 and 1930. Seen here at Exchange station on 11 August 1948, No 391 was one of 14 of the type that survived through to closure in January 1949. It is seen on route No 35, from Exchange to Hazel Grove, which was the last Manchester route to close.

lems of traffic congestion. Whilst Mattinson had sought to increase the capacity of the tram fleet by converting four-wheel cars to bogie vehicles, his successor was much less convinced about the future role of the tramcar in Manchester. Although the final extensions were not yet complete (and sanction had been given to construct the Wythenshawe route — never fulfilled), Pilcher moved rapidly to evaluate buses as replacements for the city's trams. The first route to succumb was the famous route No 53 with its single-deck combination cars and single-track sections. It was progressively converted from 3 March 1930 through to 6 April 1930, and the immediate success claimed for the conversion opened the way for further abandonments. The next conversion, that of the short route No 25 to Bradford Road, occurred on 26 October 1930. There was, however, still no definite conversion policy and March 1930 also witnessed the introduction of the first of 38 fully-enclosed four-wheel cars that became known as the 'Pilchers'. These cars were built over a 30-month period, the last emerging in October 1932 by which stage the tramway abandonment programme had become more definite.

In his wish to withdraw the trams, Pilcher was assisted by the need to reconstruct certain roads and bridges, since this gave an excuse for withdrawal. To avoid the costs involved in accommodating trams in the rebuilding of the road to Altrincham, the trams to Altrincham and Sale were withdrawn in 1931. These were followed by the withdrawal of the majority of the routes in Middleton and the cessation of the through service to Rochdale in 1932. Further closures occurred in 1934, all in favour of the motorbus. However, by early 1935, pressure was growing for future replacements to include trolleybuses. Although this policy was strenuously opposed by Pilcher, the Council agreed on 31 July 1935 to seek powers to operate trolleybuses and a Bill to facilitate this was promoted through the 1936 parliamentary session. On 29 July 1936 the Council voted to convert the Ashton Old Road tram route to trolleybus and Manchester joined the ranks of Britain's trolleybus operators when the new service was inaugurated on 1 March 1938. Prior to this, on 7 July 1937, the Council adopted a policy that the entire tramway system be abandoned and on 17 August 1938 Pilcher produced a report outlining a plan for abandonment over the next three years. After discussion, the plan was adopted on 8 February 1939. The first routes to be withdrawn were the two serving West Didsbury, Nos 41 and 42, which were converted to

bus operation on 12 February 1939, followed on 11 June 1939 by the conversion of routes Nos 12 to Greenheys and 13 to Chorlton. The last closure before the outbreak of World War 2 saw route No 23 from Hollinwood to Chorlton converted, although this did not lead to any track being abandoned because the route was covered by other services. Also closed to trams in 1939 was Princess Road depot.

September 1939 and the outbreak of war saw Manchester's conversion scheme progressing. Inevitably, wartime exigencies meant that the original withdrawal date of 1942 could no longer be met, and the trams were therefore given a longer life than planned. Certain work, such as the conversion of the Hyde route to trolleybus operation, was suspended; although one route, No 51 from Miller Street to Oxford Road, was converted to bus operation on 23 March 1940. The trolleybuses on order were used to replace buses to Moston and Greenheys. This closure, which released eight 'Pilcher' cars, enabled route No 38 to be extended from West Point to Fallowfield on 17 June 1940 (it had been curtailed earlier in 1938). Also reinstated, on 27 May 1940, was route No 23 from Chorlton to Hollinwood, and the number of trams on routes Nos 36 and 44 were increased to replace buses on the inner section of the Manchester-Wythenshawe route. On 16 October 1940 route No 37 was extended from Barlow Moor Road to a new crossover at the end of Princess Road.

The next resurrection occurred on 23 November 1942 when route No 13 from Albert Square to Chorlton was reintroduced as a response to the Regional Transport Commissioner's request to save 10% of bus mileage. The route was extended from Chorlton to Southern Cemetery on 21 December 1942. This was, however, to be the last such reintroduction. By 1945, Manchester still had some 364 trams in service operating over a network a fraction of the size it had been at its peak, but which still played a fundamental part in the transport of the south of the city. All the routes to the north, with the exception of the line to Oldham, had already been converted. Despite the closures there still remained through services to three adjacent operators — Oldham, SHMD (although the SHMD cars no longer operated over the route) and Stockport. Although still physically connected to Salford's system, there had been no through services with Salford (except for Salford's use of Deansgate) since July 1937.

It is evident that Pilcher regarded the arrival of peace as the time to renew the abandonment programme. However, he was frustrated in his desire to withdraw the final trams by the time of his retirement (the end of 1946) by the lack of new vehicles and the emphasis upon austerity. The first curtailment, that of reducing route No 13 to peak-hours only, occurred on 11 February 1945. At the same time route No 23 was also reduced to peak-hours only. Buses took over all the off-peak services. The last illuminated car to run in Manchester, No 639, ran on 8/9 May 1945 to celebrate VE day. In the autumn of 1945 the part day and football service, No 42F (which had been introduced in 1940), was withdrawn along with the peak-hours-only service No 27D, which linked Trafford Park with Birchfields Road. The closures of the 42F enabled the overhead in Platt Lane, Raby Street and Great Western Street (tracks that had originally carried the erstwhile route No 53) to be recovered.

In January 1946 the Corporation confirmed that it remained the intention that the remaining trams would be withdrawn as quickly as possible. Except for trolleybuses (eventually) on the Hyde

Below:
The last new trams to be acquired by Manchester were 38 'Pullman' or 'Pilcher' cars that entered service between 1930 and 1932. Upon withdrawal these trams were sold for further operation in Aberdeen, Edinburgh, Leeds and Sunderland. Ex-Manchester 'Pilcher' car No 370 is seen with a sister car in Kirkstall Road Works in Leeds on 23 October 1948. No 370 became Leeds No 286 and was finally scrapped in May 1954.

route, all the conversions would be in favour of motorbuses. Also in January 1946, it was agreed with Salford (then pursuing its own closure policy) that the track in Deansgate could be abandoned. The first conversion of 1946 saw trams withdrawn from route No 32 (Exchange-Reddish) on 17 February. With this closure and the start of the removal of the overhead, Stockport's peak-hours-only service to Gorton Library was diverted to Belle Vue during April. On 4 May the remaining peak-hours-only trams on routes Nos 13 and 23 ran for the last time. On the same day peak hour services from Piccadilly to Trafford Park were also withdrawn. This was to be the last closure under Pilcher's auspices. Although scheduled to retire at the end of the year, he in fact resigned as from 30 June 1946 (to join the Traffic Commissioners) and was replaced by A. F. Neal, who, coincidentally, also came to Manchester from Edinburgh. The new manager perpetuated the closure policy. On 7 July 1946 trams were withdrawn (except at peak periods) from route No 39 East Didsbury-Exchange. Also in July, Manchester offered the 38 'Pilcher' cars for sale. These were disposed of over the next two years to Leeds, Sunderland, Edinburgh and Aberdeen. On 3 August 1946 Oldham abandoned its trams, which led to the withdrawal of joint service No 20 from Manchester to Waterhead. Manchester cars continued to serve the route, as far as the borough boundary at Hollinwood, until routes Nos 21 and 23 were converted to bus operation at the end of December 1946. On 24 August the remaining Manchester services to Trafford Park ran for the last time. The next day saw route No 37 Levenshulme-Southern Cemetery curtailed to run from Exchange to Levenshulme. This closure removed Manchester trams from most of Deansgate, although Salford's trams were to serve the street until March 1947.

The next withdrawal, on 2 February 1947, saw route No 40, Albert Square to East Didsbury, replaced by buses, although occasional peak-hours trams continued to operate. By 31 March 1947 the number of trams in service had been reduced to 233. With the closure of Salford's system on 31 March 1947, Deansgate lost the majority of its tram traffic. On 1 June 1947 route No 36, Albert Square to Southern Cemetery, ran for the last time. The Princess Road reserved track beyond Whitchurch Road was thereafter used only at peak periods. The declining condition of the reserved track sections, which had led to the derailment of car No 993 on Princess Road on 6 May 1947, led to a speed limit of 15mph being imposed on these sections of track. Shortly afterwards, 7 June 1947 saw the last football cars operate over route No 36 to the ground of Manchester City at Maine Road. Also in June 1947 the 'hospital' tram from Birchfields Road to Piccadilly ran for the last time. On 6 July route No 44, Southern Cemetery-Piccadilly, was operated by trams for the last time. This was followed on 10 August by the curtailing of route No 33 in Reddish (from Vale Road to the Bull's Head) and on the 16th of the same month by the curtailing of route No 38 from Fallowfield to Moseley Road. On 15 November 1947 peak-hours routes Nos 39X (Exchange-East Didsbury) and 40X (Albert Square-East Didsbury) were cut back to Mauldeth Road. This marked the closure of most of the Kingsway reserved track section to East Didsbury. The newly curtailed services to Mauldeth Road were destined to have only a short life, being finally withdrawn on 20 December 1947. This meant the end of all reserved track operation in the city, except for a short stretch along Kingsway to give access to Birchfields Road depot. A week prior to this closure, on 13 December, route No 38 had been reduced to peak-hours only. The final closure of 1947, on 30 December, saw the through service to Hyde, route No 19, 'temporarily' cut back to Broomstair Bridge. The track from Broomstair Bridge onwards was not, however, formally abandoned until 14 February 1948. During the winter of 1947/48 Birchfields Road depot was converted for use by the replacement buses although it remained in use by the trams until the final closure.

The first route to succumb in 1948 was the peak-hours service No 38X, Albert Square-Moseley Road, which operated for the last time on 31 January. It was followed next day by the withdrawal of service No 33, Piccadilly-Reddish, and on 15 February trams ceased to serve Albert Square with the conversion of route No 35B to Stockport. From the same date route No 35C, from Piccadilly to Stockport, was combined with Stockport route No 4A, Hazel Grove to St Peter's Square, to form a through service. A month later, on 14 March, the trams were withdrawn from the Broomstair Bridge route, No 19, although trams continued to serve Reddish Lane and Belle Vue at peak hours until the middle of May. Earlier in May the last of the Stockport peak-hours-only service to Belle Vue was withdrawn. May 1948 also saw the closure of Hyde Road as an operating depot, although it remained connected to the system so that withdrawn cars could be moved there for scrapping. By now the Manchester system had been reduced to three basic services, all using Stockport Road.

Above:
Manchester Exchange station on 11 August 1948, No 929 on route 35A, was one of a batch of 86 bogie cars built by English Electric or Manchester Corporation Transport Department between 1920 and 1922.

The first of these three routes to close was the peaks-hours service No 37E from Grosvenor Street to Levenshulme. This was followed, on 3 October, by the withdrawal of route No 37, Exchange-Levenshulme. This left one route and some 35 trams to soldier into the new year. The final end was not long in coming, however; on 9 January route No 35, from Exchange to Hazel Grove, the joint service with Stockport, was converted. The final passenger service by Manchester trams occurred during the morning peak on the 10th, when five cars were operated. Four cars then participated in the closing procession, including No 1007 which was suitably decorated and which carried the civic party. All the withdrawn trams were transferred to Hyde Road, where all 35 remaining passenger cars were destroyed in one huge bonfire on 16 March 1949. The four remaining works cars were similarly dealt with on 4 May.

At this stage no Manchester tram survived. However, one of the single-deck combination cars, No 765, was subsequently rescued and, after a short sojourn at Crich, was eventually restored. Now displayed at Heaton Park, No 765 has made visits to both Blackpool and Crich. A second Manchester tram, No 173, one of 81 cars supplied by Brush in 1901, has also been rescued and is undergoing restoration. Possibly even more significant, it is now again possible to ride on an electric tram on a section of original Manchester tram track. When the various routes towards Middleton via Cheetham were converted in the 1930s, the short branch that served Heaton Park was merely resurfaced leaving the track *in situ*. So 40 years on, in 1976, work started to create an electric tramway, using the branch as a basis, and the first services were inaugurated on 11 July 1979.

Subsequently, the line has been extended and trams from a number of operators (including Hull and Blackpool) can now be ridden. Street tramways are also destined to return to Manchester during 1992 with the introduction of the first Manchester Metrolink services. But that is another story.

Manchester Closures

11 February 1945	13 — Albert Square to Southern Cemetery reduced to peak-hours only
11 February 1945	23 — Hollinwood to Chorlton reduced to peak-hours only between Piccadilly and Chorlton
Autumn 1945	To allow overhead equipment to be recovered 42F (Exchange to Platt Lane) (part day and football service) and 27D (Birchfields Road to Trafford Park) (peak-hours-only service) were discontinued. Overhead in Platt Lane, Raby Street and Great Western Street recovered by 21 November 1945
17 February 1946	32 — Exchange to Reddish via Clowes Street
4 May 1946	13 — Peak-hour services withdrawn
4 May 1946	23 — Peak-hour services withdrawn
7 July 1946	39 — Exchange to East Didsbury reduced to peak-hours only
3 August 1946	20 — Manchester to Waterhead, end of Oldham trams and joint service
24 August 1946	Remaining Manchester tram operation into Trafford Park from City withdrawn
25 August 1946	37 — Levenshulme to Southern Cemetery via Deansgate — replaced by buses between St Mary's Gate and Southern Cemetery — end of tramway operation in

	Stretford UDC
29 December 1946	21/23 — Piccadilly to Hollinwood
2 February 1947	40 — Albert Square to East Didsbury, certain trams continued to operate at peak hours
1 June 1947	36 — Albert Square to Southern Cemetery. Princess Road track beyond Whitchurch Road now used only at peak hours
7 June 1947	Last football cars over 36 route from Great Jackson Street to Bowes Street and from City to Wilmslow Road
June 1947	'Infirmary' tram — Birchfields to Piccadilly via Oxford Road withdrawn — one tram per day. 1 July 1947 wires removed from Dickenson Road
6 July 1947	44 — Piccadilly to Southern Cemetery
10 August 1947	33 — Cut back from Reddish (Vale Road) to Reddish (Bull's Head)
16 August 1947	38 — Albert Square to Fallowfield cut back to Moseley Road
15 November 1947	39X/40X — Peak-hour services cut back from East Didsbury to Mauldeth Road
13 December 1947	38 — Reduced to peak-hours only
20 December 1947	39X/40X — Exchange/Albert Square to Mauldeth Road
30 December 1947	19 — Exchange to Hyde cut back to Broomstair Bridge
31 January 1948	38X — Peak-hour

Manchester

Fleet Numbers	Date	Trucks/Bogies	Body	Withdrawn
102/5/8-14/6/7/9/123/7/8/34/7-9/147/51/4/7/60/2/ 164/5/70/1/181-4/186/7/220/38/9/243/5/6/8/51-3/ 9/267/77/8/83/4/9/290/2/4/309/10/5/319/21/6-8/30/1/ 336/40/8/52/3/6-8/360/76/7/9/82/3/8/391/3/4/8, 402/ 4/406/7/10/7/9/21/422/4/6/7/9/31/2/434/90/2/5/7/9/ 505/6/11**1**	1924-30	MCTD bogies	MCTD	1945-49
104/6/21/5/31/41//144/61/3/73/6/96/217/25/8/31/42/ 263/6/70/2/4/87/349/70/80/1/9/420/93/502/3/10/538/ 610/69/71/6**2**	1930-32	Peckham P35	MCTD	1946-48
192/219/26/7**3**	1901	Brill 22E	Brush	1946-48
438/9/43-5/8/9/453/8/71/7**4**	1902-03	Brill 22E	Brush	1939-48
556/9/60/2/7-71/574/5/8-82/6-94/596-8/602/4/607- 9/11/4/6/618-23/6/30/1/3/634/7/9-41/3/8**5**	1904-05	Brill 22E	Brush	1945-48
685/6**6**	1910	Brill 22E	MCTD	1948
812/20/5/30**7**	1920	Brill 22E	EE	1946-47
847**8**	1921	Brill 22E	EE	1947
849/50/5/7/63-5/868-76/83/5/6/8/889/91/2/4-7/9/ 903/8-13/9/20/922-5/7-9/32**9**	1920-22	Brill 22E (1928 903/27 given MCTD bogies)	860-909 EE, 910-933 MCTD	1945-48
934-93**10**	1924-25	MCTD	EE	1945-49
1004-46/8-53**11**	1926	MCTD	EE	1945-49 (1047 withdrawn 1940)

1 'Replacement' bogies.
2 'Pilcher' cars — sold to Leeds (7), Sunderland (6), Edinburgh (11) and Aberdeen (14).
3 Batch 188-237. Originally open-top, 192/219/26/7 rebuilt 1924-29.
4 Batch 437-86. Originally open-top — top-covers 1907-16. Those that survived post-1939 were rebuilt fully enclosed 1924-27.
5 Batch 549-648. Rebuilt fully enclosed 1923-26.
6 Batch 680-717. No 685 rebuilt as fully enclosed 1925. No 686 retained after 1940 as 'trolleyhead' car.
7 Batch 793-835.
8 Batch 836-847. Single-deck combination cars. No 847 retained post-1935 for carrying sand.
9 Batch 848-933.
10 Fully enclosed as new.
11 No 1007 Manchester's official last tram.

One of three tramways to survive on the Isle of Man, the 3ft 0in gauge Manx Electric Railway is, at 17 miles, the longest of all the remaining British tramways. Its survival is, however, not without incident and the line could have disappeared on a number of occasions.

In the late 19th century speculators were interested in developing the area to the north of Douglas, and in 1892 the Douglas Bay Estate Ltd obtained an Act from Tynwald (the Manx Parliament) to enable it to build a tramway north from Douglas to Groudle Glen. Before services over the route commenced the original company was taken over by a new company, the Douglas & Laxey Coast Electric Tramway Co Ltd — the first of many such transfers — which had been incorporated on 3 March 1893. With Mather & Platt undertaking the electrical work and with a line voltage of 500V dc adopted, the first public services over the new line started on 7 September 1893.

The new company obtained powers to double the original line and extend it northwards to Laxey. Work started in February 1894 and the extension was opened on 23 July 1894. Meanwhile, the company changed its name to the Isle of Man Tramways & Electric Power Co Ltd. This company, which also eventually owned the horse and cable tramways in Douglas and the Snaefell Mountain Railway, was the brainchild of a local entrepreneur, Alexander Bruce. The company's aim was an electrified tramway from the esplanade in Douglas right through to Ramsey and, although powers to electrify the horse-

tramway in Douglas were rejected, the company did obtain permission to extend to Ramsey in 1897. The same year witnessed the changeover from the two fixed bow collectors (which are still used on the Snaefell line) in favour of more conventional trolley booms. The first section, to Ballure (where a temporary depot was built) was opened on 5 August 1898 and the line through to Ramsey was completed on 24 July 1899. A new depot, replacing the structure at Ballure, was opened in Ramsey. Additional work in 1899 saw the installation of a water-powered generating station at Laxey to supplement the existing sources of power.

However, in February 1900 Dumbell's Bank, in which Alexander Bruce was also heavily involved and which had played a central role in the development of the line, failed, with the company's tramways and land holdings passing into the hands of the receiver. The lines in Douglas passed to the Corporation, but the remainder, both the Manx Electric and the Snaefell, passed on 18 August 1902 to the Manx Electric Railway Co Ltd. This new company, formed primarily of Lancashire businessmen, was officially incorporated on 20 November 1902. Despite trials and tribulations, it was to run the tramway for the next half century.

The new owners acted quickly to improve the tramway, employing consultants to advise on how to upgrade the line. The result was to see many of the cars receiving new electrical equipment, and trucks and major changes to the electrical supply equipment. The majority of the elec-

Left:
On 25 August 1971, Milnes-built crossbench tram No 14 is seen hauling trailer car 54, also built by Milnes, at Laxey. No 14 dates from 1898 and the trailer from five years earlier. Laxey is one of the main intermediate stops on the Manx Electric Railway and the point where passengers change if they are intending to travel on the Snaefell Mountain Railway.
P. H. Groom

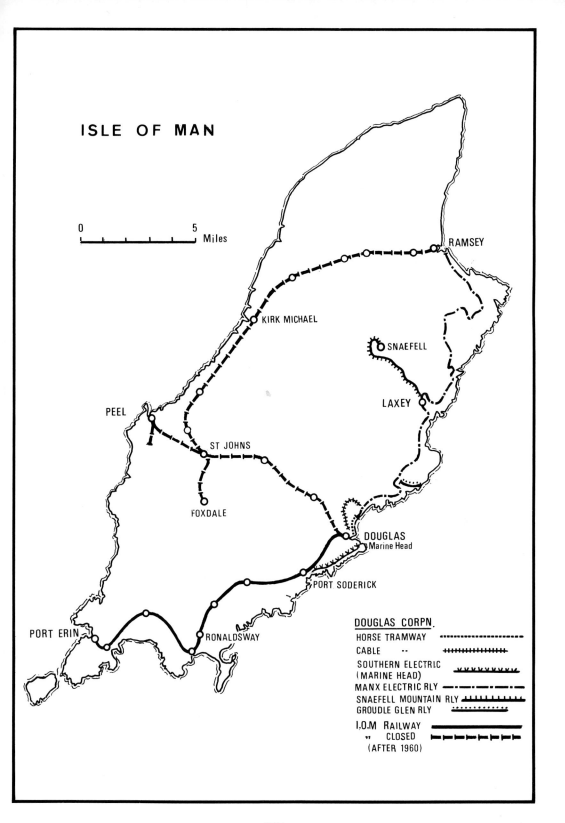

ISLE OF MAN

0 ____ 5 Miles

RAMSEY

KIRK MICHAEL

SNAEFELL

PEEL

LAXEY

ST JOHNS

FOXDALE

DOUGLAS
Marine Head

PORT SODERICK

PORT ERIN

RONALDSWAY

DOUGLAS CORPN.
HORSE TRAMWAY
CABLE
SOUTHERN ELECTRIC
(MARINE HEAD)
MANX ELECTRIC RLY
SNAEFELL MOUNTAIN RLY
GROUDLE GLEN RLY
I.O.M RAILWAY
  „   CLOSED
(AFTER 1960)

trical distribution equipment was converted from dc to ac although the generating equipment at Snaefell remained dc until 1924.

This period was the golden age of the line, with passenger traffic buoyant and the freight traffic at its peak, with both livestock and stone carried. Additional passenger traffic came from the continuing development of the holiday industry, with, for example, a holiday camp at Howstrake opening during the 1920s. 1930 was, however, to witness a major disaster when a serious fire hit the depot at Laxey in April, destroying four of the motor cars and seven trailers — although three of the latter were rebuilt. By the 1930s the financial position of the line was growing increasingly precarious and its survival depended upon the willingness of the debenture holders to allow the company to pass payments. Although 1934-35 saw a further change in the electrical supply, with power now being taken from the public supply, and further investment saw the introduction of signalling to control a number of the level crossings, it is possible that the line would have succumbed had war not broken out.

After the war the Isle of Man experienced a great deal of tourist traffic, and the MER benefited as a result of fuel restrictions. Nevertheless the finances of the Manx Electric were becoming increasingly stretched and were soon worsened further by the increasing coach competition once fuel became more widely available. In the winter of 1951-52, for the first time since the line opened, no service was operated on Sundays, although work on vehicle maintenance was continued, with No 19 undergoing a major rebuild. An unusual source of traffic at this time came from the Air Ministry, which used the line (and the Snaefell Railway) to ferry both men and materials in the construction of a radar station. The Ministry used a small Wickham trolley for the purpose and built a small shed at Laxey to house it. Despite this, the economic position continued to deteriorate. In 1954 Tynwald gave the Railway permission to increase fares to a maximum of 3d per mile but rejected the company's application to suspend winter services entirely. The company stated that not operating winter services would save £3,638 per annum. As if the financial position wasn't enough, on 14 August 1955 the tramway suffered a serious collision which saw four people injured and cars Nos 14 and 22 damaged. At the end of 1955 the Board of the company announced that if no government support was forthcoming the operation of the line would cease at the end of 1956 and that steps would be

taken to wind up the company. The dire position was emphasised in the annual report for the year which showed that, although the company had made a profit (the first since 1952), it was £22,974 in arrears to the debenture holders.

These announcements stimulated Tynwald to take action. On 22 January 1956 the Isle of Man Tourist Board was instructed to submit definite proposals for the future of the line. A sub-committee was established by Tynwald to investigate the subject and this committee approached British Railways for advice. The report produced by BR costed retention at some £674,000 and recommended that the tramway be abandoned in favour of buses. This recommendation was accepted by the sub-committee, but on 20 June 1956 the proposed closure was rejected by Tynwald, the importance to the island of the tourist potential of the line being a considerable factor in the decision. The tramway received a further year's stay of execution whilst discussions progressed and finally, on 21 November 1956, the special committee appointed recommended that the government buy the line at an agreed price of £50,000 and that it be operated as a national undertaking. The report was debated in Tynwald on 12 December and the proposed purchase was agreed.

On 1 June 1957 the railway passed officially to the newly created Manx Electric Railway Board and the old company was placed in receivership. The initial expectation, however, that an annual subsidy of £25,000 would be sufficient to keep the line operational was to prove misplaced and the new Board approached Tynwald for an additional £20,000. When this request was rejected all bar one of the new directors resigned. The new Board agreed to accept the £25,000 figure, but reduced the rate of reconstruction as an economy measure. To mark the change of ownership a new livery of green and white was adopted in 1958, but this was short-lived and the cars soon reverted to the traditional varnished teak or brown, red and white with full lining out.

The next five years saw dramatic progress on the railway, partly funded through loans and additional grants and partly through reduced losses which enabled some of the subsidy to be transferred to capital expenditure. By 1962 more than half of the track had been relaid and much of the overhead had been replaced by new grooved wire. Work was also undertaken on the vehicle fleet, with, for example, 12 compressors bought from Sheffield in November 1960 and a further four from Glasgow in 1962. Over the winter of 1963-64 new stations were constructed at

Douglas and Ramsey. Also in 1963, the Manx government changed the method of assessment. In place of the £25,000 subsidy and an additional grant for capital work made to alleviate unemployment, both payments were combined. By 1964 the 1962 scheme to make all the substations fully automatic was completed; all, bar that at Laxey, were now unstaffed. Despite all the measures, however, the line's continued reliance upon seasonal traffic was to lead to problems. The deficit for 1963 reached more than £32,000 when poor weather severely affected passenger levels.

The financial position of the line through the 1960s was not good and the future of sections of the line was regularly under threat. Although a new station was opened at Ramsey in 1964 the Report of the Transport Commission to Tynwald published in early 1966 raised serious doubts over the survival of the section of line north from Laxey to Ramsey. The threatened section suffered a further setback when, on 25 January 1967, the trackbed at Bulgham Bay collapsed. Temporary provisions enabled services to operate both north and south of the breach, with passengers walking around the obstruction, until, after repair work, through services were restored on 10 July 1967.

The threat to the Laxey-Ramsey section proved all too real in October 1975 when, with the loss of the Post Office contract, the service was withdrawn. With the simultaneous suspension of the service between Douglas and Laxey for the winter, for the first time since the line opened 80 years earlier there was no MER service of any kind. The closure was, however, unpopular and this, combined with the continuing threat to the remaining section of the Isle of Man Railway, led to transport being a major issue at the elections to Tynwald in September 1976. The result was that the through services to Ramsey were reinstated with the summer 1977 timetable and that both the Isle of Man Railway and MER was united under the control of the MER board (although jointly operated under the title of Isle of Man Railways). Since 1977 the MER has seen much maintenance work undertaken to ensure that the tramway will continue to operate into its second century.

Nevertheless, the Manx Electric Railway continues to play an important part in the life of the Isle of Man. With the closure of the Isle of Man Railway route from Douglas to Ramsey, the line now forms the only rail link between the two towns, and as part of the nationalised Isle of Man Railways it would seem to have a secure future. With its continuing reliance upon the original fleet of cars (proposals in 1956 to acquire four replacement cars having come to nothing), the line retains a great deal of its historic charm. Long may it continue!

Left:
Built by Milnes in 1899, MER No 22 was one of four power cars delivered in that year. It is pictured hauling an open toastrack on the gradient out of Laxey. With many of the trams well into their 10th decade, the MER is looking forward to the line's centenary in 1993 when a whole series of celebrations are planned. *MER*

Manx Electric

Fleet Numbers	Date	Trucks/Bogies	Body	Withdrawn
Motors				
1/2[1]	1893	Brush	Milnes	—
5/6/7/9[2]	1894	Brush	Milnes	—
14/5/7/8[3]	1898	Milnes	Milnes	—
16[4]	1898	Brush	Milnes	—
19-22[5]	1899	Brill	Milnes	—
23[6]	1925	Brill	MER	—
25-7[7]	1898	Brush	Milnes	—
28-31[8]	1904	Milnes	UEC	—
32/3[9]	1906	Brill	UEC	—
Trailers				
36-7[10]	1894	Milnes	Milnes	—
40/1/4[11]	1930	Milnes	EE	—
42/3[12]	1903	Milnes	Milnes	—
45-8[13]	1899	Milnes	Milnes	—
49-54[14]	1893	Milnes	Milnes	—
55/6[15]	1904	Brill	UEC	—
57/8[16]	1904	Brill	UEC	—
59[17]	1895	Milnes	Milnes	—
60[18]	1896	Milnes	Milnes	—
61/2[19]	1906	Brill	UEC	—

1	Unvestibuled saloons.	**11**	Crossbench, rebuilt after fire 1930.
2	Unvestibuled saloons.	**12**	Crossbench.
3	Crossbench.	**13**	Crossbench.
4	Crossbench.	**14**	Crossbench.
5	Winter saloons.	**15**	Crossbench.
6	Locomotive. Borrows trucks from either No 32 or No 33.	**16**	Saloon.
7	Crossbench.	**17**	Short saloon.
8	Crossbench.	**18**	Crossbench.
9	Crossbench.	**19**	Crossbench.
10	Crossbench.		

Note: Nos 3/4/8/24/34/5/8-41/4 destroyed by fire in 1930. Only Nos 40/1/4 rebuilt.

Left:
On 2 October 1967 MER car No 19 is pictured at Laxey with the 3.30pm service to Douglas.
R. E. Ruffell

With a route mileage at its peak in excess of 50 miles and with some 300 tramcars in operation, the tram system of Newcastle-upon-Tyne was by far the largest of northeast England. Despite its size, however, it was one of the many systems that only saw an extended existence as a result of World War 2.

The first tramways in Newcastle were all built by the Corporation and leased to the Newcastle & Gosforth Tramways & Carriage Co Ltd for a period of 21 years expiring on 21 November 1899. These first routes, all operated by horse-trams, were inaugurated in late 1878. To extend the tramway outside the borough boundary towards Gosforth, the company itself built an extension. Although there were experiments with steam power between 1879 and 1882, the horse-tram remained pre-eminent until the electrification of the system two decades later. In 1899 the Corporation obtained an Act, the Newcastle-upon-Tyne Tramways & Improvement Act, which empowered the Corporation to build some 21 miles of new tramway, to electrify the lines, and to purchase — compulsorily if necessary — those tramways outside the city. Work on electrification began on 19 April 1900. Efforts to ensure that some form of tramway operation was maintained during the transition period ended in failure and the last company-operated horse-tram ran on 13 April 1901, which meant that there was no further tram service until the new electric services were inaugurated on 16 December 1901. By that date some 14½ miles of route were completed and other sections followed quickly.

Outside the borough boundary, the Tyneside Tramways & Tramroads Co built two routes of later significance to the Corporation. These were from Wallsend to North Shields and from Wallsend, along the Great North Road, to Gosforth. This latter route opened in two stages, to Rothwell Road on 29 September 1902 and to Gosforth Park Gates on 18 April 1904. After a protracted dispute and the promotion of a private Bill in Parliament, agreement was reached between the Corporation and the company over through running, with through services starting later in 1904.

In the period leading up to the outbreak of World War 1 there were numerous extensions built to Newcastle's tramway system. These included Scotswood Bridge on 5 April 1906, Fenham on 5 September 1907 and Shieldfield on 4 October 1912. There were also two extensions opened during the war: Newburn to Throckley on 23 April 1915; and Benton Road to Benton on 25 February 1916. This expansion was also to continue into the postwar era: in the decade after 1918 some £686,000 was spent in expanding and modernising the tramways. Some of this expenditure went into improving the existing tramcar fleet and in buying new cars, such as the 'B' class of 1926, but much of it went into the further

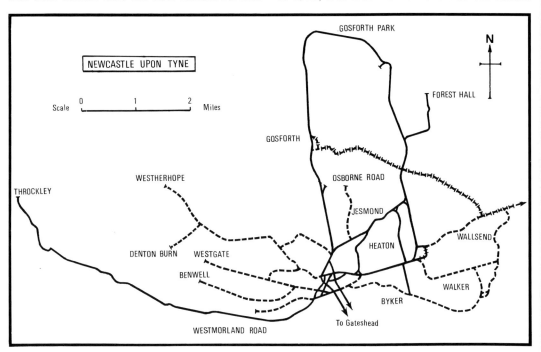

expansion of the network. The first postwar extension, from Benton to Forest Hall and to Gosforth, opened on 8 April 1921. The extension to Gosforth was later to be extended by the construction of the Gosforth Park Light Railway to link up with the Tyneside Co's line to form a circular. Further significant extensions saw the trams reach Slatyford in 1922, Benwell and Melbourne Street in 1923, Westerhope and the Fox and Hounds (an extension of the Westgate Road route) in 1925, and Denton Burn in 1926. More significantly, the two links across the Tyne, linking Newcastle's trams with those of Gateshead, opened on 12 January 1923 and 10 October 1928. But, by 1928, even with the expenditure made over the previous decade, the position of the tramcar was under threat. There was considerable opposition to the decision to run trams over the new High Level Bridge, and this link was destined to be the last wholly new track built in the area.

Elsewhere the tramcar was on the retreat; as early as 1912 Newcastle had experimented with a bus service (to Westerhope) and by the mid-1920s there were five bus services operating in the city. This trend was destined to continue as much of the new housing development occurred beyond the termini of the existing tram routes. On 6 April 1930 the Tyneside Tramways & Tramroads Co ceased to operate trams. Newcastle took over the section of track in Gosforth along the Great North Road from that date and continued to operate on the through services to Wallsend until 25 May 1930, when a new joint

bus service was introduced. At the opening of the Gosforth Light Railway in 1924 the Corporation produced a special film to celebrate the opening; six years later the Corporation adopted a policy that 'in every case when the permanent way of a tram route becomes worn out, and must be renewed if a tram service is to be continued, careful consideration must be given to . . . whether the route could be more efficiently served by a form of transport other than trams'. There could be no better indication of the contemporary shift in attitudes. Already, on 3 June 1929, after barely three years, the Denton Burn service was converted to bus operation. This was partly the result of bus competition but also, and more significantly, the consequence of Newcastle's policy of building these later extensions as effectively single-track with passing loops.

However, although trolleybuses were first considered as a replacement in 1931, it was decided that the tram system would be patched up. Three years later, in 1934, the question of tram replacement surfaced again and it was agreed to adopt trolleybuses on the route to Wallsend. The necessary powers were obtained in the Newcastle-upon-Tyne Corporation Act of 1934, and this was extended by a further Act the following year to enable trolleybus operation over all routes. Work started on 8 April 1935 and the new service, linking Denton Burn with Wallsend, was inaugurated on 1 October 1935. The success of the new service led to a policy of tram conversion. The next tram-to-trolleybus conversion was Brighton Grove to Welbeck Road (Walker) via Stanhope

Above:
**The Class B fully-enclosed double-deck trams were
the last new tramcars to be delivered to Newcastle.
The first five (Nos 232-36) were constructed in the
Corporation's own workshops from 1917 to 1920
whilst the remainder were built by Brush and
delivered in three batches from 1921 to 1926.
No 270, seen here at Scotswood on 20 March 1949,
was one of those delivered in 1923. The Scotswood
route was to close finally some seven months later
on 10 September.**

Street and Shields Road, which occurred on 19 September 1937. In the same month the Council met and agreed further conversions. The trolleybus system grew considerably over the next year, with routes such as that from Westerhope to Central station and Osborne Road to Central station being converted. By early 1939 the tram route mileage had declined to 31. The next conversion, however, the Westmorland Road route, on 2 July 1939, was in favour of buses. The policy of conversion was to be considerably delayed by the outbreak of war; the next proposed closure, that of Elswick Road, was delayed for almost five years from the originally scheduled date of September 1939.

By 1939 Newcastle had a considerable surplus of tramcars. These included a number of 'C' class single-deck cars of 1901 and some of the 'D' class double-deck cars of the same year. Survivors of both types were offered to Sheffield, but rejected, although a number of the 'C' class were subsequently sold to both Gateshead and Grimsby & Immingham in 1947-48. The remainder were scrapped. Sheffield did, however, acquire 14 of

the 'A' class double-deck cars in 1941 for the temporary replacement of cars damaged in the Blitz. On 11 June 1944 the long delayed conversion of the Elswick Road route was completed using second-hand trolleybuses bought from Bradford. No trams were scrapped after this closure.

Thus, by 1945, Newcastle's tramways had contracted to about half their peak. Apart from the long route to Throckley, the trams were now concentrated on the east and north of the city and on the joint services to Gateshead. To operate the services there were about 200 tramcars of varying vintages, the most recent of which were the final 'B' class cars of 1926. It was clear that the policy of tramcar abandonment was to be renewed, although the complication of the joint services with Gateshead was still to be resolved.

Further trolleybus powers were obtained in the 1945 Act and formal powers to convert the remainder of the system were set out in the Newcastle-upon-Tyne Corporation Act of 1946. In February 1946, some 36 new trolleybuses were ordered, followed in November by an order for a further 50. At the same time, infrastructure work took place to enable conversions to proceed. On 1 June 1946 the first postwar conversion, the Throckley route to bus, took effect with 'B' class car No 253 operating the final service. Not all was negative, however, as the Gosforth Park Light Railway saw its first services since 1939 at the end of July 1946. This was marred by a serious collision in Gosforth between cars Nos 276 and 300 in which one person was killed and several injured.

Work progressed on the conversion scheme. In early 1947 additional land was acquired at Gosforth to enable a trolleybus turning circle to be built — the Light Railway's private right of way and the circular route were to be abandoned with the closure of the tramway — and in October 1947 some 50 further trolleybuses were ordered. At the same time 46 trams were put up for sale; there was no taker but the scrapman. On 16 April 1948 No 290 operated to Gosforth as the last tram on the route. In future the only tramcars to be found in the Park would be there for scrapping.

On 31 October 1948, buses, rather than trolleybuses, replaced trams to Forest Hall, West Moor and Chillingham Road/Shieldfield. The service from New Bridge Street to Chillingham Road via Byker Bridge, which was abandoned at this date, had only been introduced following the Gosforth closure on 18 April 1948. The overhead was retained on the West Moor route to enable trams to reach Gosforth Park on their final journey.

Newcastle-upon-Tyne Closures

1 June 1946	Throckley to Scotswood Bridge
16 April 1948	Gosforth
31 October 1948	Forest Hall
31 October 1948	West Moor
31 October 1948	Chillingham Road/Shieldfield
10 September 1949	Scotswood Bridge
4 March 1950	Saltwell Park
4 March 1950	Wrekenton

Last tram: Not recorded

Above:
With Class B No 262 in the background, 1912-built balcony car No 196 is seen at Central station on 13 March 1948. One of a batch of 17 cars built by Newcastle Corporation on Brill 21E trucks, No 196, like the remainder of the class, remained as a balcony car throughout its life, unlike many of the older cars which had been rebuilt fully enclosed.

Above right:
With seating for 84 passengers, the Class F double-deck trams of Newcastle Corporation were amongst the largest tramcars built for operation in Britain. Dating originally from 1901, the 22 cars of the type were rebuilt as open-top double-deckers in 1903-05 from their original single-deck form. With many of the type surviving into the late 1940s, Newcastle was one of the last places in Britain where it was possible to travel regularly on an open-top tram. No 91 is seen here on 15 March 1948 outside Newcastle Central station. One of the class, No 102, is now preserved and restored at the National Tramway Museum.

The effects of the 1948 closures included the cessation of the joint routes beyond Central station and the Museum, and for the next 18 months Newcastle's tramway operations would be limited to the joint services from Central station and the Museum over the Tyne bridges to Wrekenton and Saltwell Park. There remained the problem of resolving the dispute with Gateshead over the future of the joint services but, as already described in the section on Gateshead, by 1950 it seemed clear that Gateshead would never adopt trolleybuses and that the future of the joint services lay in the diesel bus. Newcastle's final trams operated on 4 March 1950, leaving Gateshead in the curious position of operating the final trams into New-

castle until its final closure in August 1951.

After closure the remaining Newcastle trams were scrapped at Byker depot, rather than at Gosforth Park with one notable exception — 1901-built 'F' class open-top car No 102, which was preserved. After display at a number of sites, including the Motor Museum at Beaulieu, No 102 now resides at the National Tramway Museum at Crich. The body of four-wheel car No 114 has subsequently been rescued for restoration at Beamish.

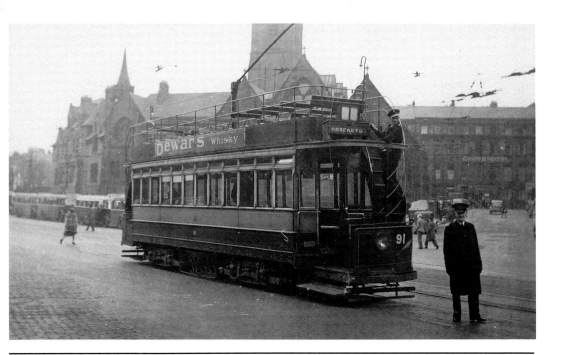

Newcastle-upon-Tyne

Fleet Numbers	Date	Trucks/Bogies	Body	Withdrawn
1-28/192[1]	1906-10	Brill 21E	Newcastle CT	1946-49
29/42/3/52/4/77/ 80/8[2]	1902	Brill 27G (25 received Peckham P25 bogies in 1932-33 including those sold in 1948)	Hurst Nelson	All withdrawn by 1948. 29/42/77 to G&I in 1948. 43/52/4/80/8 to Gateshead
89-97/9-110[3]	1901	Brill 27G	Newcastle CT	1946-49 (98 withdrawn 1917 after fire)
111/5/20/1/7/130[4]	1905-07	Brill 21E	Hurst Nelson	1947
131-65[5]	1901	Brill 21E	Brush	All by 1939 (except those used for works)
170-91[6]	1903-04	Brill 21E	Newcastle CT	By 1949
193-229[7]	1912-16	Brill 21E (except 203/4/206/ 7/10/1/5/6 on Peckham P22)	Brush (210-24), Newcastle CT (225-9)	1947-50
232-6/240-50/2-309[8]	1917-26	Peckham P22	Newcastle CT (232-6), Brush (rest)	1947-50
237[9]	1921	Peckham P22	Newcastle CT	By 1949
310-2[10]	1921-23	Brill 21E	Newcastle CT	By 1949

1 Class H. Built to replace single-deck trams and possibly incorporated parts. 1946 Nos 1/3/13/7/22/4/6 renumbered 24/26/17/13/1/22/3.
2 Class C. Most had been rebuilt 1916-33.
3 Class F. Single-deck bogie cars. Rebuilt as open-top 1903-05. Nos 96, 105/8 rebuilt with balcony tops 1905-07. No 105 lost top-cover c1918. Nos 96/108 were vestibuled 1938. No 102 preserved.
4 Class A. Batch 111-30. Nos 111/5/20/121/7/30 vestibuled 1933. Remainder sold to Sheffield 1941. No 120 renumbered 24 1947.
5 Class D. No 143 was breakdown tram; 168 was sand tram. Certain others survived 1939 — offered to Sheffield 1941 but declined and scrapped 1947-48.
6 Class G. Originally open-top, converted to fully-enclosed 1927-29.
7 Class E.
8 Class B.
9 Rail grinder.
10 Sand cars.

Situated on the western slopes of the Pennines, Oldham owed its prosperity to cotton. Although always overshadowed by its neighbour in the west, Manchester, the town grew rapidly during the 19th century. Like all the south Lancashire tramways, Oldham tramways were constructed to the 4ft 8½in gauge and even after the closures of the 1930s formed part of an interlinked tramway network that included Manchester and Stockport.

The Corporation of Oldham was granted parliamentary powers in 1870 and 1878 to construct, but not operate, a tramway system. The first route from Hollinwood to Asa Lees (later extended to Waterhead) was opened on 16 September 1880 and leased to the Manchester Carriage & Tramways Co. This route was operated by horse-trams, but the next two routes, from Royton to the boundary of the borough at Werneth and to Hathershaw via the town centre, were both operated by the steam-trams of the Manchester, Bury, Rochdale & Oldham Steam Tramways Co. These routes, which opened in November 1885, subsequently passed to the Bury, Rochdale & Oldham Tramways Co Ltd when the original company went bankrupt.

In 1899 the Corporation obtained further powers to enable it to both operate tramways and to build a new electric-operated system. The first electric route, from Chadderton to Rochdale Road (where it met the steam-tram service to Royton), was opened on 15 December 1900. Further extensions followed during 1901, but these early extensions were all separate due to the continuing existence of both the company-operated systems. On 31 October 1901 the lease on the horse-tram route expired and the lease on the steam-tram network was surrendered, although the latter still had some two years to run. On 1 November 1901 the horse-trams ceased to operate and for six months there was no service on the key Hollinwood-Waterhead service whilst it was converted to electric traction. It was finally reopened on 17 May 1902. Steam-trams were withdrawn on 19 November 1901, but were temporarily reintroduced over sections of the system whilst conversion work progressed. On 7 March 1902 the first section of the converted steam-tram route was reopened.

Whilst the conversion work was proceeding on the former horse- and steam-tram routes, the Corporation was also proceeding rapidly with the extension of the electric tramway network, both inside the borough and also in outlying areas where the track was leased from other local authorities (in Lees, Royton and Shaw). In 1906, through electric tram operation to Rochdale was inaugurated followed later the same year by services to Manchester. The former was destined to be relatively short-lived, being abandoned in 1913 due to a low bridge precluding the use of top-covered trams, but that to Manchester continued right until the end of tramway operation in the town. A third through service, linking the town with Ashton, was started in 1921, but abandoned in 1925 when Ashton converted to trolleybus operation. The desire to maintain a through service between the two towns led Oldham to install trolleybus overhead on the route and to buy a couple of trolleybuses. This conversion was, however, less than successful and led to motorbuses replacing the through trolleybuses in April 1926. Oldham's trolleybuses were themselves finally withdrawn in September 1926.

The last route extension in the borough was opened on 4 June 1914 along the Ripponden Road to Grains Bar. This was not the final increase in Oldham's track mileage, however, as in August 1925 the Corporation bought the section of track from Chadderton to Mills Hill Bridge from the Middleton Electric Traction Co Ltd.

The 1920s were a period of contradiction in Oldham. The experiment with trolleybuses led to the temporary withdrawal of trams on the Hathershaw-Summit route although the same year was to witness the delivery of the last new trams delivered — a batch of 12 fully-enclosed trams built by English Electric. In 1928 the conversion of the Lees route was advocated on the grounds that the track needed replacement and this led, on 1 May 1928, to the trams reappearing on the Hathershaw-Summit route but being withdrawn the following day from the Mumps-Lees

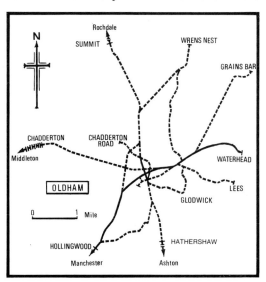

Left:
Oldham No 16, one of a batch of balcony-top double-deck trams delivered in 1921, waits at Hollinwood where the Oldham and Manchester tram systems met. *Modern Transport*

ervice. This closure was followed on 24 December 1928 by the closure of the Ripponden Road oute to Grains Bar. Part of this route was, however, retained for a further four years to serve the ugby ground.

After the closure of the Grains Bar route there ere no further closures until 1935. It had been ecided the year earlier that the trams would be rogressively withdrawn over a five-year period. On 11 June 1935 the services from Middleton Iills to Market Place and from Chadderton Road o Shaw via the Market Place were converted to notorbus operation. These were followed on 1 December 1935 by the service from Hollinwood, via Hollins, to the Market Place. Three routes were converted on 6 November 937: Hathershaw-Star Inn-Summit (for the second time); the Glodwick circular; and the peak-our service from Waterhead to Star Inn.

These closures meant that there were now only two routes running and these were scheduled for closure in September 1939. The outbreak of World War 2 intervened and gave the nain Hollinwood-Waterhead service a reprieve, but the second route, from Shaws Wren Nest to Hollinwood, was converted to bus operation on 2 December 1939 due to the condition of the tram track. Oldham retained some 26 trams to operate its remaining service, although these were supplemented by trams from Manchester Corporation on the joint through service from Waterhead (via Hollinwood) to Manchester.

With the end of World War 2 it proved possible for Oldham to obtain a sufficient quantity of buses to enable the final withdrawal of the trams to take place, the last tram, No 4 suitably decorated, operating on 3 August 1946. Manchester's trams continued to serve the route to Hollinwood from the south for a further few months. This was, however, not quite the end of Oldham's trams for six (Nos 17, 18, 24, 125, 126 and 128) were sold to Gateshead, where they remained in service for a further four years.

Oldham Closure

3 August 1946	Hollinwood to Waterhead

Last tram: No 4

Oldham

leet Numbers	Date	Trucks/Bogies	Body	Withdrawn
-6/8-12/14/6[1]	1921	Preston 21E	EE	1946
7/8/22/4[2]	1924	Preston 21E	EE	1946
21-32[3]	1925-6	Preston 21E	EE	1946

1 Balcony top.
2 Fully enclosed. Nos 17/8/24 to Gateshead 1946 and renumbered 72, 71 and 35 respectively.
3 Fully enclosed. Nos 122/5/8 to Gateshead 1946 and renumbered 68-70.

Whilst the majority of British tramways adopted the standard gauge of 4ft 8½in, most of the tramways constructed in the southwest adopted their own standard gauge of 3ft 6in. The only one of these latter systems to survive into the postwar era was that of Plymouth, and even this survival was but a fraction of a much larger network.

The first tram route in Plymouth, paradoxically constructed to the gauge of 4ft 8½in, was opened by a subsidiary of the Provincial Tramways Co in 1872. This initial route, linking Derry's Clock with Cumberland Gardens, was subsequently extended to Devonport in 1874. The first incursion by 3ft 6in-gauge trams came in 1880 when the Plymouth, Devonport & District Tramways Co opened a steam-operated tramway from Millbay station to Hyde Park Corner (Mannamead). After a period of steam operation this latter operator converted to horse operation under the aegis of the Plymouth Tramways Co. In 1892 Plymouth Corporation acquired the 3ft 6in-gauge system and over the next decade progressively extended it to, inter alia, Mutley.

In 1896 Plymouth Corporation received the Royal Assent to its Bill to allow for the electrification of the Corporation-owned tramways and the first section, from Theatre Royal to Prince Rock, opened on 22 September 1899. Further extensions were built, such as Peverell Park Road in January 1903, and the old horse-operated routes were converted. The last Corporation-owned horse-tram operated, on The Hoe and Piers route, on 22 June 1907.

Until 1914 Devonport formed a completely separate settlement to Plymouth and saw the development of a distinct 3ft 6in-gauge electric tramway under the ownership of a subsidiary of British Electric Traction. This, the Devonport & District Tramways Co, constructed a small network of tramways to serve the town, linking the centre to Stoke, Camel's Head, Keyham and Millbridge. The section from St Budeaux to Saltash Passage was physically separated from the rest of the Devonport & District system until 1903 when the existing footbridge was rebuilt into an embankment. Devonport retained its separate identity until October 1914 when the towns of Plymouth and Devonport were united. As a consequence BET sold its interests in Devonport & District to Plymouth Corporation and connections were completed, linking the two systems where they met.

Whilst all these developments were occurring there still remained the solitary 4ft 8½in-gauge line of the Plymouth, Stonehouse & Devonport Tramways Co. The original horse-tramway in the town was converted to electric traction in 1901 having already been converted to 3ft 6in gauge.

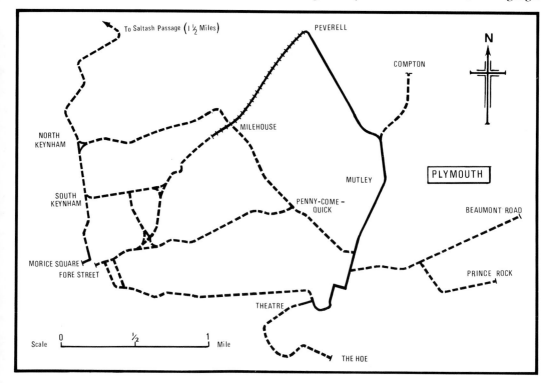

Above:
Plymouth No 158 was one of a batch of 15 open-top trams built in the operator's own workshops in 1927-28. Originally constructed as bogie trams, all were converted to four-wheel in 1930-31. No 158 was seriously damaged during the war, but was repaired and survived to become the system's official last tram. *F. N. T. Lloyd-Jones*

The company also sold its track in Devonport and Stonehouse to the respective Corporations, retaining ownership of the short section from Stonehouse Bridge to Manor Street, in exchange for a 21-year lease of the operating of the route. In 1914, with the union of Plymouth with Devonport and Stonehouse, new connections were made linking the Devonport & District to the Corporation tramways at Peverell and Pennycomequick in 1915. The PS&D was allowed to continue operating trams until the expiry of its lease in 1922.

In 1919 a new manager was appointed and he energetically improved the main depot and workshops at Milehouse and proposed a number of tramway extensions. Of these extensions only one, along Alma Road linking Pennycomequick with Milehouse, was actually constructed, being

opened in June 1922. By this time, however, the Corporation had already introduced its first motorbuses, powers for which had been obtained in 1915.

Although tramways were falling out of favour elsewhere in the southwest, Plymouth continued to modernise its fleet, constructing 16 new tramcars at Milehouse in the period 1925-28. Like all previous Plymouth double-deck trams these were open-top; repeated requests to the Board of Trade for permission to operate enclosed trams were rejected, despite the precedent of Halifax in terms of operating enclosed trams on hilly 3ft 6in-gauge systems.

Despite the relatively recent investment in new tramcars, the 1930s were to witness the almost total dismemberment of the Plymouth tramway system. The first route to close was that from Morice Square (via South Keyham) to St Budeaux in October 1930, although other routes were extended in part compensation. Although now pursuing a policy of withdrawal, second-hand trams were acquired from both Exeter and Torquay (in 1932 and 1934 respectively) and this allowed for the withdrawal of Plymouth's older trams. The period witnessed an almost relentless decline in the Plymouth tramway network, so that by September 1939, on the outbreak of World War 2, only one route — Theatre to Peverell (with access to Milehouse depot) — remained. This would have closed but for the outbreak of war.

As one of Britain's most important naval towns it was inevitable that Plymouth would face severe air attack from the Luftwaffe and during the course of the war much of the town centre was destroyed. In one air raid on 29 March 1941, tram No 153 was destroyed and No 158 was seriously damaged. This attack also led to the temporary suspension of the tramway service. When it was reintroduced the town section was foreshortened so that for the last four years the service started from Old Town Street. By 1945 only four trams remained available for service (Nos 154, 157, 158 and 165) and on 29 September 1945 Plymouth became the second postwar system to close when No 158, which had been repaired after its wartime damage, carried the official party to Milehouse depot.

Plymouth Closure

29 September 1945 (Theatre)-Old Town Street to Peverell

Last tram: No 158

Plymouth

Fleet Numbers	Date	Trucks/Bogies	Body	Withdrawn
151[1]	1925	MSCC/Plymouth CT bogies. Retrucked with Peckham P22 trucks 1930-31	PCT	1945
152/4/5/7-62/165/6[2]	1926-28	MSCC/Plymouth CT bogies. Retrucked with Peckham P22 trucks 1930-31	PCT	1945

1 Experimental bogie car, open top.
2 Batch 152-66, open-top bogie trams. No 158 damaged World War 2 but repaired and acted as official last tram.

Left:
No 165 was the penultimate of Plymouth's last batch of trams to enter service. Like so many of the narrow gauge systems, Plymouth suffered restrictions in terms of vehicle design.
F. N. T. Lloyd-Jones

Of the two tramways that survived World War 2 in what now constitutes South Yorkshire, Rotherham's was by far the smaller of the two, although it could lay claim to some of the most unusual tramcars to have operated in Britain and, arguably, one of the more unusual tramway histories.

Although there were several early proposals for a horse-tramway in the town, with the first in 1876 and powers being obtained in 1881, these early schemes came to nought. It was not until the last year of the 19th century that more concrete developments occurred, when the twin authorities of Rotherham and Rawmarsh began to support the idea of tramway networks. Unfortunately, despite their proximity, they were unable to agree a joint approach, and this was to have a considerable bearing upon the development of public transport in the area. The initial result was that both local authorities promoted Bills for the construction of tramways, both receiving the Royal Assent at the end of July 1900. Whilst Rotherham proceeded with its proposals, Rawmarsh had second thoughts and ultimately transferred its powers to what became the Mexborough and Swinton Tramways Co Ltd.

The first sections of the new electric tramway, built to the gauge of 4ft 8½in, were opened officially on 31 January 1903. These two routes, from College Square along the Rawmarsh Road and from Effingham Street to the Pumping Station on the road to Dalton, were quickly followed by further extensions. The route to Kimberworth was opened on 8 April 1903, that to Canklow on 6 June 1903 and the Templeborough route on 8 June 1903. The last was further extended to Tinsley on 31 July 1903. At Tinsley, Rotherham's tramways met those of Sheffield, but it was not until 20 June 1905 that agreement was reached with the southern neighbour to start through running, services commencing in September 1905.

Although parliamentary powers were obtained at the same time as Rotherham's, the construction of the Mexborough & Swinton route was a long-drawn-out affair. It was not until February 1906 that work started and, to complicate matters yet further, the company adopted the French Dolter stud method of current collection. The first section of the tramway was opened in February 1907 but it was not until August 1907 that the full route to Swinton was opened — and by this date it was apparent that the Dolter stud system was a disaster. Although the Rotherham-owned line from Rawmarsh into College Square was fitted with studs to facilitate the through service, and although the Rotherham General Manager contemplated the fitting of Dolter studs to two Rotherham trams, the problems with the stud system (which included a number of horses being killed through electric shocks) meant that the pick-ups were never fitted. The situation deteriorated to such an extent that, on 30 July 1908, Swinton Council sent a telegram to the Board of Trade requesting the withdrawal of the stud system and the Board responded the same day acceding to the request. By this date the bulk of the Mexborough & Swinton route had already been fitted with conventional overhead and only the section within Swinton remained. The conversion work was completed on 29 August and from 20 October 1908 Rotherham operated a second through service, this time northwards.

Further extensions to the Rotherham system were opened on 1 October 1906 (to Dalton) and on 2 March 1910 along the Wellgate. There remained a need to serve other districts, but there were severe doubts as to the viability of some of them. In October 1910 it was decided to seek parliamentary powers to operate trolleybuses, and an Act allowing for this, along with two further tramway extensions to Broom and Thrybergh, was obtained. The initial trolleybus route was designed to provide a link between the new tram terminus at Broom and the mining settlement at Maltby. The two new tramway extensions and the trolleybus route all opened during 1912.

Although the through service to Sheffield had been established in 1905, there were problems over fares and workmen's services that led to friction between the two operators, a situation which was exacerbated by the incorporation of the Parish of Tinsley into Sheffield in 1912. Disagreement led to the cessation of the through

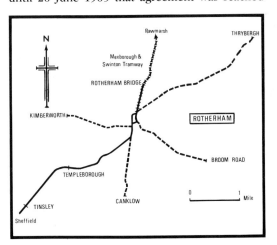

service in September 1914 and, although rein-stated in May 1915, the various disputes were not resolved until arbitration in 1916. Ultimately, however, the section of track between Tinsley and Templeborough, the disputed section, passed to Sheffield's ownership in January 1926 at the end of Rotherham's lease.

After World War 1, there were a number of proposals for tramway extensions, including the partial replacement of the then unpopular trol-leybus service to Maltby. In the event the only sig-nificant changes to Rotherham's trams in the immediate postwar years saw a number of alter-ations in the town centre to ease congestion. The last of these opened in September 1922 and this meant that the tramways had reached their maxi-mum extent.

The start of the decline of Rotherham's trams can be dated to 1924 when trolleybus services were extended from Broom to the town centre to duplicate the existing tramway. Much more seri-ous, however, was the joint decision, between Rotherham and Mexborough & Swinton in November 1926, to convert the Rawmarsh route to trolleybus operation. After Mexborough & Swinton obtained powers, work started on the conversion in 1928 and the through trolleybus services were completed to Conisborough on 10 March 1929. For Rotherham, however, the conversion did not lead to a great deal of track closure, since the fleet's depot was situated on the route. Further closures followed soon, as the final trams ran on the Broom route on 10 June 1929. This closure was followed on 16 May 1931 by the conversion of the Kimberworth to Dalton and Thybergh services to trolleybus operation.

These closures meant that the Rotherham sys-tem was now reduced to two routes — the joint service to Sheffield and the line to Canklow. Rotherham had already suggested, in July 1930, that the through service be converted, but this was rejected by Sheffield. As a consequence Rotherham, in pursuance of the 1930 Rotherham Corporation Act, undertook a number of improvements and, in addition, acquired 11 single-ended tramcars, delivered in 1934-35, from English Electric. Prior to the delivery of these trams, however, the route to Canklow was converted to bus operation on 9 July 1934.

To facilitate the operation of the new single-ended tramcars, which had the appearance of trolleybuses on rails, a reversing triangle was con-structed at Templeborough for short workings. The construction of the various loops in Rother-ham town centre in the early 1920s had already provided a loop in the centre. With the exception of one older car, No 12 (although not the original car of that number), all the non-single-ended trams were scrapped. No 12 was retained for a variety of operational reasons, and was regularly pressed into service to alleviate an acute vehicle shortage. In 1939 No 12 was fitted with platform vestibules and three years later was again rebuilt, to emerge as a fully-enclosed car.

The through service was maintained through-out the war, and although Rotherham did extend trolleybus overhead to the boundary at Temple-borough to improve workmen's services, the experiment proved short-lived and unsuccessful. Whilst Rotherham's trams were generally limited to the normal route, Sheffield did, on occasion, extend the through service to outlying termini,

such as Intake. Rotherham continued to experience vehicle shortages and so the heaviest load in maintaining the service fell upon Sheffield. In order to improve the situation, Rotherham obtained the loan of (and subsequently bought) an elderly Leeds tram. This vehicle, No 125A in the Leeds fleet, was rebuilt fully enclosed and numbered 14 in the Rotherham fleet.

Although Rotherham had earlier been keen to abandon the through route, the immediate post-war era saw the Corporation undertake track repairs and the Transport Department was authorised to reconstruct the depot fan. However, despite the continuing shortage of vehicles, Rotherham did not increase its fleet and the bulk of the service continued to rely upon Sheffield. In 1948 it emerged that the combined railway and canal bridge at Tinsley was in urgent need of repair. To facilitate work on the bridge the through service was suspended on 11 December 1948. It would never be reinstated. During 1949 it was jointly decided that the reconstructed bridge would not carry tram track and Sheffield

decided to close the section from Vulcan Works to Tinsley. With the termination of the through service and its replacement, after the completion of bridge work, by buses, Rotherham's tramways lost their sole *raison d'être*. It came as no surprise, therefore, when the final Rotherham tram was run on 13 November 1949. The last car, No 11, operated without a formal ceremony. Despite their relative youth (they were only 14 years old), all the single-ended cars were scrapped, bringing to an end one of the more unusual operations amongst British tramways.

Rotherham Closure

13 November 1949   Rotherham to Templeborough (joint service to Sheffield suspended in 1948)

Last tram: No 11

Rotherham

Fleet Numbers	Date	Trucks/Bogies	Body	Withdrawn
1-6[1]	1934	EMB Hornless	EE	1949
7-11[2]	1935	EMB Hornless	EE	1949
12[3]	1902	Brill 21E	ERTCW	1949
14[4]	1942 (acquired)	Brill 21E	Leeds CT	1949

1   Single-ended for use on the through service to Sheffield.
2   As Nos 1-6.
3   One of the original batch 1-12, rebuilt with domed top 1935 and fully enclosed 1942.
4   Leeds No 125 (125A from 1927) built originally 1908.

With the majority of its tram routes terminating in the city of Manchester, the tramway history of Salford was inextricably interwoven with that of its larger neighbour across the River Irwell. However, relations between the two operators were not always harmonious and in the early days of electric traction a full-scale 'tram war' was nearly the result.

In 1875 Salford Corporation obtained powers to build a number of tram routes. The first two routes, opened in 1877, linked Pendleton to Albert Bridge and from the borough boundary in Bury New Road to Kersal Bar. As elsewhere the actual operation of the horse-tramways was leased out, the lease eventually passing, in 1886, to the Manchester Carriage & Tramways Co. This company, which dominated the pre-municipal era in this part of Lancashire, eventually operated a network of some 143 route miles. On 27 April

1901 the company's lease expired and Salford Corporation acquired some 50 miles of track within the borough's boundaries for £42,500.

Salford Corporation moved quickly to electrify the system. The first two electric routes, from Kersal Bar along Bury New Road to Blackfriars Bridge in Manchester, and Grove Inn to Kersal, were opened on 4 October and 14 October 1901 respectively. Further conversions followed quickly: from Chapel Street to Irlams O'Th'Height on 21 November 1901; from Blackfriars to Great Clowes Street on 5 January 1902; Oldfield Road, Cross Lane and Trafford Road in February 1902; Regent Road and Eccles New Road on 4 April 1902; and so on. By October 1903, and the opening of Eccles station to Monton Green, Ordsall Lane and New Oldfield Road, the last horse-trams had been withdrawn. To operate the new fleet of electric trams, the Cor-

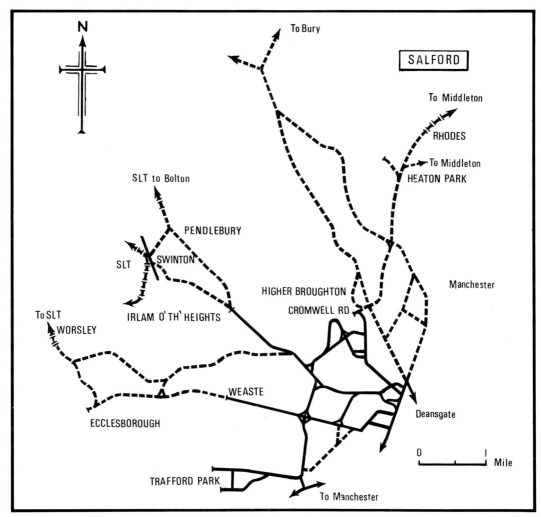

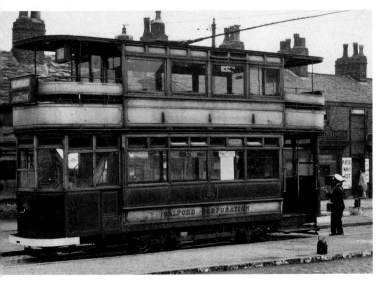

poration built a brand-new depot/works at Frederick Road, which also opened in 1901 and replaced the horse-tram depots inherited from the Manchester Carriage & Tramways Co.

The next three years were to witness the continuing expansion of the tramway network. Numerous extensions were built into adjacent districts, such as Swinton and Pendlebury in May 1903, from Kersal Bar progressively via Prestwich and Whitefield to link up with the trams of Bury at Radcliffe between 1902 and 1905, linking into the Trafford Park tramway on 30 October 1905 and, finally, the line from Winton to Worsley on 2 October 1906. This extension, which provided Salford with a further connection to the South Lancashire Tramways (which were also met at Swinton and Pendlebury) was, however, destined to be the final tramway extension built.

Thus, by 1906, Salford had come to form a centre-piece of the South Lancashire tramway network, bounded on the east by Manchester, on the west by South Lancashire Tramways and by Bury in the north. The opportunities for through running were great but these had taken their time to be established. Due to a dispute over the allocation of receipts (the two Corporations had, in theory, an agreement not to make profits in the other operator's area), Manchester excluded all Salford trams from Deansgate as and from 28 June 1901 with the consequence that all Salford services had to terminate on the bridges crossing the River Irwell. This dispute lasted for almost two years and through running was only reinstated on 31 May 1903. It was not for another two decades, however, that full advantage was taken of the interlinked systems. It was only in

early 1926 that a through service linking Manchester with Bury via Whitefield was established and a similar agreement saw a service to Walkden via Swinton and the South Lancashire Tramways. Between August and October 1926 a further five joint services were established between Salford and Manchester, such as service No 34 from Weaste to Belle Vue via Oldfield Road, Deansgate, Market Street and Ardwick.

However, by the late 1920s unbridled bus competition, in the era before regulation, critically undermined these new through services, indeed Salford Corporation was forced to operate buses in competition with corporation-owned trams in an effort to defeat the pirate operators, and it was inevitable that the joint services would cease. Thus from December 1930 service No 33 ceased to operate beyond Deansgate to Reddish. Other joint services were similarly reduced. Although the early 1930s witnessed the closure of the joint services, it was not until the middle years of the decade that the tramway system saw massive retrenchment in favour of the motorbus.

The first motorbuses had been introduced to Salford in 1920 but in 1925, when the trams numbered some 230, there were still only 19 motorbuses in service. This had increased to 76 by 1930. The first significant closure occurred on 19 March 1932 when the Victoria-Middleton via Rhodes service was abandoned. This was followed on 9 March 1935 by the abandonment of the services beyond Irlams O'Th'Height into Swinton and Pendlebury. Trams continued to serve Irlams O'Th'Height for a further decade. On 16 March 1935 the Kersal-Whitefield section of route No 63 was converted; until 1933 this had formed the through service to Bury. 1936 saw the closure of route No 37 from Kersal to Victoria on 30 April, route No 65 from Deansgate to Worsley on 7 October and route No 73 from Victoria to Whitefield on 7 November. The following year saw the conversion of route No 36 from Kersal to Victoria on 21 June and the section of route No 63 from Broughton to Kersal on 19 December. 1937 also probably saw the final running of route No 75, a part-day service from Deansgate to Weaste, route No 78, from Trafford Park to Deansgate via Cross Lane, and route No 79, a part-day service from Deansgate to Broughton via Great Clowes Street.

Despite all these closures it was not until 1938 that Salford operated more buses than trams. 1938 was to be the final year of operation for

route No 66 from Deansgate to Peel Green (via Monton) and route No 64, the alternative route from Deansgate to Peel Green via Patricroft, which closed on 1 May and 10 July respectively. It is likely that service No 68, from Pendleton to Broughton, which was latterly only a peak-hours service, also ceased operating in 1938.

In theory, 1939 was to be the penultimate year for Salford's trams, and it certainly witnessed a considerable acceleration in closures with five routes succumbing. The first closure of the year occurred on 18 March when two routes, Nos 67 and 76 from Cromwell Bridge via Deansgate to Peel Green and from Victoria to Eccles respectively, were closed. Part of the latter route as far as Weaste was reopened in June 1942 as a wartime emergency measure. It is likely that March 1939 also saw the final operation of route No 80, from Blackfriars Street to Weaste, which was a short working of route No 76. These closures were followed by route No 82, from Deansgate to Eccles station, on 30 April and route No 63, from Victoria to Broughton, on 11 June.

By 1940 the Salford tram fleet had declined to 61 operating three main services (four after the

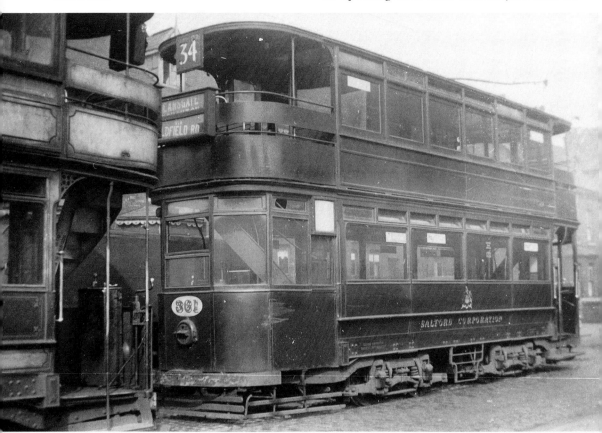

reopening of the Weaste route in 1942), from Deansgate to Irlams O'Th'Height, from Victoria to Cromwell Bridge and the Deansgate/Docks circular. In addition there remained a peak-hours service linking Pendleton with Trafford Park. World War 2 had few effects in Salford, apart from the reintroduction to Weaste, although some 30 trams appeared in a wartime grey livery after 1941. However, the war years were to witness the next closure, albeit unplanned, when on 29 May 1944 the service from Deansgate to Irlams O'Th'Height was, in theory temporarily replaced by buses due to a collapsed sewer in Bolton Road, between Pendleton and Irlams O'Th'Height. Peak-hour trams continued to serve Pendleton until the official date of conversion, 18 November 1945. The decision to make the conversion permanent had been taken the previous April.

On 10 August 1946 the General Manager, J. W. Blakemore, retired, and he was replaced by C. W. Booth. Salford's tram fleet now numbered some 38 in total — more than 20 others remained, however, but were not fit for service. A fortnight later, on 24 August 1946, the peak-hours only service linking Pendleton with Trafford Park was closed. During September, the official name of the department was changed to Salford City Transport and, as if to emphasise the break with the past, a new livery of green, rather than red, was adopted for the buses on 18 October.

1947, the last year of Salford's trams, was to see the closure first of all, in January, of route No 69, the peak-hours service from Victoria to Cromwell Bridge via Lower Broughton Road. Two months later, on 2 March, the restored services from Deansgate to Weaste (routes Nos 34 and 76) were again converted to bus operation

and Weaste depot (which had been originally built in 1929) was closed to trams. This left only the Deansgate and Docks circular route (Nos 70/71 — one number for each direction) in service. Final closure was not long delayed. The last Salford trams operated on 31 March 1947, with No 350, which dated originally from 1903, being the official last car. By early June 1947 the last trams had been taken to Hyde Road Works in Manchester for scrapping and work had started on dismantling the remaining overhead. No Salford tram survived into the era of preservation and thus only photographs can keep alive the memory of this important operator.

Salford Closures

18 November 1945	81 — Deansgate to Irlams O'Th'Height. Conversion made permanent — had been temporarily run by buses following a sewer collapse on 29 May 1944
24 August 1946	Peak-hour trams linking Pendleton with Trafford Park
January 1947	69 — Victoria to Cromwell Bridge via Lower Broughton Road (peak-hours service)
2 March 1947	34/76 — Deansgate to Weaste
31 March 1947	70/71 — Deansgate and Docks circular

Last tram: No 350

Salford

Fleet Numbers	Date	Trucks/Bogies	Body	Withdrawn
154-6/8[1]	1913-14	Brill 21E	Brush	1946-47
201-12	1915	Brill 61E bogies	Brush	1946-47
214-9/21/2[2]	1915	Brill 61E bogies	Brush	1944-47
225-30[3]	1923-24	Peckham P22, replaced by Brill 21E	Brush	1946-47
333-5/8/9/41/344/6-53/6-8[4]	1902-03	Brill 27G bogies	Milnes	1946-47
361/3-5/7/9-371/3/6[5]	1903	Brill 27G bogies	BEC	1944-47
380[6]	1905 (acquired)	Brill 27G bogies	BEC	1947

1 Batch 151-60. Delivered with vestibules, top-covers fitted 1923. No 154 had top-deck vestibules fitted 1928.
2 Batch 213-24. Open-top, built for Worsley-Whitefield route due to low bridges. Top-covers fitted 1922.
3 Specially-built low-height fully enclosed.
4 Originally open-top, top-covers fitted 1923-24. Batch 101-30 renumbered 330-59 1929-35.
5 Open-top originally. Top-covers fitted pre-1914. No 364 received top-deck vestibules. Batch 131-50 renumbered 360-79 1926-35.
6 Trafford Park No 10 built 1903. Rebuilt 1924. Renumbered from 161 c1935.

Sheffield's immaculate fleet of four-wheel cars, painted in their familiar blue and cream livery, were amongst the most attractive of all British tramcars, and the Sheffield system was the last municipal tramway to close in England.

In 1872 the Sheffield Tramways Co obtained an Act to construct nine miles of tramway within the city. Within the Act there was a clause enabling the Corporation to build the lines and to lease them to the company if the Corporation so decided. The Corporation decided to exercise these powers. The first route, from Lady's Bridge to Attercliffe (later extended to Tinsley) was opened on 6 October 1873, and over the next four years four additional routes were built. All of these, built to standard gauge, were horse-operated. In December 1895 the Corporation decided to promote a Bill for the takeover of operations when the company's lease expired in 1896. The takeover was effective from 11 July 1896 and was confirmed by the Sheffield Corporation Act of 1897. This Act also allowed for the construction of new tramlines and for the adoption of mechanical power. In August 1897 it was decided to utilise electricity. Work started on the actual conversion in February 1898 with the start of work on building the power station at Kelham Island. The first section of electrified line, from Tinsley to Nether Edge, was opened on 5 September 1899 using four cars (Nos 46-49) converted from horse-trams. Over the next few years the conversion programme was rapid, and the last horse-tram operated on 11 November 1902 on the Hillsborough route, and this was also the last ex-horse-tram route to see electric services when these were inaugurated on 30 May 1903.

In addition to the conversion of the existing horse-tram routes, work also proceeded on the extensions authorised under the 1897 Act. These included Darnall (11 April 1901), Intake (17 April 1902) and culminated with Wolseley Road on 25 December 1904. By 1904 there were some 241 cars in service, including a number of single-deck trams for use on hilly routes and those with low bridges. The latter aspect was a serious problem and was only gradually solved by a programme of road-lowering, which enabled double-deck trams to operate over those routes. The next major advance occurred on 20 June 1905 when Rotherham's trams met those of Sheffield at Tinsley. Through running commenced on 11 September 1905. 1905 also witnessed the erection of permanent buildings at Queen's Road, where many of Sheffield's future tramcars were to be built.

After the Rotherham link there was to be a period of consolidation before the next period of expansion between 1908 and 1912. On 19 May 1908 the line from Holme Lane junction to Malin Bridge was opened and this was followed on 1 August by the line to Banner Cross. On 29 May 1909 the Darnall service was extended to Handsworth, and that to Pitsmoor was extended to Firth Park on 25 August of that year. February 1911 saw Shoreham Street depot opened. In December 1912 a loop was constructed at Hunters Bar, and the Middlewood route was opened in two stages during 1913. The final pre-World War 1 extension saw the Crookes service extended to Heavygate Road on 26 November 1913. 1913 also witnessed the first motorbus service, from Broomhill to Lodge Moor, in pursuance of powers obtained in 1907. Trolleybus powers, too, were obtained, in 1912, but these were never pursued. During World War 1, 20 ex-London County Council 'B' class double-deck trams were acquired to strengthen the fleet.

As elsewhere, the 1920s were a period of considerable economic depression and during 1921-27 some £900,000 was spent on civil engineering projects to reduce unemployment. Many of these schemes, such as road widening, had a direct effect upon the tramways. In addition to a new depot at Crookes, opened in 1921, there were also extensions to Millhouses Lane (from Banner Cross) on 14 April 1922, from Woodseats to Abbey Lane on 22 January 1923, from Nether Edge to Fulwood on 12 July 1923, to Wadsley Bridge on 7 June 1924 and, finally, along Exchange Street on 22 September 1924. There were, however, a number of proposed extensions that were never built, and the failure of the pro-

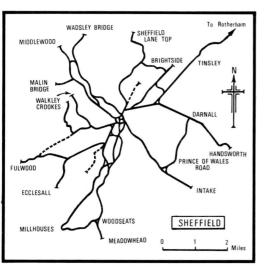

Left:
On 22 May 1949 the LRTL hired the prototype postwar car No 501 on a tour of the Sheffield system. It is seen here, at Crookes, in the company of 1939-built car No 303. This latter car was the last of the domed-roof cars to be delivered during the 1930s and was one of a total of 73 built between 1936 and the outbreak of World War 2. One of the type, the second No 264, is now preserved at the National Tramway Museum.

Below left:
No 451, seen here in the City Square on 22 May 1949, was the first of a batch of 50 trams delivered to Sheffield between 1926 and 1927 by the local firm of Cravens. The entire class was withdrawn between 1950 and 1957. Although none were preserved at that time, the body of No 460 has subsequently been rescued and is currently undergoing restoration at the Sheffield Transport Museum.

posed extension and the prohibitive cost of track re-laying spelt the end of the short Petre Street route, which was converted to bus operation on 19 April 1925.

The next year, 1926, witnessed further expansion, with the takeover of the section of track from Tinsley to Templeborough from Rotherham (the result of boundary readjustment) along with a further eight ex-LCC 'B' class cars that Rotherham had acquired on 1 January and a further extension to the Millhouses route on 31 July. This was followed, on 14 April 1927, by the opening of a link line between the Millhouses and Woodseats routes. Also in 1927, Cravens-built car No 1 entered service. This car, the first with flush rather than rocker panels, was to set the standard for 154 further cars built over the next few years. 1928 saw the link line along Prince of Wales

Road, between the Intake and Darnall routes, opened on 24 February, whilst on 23 October 1928 the new depot at Tenter Street opened. 1928 was also a significant year in that it saw the creation of the Joint Omnibus Committee between the Corporation and the local main line railway companies.

There was now a period of consolidation as the new 'Standard' cars gradually replaced the older cars, including the ex-LCC 'B' class. Then came a further series of extensions in the mid-1930s. The Handsworth route was extended on 7 September 1934, the Firth Park route reached Sheffield Lane Top on 18 November 1934, whilst the Intake route was extended twice during 1935. The last of these was, however, destined to be the final route extension; further proposals, such as that to Dronfield, were delayed by the war and never resurrected. 1935 also witnessed the introduction of the new cream with blue lining livery which was to remain standard right through the remaining years of tramway operation. There were two further abandonments: Nether Edge on 24 March 1934 and Fulwood via Broomhill on 22 August 1936. These closures did not foreshadow any great change in policy; indeed, 1936 was to witness the first appearance of a new standard class, the 'Domed Roof' cars, and during the interwar period 433 trams were placed in service.

Inevitably, with its concentration of steel industry, Sheffield was to suffer several heavy air raids. In total some 14 trams were destroyed by enemy action, although all were rebuilt as 'Domed' cars and returned to service between 1941 and 1944. The war also led to a considerable increase in the level of traffic, such that additional cars were required. In 1941 this led to the acquisition of 14 cars from Newcastle and 10 from Bradford in 1942. All were fully enclosed before entering service in a wartime grey livery and, in the case of the Bradford cars, regauged from 4ft 0in. As a consequence, in 1944, Sheffield's tramcar fleet reached a peak of 468.

1945 saw Sheffield with one of the most modern tramways in Britain; although it largely lacked the segregated tracks of recent extensions built in other towns (most notably Leeds and Liverpool) the tram seemed certain to dominate public transport in the city for some time. The appointment of a new manager, R. C. Moore, in 1945 did little to herald any great change in policy and the appearance of a brand-new car,

No 501, in August 1946 seemed to support the view that Sheffield was amongst the most secure of British tramway operators. No 501 marked a revolution in Sheffield tramcar design, but was destined to be the last car built at Queen's Road. A further 35 new cars, to a similar design to No 501 but with differences in materials and construction, were produced by Charles Roberts between 1950 and 1952. Ironically, by the time that the last of these entered service, in April 1952, the decision to abandon the tramways had been taken.

An indication of the future occurred in 1948 when, due to the need to rebuild the railway bridge at Tinsley, the through Sheffield-Rotherham service was suspended on 11 December. In consultation with Rotherham it was decided not to reintroduce the trams, and this led to Sheffield abandoning the Vulcan Road-Templeborough section at that date. (Rotherham continued serving its section until 13 November 1949.) This closure allowed for some 25 cars to be withdrawn, including many of the wartime second-hand buys.

In early 1951 the future of the tramway system was under threat. The *Star* newspaper undertook a survey on 28 February 1951 and discovered that 84.5% were in favour of the tramcar; this public support was not enough to reprieve the tramcar and on 4 April 1951 the Council adopted a policy advocating complete abandonment over a 15-year period. The opponents of abandonment formed the Sheffield Tramways Development Association but the decision to abandon had become 'political' and the efforts of the Associa-

Left:
Originally built in 1907 as part of a batch of 15, No 342, seen here in September 1949, was one of eight of the batch to survive into the postwar era. On withdrawal, No 342 was preserved at the Museum of British Transport in Clapham. After the dispersal of the Clapham collection, No 342 passed to the North of England Open Air Museum at Beamish, where, controversially, the tram was rebuilt into a fake open-top condition. Subsequently, the tram has been fully restored to Sheffield condition and has had its original fleet number, No 264, restored to it. This means that there are now two Sheffield trams numbered 264 preserved.

tion came to nought. The first closure, Fulwood to Malin Bridge, took place on 5 January 1952 and led to considerable public disquiet. The STDA presented a petition with 7,868 names and a 20pp report to the Council seeking the restoration of the service, but again to no avail.

1952 was to witness another controversial move with the repainting of 23 cars in two varieties of green livery. The Council was, however, more receptive to public outcry on this issue and all 23 cars were repainted in blue and cream by the middle of 1953. Although the policy was now one of abandonment there were still a number of positive developments. Between 1952 and 1956 a total of 23 'Standard' cars had their lower decks rebuilt, whilst in July 1955 the track layout in

Angel Street was modified so that a bi-directional single track in a central reservation was possible.

The next closure, Ecclesall to Middlewood, took place on 27 March 1954 again despite a petition (this time with 11,000 names). By 31 March 1954 the tramcar fleet had been reduced to 369 passenger cars. All of the ex-Bradford and Newcastle cars had succumbed, with the exception of ex-Bradford No 330 which had been cut down for works' duties, as had some of the rocker-panel cars. The next closure, Walkley to Intake on 7 April 1956, left only four of the rocker-panel cars (Nos 42, 52, 456 and 497) in service, although these were destined to last until 28 April 1957 when three of them ran a farewell tour. The last tramcar operated over the Intake-East End service (via Elm Tree, Prince of Wales Road and Darnall) on 6 October 1956. By 31 March 1957 only 265 cars remained in service. The next casualty was the Crookes-Handsworth service, which operated for the last time on 4 May 1957. This closure also meant the end of the peak-hours service from Crookes/Handsworth to Brightside and Vulcan Road. Crookes depot, too, was closed to trams from this date. On 26 October 1956 trams were withdrawn from Exchange Street to Sheffield Lane Top. The only track lost as a consequence of this closure was Exchange Street. The next closure, on 4 January

1958, was not a route but Furnival Street and Paternoster Row in the city centre, which meant that cars no longer served the Midland station.

Apart from this closure, 1958 also saw the other significant withdrawals: on 12 April trams operated for the last time from Prince of Wales Road to Fitzalan Square via Darnall; and, on 6 December trams were removed from the Fitzalan Square-Brightside (via Savile Street) service and the peak-hours-only service from Brightside to Sheffield Lane Top. By this date considerable inroads were being made into the 'Standard' and 'Domed' trams and it was also clear that the initial 15-year timescale was generous.

The next closures were both on 28 February 1959. These were the routes from Beauchief to Woodseats via Abbey Lane and from Fitzalan Square to Sheffield Lane Top (via Savile Street). These closures also meant that Shoreham Street depot was no longer required to house trams. The final closure of 1959, on 3 October, saw trams withdrawn on the two routes (via Queen's Road and via Shoreham Street) between Wadsley Bridge and Woodseats. This date also marked the closure as an operational depot of Tinsley: in

future it would simply act as a store for cars on their one-way journey to Wards scrapyard. The fleet now numbered about 100, all were housed in Tenter Street depot.

1960, destined to be the last year of operation, saw the conversion of the Sheffield Lane Top to Woodseats/Meadowhead service on 2 April 1960. Four months later, on 29 August, the loop at Mill-

Sheffield Closures

12 December 1948	Vulcan Road to Templeborough
5 January 1952	Fulwood to Malin Bridge (via Hunters Bar)
27 March 1954	Ecclesall to Middlewood
7 April 1956	Walkley to Elm Tree
6 October 1956	Elm Tree to Intake
4 May 1957	Crookes to Handsworth
26 October 1957	Exchange Street to Sheffield Lane Top (via Newhall Road)
4 January 1958	(Furnival Street and Paternoster Row)
12 April 1958	City to Elm Tree (via Prince of Wales Road)
6 December 1958	Brightside to Savile Street and Fitzalan Square — also factory-hours service from Brightside to Sheffield Lane Top via Upwell Street and Firth Park — only track abandoned was Brightside Lane beyond junction with Upwell Street to Brightside terminus
28 February 1959	Fitzalan Square to Sheffield Lane Top (via Savile Street)
28 February 1959	Beauchief to Woodseats (via Abbey Lane)
3 October 1959	Wadsley Bridge to Woodseats (and peak-hour Vulcan Road to Meadowhead via Shoreham Street)
2 April 1960	Sheffield Lane Top to Woodseats/Meadowhead
8 October 1960	Beauchief/Millhouses to Weedon Street/Vulcan Road

Last tram: No 510

Below:
Sheffield No 15, one of the Sheffield Transport Department-built 'Standard' cars of 1928-30, is seen at Tinsley on 22 May 1949. At this date the car still retained its prewar livery.

houses was taken out of service so that it could be converted for use by the replacement buses. The scene was now set for the final closures on 8 October 1960 when trams were withdrawn from the Beauchief/Millhouses to Weedon Street/Vulcan Road routes. As befitted a long and faithful servant of the city, the tramcars were given a rousing send-off, with a procession of cars concluding with No 510 as the official last car. The final rites were acted out some two months later, on 21 December 1960, when No 536 became the last car to make its short final journey to Wards scrapyard. Even this was destined to be not the final chapter in Sheffield's tramway history because in December 1961 preserved horse-car No 15 operated over the still-extant track in the Moor for Christmas shoppers.

As one of the last British tramway systems to close, there are inevitably a number of Sheffield cars preserved. In addition to horse-car No 15, No 46, one of the original Milnes-built single-deck cars of 1899, was restored for the closure procession and is now at Crich. The National Tramway Museum also houses 'Standard' class

Left:
One of the most controversial of postwar decisions in Sheffield — apart from the actual closure decision — was that to paint some trams in green liveries. No 83, one of the 23 trams so treated, is caught in the unpopular livery on 29 March 1953. The cars soon reverted to their cream and blue livery. *D. Trevor Rowe*

Left:
The 35 Roberts-built trams of 1950-52, Nos 502-36, were the last new trams to be bought by Sheffield, and showed minor detail differences from the prototype car built in 1946 by Sheffield Transport Department. These differences included a steel frame rather than composite construction and the location of the side-lights, which on the production batch were situated below the blue waist-rail, whereas on No 501 they were located within the blue band. Seen at the Crookes terminus on New Year's Day 1954, No 526 awaits departure on the cross-town route to Handsworth. The Crookes-Handsworth route was to survive for a further three years before conversion in May 1957. Two of the Roberts cars survive: No 510 at Crich; and 513, now at Beamish after a well-travelled career.

183

No 189, 'Domed' car No 264 and 'Roberts' car No 510. Two Sheffield cars are operated at the North of England Open Air Museum at Beamish: 'Preston car No 264 (which had been renumbered 342 during the 1930s) went to the museum after a sojourn at Clapham and has recently been fully restored after spending some time, controversially, as an open-top car; and a second 'Roberts' car, No 513, which like No 510 featured in the closure procession, has also been restored, albeit now without the specially-painted panels. One of the ex-Bradford cars, No 330, also survives at Crich, although still as a works car. The Sheffield Transport Museum houses the lower deck of Cravens-built rocker-panel car No 460 of 1926.

Sheffield

Fleet Numbers	Date	Trucks/Bogies	Body	Withdrawn
1[1]	1927	Peckham P22	Cravens	1957
2-35[2]	1928-30	Peckham P22	STD	1951-57 (25/7 withdrawn 1960)
36-60[3]	1924-25	Peckham P22	Brush	1950-57
61-130 (except 83/5/100/12/9/29)[4]	1930-33	Peckham P22	STD	1951-60
131-55 (except 133)[5]	1929-30	Peckham P22	Hills	1956-60
156-201 (except 192 and 201)[6]	1933-34	Peckham P22	STD	1957-60
202-30 (except 227)[7]	1935	Peckham P22	STD	1958-60
231-42[8]	1936	Peckham P22	STD	1957-60
243-8[9]	1936	Peckham P22	STD	1958-60
249-303 (except 261/74)[10]	1936-39	Peckham P22	STD	1957-60
311-24[11]	1941 (acquired)	Brill 21E	Hurst Nelson	1948-52
325-34[12]	1942 (acquired)	Brill 21E	EE	1950-51
83/5/100/12/9/129/33/92/201/227/61/74/430/83[13]	1941-44	Peckham P22	STD	1957-60
336/9/42-50[14]	1907	Peckham P22 fitted 1918-20	UEC	1950-54
352-65[15]	1919-33 (converted)	Various	Various	1952-60
366-9[16]	1918-21	Peckham P22	STD	
370[17]	1931	Peckham P22	STD	
371-5[18]	Pre-1919	Various	Various	1946-57
376-430 (except 430)[19]	1919-22	Peckham P22	Brush	1950-57
451-500 (except 483)[20]	1926-27	Peckham P22	Cravens	1950-57
501[21]	1946	M&T 588	STD	1960
502-36[22]	1950-52	M&T Hornless 588	Roberts	1960

1 –
2 Nos 25/27 rebuilt.
3 –
4 Nos 68/9/72/3/5/87/9/97/8/102/15/22/8 rebuilt.
5 No 151 rebuilt.
6 Nos 161/7/70/3/4/83/91 rebuilt. No 189 preserved at Crich.
7 –
8 –
9 –
10 No 264 preserved at Crich.
11 Ex-Newcastle CT new 1905-07. Rebuilt fully enclosed by Sheffield. Were Newcastle Nos 122/24/13/29/18/17/14/16/12/19/25/26/23/24 respectively.
12 Ex-Bradford CT new 1919-21. Regauged to 4ft 8½in and fully enclosed. Were Bradford Nos 214/43/42/16/37/51/57/15/19/17 respectively. No 330 converted to works car and preserved at Crich.

13 Wartime replacements.
14 Originally open-balcony cars Nos 258-72, renumbered 1937 to 336-50. Fully enclosed 1924-27. Nos 337/8/40/1 withdrawn 1938-39. No 342 now preserved at Beamish. Nos 349/50 to works duties 1951/53.
15 Snowploughs. No 354 now restored as passenger car No 46 at Crich.
16 Experimental cars.
17 Experimental.
18 Works cars. No 375 preserved and restored as horse-car No 15.
19 –
20 –
21 –
22 Nos 510/3 specially repainted for closure. Now preserved at Crich and Beamish respectively.

The immortally named Stalybridge, Hyde, Mossley & Dukinfield Tramways & Electricity Board can lay claim to having possibly the longest name of any of the postwar British tramways. It also possessed one of the most complex small tramway systems, a reflection of the fact that it was designed to serve four small towns on the Lancashire side of the Pennines. In the postwar era it was also to witness a curious after life whereby trams continued to serve the district for some two years after the Board had officially abandoned its tramways.

The first electric tramway in the area later served by the SHMD Board was operated by a subsidiary of British Electric Traction, the Oldham, Ashton & Hyde Electric Tramways Ltd, over a route linking Ashton and Gee Cross via Denton and Hyde. This line was opened on 12 June 1899. An extension, built by Hyde Corporation but leased to the company, linked the line to Stockport's system in 1902; and from 1 January 1903 a through service between Stockport and Hyde was instituted. Efforts by the company to extend its area of operation by new lines to Newton Wood and Dukinfield were, however, thwarted by the local authorities which had themselves sought powers to operate trams. In 1899 the Corporations of Hyde and Dukinfield jointly applied to the Light Railway Commissioners for

permission to build a tramway linking the two towns. Following discussions with the neighbouring towns of Stalybridge and Mossley a joint Board was established following an agreement on 23 October 1899. On 9 August 1900 the Stalybridge, Hyde, Mossley & Dukinfield Tramways & Electricity Board Act received the Royal Assent. This authorised the construction of a network of routes in the area of the four towns.

Following investigations, work commenced on the building of the electric tramway on 23 October 1902. On 31 March 1903 the Manchester Carriage & Tramways Co's lease on the horse-tramway from Stalybridge Town Hall to Ashton expired (this was the only pre-electric tramway route in the Board area and had commenced operation on 4 June 1881) and was taken over by the Board with the intention that the line be converted to electric traction. However, it was felt that some form of tramway operation was required in the interim whilst the conversion took place. Following discussions, horse-trams from Manchester Corporation provided a service under contract to the Board.

The last horse-tram operated on the Ashton-Stalybridge route on 14 October 1903. After a test run on 7 October 1903 from Stalybridge to the boundary with Ashton (using an Ashton car since the Board had yet to receive its first trams) and the official inspection on 13 October, public services started on 15 October 1903 again using Ashton cars alone under an operating agreement with the Board. This temporary arrangement was to last until the Board received its first trams.

On 19 May 1904 power was supplied by the Board's power station at Park Road, Stalybridge (where the main depot was also situated), to the tramways for the first time and, with the arrival of the Board's first trams, services were introduced from Stalybridge to Hyde on 22 May 1904. Further services followed over the next few months, such as those from Stalybridge to Mossley station, Millbrook and Mottram Road on 22 July 1904. However, with the arrival of the Board's own trams the question of the receipts from the through service to Ashton remained unresolved. The dispute led to the cessation of the through service on 13 June 1904, until they were reintroduced as late as 20 July 1905 following an agreement on the allocation of receipts. By the end of 1904 all the authorised sections of track had been completed with the exception of three lines. Of these, two were additional connections between the Board's lines and those of Ashton Corporation, whilst the third, linking Dukinfield with Hyde, was delayed whilst a railway bridge was

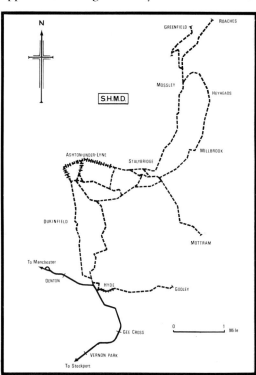

pany's lines (in conjunction with the other local authorities). The final takeover occurred on 24 May 1921. Ownership of the track in the Board area passed to Hyde Corporation (it was never actually owned by the Board) and operation passed to the Board. This enabled the Board to participate in the through Stockport service for the first time and, following the reconstruction of the junction in Denton in August 1921, a through Hyde-Manchester service was introduced for the first time on 5 March 1922.

In 1923, for the first time ever, the trams made a profit, but by this date events were moving against the tramways. Although the SHMD Tramways & Electricity Board Act of 1923 allowed for the construction of further tramways (none of which was actually built), it also permitted the Board to operate buses. The first buses in the region were, however, those operated by the North Western Road Car Co in 1924 in competition with certain of the tram routes. This inevitably led to a decline in the level of passenger traffic on the tramways and the Board was forced to respond. The first SHMD bus service, linking Hyde with Woolley Bridge, was introduced on 29 May 1925 and led, eventually, to the withdrawal, except at peak periods, of the trams from Hyde to Godley. During the late 1920s the tramcar was gradually on the retreat but, unlike other systems where closures occurred at a definite date, many of the SHMD routes simply faded away. The main service could be withdrawn, but occasional peak-hour and holiday services might remain, with the result that the track and overhead remained *in situ* with a ghostly after-life.

The gradual elimination of the trams effectively got underway in 1928. On 12 January the trams were withdrawn from the Ashton-Hyde service, and this was followed by two further closures on 30 August 1928 – Acres Lane-Ashton and Dukinfield-Ashton. The Ashton-Stalybridge-Mottram service was partially converted to bus operation on 1 January 1929; the Saturdays-only service was withdrawn on 14 December 1929. On 3 February 1930 buses replaced trams on the route from Hyde to Stalybridge, and, five days later, on 8 February, buses took over the Ashton (via Heyheads) to Mossley service. In 1931 it was decided,

reconstructed. These final three sections were inspected in May 1905. 1905 also saw the opening of the additional depots at Hyde and Mossley.

The town of Hyde was in the curious position of being served by the electric trams of two different operators – the Board and the company – which were not connected. However, following an agreement between the Board and company on 1 October 1905 a new link, opened in June 1906, was built, thereby allowing the Board's trams access to Hyde Market Place. Except for the transfer of the company lines on the expiry of the lease after World War 1, this was destined to be the last extension to the Board's system. Whilst there were many attempts to extend the tramways, in particular towards Saddleworth, the continuing parlous financial position of the Board made this impractical. In the period leading up to the outbreak of World War 1 the Board never made a profit from its tramway operations; indeed, in 1913, it recorded the biggest loss of any of British tramway operators, partly as the result of paying accident compensation. Despite the losses, the Board remained pro-tram and in September 1918 Hyde Corporation gave the Oldham, Ashton & Hyde company notice, delayed by the war, that it intended to take over the com-

all tramway services would be converted, the lines from Ashton to Stalybridge and Ashton to Roaches being converted during that year. Formal application to abandon many of the routes was only made in 1934, even though many had not seen a tramcar in several years! By 1935, when the Board opted out of operating the joint service to Manchester leaving the service to the latter's trams alone, there remained no more than 20 of SHMD's green and white trams in service.

Elsewhere, in both Ashton and Manchester, the trolleybus was being adopted as a tramway replacement vehicle and under the SHMD Transport & Electricity Board Act of 1936 the Board was empowered to convert the tram routes to trolleybus operation. Although the Board never actually operated trolleybuses, it was responsible for the erection of trolleybus overhead within its area, following an agreement in May 1937 with Ashton and Manchester Corporations, from the Board's boundary to Stalybridge. The new through trolleybus service from Stalybridge, via Ashton, to Manchester was inaugurated on 1 March 1938 and led to the final abandonment of the track in Stalybridge. This meant that for the trams' last seven years of service they were isolated from the Board's main workshops! All the remaining trams were housed at the out-depot at Hyde, where all routine maintenance was undertaken; any major work required was undertaken at Stockport. Thus by 1939 the Board retained two tram routes: from Hyde towards Manchester and from Hyde towards Stockport. Proposals made by Manchester in early 1939 for the conversion of the Manchester-Hyde service to trolleybus operation later that year were delayed by the outbreak of World War 2 and were only finally completed in January 1950, long after the last SHMD trams had operated.

World War 2 ensured that the Board's trams had a longer life than otherwise expected, although only six cars (Nos 18, 42, 61-64) remained in service, over track which was owned by Hyde Corporation rather than the Board. In November 1943 the Board was made aware of the dangerous condition of the track and it rec-

ommended that the route to Stockport be converted to bus operation. This, however, was rejected by Stockport Corporation. Although the conversion was not proceeded with, SHMD cars were withdrawn from the weekdays service to Stockport and Edgeley, being limited to the shuttle service to Gee Cross, on 2 March 1944. As there was no Hyde-Gee Cross service on Sundays, SHMD cars continued to operate through to Edgeley on Sundays until 20 September. Thereafter, SHMD cars were limited to the Hyde-Gee Cross service until final closure.

In May 1945 the Board petitioned the Ministry of War Transport for permission to withdraw the final trams. Following inspection, the Ministry accepted the withdrawal of the SHMD cars but ordered that the tracks be maintained for use by Stockport and Manchester cars. The last public operation of SHMD trams took place on 12 May 1945, although following the tradition of a slow death the actual last car, No 18, operated on 29 May 1945 in connection with a BBC recording. Following the closure the remaining six cars were quickly disposed of. This was not the end of tramway operation in the area, however, since the Hyde Corporation owned track from Broomstair Bridge (on the Manchester route) to Gee Cross (on the route to Stockport) remained in use for a further two years until the section from Gee Cross to Hyde was abandoned on 1 March 1947 and that from Broomstair Bridge to Hyde on 30 December 1947.

SHMD Closure

21 May 1945	Hyde Market Place to Gee Cross. (Track used by Stockport until 2 March 1947. Manchester trams also terminated in Hyde Market Place on route 19 from the boundary at Broomstair Bridge until 30 December 1947.)

Last tram: No 18

SHMD

Fleet Numbers	Date	Trucks/Bogies	Body	Withdrawn
18[1]	1904	McGuire 21EM	BEC	1945
42[2]	1905	Peckham P22 (originally M&G 21EM)	Hurst Nelson	1945
61-4	1924-25	M&G 21EM	SHMD	1945

1 Originally open top — balcony-top fitted pre-1912.
2 Originally open top — balcony-top fitted post-1912.

At almost 2,100ft, Snaefell is the highest peak on the Isle of Man. From its summit it is possible, on a clear day, to see Ireland, Scotland, England and Wales and it was inevitable that such a view would inspire the Victorians to provide some form of transport to the top.

The first proposal for a line up Snaefell was made in 1887-88 by G. Noble Fell, the inventor of the 'Fell' mountain railway system. Although these proposals failed, eight years later, in 1895, a more determined scheme was destined to succeed. In January of that year, the Snaefell Mountain Railway Association was formed to construct the line. It had close links with the company then constructing the Manx Electric line, and the ubiquitous Alexander Bruce was again deeply involved.

Construction of the line was able to proceed quickly because, as the line was entirely over private property or on land that was readily available, no Act of Tynwald was required. Such was the pace of construction that the first passenger services were run on 21 August 1895.

The Snaefell line adopted the unusual gauge for the Isle of Man of 3ft 6in rather than the more common 3ft 0in. The reason for this is that the 3ft 0in gauge would not have allowed sufficient clearance for the 'Fell' gear and braking system, although a temporary third rail, laid to the 3ft 0in gauge, was installed during construction to enable the Manx Northern Railway's locomotive *Caledonia* to operate certain of the construction trains.

Installation of the 'Fell' system was supervised by its inventor. It seems likely that Fell had initially suggested the system in 1887-88 when it was believed that steam was the most likely method of traction. The adoption of electricity meant that the additional tractive power that the 'Fell' system offered was essentially unnecessary, since trams are well capable of handling gradients worse than the line's maximum of 1 in 12 (witness Church Bank in Bradford), and the primary use of the system is as a safety device to prevent derailment. Nevertheless, the success of the system over almost 100 years is that there has never been a serious incident along the route.

To operate the line, six single-deck cars were delivered from Milnes. The cars were fitted with the peculiar double bow collectors (patented by John Hopkinson, who supervised the installation of the line's electrical supply by Mather & Platt), which were also fitted to the Manx Electric cars for a time. Although the latter's trams were subsequently fitted with conventional trolley booms, the double bow collectors on the Snaefell cars remain to this day. Of the six original cars, five survive; the sixth was destroyed by fire in 1971, but was rebuilt by the Manx Electric Railway in an original form. Since then, all the cars have been given new motors and control gear purchased in Germany, with new bogies made by London Underground at Acton Works.

As a subsidiary of the Manx Electric Railway, the Snaefell's history is closely allied with that of its parent. From the collapse of Dumbell's Bank

Note: **For map please see page 157.**

Right:
Snaefell No 3 approaches the Summit station on 28 July 1959. Note the unusual pointwork and the retention of the twin large 'pantographs'. Trams on the associated Manx Electric Railway had similar pantographs prior to their replacement with trolley booms. *Frank Church*

Snaefell Mountain Railway

Fleet Numbers	Date	Trucks/Bogies	Body	Withdrawn
/6	1895	Milnes	Milnes	—
	1971	Milnes	MER/Kinnin	—

Rebuilt after original No 5 destroyed in fire.

ght:

aefell No 1 ascends from Laxey on 27 July 1959 ssed the railway's sheds. The more modern shed the middle of the picture housed the Air nistry's Wickham trailers used in connection with e radar station. *Frank Church*

rough to the takeover by the Manx government 1957, the fortunes of the two lines have been sely interwoven. There are, however, differces between the two lines. Whilst the Manx ectric was very much an essential link in the and's transport network, the Snaefell line was vays operated only for tourists, and normally it ly ever runs during the summer season. The e exception, during the early 1950s, was when e Air Ministry used both lines to facilitate the nstruction of a radar station. Almost 100 years er the first cars climbed up the mountain, the aefell Mountain Railway continues to fulfil its iginal function – that of carrying tourists up to e summit of the highest peak on the island.

low:

e Snaefell Mountain Railway has a centre third-l for much of its length to assist with braking on e steep gradients. This is the centre rail-brake as ically fitted to the six cars. *W. S. Garth*

Although the tramways of Southampton boasted some of the more unusual designs of trams — with a special profile to enable them to be operated through the Bargate — the particular importance of Southampton in tramway history is that it saw the launch of the private preservation of tramcars and laid the foundation of what has subsequently become the collection of the National Tramway Museum at Crich.

It was on 5 May 1879 that the first tramway opened in Southampton. Operated by the horse-trams of the Southampton Tramways Co, this first route linked Floating Bridge with Avenue (Alma Road) via Canute Road, Oxford Street, High Street and Above Bar. A month later, on 9 June, a second route from Above Bar to Shirley via Commercial Road was opened and this launched 20 years of company-operated tramways in the town, until 30 June 1898 when Southampton Corporation, having already bought the Southampton Electric Light & Power Co, compulsorily bought out the Southampton Tramways Co with the intention of converting the tramway to electric operation.

The first section of the new electric tramway, from Junction to Shirley, was opened on 20 January 1900, and it was quickly followed by further extensions and conversions. After the construction of the initial system, further extensions were opened in 1910 (Clock Tower to Northam), 1911 (Royal Pier), 1922 (Hampton Park to Swaythling), 1923 (Bullar Road) and, finally, 1930 (along Burgess Road to link the Swaythling and Bassett

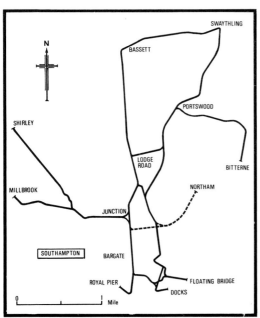

routes). In the central area, however, there remained a significant problem — the Bargate. One of the original gates to the mediaeval walls, originally dating from the end of the 12th century and described as 'probably the finest, and certainly the most complex, town gateway in England', the Bargate formed the only link between Above Bar and the High Street — and, as such, it had to be utilised by the trams. It was, however, wide enough for only a single track and its height precluded the use of enclosed-top trams until the construction of the special Bargate-profile trams in the early 1920s.

As early as 1899, a special committee had been formed to advise on the construction of a route around the Bargate, but nothing was achieved. Then, before World War 1, when trams were passing through the Bargate every 30sec, serious consideration was given to the demolition of the Bargate as a means of saving the cost of the policemen required manually to signal the trams through. Fortunately this piece of municipal vandalism was avoided by the introduction of electric signalling. Despite the obvious problems, however, little was done until the early 1930s: in 1932 the eastern bypass was constructed and this enabled a new southbound track to be constructed, leaving the northbound trams to continue passing through the Bargate. Finally, in 1938 the western bypass was opened, and trams ceased to use the Bargate at all — the final tram through the Bargate, No 8, passed through on 4 June 1938.

By this date Southampton had witnessed its first tramway closures. Buses had already been introduced to the town in 1919, but it was not until 2 October 1935 that the first route, that to Millbrook, was closed. This closure was destined to be short-lived, and the service was reintroduced in 1939. The next closure was to be permanent — on 4 June 1936 trams were withdrawn from the Clock Tower to Northam Bridge service.

As a port city it was inevitable that Southampton would be a target for German air raids, and considerable damage was inflicted upon the town during the war. Despite this, only one tram (No 13) was completely destroyed by enemy action although the transport department offices were destroyed and the service to Royal Pier was suspended for the duration. One factor reducing the potential for destruction was the building of two dispersal sidings in the woods on the Common near Burgess Road, to which some trams were sent for overnight storage. By 1944 the Corporation was looking to the future and to the need to reconstruct the town. In mid-1944 the

One of Southampton's famous knifeboard open-top trams, No 43, is seen being dismantled at Shirley depot on 8 January 1949. Originally built by Hurst Nelson in 1903, No 43 was one of four rebuilt in 1906-07. Of the 10 cars of this type built, eight survived into the postwar era, all being finally withdrawn in 1948. It was the imminent threat of scrapping that led to the acquisition by the LRTL of sister car No 45 for preservation in late 1948 — the first British tramcar to be preserved privately and the first of many to pass eventually to the National Tramway Museum.

chairman of the Transport Committee announced that the trams were to be withdrawn as part of the reconstruction policy. It was further announced that whether the trams would be replaced by trolleybuses (as earlier in neighbouring Portsmouth) or by motorbuses would be decided later. Although Southampton had gained powers for trolleybus operation in 1937, the motorbus was destined to be the chosen mode.

Although abandonment was now the official policy, the Transport Department had to wait to put it into practice. It was, therefore, not for another three years until the closure policy could be put into effect. The first abandonment, the route from the Docks via St Mary's to Bitterne Park, occurred on 15 May 1948, followed on 30 October 1948 by the route from Swaythling to Stag Gates. Numerous trams were withdrawn as a consequence, many finding their way to the

scrapyard of A. F. Harris at Bevois Valley where they were slowly dismantled.

It was during the August of 1948 that an all-important tram tour occurred; all-important because it was this tour that led to the first tram-car to be acquired by enthusiasts for preservation. The day in question had proved to be hot, and the participants on the tour rejected the all-enclosed tramcar that they had been allocated in favour of one of the surviving open-top cars. Upon the completion of the tour it was politely enquired of the officials as to the ultimate fate of the tram. Upon being told that it was due for scrapping, with a value of £10, an appeal to raise that sum was launched through Modern Tramway which resulted in the saving of No 45. The purchase of No 45 was the easy part: storage of it was a headache that lasted for more than 10 years until the acquisition of the site at Crich.

The next closure occurred on 5 March 1949 when the route from Swaythling to Junction (via Burgess Road, Bassett Crossroads and Avenue) was converted to bus operation. Although not definitely recorded, the section between Roberts Road and Millbrook was closed at some point between September 1948 and March 1949. The final closure, from Floating Bridge to Shirley, from Holy Rood to Royal Pier (via High Street). The section from Roberts Road to Millbrook, originally closed in 1935 (except for workmen's services) and reinstated in 1939, certainly survived into the second half of 1947 although a definite closure date is not recorded. The final tram, No 9, suitably decorated, arrived at Shirley depot just before midnight.

This was not, however, destined to be the final movement of a Southampton tram under its own power, either in its own town or elsewhere. The last recorded movement of a Southampton tram in Southampton occurred on 4 February 1950 when Nos 21 and 101 made their way from Shirley to Portswood depot. Moreover, a number of Southampton trams were sold to Leeds for further service. Of the 22 trams acquired by Leeds (allocated the fleet numbers 290-308, 310 and 312), only the first 11 (290-300) entered service. Of the remaining 11, some found their way to Leeds whilst the remainder were dismantled in Southampton. The life of Nos 290-300 was destined to be relatively short in their new home, as the decision was made in Leeds to acquire the ex-London 'Feltham' cars. The last tram in service, No 297, was withdrawn in December 1953. Ironically, the cars that entered service were outlived by those sent to Leeds but which never entered service. These were sent to a scrapyard at Stanningley (between Leeds and Bradford) where they remained until 1958.

Apart from No 45, a number of other Southampton trams have been rescued subsequently and preserved, and are currently undergoing restoration. These include No 57, a knifeboard car dating from 1910, which is, like No 45, an open-top car, and was discovered in 1972; and No 11.

Southampton Closures

15 May 1948	Portswood to Bitterne Park
15 May 1948	Lodge Road to Docks (via Bevois Hill and St Mary's)
30 October 1948	Swaythling to Stag Gates (via Portswood and Lodge Road)
5 March 1949	Swaythling-Junction (via Bassett)
31 December 1949	Floating Bridge to Shirley
31 December 1949	Holy Road to Royal Pier (via High Street)

The workman's service to Millbrook closed by March 1949. Ordinary services on this route ceased on 2 October 1935, but it was used by workmen's trams after that date and was certainly passable at least until 5 July 1947 and was used on the LRTL special on 29 August 1948. The actual last tram movement — from Shirley to Portswood depots — occurred on 4 February 1950 and was by No 101. Overhead had been retained after the official last closure to facilitate inter-depot movement.

Last car: No 9

Left:
Seen at the Royal Pier on 8 January 1949, No 106 was one of a batch of eight trams built in Southampton's own workshops in 1929-30. After withdrawal in Southampton, all eight were sold to Leeds, where, as Leeds No 293, No 106 was to give a further three years of service before again being made redundant.

eet Numbers	Date	Trucks/Bogies	Body	Withdrawn
6[1]	1902	Brill 21E	Milnes	1945-49
11[2]	1920-26	Peckham P35 (7/8/10), Brill 21E (9/11)	Southampton CT	1949
⁾3	1923	Peckham P35	Southampton CT	1949
⁾-20[4]	1920-26	Peckham P35 (14/6-20), Brill 21E (15)	Southampton CT	1949
⁾5	1930	Peckham P35	Southampton	1949
⁾6	1928-29	Peckham P35	Southampton	1949
⁾7	1930-31	Peckham P35	Southampton	1949
⁾8	1901	Brill 21E	Milnes	1948-49
⁾9	1931-32	Peckham P35	Southampton	1949
⁾10	1901	Brill 21E	Milnes	1948
⁾/9/30[11]	1902	Brill 21E	Milnes	1948-49
12	1924-25	Peckham P35	Southampton	1949
13	1931-32	Peckham P35	Southampton	1949
⁾/4[14]	1900	Brill 21E	Milnes	1945-48
15	1931-32	Peckham P35	Southampton	1949
16	1899	Brill 21E	Milnes	1949
⁾17	1928-29	Peckham P35	Southampton	1949
18	1903	Brill 21E	Hurst Nelson	1948
	1899	Brill 21E	Milnes	1948
⁾-5/8/9[19]	1903	Brill 21E	Hurst Nelson	1948
20	1931-32	Peckham P35	Southampton	1949
	1918	Brill 21E	Southampton	1948
-61[21]	1908-11	Brill 21E	Southampton	1945-49
-8	1911-12	Brill 21E	Southampton (63 UEC)	1948-49
-73[22]	1912-15	Brill 21E	Southampton	1948-49
23	1917	Peckham P35	Southampton	1949
-80[24]	1918-19 (acquired)	Brill 21E	ERTCW	1946-48
	1918-19	Brill 21E	Southampton	1948
-7/9-91[25]	1919-20	Brill 21E	English Electric	1945-49
-101[26]	1925-28	Peckham P35	Southampton	1949
2-9[27]	1929-30	Peckham P35	Southampton	1949

Rebuilt 1930-31.
Rebuilt 1924-26. Nos 7/8/10 sold to Leeds, only 10 sent but did not enter service. No 11 now restored.
Sold to Leeds, but never sent.
Nos 14/6-20 sold to Leeds — only 14/8/9 sent, but did not enter service.
Sold to Leeds, not used.
As No 21.
Sold to Leeds, used.
Rebuilt 1921-22.
As No 23.
Rebuilt 1921-22.
Rebuilt 1921-30. No 28 withdrawn 1930.
Sold to Leeds, not sent.
As No 23.
No 33 rebuilt 1913.

15 As No 23.
16 Rebuilt 1915.
17 As No 21.
18 Rebuilt 1921.
19 Rebuilt 1906/07 (43/6-8), 1921/22 (40-2/4/9), 1929 (45). Nos 46/7 withdrawn 1929-31. No 45 preserved.
20 As 23.
21 Rebuilt at various dates. Remains of No 57 preserved.
22 —
23 —
24 Ex-London County Council built 1903 as open top. All altered 1919-22. No 75 withdrawn 1934.
25 No 88 withdrawn 1932.
26 Sold to Leeds, Nos 93/4 never left Southampton, none entered service in Leeds.
27 Sold to Leeds, all bar 102/3 entered service.

Of the four tramways that survived World War 2 in northeast England, South Shields was both the least-known and the shortest-lived. Nevertheless, it was a system that, despite its size, was one of the most forward-looking until the 1930s, and, had the two-mile gap with Sunderland been connected, could have formed an important interurban operator.

The first horse-trams in South Shields, on a route linking Tyne Dock with Pier Head, opened for public service on 1 August 1883. Although from the outset the track was owned by the Corporation, the actual operation was leased out to a company — the South Shields Tramways Co. This company soon collapsed, however, and the six trams were sold to Douglas on the Isle of Man, where they were eventually numbered 13-18. After more than a year without trams, a new company, the South Shields Tramways & Carriage Co Ltd, obtained a 14-year lease on the line from January 1887, and a new service was started in March of that year.

In 1899 the company was taken over by British Electric Traction (BET), which already owned the neighbouring Jarrow & District company. This takeover was agreed following the decision by the Corporation to grant the company a further seven years on its lease. However, the new lease had a clause allowing the Corporation to terminate the arrangement after five years, and in 1906 this clause was enforced. The last company-owned horse-tram operated on 31 January 1906. The company and Corporation had been in dispute for a number of years over BET's proposals for an electric light railway linking South Shields with Sunderland. Moreover, the Corporation had already gained parliamentary power to operate electric trams in the town in 1903.

The new electric system, owned and operated by the Corporation (although the possibility of offering a lease had been considered), was inaugurated on 30 March 1906. The first route linked Fowler Street with Laygate and Stanhope Road. Three months later, on 23 June 1906, the route was extended to Tyne Dock by two different routes: along Stanhope Road; and, secondly, a route parallel to the original horse-tram line. The actual horse-tram route to Tyne Dock was abandoned, although there was pressure to electrify it. On 2 August 1906 the former horse-tram line from Market Place to Pier Head was reopened as an electric service. This was followed on 28 September 1906 by the section from the Market Place to Laygate and, finally, the section along Boldon Lane and Hudson Street (linking the two Tyne Dock termini) opened on 26 March 1907. At Tyne Dock a direct connection with BET's Jarrow & District trams was made and a through service commenced in June 1908. This was only to last until 1911, but was reinstated from 1922 until 1927, when it was again withdrawn. The Jarrow & District trams were to operate for a further two years.

The last extensions to the South Shields tramway system — the short Mile End route and the much longer Cleadon Light Railway — were both opened in 1922. The former gave South Shields one of the few 'Grand Union' tramway junctions in Britain and, with a route mileage of 7½, South Shields was possibly the smallest tramway operator in Britain to possess one. The Cleadon Light Railway took South Shields to within a few miles of Sunderland's trams but, despite several proposals, the gap was never bridged. Despite its relatively small size the South Shields system was to witness considerable modernisation over the next decade, although not without controversy both over personalities and over finance.

Apart from the dramatic rebuilding of a number of its own fleet, South Shields took advantage of closures elsewhere by acquiring between 1929 and 1932 some dozen second-hand trams. These included two from Jarrow & District, six from Wigan (of which only four entered service) and two from Ayr. More impressively, the short stretch of track along Ocean Road was completely reconstructed, despite arguments about the cost, in 1934-35, and in 1936 the brand-new streamlined tram, No 52, was delivered from Brush.

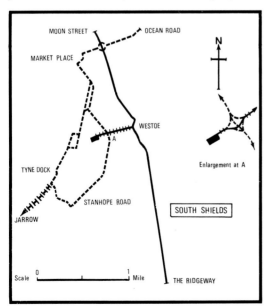

Elsewhere, however, things were not quite so promising. A witch-hunt over allegations of certain irregularities had led to the forced resignation of the general manager. His replacement, Fitzpayne from Edinburgh, who was later to make his name at Glasgow, remained at South Shields for just over a year, but during this time the decision to seek powers to operate trolleybuses was taken by the council on 6 June 1934.. The initial idea was that the trolleybuses would supplement the trams rather than replace them, but the Act empowering the use of trolleybuses covered some 13 different routes. Having just missed the 1934 parliamentary session, the Bill went through the following year and gained the Royal Assent on 2 August 1935.

Work started in April 1936 to erect the trolleybus overhead, and by this stage the tram track along Stanhope Road was giving cause for concern. Consequently, it was decided to replace the trams with trolleybuses over this section. The first of the new trolleybus routes, from Laygate to Marsden via Prince Edward Road, was opened on 12 October 1936 and that along Stanhope Road was to follow in March 1937. This was the first tramway abandonment. It was now decided, however, that all tramways with the exception of the Moon Street-Ridgeway and Ocean Road routes would be converted to trolleybus operation. On 11 April 1938 the Pier Head-Laygate-Tyne Dock route was converted to trolleybus operation, followed three days later, on the 14th, by the Chichester-Westoe-Fowler Street service. This meant that only 12 trams were required, as opposed to the peak number of 49 in 1931. The fleet continued to be maintained at the Dean Road depot, which required the retention of s short stretch of the erstwhile town route for access.

Situated adjacent to the River Tyne, it was inevitable that South Shields would suffer damage during World War 2. Although no trams were destroyed, enemy action did lead to the destruction of three trolleybuses and one bus and to a certain amount of dislocation of service. One of the surprises of the wartime era was the reintroduction of trams to the Ocean Road service between 25 January and 18 December 1943, when the service was replaced by trolleybuses. The one remaining route continued to soldier on through 1945 until final withdrawal on 31 March 1946. The official ceremony to mark the closure of the tramway system took place the following day, when No 39 carried the official party. Of the fleet, only No 52 was to receive a reprieve, being sold to Sunderland (where it was renumbered No 48). The remainder were dismantled and either sold for scrap or for use as farm buildings. Thus disappeared one of the smaller of the northeastern tramways. Despite its size, South Shields was, in its time, an innovative operator and one which put to shame many of its larger brethren.

South Shields Closure

31 March 1946   Moon Street to Ridgeway

Note: Closing ceremony held on 1 April 1946.

Last tram: No 39

South Shields

Fleet Numbers	Date	Trucks/Bogies	Body	Withdrawn
6[1]	1932 (acquired)	Peckham P22	EE	1946
23, 33, 50/1[2]	1931 (acquired)	Brill 43E bogies	EE	1945 (33/50), 1946 (23/51)
39[3]	1914	Peckham P35	Brush	1946
1-5	1921	Brill 76E bogies	EE	1946
29[4]	1929	Smith Pendulum; to Hurst Nelson 21E 1932	South Shields CT	1946
52[5]	1936	M&T swing-link bogies	Brush	1946

1   Originally Dumbarton No 31 built 1921, to Ayr (No 29) 1928. Rebuilt by South Shields as fully enclosed.
2   Originally Wigan Nos 4, 2, 6 and 1 built 1914. Rebuilt by South Shields 1932-35. No 33 renumbered from 52 in 1935.
3   Survivor of batch 36-40. Originally open canopied and non-vestibuled. Fully-enclosed 1931 — only one of class so treated.
4   Rebuild of No 29 originally built by UEC 1907.
5   Sold to Sunderland for £250 1946 and renumbered 48.

The last tramway to operate in Cheshire and in the area that was eventually to form Greater Manchester was Stockport. The town's trim red and cream trams outlasted those of its much larger northern neighbour by more than two years. Indeed, for much of the postwar decade Stockport was considered to be relatively secure for the tram, with the contemporary press reporting the imminence of major track renewals.

The first tramway in Stockport arrived with the opening of the Manchester Tramways & Carriage Co's line from Piccadilly to Stockport via Levenshulme, which opened on 7 May 1880. This was operated by horse-trams, as was the next route, that of the Stockport & Hazel Grove Carriage & Tramways Co Ltd, which opened a route from Stockport to Hazel Grove at Easter 1890. In 1900 Stockport Corporation, empowered under an Order made after the 1870 Tramways Act, started to construct its own electric tramway system. The first route, to Woodley station, was opened on 26 August 1901. This was followed by the first stretch of the Reddish line, to Sandy Lane, on 3 September 1901. The first part of the Cheadle route was opened on 23 January 1902. Next, 30 May 1902 witnessed the opening of two extensions: to Pole Bank (Woodley) and to Houldsworth Square on the route to Reddish. Two days later, on 2 June, electric services were introduced to the Levenshulme-Stockport route. The service from Manchester, via Levenshulme, to Stockport was the first to be municipalised, in pursuance of the Manchester Corporation Tramways Act of 1899, and it is likely that Manchester undertook the actual electrification of this particular route. On 25 July 1903 the Cheadle route was extended to Cheadle Heath Bridge and on 25 November 1903 the Reddish route was

extended to the Bull's Head in Reddish, where a second connection with Manchester's tramways was made. 1904 was to witness the final extensions: to Cheadle Green on 5 February and thence onwards to Gatley on 24 March; and, finally, the Stockport & Hazel Grove Co was taken over at a price of £24,000 and the route was electrified from 5 July 1905, at which time the through Manchester-Stockport service (route No 35) was extended to run through to Hazel Grove. The tramway system of Stockport was now complete.

By 1907 Stockport had a fleet of 50 trams operating, and there was little change for the next decade. In 1911 a programme of car modernisation was started which saw some of the earlier open-top cars fitted with balcony covers manufactured by the United Electric Car Co of Preston, but the next significant development, on 10 March 1913, was the introduction of trolleybuses on a two-mile route south-westwards from the town centre to Offerton. Stockport's trolleybuses, which were short-lived and officially abandoned on 7 October 1919 (although journeys were recorded well into 1920, finishing on 11 September of that year), were unique in Britain in that they were fitted with the Lloyd-Kohler type of overhead. Under this system the positive and negative feeds were strung vertically above each other and the trolleybuses had trolley carriages and cables which were exchanged when two vehicles met.

During the 1920s the tramway fleet was expanded considerably and many of the earlier cars were further modernised. This process of modernisation continued right through the 1930s and into World War 2. Indeed, the last two open-top cars (Nos 1 and 13) received top covers for the first time in 1941 and 1944 — No 13 being the last tram in Britain to be so treated. The last wholly new cars were, however, two bought in 1928-29, which were unique in that the bodies were built in Stockport's own workshops. Although the period did not witness any major alteration to the tramway network, it did see the first abandonment when, on 21 September 1931, the section of line from Cheadle to Gatley was abandoned — a section of line which was, however, outside the Stockport boundary and was owned by Cheadle & Gatley Urban District Council. Elsewhere, and in particular in Manchester, the gradual trend towards tramway abandonment was soon to have an impact.

In March 1944 Stockport undertook a partial renumbering of its fleet so that cars were now numbered together in three distinct groups:

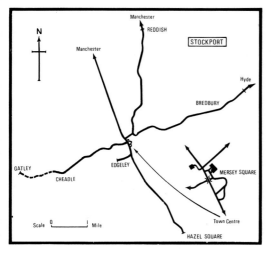

Above:
Originally built in 1902 as an open-top car by the Electric Railway & Tramway Carriage Works, Stockport No 17 was rebuilt fully enclosed in 1923. Seen at the terminus of the Cheadle Heath route on 14 May 1949, No 17 has the double 'H' on the dash to indicate that this was a low-bridge car capable of passing under the two low railway bridges on the through route to Hyde. The tramway originally went beyond Cheadle Heath to Gatley, but this section was the first part of the Stockport system to close during the 1930s. Although No 17 was shortly to be withdrawn — the route to Hyde had already closed by this date — the Cheadle Heath route was to survive for a further two years.

Nos 1-29 were reserved for the low-bridge cars used on the joint service through to Hyde; Nos 34-45 were reserved for normal-height balcony-top cars; whilst Nos 46-83 were designated for normal-height fully-enclosed cars. In late 1944 it was rumoured that the through service to Manchester was to be abandoned, but this led to considerable opposition, and the Ministry of War Transport also refused consent to closure. As a consequence, Stockport Town Council decided on 31 October 1944 to re-lay the track along Wellington Road. This work was undertaken during the summer of 1945, utilising a labour force made up almost entirely of German prisoners of war. At the same time a number of track modifications were undertaken, including the installation of a new crossover at Belmont Bridge. Other remedial work included the replacement of the feeder cable on the Hazel Grove route — but only as far as the borough boundary since the track in Hazel Grove was only leased to Stockport on an annual basis.

Earlier in 1945, following condemnation of its remaining cars by the Ministry of War Transport, the last SHMD trams operated on 12 May 1945, leaving the through route from Hyde to Stockport to be operated by Stockport's low-bridge cars alone. Elsewhere Manchester Corporation in January 1946 reconfirmed its intention to abandon its remaining tramways as soon as possible. Whilst Stockport was continuing to re-lay the through route, the council's Planning Committee noted, ominously, that 'it is anticipated that the tramway track will be removed'. In April 1946 Stockport's peak-hour trams to Gorton Library were diverted to Belle Vue as a result of Manchester dewiring the erstwhile route No 32. Stockport itself contemplated the future based on the motorbus 'because Manchester will not have anything else'.

Although 1947 started badly for the tramcar in Stockport, with the section of the through service to Hyde being abandoned beyond Bredbury Bar on 1 March 1947, Stockport's own tramcars continued to serve Vernon Park all day with a peak-hours extension to Bredbury Bar. The closure of the Hyde service rendered redundant the 'H-H' symbol on the dashes of the low-bridge cars, since trams no longer passed under the low bridge at Bredbury. Despite this abandonment the tramcar was still receiving investment; 1947 saw track being relaid on a number of sections, and car No 16 was rebuilt following serious accident damage. On 3 May 1947, however, the peak-hours extension to Bredbury Bar was abandoned. Although the contemporary press recorded the acquisition of replacement track to re-lay the complex Mersey Square layout in the centre of Stockport, this work was never undertaken and, increasingly, the abandonment of Manchester's trams influenced the destiny of Stockport's.

On 15 February trams last ran on one of the through Manchester to Stockport services, when route No 35B was converted to bus operation. This marked the end of tramway operation in Albert Square in Manchester. On the same day route No 35C from Piccadilly to Stockport was combined with Stockport's route No 4 to form a through Manchester-Hazel Grove route, with the result that the last trams were withdrawn from St Peter's Square in Stockport. Two months later, on 1 May 1948, the Stockport peak-hours-only service to Belle Vue via Reddish operated for the last time. Then, on 3 October 1948, Manchester withdraw its trams from route No 37, Exchange to Levenshulme, leaving the through Stockport route as its last service. Three months later, on 9 January 1949, the last Manchester route was converted to bus operation, leaving Stockport to continue to operate the southern rump of the through service to the borough boundary at Crossley Road. With Manchester's trams finally abandoned, it was inevitable that Stockport would eventually follow suit, and on 8 July 1949 the Town Council agreed on a policy of abandonment in favour of 68 new buses. The first phase of the abandonment policy saw cars withdrawn from the Hazel Grove to Levenshulme route on 14 January 1950. Some 45 cars were retained for other services. It was reported that the new track bought for the re-laying of Mersey Square was languishing unused behind the depot.

By now, standards of maintenance were declining. The last car to be repainted, No 53, emerged in March 1950, and other work was

Below:
The focal point of the Stockport tramway network and one of the most complex tram track layouts in the area was at Mersey Square in the town centre. Mersey Square was the terminus of most of Stockport's tram routes as well as the location of the main depot and workshops. With a fine array of vintage buses in the background, Stockport No 54, one of a batch of 10 cars built by English Electric in 1920, traverses the square in stately fashion on 14 May 1949.

allowed to decline gradually. By early 1951 it was reported that a number of traction columns had rusted through and that the span wires were now either tied back onto adjacent poles or affixed to trees. Thus the end for this once-proud system was not far away. On 3 March 1951 the service from Vernon Park to Edgeley was replaced by

Stockport Closures

1 March 1947	Vernon Park to Hyde (the end of Stockport operation within SHMD area)
15 February 1948	Alterations to services to Manchester allowed Stockport to withdraw trams from St Peter's Square, Daw Bank, Lord Street and Wellington Street — services now operated through to Hazel Grove
14 January 1950	Levenshulme
14 January 1950	Hazel Grove
3 March 1951	Vernon Park to Edgeley
10 March 1951	Mersey Square to Cheadle
25 August 1951	Mersey Square to Reddish

Last car: No 53

buses and the line from Mersey Square to Cheadle succumbed exactly one week later. At the same time the one remaining route to Reddish was curtailed from its previous terminus in Mersey Square to a new terminus in the congested Princes Street. Heaton Lane depot was closed to tramcars, and a total of 30 cars remained in service (Nos 50-61, 65-68 and 70-83). Stockport's last tramcar, an illuminated No 53, operated on 25 August 1951 — the following day would have been the 50th anniversary of municipal electric tramway operation in the borough. Of the trams, none was to survive immediately into preservation, but the remains of No 5 have subsequently been rescued and are

Above:
The history of Stockport's trams was closely interwoven with that of its much larger neighbour — Manchester — to the north. Stockport No 73, built by Cravens in 1923, is seen in Piccadilly Manchester on 11 August 1948 with a Manchester Corporation diesel bus, in the then-fashionable streamlined livery, alongside. It was the decision of Manchester Corporation to complete its tramway abandonment programme that was one factor in the eventual decision to convert Stockport's tram routes to bus operation.

undergoing restoration — a fitting tribute to one of the more compact and typical British tramways.

Stockport

Fleet Numbers	Date	Trucks/Bogies	Body	Withdrawn
1[1]	1902-03	Brill 21E	ERTCW	By 1950
2[2]	1907	Brill 21E	UEC	By 1950
3[3]	1901	Brill 21E	ERTCW	By 1950
4[4]	1907	Brill 21E	UEC	By 1950
5[5]	1901	Brill 21E	ERTCW	By 1950
6[6]	1919-20	Brill 21E (replaced by Cravens)	EE	By 1950
7[7]	1907	Brill 21E	UEC	By 1950
8[8]	1901	Brill 21E	ERTCW	By 1950
9-11[9]	1919-20	Brill 21E (replaced by Cravens)	EE	1951
12/4/5[10]	1902	Brill 21E	ERTCW	12/5 1951, 14 by 1950

Stockport

Fleet Numbers	Date	Trucks/Bogies	Body	Withdrawn
16[11]	1907	Brill 21E	UEC	1951
17-20[12]	1902	Brill 21E	ERTCW	By 1950
21-5[13]	1902-03	Brill 21E	ERTCW	21-4 by 1950, 25 1951
26[14]	1929	Cravens	SCT	By 1950
27[15]	1907	Brill 21E	UEC	1951
28[16]	1902-03	Brill 21E	ERTCW	By 1950
29[17]	1919-20	Brill 21E	EE	By 1950
30[18]	1901	Brill 21E	ERTCW	By 1950
31-40[19]	1905	Brill 21E	Brush	By 1950
41[20]	1906	Brill 21E	UEC	By 1950
42[21]	1901	Brill 21E	ERTCW	By 1950
43[22]	1902	Brill 21E	ERTCW	By 1950
44[23]	1906	Brill 21E	UEC	By 1950
45[24]	1902	Brill 21E	ERTCW	By 1950
46-8[25]	1906	Brill 21E	UEC	1951
49[26]	1901	Brill 21E	ERTCW	1951
50[27]	1925-26	Cravens	Cravens	1951
51-60[28]	1920	Peckham P22	EE	1951
61[29]	1928	Brill 21E	SCT	1951
62/3[30]	1901-02	Brill 21E	ERTCW	1950-51
64[31]	1902-03	Brill 21E	ERTCW	By 1950
65[32]	1925-26	Cravens	Cravens	1951
66-75[33]	1923	Cravens	Cravens	1951
76-83[34]	1925-26	Cravens	Cravens	1951
100[35]	1902	Brill 21E	Dick Kerr	1951
101[36]	1902-03	Brill 21E	ERTCW	1951
102[37]	1901	Brill 21E	ERTCW	1951

1 UEC balcony-top 1911-19; Brush balcony-top 1919-26. Fully enclosed c1926. Renumbered from 30 in 1944.

2 Balcony-top — fully enclosed 1926-36. Renumbered from 49 in 1944.

3 Brush balcony-top fitted c1920.

4 Balcony-top. Fully enclosed 1926-36. Renumbered from 46 in 1944.

5 Brush balcony-top fitted c1920. Now preserved.

6 Fully enclosed 1926-36. Renumbered from 61 in 1944.

7 Fully enclosed 1926-36. Renumbered from 48 in 1944.

8 Brush balcony-top fitted c1920.

9 Fully enclosed 1926-36. Renumbered from 62, 65, 63 in 1944.

10 Nos 12/5: UEC top-cover fitted 1911-12; fully enclosed 1923-36. No 14: Brush top-cover fitted c1920.

11 Fully enclosed 1926-36. Renumbered from 47 in 1944.

12 No 17: fully enclosed 1923; No 18 Brush balcony-top fitted 1920; No 19 UEC top-cover fitted 1911-12 and fully enclosed 1926-36; No 20 Brush balcony-top fitted c1920.

13 Nos 21-4: Brush top-covers c1920; No 23 was fully enclosed 1926-36; No 25: UEC top-cover fitted 1911-12.

14 Fully enclosed from new.

15 Fully enclosed 1926-36. Renumbered from 50 in 1944.

16 Brush top-cover fitted c1920.

17 Fully enclosed 1926-36. Renumbered from 64 in 1944.

18 Balcony top fitted 1941. Renumbered from 1 in 1944.

19 –

20 –

21 UEC top-cover fitted 1911-12. Renumbered from 4 in 1944.

22 UEC top cover fitted in 1911-12. Renumbered from 16 in 1944.

23 –

24 Balcony-top fitted 1944 — was last open-top tram. Renumbered from 13 in 1944.

25 Fully enclosed 1926-36. Renumbered from 42/3/5 in 1944.

26 UEC top fitted 1911-12. Renumbered from 2 in 1944.

27 Fully enclosed from new. Renumbered from 85 in 1944.

28 Fully enclosed from new.

29 Fully enclosed from new. Renumbered from 6 (ii) in 1944.

30 UEC tops fitted 1911-12. Renumbered from 9 and 11 in 1944.

31 UEC top fitted 1911-12. Fully enclosed 1926-36. Renumbered from 29 in 1944.

32 Fully enclosed from new. Renumbered from 84 in 1944.

33 Fully enclosed from new.

34 Fully enclosed from new.

35 Water car.

36 Converted to breakdown car in 1923. Renumbered from 26 (i) in 1929.

37 Converted to rail grinder 1925. Renumbered from 6 (i) in 1929.

With their distinctive livery, complete with 'Shop at Binns' legend, and with their pantographs, the trams of Sunderland were amongst the most noticeable of all those that survived World War 2. Moreover, in 1945, Sunderland was one of the few relatively small operators not to have definite plans for closure and, indeed, opened one of the last conventional tramway extensions in Britain.

In 1878 the Sunderland Tramways Co was authorised to construct and run trams on a network of routes from the centre to Roker, Christ Church, Tatham Street and the Docks. The first section, from Monkwearmouth (on the north side of the River Wear) to Roker, opened on 28 April 1879 and was operated by horse-trams. The remainder of the authorised system was opened on 11 June 1879. At the same time Sunderland Corporation was also empowered to build (but not operate) tramways, although not all the authorised sections were constructed. Corporation-built tramways extended the horse-tram network to *inter alia*, Southwick. During 1880 the Sunderland Tramways Co undertook experiments with steam-trams, but these were not deemed a success and the system remained horse-operated until the Corporation took over.

In 1896 the Corporation decided that it would seek powers to take over and electrify the system.

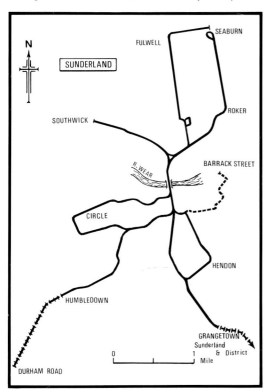

The actual Bill was, however, not promoted until November 1898, receiving the Royal Assent on 1 August 1899. The date of the takeover was set as 31 December 1899, although the actual purchase was not completed until some three months later. With its powers already confirmed, the Corporation started the work of converting the horse-tramway in November 1899. The official opening of the first stretch of electric tramway, from Roker to Christ Church, took place on 15 August 1900. This opening was followed rapidly by others over the succeeding months and the final horse-tram operated barely six months later on 19 February 1901.

With the completion of the old network, the Corporation turned to the building of a number of extensions. On 22 May 1901 the Roker route was extended to Seaside Lane; on 16 July 1901 from St Barnabas to Villette Road (this route, with its low railway bridge in Suffolk Street, required the provision of single-deck trams); and on 12 August 1901 from Christ Church to Grangetown. Further extensions, to Fulwell and to Barrack Street, were opened on 27 March 1903 and 23 January 1904 respectively. The next opening in the area, from Grangetown southwards to Ryhope in 1905, was under the aegis of the Sunderland & District Tramways Co and, despite the proximity of the two termini at Grangetown, it was not until 1920 (and the threat from the new motorbuses) that agreement was reached to operate through services. These lasted barely five years as the Sunderland & District trams were abandoned on 15 July 1925.

The next two decades were a period of consolidation. Extensions were proposed, but none were progressed. Nonetheless, there were minor improvements to the existing layout, for example the widening of Ryhope Road in 1921 allowed for the tram track to be realigned. However, the mid-1920s saw two conflicting actions. Firstly, in 1924 it was proposed that the tram service to Barrack Street (The Docks) should be replaced by buses and, secondly, the first stage of the Durham Road route was opened on 17 November 1925 — the first extension for 20 years. The proposal to convert the Barrack Street route was held in abeyance as the Corporation did not receive powers to operate motorbuses until July 1927 and the final decision to convert the Barrack Street route was taken. Trams continued to serve the route until July 1929. Less than a month later, on 4 August 1929, the Durham Road route was extended to Humbledon.

For the next 20 years the life of Sunderland trams was dominated by Charles Albert Hopkins.

Appointed general manager in May 1929, Hopkins' first duty was to provide a report on the future of Sunderland's transport. Widely considered to be pro-bus, Hopkins' report surprised many by advocating the retention of the trams, including the Villette Road route which had already been approved for closure. The 1930s witnessed a considerable revolution both to the fleet and to the infrastructure.

On 27 August 1930 the Villette Road route was suspended, reopening in March 1931. There would seem to have been little intention to abandon the line because new single-deck tram No 85, nicknamed 'The Covered Wagon', was delivered in February 1931. Nevertheless, this vehicle was effectively rendered superfluous by the 1932 agreement with the London & North Eastern Railway to raise the Suffolk Street railway bridge and to lower the roadway, thereby enabling the operation of double-deck trams. To allow for the conversion the service was suspended again, but when resumed on 11 January 1933 the double-deckers appeared. A further development saw the extension of the Fulwell route along Dykelands Road to Seaburn which opened on 10 May 1937. This was the final extension to be opened prior to the outbreak of World War 2.

To operate the tram services Hopkins adopted a three-fold policy: rebuilding a number of older cars; acquiring second-hand cars from other operators; and, finally, acquiring a number of completely new cars. The first second-hand trams to be acquired were two from Accrington in November 1931. These were followed by two trams which incorporated bodies acquired from Mansfield in 1933. In 1934 new car No 99 was delivered from English Electric, the first of a number of streamlined cars delivered in the period up to 1940 in addition to a number of more conventional designs (including one delivered in an experimental mustard livery which was nicknamed 'The Yellow Peril'). During this period Sunderland became home to a number of notable cars, including Portsmouth No 1 (bought for £90 in 1936 at a time when the cost of a new tram was almost £3,000) and Metropolitan Electric Tramways No 331, one of the prototype 'Feltham' trams. Larger batches of second-hand trams followed from Ilford (nine cars) and Huddersfield (eight). In this latter case the trams had to be regauged from Huddersfield's 4ft 7¾in before entering service. Sunderland's tram fleet was notable for the use of the pantograph. This was first adopted in 1933 on tram No 98 replacement of the more common bow collector which had been adopted three years earlier.

In September 1939, therefore, Sunderland was able to enter World War 2 with an up-to-date tramway system and, indeed, the last completely new tram, No 52, did not enter service until 1940. Prior to this, however, the need for coastal defence meant that the tram service from Roker to Seaburn was suspended (from 15 December 1939) and replaced by a motorbus service. The alternative tram route to Seaburn (via Fulwell) was not affected. As a port and shipbuilding centre, it was inevitable that Sunderland would face aerial attack during the war and a certain amount of damage to the tramway resulted, including damage to both Wheat Sheaf and Hylton Road depots during 1943. During the war the tram fleet remained largely unchanged, the most significant alteration being the sale, in November 1944, of single-deck tram No 85 to Leeds.

With the end of the war in Europe it was possible to revert to prewar services, and the suspended line from Roker to Seaburn was reintroduced on 4 June 1945. This period was, however, marked by two strikes over running times. Work also proceeded on a number of tramway improvements, including a further extension to the Durham Road route to serve the newly-constructed housing estates along the road. In addition, the loop at Roker Park football ground was relaid to allow trams to run via Cardwell Street; at the same time the crossover in Gladstone Street was removed in January 1946; and three months later the junction between Ryhope Road and Villette Road (which had lain disused after the closure in 1929 and subsequently been removed) was relaid and a peak-hours circular route operated. This innovation was to prove less than successful and was withdrawn from July 1946, whereupon the newly-laid junction reverted to a moribund condition.

The Corporation believed that it required at least 18 new trams to operate existing services and the Durham Road extension under construction. It proved impossible to obtain these vehicles and the search for second-hand cars was resumed. The unique South Shields streamlined car (No 52) was bought in July 1946 and this was followed by six of the Manchester 'Pilcher' cars during 1947-48. Finally, a single tram was acquired from Bury. This car, numbered 85 by Sunderland, was destined to be the last car bought by Sunderland.

By the time that No 85 had been delivered the Corporation had already taken the decision to scrap the tramway system despite the work continuing on the Durham Road extension. The chosen form of vehicle for replacement was the diesel bus; the Corporation had considered, but rejected, trolleybuses in 1938. The policy of replacement was considered as a long-term option as there were few replacement buses available. In the meantime the first part of the new Durham Road extension (some 630yd to Grindon Road) opened on 21 February 1948. The final extension (to Thorney Close Road) was opened a year later on 7 February 1949. Hopkins, however, did not live to see this final extension. He died on 16 October 1948 and was replaced by his assistant, H. W. Snowball.

The start of the new decade did not see any immediate signs of the policy of abandonment until 5 November 1950 when the Villette Road route was converted. In March 1951 work started on replacing the railway bridge at Southwick Road, and although a single track was retained — given that the official policy was now abandonment — the costs of tramway reinstatement were considered prohibitive and the Southwick route was abandoned suddenly on 2 September 1951.

The final phase of Sunderland's tramways came with the death on 1 January 1952 of Snowball and the appointment in July of his successor Norman Morton. Morton was a 'bus-man' and it came as little surprise that in September 1952 it was decided that there would be an accelerated abandonment policy so that all trams would be withdrawn over a two-year period.

On 20 September 1952 buses replaced trams on the Roker Park football specials, although the loop was retained for operational purposes until the final closure. This was followed on 30 November 1952 by the closure of the Grangetown route. Thereafter trams terminated at the

Left:
Another source of second-hand trams was Huddersfield. Sunderland No 32, originally Huddersfield No 140, was built by English Electric in 1931 — one of a batch of eight which were Huddersfield's last new trams — and sold to Sunderland in 1938. Built to the unusual gauge of 4ft 7¾in, the eight cars had to be regauged prior to use on Wearside.

Borough Road crossover, on a stub of track left after the Villette Road closure. On 3 January 1954 the Circle route and the Seaburn via Roker route were both converted. This meant that there remained only 29 trams in service and final closure was not long delayed. The next section to be abandoned was the Durham Road route (including the section barely five years old) which succumbed on 28 March 1954. This left the final route from Borough Road to Seaburn via Fulwell, which closed seven months later on 1 October 1954. The last car, suitably decorated, was No 86, bringing to an end 54 years of electric tramcar service by the Wear.

Of Sunderland's tramcar fleet the majority were quickly scrapped. After an appeal in 1952, No 100 (the erstwhile MET No 331) was preserved. As with many of the other trams preserved prior to the acquisition of the Crich site, No 100 led a nomadic existence, being stored at a variety of sites, including Thornbury depot in Bradford. Often regarded as a 'forgotten' tram due to the complexity of construction and the apparently prohibitive cost of restoration, No 100 was finally restored during 1989 through the

sponsorship of the Gateshead Garden Festival and British Steel and spent the summer of 1990 operating in Gateshead, albeit in an unauthentic livery. Now back at Crich, it has been retored to its original London livery. Sunderland No 16 has been recovered and is at Beamish, but it remains to be seen if it will be restored.

Sunderland Closures

5 November 1950	Villette Road
2 September 1951	Southwick
30 November 1952	Grangetown
3 January 1954	Circle
3 January 1954	Seaburn (via Roker)
28 March 1954	Durham Road
1 October 1954	Seaburn

Last car: No 86

Openings:
The Durham Road extension opened in two phases on 21 February 1948 and 7 February 1949.

Fleet Numbers	Date	Trucks/Bogies	Body	Withdrawn
-9[1]	1937/38 (acquired)	Peckham P22, replaced by M&T Hornless trucks 1946-48	Brush	1954
3-8[2]	1900	Originally Brill 22E bogies. 1901 Brill 21E trucks, Brill Radiax on rebuilding 1920-22. Again retrucked 1930-34: 14/5/8 P22, 13 M&T, 16 P35 (later P22), 17 EE swing link	ERTCW	1953-54
9-20[3]	1931 (acquired)	Peckham RB	Brush	1953
1/4[4]	1933	EMB Hornless	SCT	1953/54
2/3/5[5]	1901	Brill 21E, later P22. 22 to EMB 1931, 22/5 to M&T 1933/34	ERTCW	1954
6-8[6]	1935	EMB Hornless	SCT	1953
9-36[7]	1938 (acquired)	M&T Swing-link	EE	1953-54
7-42[8]	1947 (acquired)	Peckham P35	Manchester	1953/54
8[9]	1901	Brill, later P22 1926	ERTCW	1953
10[10]	1902	Brill 21E, 1930 EMB Hornless	ERTCW	1953
5[11]	1936 (acquired)	EMB Flexible axle	Portsmouth	1953
3[12]	1946 (acquired)	M&T Swing-link	EE	1954
9-52[13]	1938-40	EE	Sunderland	1953-54
3[14]	1936	EE	EE	1954
4-5[15]	1935-36	M&T	55 Brush, 54 SCT	1953-54
6/7/60-4[16]	1902	Brill 21E	ERTCW	1951-54
6-71[17]	1906	Originally M&G radial, later: 66 P35, 67 P22, 68 EE, 69 P22, 70 EE, 71 EMB Hornless	Brush	1953-54
2-83[18]	1921	Originally P22, later: 77/81 Peckham P35, remainder EMB	EE	1953-54
4[19]	1926	P22 replaced by EMB Flexible axle in 1931	SCT	1953
5[20]	1948 (acquired)	EMB Flexible axle	Milnes	1954
5[21]	1932	EMB Hornless	SCT	1954
7-98[22]	1933	EMB Hornless	87-95 EE, 96-8 SCT	1954
9[23]	1934	EE bogies	EE	1951
0[24]	1937 (acquired)	UCC bogies	UCC	1951

1 EX-LPTB (Ilford Nos 33-40) built 1932. Rebuilt with fully-enclosed top decks.

2 Rebuilt fully enclosed 1920-22. Remains of No 16 at Beamish.

3 Ex-Accrington Nos 42/3 built 1926, regauged from 4ft 0in to 4ft 8½in.

4 Incorporated the body shells of Mansfield & District Nos 27/8 built by EE 1925.

5 Batch 19-26, originally single-deck. Nos 22/3/5 rebuilt as double-deckers 1925, remainder withdrawn 1930.

6 First Sunderland cars with glass roof-lights.

7 Ex-Huddersfield 137-44 built 1931. Regauged from 4ft 7⅞in to 4ft 8½in. Nos 31/2/4/5 in closure procession.

8 Ex-Manchester 'Pilcher' trams Nos 228, 503, 163, 176, 380 and 131 respectively. Built 1930.

9 Rebuilt fully enclosed 1925. Renumbered from 32 in 1938. Used as works car 1951-54.

10 Rebuilt fully enclosed 1930.

11 Portsmouth CT 1 built 1930. Retrucked before entering service.

12 Ex-South Shields No 52 built 1936.

13 EE design streamlined, centre entrance.

14 Streamlined, centre entrance.

15 Streamlined, centre entrance.

16 Batch 56-65, all rebuilt 1926-34. No 58 withdrawn 1938, 59/65 to works cars 'C' and 'D', withdrawn 1951.

17 Rebuilt 1922/23 and again 1932/34.

18 All rebuilt 1929-31 when retrucking occurred.

19 Incorporating parts of Sunderland District lower saloon of 1908.

20 Ex-Bury No 30 built 1905; heavily rebuilt by Bury CT 1931.

21 Nicknamed 'The Ghost Tram'. Official last tram.

22 –

23 Streamlined bogie; stored 1940-45, repainted prewar livery 1946. Withdrawn 1951 and offered for sale. Scrapped 1953.

24 Prototype 'Feltham', MET 331 built 1930. To LPTB 2168 in 1933. Stored 1939-45, now preserved.

The honour, if honour it be, of being the last electric tramway in Wales fell to the Swansea & Mumbles Railway. There was a certain irony in this inasmuch as the railway not only claimed its descent from the world's oldest passenger-carrying railway but it was also the last 'new' electric tramway to open, postdating the Dearne District Light Railways by some five years.

The origin of the Swansea & Mumbles dated to the early 19th century when the Oystermouth Railway received its parliamentary Act in 1804. The railway was built from Swansea to Oystermouth and initial freight services started over part of the line in April 1806. Passenger services were introduced on 25 March 1807, the first known case of the regular conveyance of passengers by rail. These services were, however, destined to be relatively short-lived. In 1826 a turnpike road was built paralleling the railway, and the passenger services were withdrawn in favour of a new service on the road. The road also led to an overall decline in the railway's fortunes, for by the mid-1850s the line was considered to be derelict.

The late 1850s witnessed the reconstruction of the railway, horse-drawn passenger services being reintroduced progressively during 1860. Then, by the 1860s, tramway development was occurring elsewhere in Britain, and the Swansea area soon followed the fashion. In 1874 the Swansea Improvement & Tramways Co received its Act of Parliament. Amongst the clauses in the Act were powers for the new company to lease the Oystermouth Railway and to improve it. On 17 August 1877 the line saw the first operation of steam trams in Britain. (This method of operation was possible because the original Act for the railway predated the 1870 Tramways Act. The 1870 Act effectively precluded the use of anything other than the horse operation of tramways, and it was not until 1879 that the Board of Trade was empowered to allow the use of steam or other mechanical traction.)

In March 1879 the Swansea & Mumbles Railway Co Ltd was incorporated, which exacerbated an already confused position regarding the ownership and running of the railway. At one point the new company was operating steam trams whilst the Swansea Improvement & Tramways Co had reverted to horse-tram operation! The confusion continued for many years until the creation of a further company, the Swansea & Mumbles Railway, in July 1893. Already, in 1889, an Act to extend the railway from Oystermouth to Mumbles and to construct a deep-water pier at Mumbles had been passed. The Act also allowed for the realignment of the existing railway from Oystermouth to Black Pill. These works were finally completed in 1898, the original line from Oystermouth to Black Pill being abandoned.

Also in 1898, the Swansea Improvement & Tramways Co was taken over by BET and electric tramcars were introduced into Swansea itself in 1900. With BET's involvement it was inevitable that efforts would be made to convert the Swansea & Mumbles, although it was not until 1925 that an Order allowing for the conversion was passed. In January 1927 the lease by which Swansea Improvement & Tramways Co operated the railway was transferred to an associated company, South Wales Transport Co Ltd, and initial trials of electric traction were held in July 1928. The full electric service was introduced on 2 March 1929.

To operate the new electric service, 13 huge fully-enclosed double-deckers were acquired from Brush. Each of these trams could seat 106 passengers and they were amongst the largest tramcars ever built. Unusually, the trams had entrances on only one side, the reason being that access was only possible from the landward side. The trams, often operating in multiple, were essential for the huge numbers that used the services. In 1945 almost 5 million passengers travelled on the trams and even in 1953 more than 3 million did so. The 13 trams operated the service throughout the electric era.

In June 1954 there were great celebrations to mark the 150th anniversary of the world's first passenger-carrying railway. But by this date the writing was already on the wall. A third of the passenger traffic had disappeared in the eight

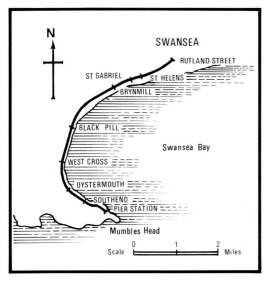

years since the end of World War 2 (although levels were still above prewar figures) and the situation was not helped by the temporary closure of the pier at Mumbles. This was not reopened until 1956, but by now the tramway was losing money. South Wales Transport was faced by the prospect of having to spend £350,000 to renew the tramway at a time when there was no profit in its operation.

South Wales Transport examined the possibility of replacing the trams with a bus service, but the company, as leaseholders, would still have faced a liability of £14,242 per annum in rent to the owners. Thus, in September 1958, South Wales Transport made a formal offer for the shares of Swansea & Mumbles Railway Ltd and of the Mumbles Railway & Pier Co. The existing shareholders accepted the offer and South Wales Transport was thus in a position to move towards the closure of the line.

To achieve this the company had to promote a private Act, the South Wales Transport Act, which was passed on 29 July 1959 despite a petition of 13,966 objectors raised by the Mumbles Railway Passengers Association. This Act allowed for the formal abandonment of the railway. The first stage of the abandonment occurred on 11 October 1959 when the section from Southend to Mumbles Pier was closed to allow for the construction of a private road for the operation of the replacement buses. Final closure of the section from Swansea to Southend occurred on

5 January 1960 when Nos 6 and 7 were suitably decorated.

This was not the final tragedy to befall the Swansea & Mumbles Railway. One of the unique Brush cars, No 2, was preserved, finding a home on the Middleton Railway in Leeds in the company of a number of other preserved trams. Used occasionally in passenger service, No 2, like most of the other trams at Middleton, suffered severe vandalism. Despite the efforts of the Middleton Railway to find alternative accommodation, none could be found. Consequently, this survivor from the world's oldest passenger railway was destroyed. The end from another of the trams does, however, remain in Swansea.

Perhaps the greatest tragedy of the Swansea & Mumbles Railway is that, had it survived only a few more years, the growth in tourism and the leisure industry could possibly have ensured its long-term future. Recent speculation on the possible reconstruction of part of the line merely emphasises the loss.

Swansea & Mumbles Closures

| 11 October 1959 | Southend to Mumbles Pier |
| 5 January 1960 | Swansea to Southend |

Last trams: Nos 6/7

Swansea & Mumbles

Fleet Numbers	Date	Trucks/Bogies	Body	Withdrawn
1-13[1]	1928-29	Brush bogies	Brush	1960

1 Largest tramcars in Britain with seating for 106. One car (No 2) preserved on the Middleton Railway in Leeds, but scrapped after being vandalised. Swansea Industrial and Maritime Museum retains one end from No 7.

A large number of books and magazines have been consulted in the preparation of this title:

Magazines:
Buses/Buses Illustrated; Modern Tramway; Tramway Review; Modern Transport; Passenger Transport Journal; The Light Railway & Tramway Journal; Scottish Transport.

Books:
Edinburgh's Transport – Hunter (Advertiser Press)
Gone but not Forgotten – Hunter/Ludgate/Richardson (RPSI/ITT)
KHCT 1899-1979 (KHCT)
Leicester's Trams – Smith (LRTL)
Liverpool Transport – Horne/Maund (TPC)
London Transport Tramways Handbook – Willoughby & Oakley (Authors)
London's Trams – Joyce (Ian Allan Ltd)
Manchester Tramway Diary 1940-51 – Yearsley/Price/Taylor
The Manchester Tramways – Yearsley/Groves (TPC)
Manchester Transport 1: Tramway and Trolleybus Rolling Stock – Taylor (MTMS)
Middleton Tramways – Kirby (MTMS)
One Hundred Years of Leeds Tramways – Young (Turntable Enterprises)
Operation Tramaway – Joyce (Ian Allan Ltd)
Plymouth – 100 years of Street Travel – Sambourne (Glasney Press)
Scottish Tramway Fleets – Brotchie (NB Traction)
Sheffield Corporation Tramways – Gandy (Sheffield Libraries)
Short Review of Birmingham Corporation Tramways – Hardy/Jaques (HJ Publications)
The Age of the Electric Train – Gillham (Ian Allan Ltd)
The Bessbrook & Newry Tramway – Newham (Oakwood)
The Giant's Causeway Tramway – McGuigan (Oakwood)
The Dublin & Lucan Tramway – Newham (Oakwood)

The Glasgow Tramcar – Stewart (STMS)
The Golden Age of Tramways – Klapper (Routledge & Kegan Paul)
The Great Northern Railway of Ireland – Patterson (Oakwood)
The Hill of Howth Tramway – Flewitt (TRA)
The Swansea & Mumbles Railway – Lee (Oakwood)
The Tramways of the East Midlands (LRTA)
The Tramways of Gateshead – Hearse (Author)
The Tramways of Grimsby, Immingham and Cleethorpes – Price (LRTA)
The Tramways of Jarrow & South Shields – Hearse (Author)
The Tramways of North-East England (LRTA)
The Tramways of North Lancashire (LRTA)
The Tramways of the North Midlands (LRTA)
The Tramways of Northumberland – Hearse (Author)
The Tramways of Salford – Gray (MTMS)
The Tramways of South Yorkshire and Humberside (LRTA)
The Tramways of South-East Lancashire (LRTA)
The Tramways of South-West England (LRTA)
The Tramways of Sunderland – Staddon (Advertiser Press)
The Tramways of the East Midlands (LRTA)
Tramway Twilight – Joyce (Ian Allan Ltd)

Other published sources:
The fleet histories prepared by the PSV Circle/Omnibus Society have proved useful. In particular those detailing the fleets of Newcastle-upon-Tyne (PA16), CIE (PI2), Southampton (PK5), Liverpool (PC13), Blackpool (PC20), Kingston upon Hull (PB22), Gateshead (PA4), Plymouth (PH3), Bolton and Salford (PC10), Aberdeen and Dundee (PL1), Isle of Man (PC6), Edinburgh (PM1), Manchester (PC9), Blackburn (PC4), Glasgow (PM12), Leeds (PB3) and Cardiff (PG1).

Left:
South Shields No 44 was one of a batch of five fully-enclosed trams supplied in 1921 by English Electric to operate the Cleadon Light Railway. As originally built, all five were fitted with front exits but, with the exception of No 43, all later had this facility removed. *Author's collection*